Advance Praise for *Cruise Ship Squeeze*

Cruise Ship Squeeze is hard-hitting, engrossing and impeccably documented. It is a compelling and comprehensive history of the cruise ship industry. *Cruise Ship Squeeze* provides the reader with a deep understanding of the economics, laws/loopholes and public relations strategies that support this wealthy rogue industry.
A veritable "who's who" of the cruise ship industry that connects the dots. *Cruise Ship Squeeze* is an invaluable resource for decision-makers, concerned citizens, ocean stewards, and the media.

— Cha Smith, Executive Director KAHEA:
The Hawaiian-Environmental Alliance: www.kahea.org

The cruise industry should thank Klein for showing them how to vastly improve the destinations they sail into — while continuing to rake in billions of dollars.

— Lelei LeLaulu, Caribbean Media Exchange on Sustainable Tourism

Cruise Ship Squeeze brilliantly lays bare an industry that has for too long escaped the glare of public scrutiny. Klein meticulously documents the structures and strategies of the tiny group of mega corporations that have come to dominate the industry, their carefully crafted image-making and political lobbying machines. Klein demonstrates convincingly that social and environmental responsibility (like other industries from tobacco to oil) is merely a public relations tactic for the cruise ship corporations, utterly foreign to their genetic makeup. Accountability has to be imposed—through citizen and community pressure, and ultimately through effective laws and regulations.
Cruise Ship Squeeze is a masterful portrayal of how these corporate buccaneers in their relentless pursuit of profit leave social and environmental havoc in their wake. They pay little or no taxes, play port cities off against each other for concessions, maintain sweat-ship working conditions, pollute the oceans, and despite seductive promises add minimal value to local communities.

— Bruce Campbell Executive director, Canadian Centre for Policy Alternatives

Ross Klein has been the Ralph Nader of the cruise industry,
the fastest-growing major sector of the tourism market. His new book is a
powerful, well-documented, and scathing critique of new forms of piracy made
possible by anachronisms like flags of convenience and by corporate practices
of borderline legality at best. With cruising extending its reach beyond its
traditional elite base, this book provides a valuable education for new
cruisers and for industry analysts alike. Klein debunks the myths
associated with cruising and points the way towards bringing
more responsible and sustainable practices to the industry.

— Robert Wood, Professor of Sociology, Rutgers University and
Coordinating Editor of Annals of Tourism Research

Ross Klein's *Cruise Ship Squeeze* is his own "wikipedia" of the cruise ship
industry — an indispensable and comprehensive reference for every student,
development planner, environmentalist and resident of a cruise ship destination.
Klein combines great experience as an actual cruise passenger with a
genealogist's insights into the rapid couplings and family tiffs among the
major cruise ship companies. In addition, he has assembled a massive data
store of concrete measures of the size and growth of the sometimes secretive
industry over the past fifty years. There is nothing to match this book.
Even as an avid observer of the cruise ship industry in the Caribbean for the
past 20 years, I learned new facts and insights on every page. Many thanks to
Ross Klein for a major work on one of the most dynamic segments of the f
astest growing and largest industry on the planet. He provides a solid grounding
on what we know, and he provides some fascinating guideposts to what
we need to know in the future to better manage this new leviathan.
If you want to improve your port's success rate in negotiating with the cruise
industry, buy every member of the local Port Authority a copy of *Cruise Ship
Squeeze*, and make sure they carry it to the negotiating meetings.

— Bruce Potter
Island Resources Foundation
[based in St. Thomas, US Virgin Islands, the world's busiest
cruise ship port of call, since 1972]

CRUISE SHIP SQUEEZE

THE NEW PIRATES OF THE SEVEN SEAS

Ross A. Klein

NEW SOCIETY PUBLISHERS

Cataloging in Publication Data:
A catalog record for this publication is available from the National Library of Canada.

Cover design by Diane McIntosh. Images: Getty Images.
Interior design by Jeremy Drought.
Printed in Canada. First printing September 2005.

New Society Publishers acknowledges the support of the Government of Canada through the Book Publishing Industry Development Program (BPIDP) for our publishing activities.

Paperback ISBN: 0-86571-522-X

Inquiries regarding requests to reprint all or part of *Cruise Ship Squeeze* should be addressed to New Society Publishers at the address below.
To order directly from the publishers, please call toll-free (North America) 1(800) 567•6772, or order online at www.newsociety.com

Any other inquiries can be directed by mail to:

New Society Publishers, P.O. Box 189, Gabriola Island, BC V0R 1X0, Canada
1 (800) 567•6772

New Society Publishers' mission is to publish books that contribute in fundamental ways to building an ecologically sustainable and just society, and to do so with the least possible impact on the environment, in a manner that models this vision. We are committed to doing this not just through education, but through action. We are acting on our commitment to the world's remaining ancient forests by phasing out our paper supply from ancient forests worldwide. This book is one step toward ending global deforestation and climate change. It is printed on acid-free paper that is **100% old growth forest-free** (100% post-consumer recycled), processed chlorine free, and printed with vegetable-based, low-VOC inks. For further information, or to browse our full list of books and purchase securely, visit our website at: www.newsociety.com

NEW SOCIETY PUBLISHERS   www.newsociety.com

Dedication

To clear skies, calm seas, and social justice …

…and to the memory of O'Neil Persaud

Contents

Part 3 – Purveyors of Trust

Part 4 – Looking to the Future

Acknowledgments

I OWE A DEBT OF GRATITUDE TO THE MANY WHO HAVE CONTRIBUTED TO THIS BOOK. I was tempted to make a list, but it proved impractical — I was bound to leave someone off. Worse, a list would ignore the contribution of so many whose names I don't know and who don't know they contributed — those I have met in my travels or that send e-mails keeping me in touch with what's happening onboard ships and within companies constituting the cruise industry. Those who have contributed know who they are and I trust know that their help is sincerely appreciated.

Several organizations must be acknowledged for their support and dissemination of my research: Bluewater Network/Friends of the Earth, Campaign to Safeguard America's Waters, Canadian Centre for Policy Alternatives, Counterpart International, KAHEA – Hawaiian Environmental Alliance, Livable Oldtown, Ocean Advocates – Seattle, Ocean Conservancy – Monterey Bay, Oceana, Oceans Blue Foundation, and Travel Just. I also thank the universities and community groups that have sponsored lectures, and with sincere appreciation acknowledge websites that provide invaluable data: Guidestar, Follow the Money, Open Secrets, Common Cause, and various US and state government agencies (some states are better than others). The age of the Internet makes this sort of research so much easier than the "old days."

I'd be remiss not to thank my lone supporting colleague at Memorial University of Newfoundland's School of Social Work, and to thank the folks in the Division of University Relations who have promoted my work. Thanks also to Tammy Manning and Jennifer Multhana, graduate students providing invaluable research assistance for Chapter 3, "Representation without Taxation."

Finally, I want to thank New Society Publishers for their support of my work. It is much appreciated!

RK
May, 2005

Introduction

PI'RATE, n. [L. pirata.]
In strictness, the word pirate is one who makes it his business to cruise for robbery or plunder; a freebooter on the seas.

— Webster's 1828 Dictionary

THIS BOOK IS ABOUT MODERN PIRATES — the ones who sail huge cruise ships from one port to another and offload thousands of day-visitors at a time. When multiple ships stop at a port, it is more an invasion of visitors than a matter of people coming to experience a new place. They come ashore, visit sites, buy trinkets and t-shirts, and sail away. They spend most of their money on the ship.

The ships aren't much better than the passengers they bring. Passengers buy tours ashore provided by local folks in the ports they visit, but the cruise ship keeps more money from the sale than is given to the person providing the tour. On top of this, the stores where passengers shop kick back substantial sums for the privilege of having cruise passengers in their place of business, ports often provide incentives for cruise ships to stop, and governments look the other way regarding cruise industry environmental practices. Governments believe they need cruise ships more than the cruise ships need them. This power-dependence relationship only increases the pirate's greed. Ports admittedly make money, but it pales in comparison to the industry's take.

The cruise industry would argue with this characterization, but the facts speak for themselves. The North American cruise industry earned more than $2.5 billion in net profit in 2004. It pays virtually no corporate income tax and is exempt from most laws in the countries that the ships visit. If a port or country is too demanding the industry will pass it by and go somewhere else. This warns others: either put up with the relatively small crumbs they receive or they'll get nothing.

Interestingly, some of the most attractive and high-priced islands in the Caribbean are places cruise ships don't visit. When cruise ship invade, the texture of a port or an island changes. These changes are good for cruise ships day-visitors who want quick and easy access to sites, clean streets, and an absence of poverty, and also want to see a place as they think it should be — often much like home — rather than the way it actually is. The changes are often disastrous for tourists staying at a resort for a week or two. The crowds of cruise passengers, taxis and attractions may not be available on days when multiple cruise ships are in port, and the beaches of island resorts where visitors spend real money are invaded by cruise passengers at the peak of the day. As cruise passengers increasingly displace visitors to land-based resorts, the port's dependence on cruise ships increases as does the greed of the pirate.

At face value, the foregoing is provocative. Some would say it is blatant exaggerations and unfair. Before concluding that the critics are right, you must read on. The following chapters support the conclusions drawn. In fact, some may opine that my characterizations are much too generous and that they don't recognize the plundering of ports. You will need to judge for yourself.

The New Pirates of the Seven Seas

The book begins with a look at the development of cruise tourism in North America — the birth of the modern pirates of the seven seas. Though ships have been used for ocean travel for centuries, cruise tourism as we know it today began 30 to 40 years ago. Princess Cruises, Norwegian Cruise Line, and Royal Caribbean Cruise Line all began operations in the mid to late 1960s. Carnival Cruise Lines was a latecomer, starting in 1972.

The industry grew slowly in its early years, but had expanded widely and significantly by the 1980s. Cruise lines were building bigger and bigger ships; they were operating more ships, and new companies appeared on the scene. Some were successful, others went belly up, and still others were swallowed up by the "big guys."

Carnival was the leader in takeovers and mergers. It was smaller than Princess and Royal Caribbean in 1988, but by 1990 it eclipsed both. It was unsuccessful in its 1988 attempt to take over Royal Caribbean, but succeeded in acquiring Princess Cruises in 2003. Carnival Corporation today controls more than 50 percent of the North American cruise market. Worldwide it owns and operates 12 cruise lines; at least two tour companies, which own hotels, trains, buses, and tour boats; and an increasing number of port terminals used by its ships. Some would characterize it as monopolistic. Carnival's closest competitor, Royal Caribbean, has less than 34 percent market share and Norwegian Cruise Line follows with 9 percent.

The growth of Carnival Corporation is presented in Chapter 2, "I Never Saw a Cruise Line I Didn't Want to Own." It tells the story of Ted Arison and his son Micky, and how they grew a company that in 1972 had virtually no money to a company today worth tens of billions of dollars. As the chapter title suggests, there aren't many cruise lines that have either not been taken over by Carnival, or that Carnival attempted unsuccessfully to take over. The chapter is as much about the development of Carnival Corporation as it is about the history of the cruise industry. It gives insight into how the industry thinks and operates.

Most North Americans are under the impression that major operators are American-based, likely because the two largest corporations accounting for almost 85 percent of the North American market have their corporate offices in Miami. But almost every cruise line serving North Americans is foreign-registered, even if beneficial ownership is US-based. By registering in countries other than where they operate, cruise corporations avoid virtually all income tax in the country from which they sail. In the case of Carnival Corporation and Royal Caribbean Cruises Limited, the only corporate income subject to taxation is from US-based tour operations. And with friends in Congress, the industry continues to get special breaks and consideration. Chapter 3 looks at how the industry avoids taxes and how it uses lobbyists, campaign contributions, and contributions from industry-controlled foundations to influence political decision-making. In stark contrast to the Boston Tea Party's cry in the 1770s against taxation without representation, the cruise industry enjoys representation without taxation. The industry exercises its influence in national politics as well as state, provincial, and local decision-making.

Cruise Ship Squeeze

The second part of the book focuses on the cruise industry's relationship with and exploitation of ports and port cities. Chapter 4 focuses on a strongly held perception that cruise ships are "cash cows." The cruise industry, its lobbyists, and its various regional trade organizations promote this view. It is based in part on consistent claims by the cruise industry, and adopted by many ports, that the average cruise passenger spends more than $100 in each port a ship calls upon. Ports extrapolate from this and make exaggerated claims about the annual impact of cruise tourism on the local economy. On this basis, many ports invest tens of millions of dollars in port facilities and terminals so they can get in on the economic windfall. Many are quickly disappointed.

The cruise industry also makes claims about the impact of the cruise industry on the US economy and on the economy of individual states. In 2004 the International Council of Cruise Lines said the cruise industry had a $25 billion impact on the US economy. While considerable if viewed in isolation, this sum appears smaller when compared with the annual sales of the Marriott hotel chain — approximately $20 billion per year. And if put into context of the industry's past claims, the industry's contribution to the US economy has decreased since the mid-1990s rather than increased, despite an almost doubling in capacity. Chapter 4, "Cruising Cash Cows," looks at industry claims, puts them into perspective, and more accurately depicts the true impact of the cruise industry on local and national economies.

In contrast to its economic benefits, cruise tourism carries considerable economic costs. As well, the cruise industry adeptly draws on its economic power and political connections to compromise the will of local governments, including national governments of many small island states. Chapter 5, "A Game of Divide and Conquer," focuses on relationships between the cruise industry, governments, and local people. We will see how the industry extracts concessions by playing governments against one another, and compromises the will and interests of local governments and regional organizations through threats. Like a child, it kicks and screams when it doesn't get its way. The industry's opposition to a 2003 initiative by the Caribbean Tourism Organization for a $20 passenger levy for ships visiting the Caribbean is a good illustration. But there are others, such as the continuing struggle for ports to establish and charge appropriate and fair fees for use of their facilities.

Another significant change is the unbundling of the cruise product. Consumers perceive cruises as all-inclusive. With the growth of new sources of onboard revenue, and the introduction of fees for things that were previously included in the cruise fare, the cruise experience has changed, and its all-inclusiveness has been lost. Although there have always been budget cruise lines, these changes have opened the market to "no-frills" cruise ships similar to the "no-frills" budget airlines. UK-based easyJet recently introduced easyCruise,[1] a wholly unbundled product where passengers pay separately for the passage, their food, and even maid service if it is desired. Chapter 6, "Squeezing the Last Drop," looks at the unbundling of the cruise product and the implications this has had for cruise passengers and for ports. A passenger today can have a cruise for a fraction of the cost 10, 20, or even 30 years ago, but additional onboard costs today are exponentially higher than in those earlier days. And as passengers spend more money onboard, they have less to spend onshore. Unbundling helps the cruise line with its income, but undermines the potential income for ports on which cruise lines depend.

Purveyors of Trust

Part 3 of the book looks at contradictions between what the cruise industry says and what it does. This is most glaringly visible in the industry's invocation of "trust us," but then what it does shatters the foundation for trust.

Chapter 7, "The Art of Greenwashing," looks at environmental issues, where the greatest contradiction is found between image and behavior. The cruise industry unabashedly promotes itself as environmentally "green" and often counters critics by asking why cruise ships would pollute the pristine areas they visit when their continuing income depends on those areas remaining pristine. This question is compelling until the industry's actual environmental record is considered — collectively, it has paid almost $100 million in environmental fines since the early 1990s. Since 1998 Royal Caribbean has been fined more than $30 million and Carnival Corporation and its affiliated companies have been fined more than $22 million. And the violations continue. In December 2003 the State of Hawai'i reported at least 16 violations of a voluntary memorandum of understanding it had with the cruise industry with regard to environmental practices.[2] In June 2004 the vice president for Environmental Compliance for Carnival Corporation-owned Holland America Line was fined after pleading guilty to confirming environmental audits that were never performed[3] — the Court had mandated the audits after Carnival Corporation pled guilty to falsifying environmental records. And the list goes on. The industry's active "greenwashing," and how it is achieved, is contrasted with behavior that is more brown than green.

Chapter 8, "Paradise Lost at Sea," goes in two directions. It explores issues of safety and health on cruise ships. This includes safety from physical harm, safety of the ship from accidents, and safety from illness. The last item is particularly salient given the frequency of disease outbreaks aboard ships — more than 100 outbreaks affected over 10,000 people between 2002 and 2004.[4] The most common cause of illness on cruise ships is the Norwalk-like virus (also called "norovirus"). How has the cruise industry handled the virus? Following particularly nasty multiple outbreaks on each of several ships, the industry took the offensive and successfully shaped the media's view of the virus. Focus shifted from the ship as a source of the virus to the industry's now mantra-like claim that passengers bring the illness with them. This claim is made even when there are facts to the contrary. The chapter looks at how the industry has handled disease outbreaks, examines ways in which the industry's self-serving view of the virus has influenced the Centers for Disease Control and media, and offers a broader view of the causes of outbreaks and the risks faced by a passenger. Just as it has effectively used public relations campaigns to shape perceptions of environmental responsibility, the industry has effectively campaigned to make itself look like a victim of norovirus and thus not responsible for the outbreaks when they occur.

The chapter also looks at other sources of paradise lost, including issues around cruise industry's noncompliance with the Americans with Disabilities Act, and the liberties taken and arrogance shown in significantly changing itineraries before departure of a cruise. The pirate attitude carries over to the industry's dealings with consumers.

Prospects for the Future

Part 4 of this book looks at prospects for positive change. It summarizes key issues and, in turn, presents arenas for social activism and grassroots activity. The premise is that the cruise industry is not going to change its environmental practices, relationship with ports, or means for influencing political decisions. In its view, it is successfully turning a profit and any voluntary changes would cut into those profits. Any perceived need for change will only be realized by direct action by individuals, groups of individuals, and organizations. Already credible groups, nationally and locally, need additional support if they are to successfully protect against piracy.

These groups are identified, as is a range of activities to make the industry more environmentally responsible, more generous in sharing economic benefits, and more supportive and sensitive to local communities and cultures. The resulting form of tourism would be sustainable economically, environmentally, and socially. In its present form, "sustainable" would not be used to describe the new pirates of the seven seas.

Part One
The New Pirates of the Seven Seas

1

Cruise Tourism Arrives in North America

THOSE HUGE LUXURY CRUISE SHIPS ARE IMPRESSIVE! In earlier times, the clean white exteriors and opulent interiors grabbed one's attention. Today size is the most significant feature. People marveled at the *Queen Mary 2* — almost as long as four football fields, twice as long as the Washington Monument is tall.[1] At 236 feet, it is 23 stories high — taller than the length of Cunard's first ship, *Britannia*.

Cruise ship interiors, with glitz and glamour and richness, are no less impressive. And then there is the reputation of unlimited gourmet food, of wonderful ports of call, and of being pampered by attentive staff. Between the feast for one's eyes and the feast for one's stomach, not surprisingly half of Americans say they want to take a cruise.

The image of cruising and cruise ships has scarcely changed despite significant shifts in the clientele that cruises, the size of ships, and the nature and quality of services provided. Positive images of bygone days persist. A cruise is viewed as the epitome of a luxury vacation. This image doesn't always fit reality on today's cruise ships.

Leisure Cruising Lands in America

Passenger ships were the primary means for transoceanic transport before air travel. Companies such as Cunard Line, Holland America Line, and Swedish American Line established their reputation and produced an image for cruise ship travel that included opulence and luxury. They provided transportation in style, especially for those who could afford to travel in first class.

Some ships were based in North America. Canadian Pacific operated cruise ships from Canada to Europe and to China. Matson Lines in the US provided transportation between the US west coast and Hawai'i, as well as transpacific voyages to Australia and the South Pacific. And several companies provided transatlantic service, including American Export Lines, Moore McCormack Line, and Grace Line. Because the focus was on transportation, port calls were few. The cruise experience was on board the ship.

Transocean travel hit its peak in 1957 and began to decline in 1958 when Pan American Airways introduced nonstop air travel between New York and Europe. Transatlantic boardings steadily declined through the early 1960s, which led to the demise of companies such as Canadian Pacific (cruise operations), United States Lines, Hamburg-America Line, and Swedish American Line. Many of the ships idled were subsequently taken over by new companies that focused on the passenger vessel as a vehicle for leisure travel.

I Don't Want to Have to Repaint the Name

Princess Cruises, established in 1965 by Stanley B. McDonald, was the first of today's modern cruise lines to focus on the leisure travel market. McDonald began the cruise line by chartering Canadian Pacific's 6,000 ton *Princess Patricia* during the off-season of its cruises from Vancouver to Alaska's Inside Passage.[2] Keeping with the ship's name (and avoiding the need to unnecessarily paint the ship), McDonald named his company Princess Cruises and provided cruises to Mexico's west coast. After two years, with demand exceeding capacity, Princess Cruises added a second ship; it chartered the newly completed Italian ship *Italia*[3] and renamed her *Princess Italia*, also for use on its Mexican cruises from Los Angeles. Princess Cruises chartered a third vessel, Costa Line's *Carla C*, in November 1968. The charter was canceled in 1970 after Costa lost one of its other ships.

Despite its success, Princess Cruises was negatively impacted by the Arab oil embargo in 1973 and the recession that followed. In 1974 it was taken over by London-based Peninsular and Oriental Steam Navigation Company (P&O). P&O replaced the ships on charter with newer vessels — three were added in 1974: *Island Princess* and *Pacific Princess*, originally built in 1971 as *Sea Venture* and *Island Venture* for Norway-based Flagship Cruises,[4] and *Sun Princess*.[5] Princess introduced the *Sea Princess* in 1979[6] and five years later its first purpose-built cruise ship, *Royal Princess*.[7] The company expanded further in 1988 when P&O purchased Sitmar cruises, which operated four ships and had three on order.

Odd Bedfellows

A year after Princess Cruises started cruises from Los Angeles, Norwegian Caribbean Line (NCL) began sailing from Miami on December 19, 1966. NCL was a marriage of convenience between Ted Arison and Knut Kloster. Arison had reservations for cruises and no ships after the Israeli government repossessed those he had chartered when the ships' owner went bankrupt. Kloster in contrast had a ship but no passengers after plans for his brand-new ship, *Sunward*, were canceled. Arison approached Kloster and "…suggested that if Kloster would send the *Sunward* to Miami they could both make some money."[8] Thus began NCL. A second ship, *Starward*, was added in 1968, followed by *Skyward* in 1969 and *Southward* in 1971. With four ships, NCL had more than 3,000 berths to fill every week.

The partnership continued until the summer of 1971 when Kloster notified Arison he was terminating their ten-year contract effective December 31, 1971. The termination was predicated on a clause giving Kloster the option to cancel the contract if he failed to make $1.5 million for two years in a row.

The breakup between Arison and Kloster was less than amicable. Some suggest there was increasing jealousy between Kloster's Norwegian employees and Arison's Americans.

According to Ted's son, Micky Arison, even though the Norwegian company was very profitable they felt their American partners were making too much. So, it was alleged, the Norwegians ... decided to sabotage Arison's profits by purchasing needed equipment such as deck chairs and engine parts and then throwing them overboard. This ensured that the inventory would not exist on the ship, throwing a shadow on Arison's integrity and guaranteeing that he would not be able to deliver the agreed-on profit because the nonexistent inventory would not show up on the balance sheet.[9]

Arison responded by seizing all advance moneys for future NCL cruises. He believed Kloster's cancellation of the contract was not valid; at the very least he was entitled to his commission of 18 percent of the gross revenue. A lawsuit ensued and was settled out of court. Arison agreed to return half of the money he seized. He retained the other half, which amounted to $1 million.

Let's Start from Scratch

The idea for Royal Caribbean Cruise Lines (RCCL) germinated in 1967, but it was 1970 before the company began cruise operations. The primary mover was Edwin Stephan. He had begun his career in the hotel industry and in the 1960s served first as general manager for Yarmouth Cruise Lines (operator of *Yarmouth* and *Yarmouth Castle*[10]), and later as general manager of Commodore Cruise Lines.[11] Stephan's views about the direction for the new cruise line were based largely on his earlier experiences. He began with several assumptions: that old ocean-going vessels were unable to make the transition from transportation with different classes of passengers to modern-day one-class cruising, so they were not a viable option; that passengers wanted new and safe ships; that ships should be purpose-built and designed for tropical waters; and that economies of scale in marketing and purchasing dictated a fleet of ships.[12]

Stephan was connected to shipping circles in Oslo and initially met three brothers — Sigurd, Brynjulf, and Morits Skaugen — of I.M. Skaugen. Eventually a partnership was formed including I.M. Skaugen and Anders Wilhelmsen & Co. Another Norwegian company, Gotaas-Larsen, later joined the partnership. They ordered three new ships from Wartsila of Helsinki, the world leader in modern cruise ship design at the time. The first ship, *Song of Norway*,[13] began operations in 1970. *Nordic Prince*[14] entered service a year later and in 1972 *Sun Viking*[15] was delivered. The ships incorporated Edwin Stephan designs including an observation lounge located on the ship's funnel well above the highest deck and inspired by the Space Needle built for the 1962 World's Fair in Seattle.

RCCL was successful from the start, partly due to its marketing of ships before they were delivered. As well, the cruise line introduced "air–sea" packages from Los Angeles and San Francisco — the two cities accounted for 35 to 40 percent of their passenger load. RCCL chartered aircraft and kept them full. The planes took new passengers to the ship and flew disembarking passengers back home. With such efficient use of the aircraft, RCCL provided flights and a quick sightseeing tour of Miami for less than $60. A one-week cruise on the *Song of Norway*, including airfare, port charges, and transfers could be had for as little as $368 per person — equivalent to $1,811 in 2004 dollars.

RCCL continued to be profitable and slowly expanded its capacity. It "stretched" *Song of Norway* adding 300 additional beds in 1978, did the same to the *Nordic Prince* in 1980, and in 1982 took delivery of the *Song of America*, its first new ship in ten years. Like RCCL's first three ships, *Song of America* was built by Wartsila, but was larger: 37,584 gross tons and accommodations for up to 1,575 passengers. It pioneered a layout where cabin decks were stacked at the front of the ship, furthest from the engines, with public rooms farther aft. Although common on large car ferries, this layout had not been repeated much on cruise ships. The trademark Sky Lounge was even more prominent than before, completely encircling the funnel. *Song of America* was sold to Sun Cruises in 1999, and renamed *Sunbird*. Unlike previous sales to Sun Cruises, the Sky Lounge was not removed.

Barely Scraping By

Following the breakdown of the partnership between Ted Arison and Knut Kloster, Arison sought to start his own cruise line. He first attempted to reach an agreement with Cunard, which had two ships retired from service and laid up in England. After that failed he learned that Canadian Pacific's *Empress of Canada* was laid up and after viewing the ship put together plans for its purchase. But he lacked the money to purchase the ship on his own.

Arison turned to an old friend, Meshulam Riklis,[16] for assistance. Riklis was a successful entrepreneur and had become a master at corporate takeovers, often involving leveraged buyouts.[17] He was at the time the principal shareholder in Boston-based American International Travel Service (AITS), which operated group and individual tours around the world under the name Carnival. Arison convinced Riklis to set up a subsidiary of AITS, to be named Carnival Cruise Lines. Riklis purchased *Empress of Canada*[18] for $7 million[19] and, in keeping with the Carnival theme, renamed it *Mardi Gras*.

The ship entered service on March 7, 1972. After two years of losing money, Riklis severed his association with Carnival and gave the *Mardi Gras* (and its $5 million mortgage) to Arison for one dollar. Arison slashed prices, opened casinos and discos on board, and devised new ways to generate onboard revenue. The company finally turned a profit in 1975. According to Micky Arison, this was the beginning of the "fun ship" concept. It wasn't so much a grand plan as an immediate strategy to generate enough income to meet weekly payroll.[20]

With his profit, Arison bought *Empress of Britain* and renamed it *Carnivale*.[21] The ship entered service on February 7, 1976, and turned a profit its first year. In 1977 Arison bought his third ship, sight unseen. The *S.A. Vaal*[22] entered the Carnival fleet in 1978 as *Festivale* after undergoing a major refit in Japan which added extra decks and almost doubled the passenger capacity. The refit was a major learning experience for Arison and Carnival Cruise Lines. A price for the refit had been negotiated in yen, but with currency fluctuations the cost in dollars almost doubled. Plans for another building project in Japan were canceled. Carnival's first purpose-built cruise ship, *Tropicale*[23] joined the fleet in 1982. Since the *Tropicale*'s debut, the cruise industry has introduced well over 100 new ships, including more than 40 contracted by various Carnival Corporation brands.[24]

A key ingredient in Carnival's marketing was its "fun ships" label, which is attributed to Bob Dickinson who joined the company in 1973. According to Dickinson, he gathered all the cruise brochures then on the market and was struck by promotion of Commodore Cruise Line's *Boheme* as the "Happy Ship."

> This idea appealed to Dickinson because the cruise slogan applied to a specific ship and not the company. After all, the ship, not the company, is what people buy. "Happy" was taken and it sounded kind of wussy anyhow! What is the one universal question – the one ingredient everyone wants in their vacation — FUN![25]

Dickinson went with the "fun ship" idea. He was apparently unaware that *Yarmouth Castle* was often referred to as the "fun ship." Even if he was, the ship sank in 1965 and few people either remembered or cared.

The Maturing of the Cruise Industry

Obviously the industry has had other players but Carnival, Royal Caribbean, Princess, and NCL are among the few that have survived. Many cruise lines have come and gone, and many have been swallowed by the major players in the industry.

Industry Growth and Consolidation

The 1970s and 1980s were a period of moderate growth. Cunard entered the cruise business in 1970 with the introduction of two 600-passenger vessels — *Adventurer*[26] and *Ambassador*.[27] Within a couple of years other cruise lines appeared, including Royal Cruise Line,[28] Royal Viking Line,[29] and Sitmar Cruises.[30] They catered to more affluent passengers than did the mainstream product offered by mass market operators. Additional lines appeared in the 1980s: Premier Cruises in 1982, Regency Cruises and Sea Goddess Cruises in 1984, Windstar Cruises in 1986, and Renaissance Cruises and Seabourn Cruise Line in 1988. The industry's growth is reflected in the number of people who took a cruise — roughly a half million passengers in 1970, 1.4 million passengers in 1980, and 3.6 million passengers in 1990.[31]

New lines continued to spring up in the 1990s: Crystal Cruises and Celebrity Cruises in 1990; Crown Cruise Line, Majesty Cruise Line, Seawind Cruise Line, Seven Seas Cruise Line, and Star Clippers Cruises in 1991; Radisson Cruise Line in 1992; Silversea Cruises, Orient Lines, and Star Cruises in 1993; and Disney Cruise Line in 1998. By 2000, the number of North Americans taking a cruise had increased to 6.9 million – almost double the number ten years earlier. Much of this expansion came with new ship construction.

The industry's growth is not a straight line. Some attempts to begin new cruise lines failed. American Family Cruises started by Costa Cruises in 1992 and Fiesta Marina Cruises, a Spanish-speaking cruise line started by Carnival Cruise Lines in 1993, both folded within a year. There were also bankruptcies, mergers, and consolidations. Renaissance Cruises went bankrupt in 1991 and again in 2001, Regency Cruises ceased operations in 1996, and more than a dozen cruise lines went under between 2000 and 2004.[32] Had it not been for mergers and takeovers, more cruise lines would have likely gone out of business. (These mergers and takeovers are discussed in the next chapter.)

Like Viagra for Ships: Mine Is Bigger Than Yours

A large factor in the cruise industry's growth is the increasing size of new ships. In contrast to the 750- to 1,000-passenger ships used by NCL, RCCL, Carnival Cruise Lines, and Princess Cruises in their early days, new purpose-built cruise ships became larger and larger. Competition emerged for which cruise line's ship was the biggest.

The competition began in 1985, when Carnival Cruise Lines unveiled the 46,000-ton *Holiday* and touted it as the largest ship ever built for vacation cruises. It carried 1,500 passengers. Three years later, in January 1988, RCCL welcomed *Sovereign of the Seas* and branded it "the world's largest cruise ship." Costing $185 million and weighing 73,192 tons, the ship carried up to 2,852 passengers. With each new ship, the celebratory hoopla became more colorful and grand.

Though not new, NCL introduced *Norway* in 1990 following a two-month, $40 million expansion. Although advertised as the largest cruise ship afloat, its passenger capacity of 2,032 was less than ships being introduced by NCL's competition.

A building frenzy during the 1990s produced a continual flow of newer and bigger ships. RCCL's *Monarch of the Seas*, at 73,941 tons and with a passenger capacity of 2,744, became the newest cruise ship in November 1991. Though 2,000 tons lighter than *Norway*, it claimed the largest passenger capacity. In July 1992, 2,655 passengers embarked on the ship — the most passengers on a single voyage on a modern cruise ship. RCCL submitted the necessary documentation to the *Guinness Book of World Records*.

Competition for biggest renewed in 1995 when Princess Cruises introduced *Sun Princess* — the largest cruise ship ever built at 77,000 tons, but with a passenger capacity of only 1,950. Competition reached new heights in November 1996 with the entry of megaships. Carnival began with the $400 million, 101,000 ton *Carnival Destiny* with capacity for 3,400 passengers. It entered the *Guinness Book of World Records* for carrying 3,269 passengers on December 22, 1996, and 3,315 on March 29, 1997. However, its sister ship, *Carnival Triumph*, took the honor on August 22, 1999, with 3,413 passengers. Today there are seven Destiny-class ships[34] — the newest expanding to 110,000 tons with capacity for 400 more passengers than their older siblings.

> *"Cruising on a megaship compared to a small ship is like going to a cocktail party with 2,000 people compared to going to a party at someone's house. In the first instance, chances are that you will only remember the meatballs, in the second instance, you will remember the people you meet."*
>
> **— Al Wallack, president**
> **Royal Olympic Cruises[33]**

Princess Cruises re-entered the competition with *Grand Princess* in May 1998. The 2,600-passenger ship cost $400 million and weighed 109,000 tons. A year and a half later, Royal Caribbean International reclaimed the title of biggest with *Voyager of the Seas*. Costing $500 million, it was the largest in both weight (142,000 tons) and passenger capacity (3,840 passengers). *Voyager of the Seas* quickly claimed the title for most passengers on a single voyage — over 3,600 passengers on a single cruise in June 2000. Five Voyager-class vessels are now sailing.

Cunard's *Queen Mary 2* rekindled competition for biggest and best. As reported in the press worldwide, the "*Queen Mary 2* is the largest (151,400 tons), longest (1,132 feet), tallest (236 feet), widest (135 feet) and most expensive ($800 million) passenger vessel ever built."[35]

Two ships will soon eclipse the *Queen Mary 2*. At 160,000 tons, the $720 million *Freedom of the Seas* is roughly 15 percent larger than the current Voyager-class ships. It will carry up to 4,370 passengers — over 5,700 people (including crew) when booked to full capacity.[36] There are currently three Freedom-class ships on order.

Their glory as the largest will be relatively short lived. Carnival Cruise Lines' "Project Pinnacle"[37] is a ship in the 170,000- to 180,000-ton range with accommodation for close to 6,500 (5,000 passengers and 1,500 crew).[38] Originally planned for 2008, the project likely won't come to fruition until 2009. The delay is largely attributed to the weakened US dollar in relation to the Euro.[39]

The contrast between the ships Royal Caribbean and Carnival started with — *Song of Norway* at 18,000 tons and 724 passengers and *Mardi Gras* at 27,300 tons and 1024 passengers — and those being built today is staggering. The size gives a

TABLE 1.1: HOW THEY'VE GROWN: INCREASES IN SHIP SIZE BY MAJOR CRUISE CORPORATIONS*

Carnival Corporation

Year	Ship	Gross Tons	Lower Berths
1972	Mardi Gras	27,300	1,024
1982	Tropicale	36,674	1,022
1985	Holiday	46,052	1,452
1990	Fantasy	70,367	2,044
1996	Carnival Destiny	101,353	2,642
2003	Queen Mary 2	150,000	2,620
2009	Pinnacle Class	175,000 (est.)	4,000

Norwegian Cruise Line

Year	Ship	Gross Tons	Lower Berths
1971	Southward	17,270	800
1988	Seaward	42,000	1,504
1992	Dreamward	41,000	1,242
1999	Norwegian Sky	78,000	2,002
2002	Norwegian Dawn	92,000	2,240

Princess Cruises

Year	Ship	Gross Tons	Lower Berths
1971	Island Princess	20,000	640
1984	Royal Princess	45,000	1,200
1990	Crown Princess	70,000	1,590
1998	Grand Princess	109,000	2,600
2004	Caribbean Princess	116,000	3,100

Royal Caribbean Cruise Line/International

Year	Ship	Gross Tons	Lower Berths
1970	Song of Norway	18,000	724
1982	Song of America	23,000	1,004
1988	Sovereign of the Seas	73,192	2,278
1999	Voyager of the Seas	142,000	3,114
2006	Freedom of the Seas	160,000	3,600

* Weight is shown in Gross Registered Tons. Passenger capacity is based on double occupancy — actual capacity can be as much as 25 percent greater than this figure.

different cruise experience. Some people prefer a small ship, both for the smaller passenger load and the greater connection to the sea.

Others prefer a large ship with its additional amenities and activities. The Voyager-class ships, for example, have "a rock-climbing wall up the smokestack, an ice-skating rink, and most talked about, a four-story tall shopping mall (the 'Royal Promenade') deep in the bowels running a considerable length of the ship."[41] They also have amusements common on other ships: virtual reality games, a running track and gym, a basketball and/or tennis court, a miniature golf course, a full-service spa, and a wide range of planned activities. One writer says of the *Voyager of the Seas*, "The idea is to grab a larger slice of the vacation market by offering so many things to do and places to explore on board – so that even people who don't particularly care for sea cruises may want to go because the experience may not seem like they're on a ship."[42] This style of cruising is different from the norm of a decade or two earlier.

"Bigger is not necessarily better."

**— Richard Fain, CEO
Royal Caribbean Cruises Limited**[40]

Where There Is Money There Is Greed

Other changes, not so visible to passengers, were associated with the maturing of the cruise industry. In the early days of leisure cruising, cruise lines generated most of their income from the sale of passenger tickets. Alcoholic and soft drinks, bought at duty free prices, were sold cheaply. The cost for a drink in the early 1970s was between 35 and 50 cents. A decade later, the price was still a bargain, between $1.00 and $1.40. Casinos in these days were small or nonexistent, and shopping and shore excursion programs were limited and left to onboard staff to plan and organize. Consequently, the cruise director and his/her staff could generate income for themselves that the cruise line captures today.

Bingo was one source of income. Introduced as a form of entertainment, it was directed by the cruise director. In the "early days," the income generated was either kept by the cruise director or shared among the cruise staff. Not until the 1980s and 1990s did cruise lines realize the money being lost to them.[43] Increasingly, they brought bingo games under their control.

Another income source redirected to cruise line coffers has been shore excursions, port lectures, and shopping programs. These too were originally the responsibility of the cruise director and his/her staff who generated income from these activities. As late as 1994, I observed a cruise director go from store to store in each port visited, collecting his "commission" for sales the previous week to passengers from the ship. He also collected money from tour providers and other businesses benefiting from the cruise ship's visits.

TABLE 1.2: WHAT DOES IT COST TO BUILD A SHIP?

Carnival Cruise Line

Year	Ship	Cost	Cost per Berth (1990 $)
1981	Tropicale	$100m+	$140,900+
1985	Holiday	$170m	$141,667
1986	Jubilee	$131m	$104,906
1990	Fantasy	$225m	$110,078
1991	Ecstasy	$275m	$129,411
1993	Sensation	$300m	$132,353
1995	Imagination	$330m	$139,118
1997	Carnival Destiny	$400m	$122,634
1998	Carnival Paradise	$300m	$116,960
1999	Carnival Triumph	$400m	$113,124
2000	Carnival Victory	$440m	$121,246
2001	Carnival Spirit	$375m	$130,896
2002	Carnival Conquest	$450m	$119,108
2002	Carnival Pride	$375m	$130,586
2003	Carnival Glory	$450m	$115,845
2004	Carnival Valor	$500m	$116,005
2005	Carnival Liberty	$450m	$101,378

Royal Caribbean Cruise Line/International

Year	Ship	Cost	Cost per Berth (1990 $)
1970	Song of Norway	$13.5m	$62,838
1982	Song of America	$140m	$135,000
1987	Sovereign of the Seas	$150m	$75,790
1990	Nordic Empress	$180m	$111,801
1991	Monarch of the Seas	$270m	$110,110
1992	Majesty of the Seas	$300m	$118,521
1995	Legend of the Seas	$314m	$149,689
1998	Vision of the Seas	$278m	$111,200
1999	Voyager of the Seas	$500m	$125,806
2000	Explorer of the Seas	$500m	$122,580
2001	Radiance of the Seas	$350m	$129,500
2002	Brilliance of the Seas	$350m	$127,750
2002	Adventure of the Seas	$500m	$117,741
2004	Jewel of the Seas	$350m	$120,750
2006	Freedom of the Seas	$750m	$138,750 (est.)

Less than ten years earlier, companies were established to formalize this system of kickbacks and to capture the money being drawn by the cruise director. Companies such as Onboard Media[44] and Panoff Publishing were the result. They centralize the system of port lectures, shore excursions, and port shopping; provide personnel and printed materials; and share with the cruise line a portion of their income. These companies initially were lucrative; however, the cruise lines learned how much money they made and demanded increasingly larger percentages of their income.

Income from sources other than cruise fares became serious business in the late 1980s and early 1990s. Carnival Cruise Lines was perhaps the first to realize the potential of onboard revenue but Norwegian Cruise Line reportedly was the first to establish a corporate manager of onboard revenue. The goal was to get passengers on board with low fares and then to generate income by spending once passengers were on the ship. J. Norman Howard, former business director for Cunard Line, succinctly expressed the orientation: "Attract passengers with good pricing and merchandising. Entertain them at all costs. Fill them up. Strip them clean. Send them home happy."[45]

Casinos, bars, onboard shops, spa services, and shipboard photography augmented the income from shore excursions and shopping programs. By the late 1990s most ships had onboard revenue centers, including art auctions, ship-to-shore communications, in-room minibars, etc. Many new profit centers have been introduced in the current decade such that a substantial portion of company profits derive from onboard revenue, and old sources of income have been more fully exploited. Almost one-third of Royal Caribbean's profit in 2002–2003 was derived from shore excursions.[46] According to the company's vice president for commercial development, a typical Royal Caribbean ship can generates close to a half-million dollars in tour income with a single call at St. Petersburg, Russia.[47]

The Cruise Industry Today

The cruise industry today is different from the image of days gone by. Looking at the changes brings to light contradictions between the image of cruising and the reality of the cruise experience, and between the image of the cruise industry and the manner in which cruise corporations behave. The next chapter looks at the evolution of industry leader, Carnival Corporation.

2

I Never Saw a Cruise Line I Didn't Want to Own

H E WAS EMBROILED IN ANTI-WAR PROTESTS IN THE LATE 1960s and dropped out of college — by age 50 he was worth over $5 billion. He became chief executive officer of Carnival Corporation in 1979 at age 30. In 1990 he inherited from his father, a self-made man, the chair of the board of Carnival Corporation and co-ownership of the Miami Heat NBA basketball team. He bought out his partners and has been the sole owner of the team for more than a decade. In 2004, with a net worth of $5.9 billion, Micky Arison placed 68 on Forbes' list of the World's Richest People. He places second in Florida, followed in the number three spot by his sister Shari whose net worth is $4.6 billion and who ranks 94 on Forbes' list.

These are large sums of money by any standards. They have been derived mainly from the cruise industry where Carnival Cruise Lines has been an innovator and industry leader in turning water into money. One element has been a pack-em-in approach. "By equipping cabins with fold-down bunk beds on which parents can stash kids, Carnival can squeeze four guests to a room. Passengers pay less per person, but Carnival gets more bodies that will spend money once on board."[1]

Another element in Carnival's success is keeping costs tightly under control. It saves on ship design and construction by standardizing its fleet and the furnishings on its ships.[2] And it saves by avoiding costly additions such as rock-climbing walls, and by resisting unnecessary expenditures. Until 1999 Bob Dickinson, president of Carnival Cruise Lines, "refused to put shampoo or conditioner in the cabins because he calculated it would cost the company $2 million to $3 million a year."[3] He relented and stocked the amenities when Procter & Gamble and Unilever supplied them for free. With growth, Carnival has achieved even greater savings through economies of scale. Its takeover of P&O Princess in 2003 has yielded synergistic savings that exceed initial projections of $100 million per year.[4]

Carnival's success is reflected in its growth. Carnival Cruise Lines progressively grew in the 1970s and 1980s; Carnival Corporation began expanding through acquisitions in the late 1980s and early 1990s. Its forays outside the cruise industry generally failed. The nature and pattern of growth over the past 15 to 20 years (see Table 2.1) offers insight into the cruise industry and its way of doing business.

Building an Empire

Carnival Cruise Lines began in 1972 after the breakdown of Ted Arison's partnership with Knut Kloster. A decade later it had four ships, including its first purpose-built

TABLE 2.1: GROWING A CONGLOMERATE: CARNIVAL'S ACQUISITION SUCCESSES AND FAILURES

Cruise Line	Year	Cost	Details
Royal Caribbean Cruise Line	1988	$550m	Carnival's offer for 70% falls through when A. Wilhelmsen exercises right of first refusal.
Holland America Line	1989	$625m	Purchase includes Holland America Line, Windstar Cruises, and Westours.
Premier Cruises	1991	$372m	Carnival withdrew offer.
Seabourn Cruise Line	1992 1995 1998	– $10m –	Carnival acquired 25% in return for sales and marketing support, acquired an additional 25% by converting a loan to equity, and in 1998 took full control as part of the deal to purchase Cunard.
Epirotiki Lines	1993 1994	Ship Ship	Traded *Mardi Gras* for 16.6 equity interest; increased this to 43% with transfer of *Carnivale* and to 49% after restructuring. Sold interest in 1995 for $25m.

ship, *Tropicale*. Preparing for major expansion, Carnival introduced a network television campaign with celebrity Kathie Lee Gifford on July 9, 1984, and a year later launched its first superliner, *Holiday*. *Jubilee* and *Celebration* followed in 1986 and 1987. These ships established the Carnival brand name and its reputation for outrageous and opulent interior designs.[5]

Also in 1987, Carnival began an initial public offering of 23.6 million common shares. Proceeds were used to pay debt incurred in construction of the two newest ships and to finance construction of the Crystal Palace Resort and Casino in Nassau, Bahamas,[6] which opened in 1988. Carnival also continued to expand its cruise operations: it ordered three Fantasy-class ships in 1987, the first for delivery in 1990, and it looked to acquire other cruise lines. Micky Arison bought Pacific Interstate Airlines and started Carnival Airlines in 1988.

Carnival's success in cruise tourism did not carry over to other segments of the travel industry. The Crystal Palace in Nassau, nicknamed "The Purple Palace" because of its garish color schemes, was a financial failure. Carnival's hope to cross-

TABLE 2.1: GROWING A CONGLOMERATE: CARNIVAL'S ACQUISITION SUCCESSES AND FAILURES – continued:

NCL	1995 –	Bought $850m in NCL debt in 11/1995; sold NCL option to buy back $1.01bn in debt in 02/1996.
British Airtours	1996 $307m	Took 29.5% interest. Sold in 2001 for $492m.
Hyundai Joint Venture	1996 4.8m	Partnership for Asian-based cruise line dissolved after several months due to irreconcilable differences.
Costa Cruises	1997 $300m	The Carnival/Airtours partnership bought 100% of Costa. Carnival bought Airtours' interest in 2000 for $510m.
Celebrity Cruises	1997 $525m	Offered spoiler bid in RCCL's take-over of Celebrity. Unsuccessful.
Cunard Line	1998 $500m	With partners, bought 100% of Cunard Line. Bought partners' 32% interest in 1999 for $203.5m.
NCL	1999 $2.1bn	Outmaneuvered by Star Cruises.
P&O Princess	2002 $5bn+	Outmaneuvered RCCL.

sell land-based vacations to cruise passengers proved wrong.[7] The hotel was plagued by low occupancy and lost hundreds of millions of dollars. It was sold in November 1994 to the Ruffin Group of Texas for $80 million.[8]

Carnival Airlines lasted a bit longer. It started in November 1988 by flying tourists on one Boeing 727 between Fort Lauderdale and Carnival's Crystal Palace in Nassau. It expanded and began scheduled service in 1990, including feeder service to its cruise ships. Initially, it flew from New York and Puerto Rico to Fort Lauderdale. In time flights were added to include Miami, Los Angeles, Newark, New Orleans, Houston, Chicago, Orlando, Tampa, and White Plains.

By 1997 the airline served 16 cities with 50 daily departures between the northeast, Florida, California, and the Caribbean. It was the largest Florida-based airline. But intense pressure from other low-fare carriers and a crash in the Everglades by ValuJet in May 1996 took their toll on passenger loads and revenue. Previously profitable Carnival Airlines reported a $75 million loss for fiscal year 1997. On top of that, its pilots had just voted 73 percent in favor of collective bargaining.[10]

From the Golden Goose Come Lead Balloons

Despite his success in cruise tourism, Ted Arison never did particularly well outside the cruise and hospitality industry. He started an auto-loan underwriting firm in the late 1970s that went out of business after just a few years. He spent $12 million to form Hamilton Corporation, a real estate firm, which a decade later was worth less than his initial investment; he sold out in the early 1990s. His return to the maritime cargo business in the 1980s lost him $43 million by the time he sold out in 1987.

Arison's biggest fiasco was Ensign Bank, "which he created by merging two smaller savings and loan institutions in 1983. In 1989 Ensign wrote off a three-million-dollar loan to CenTrust Bank chairman David Paul, who later was indicted and jailed for banking and securities fraud; then, on Arison's say-so, Ensign loaned $750,000 to Port of Miami director Carmen Lunetta for a real estate development. Finally Ensign lost more than $19 million in the first quarter of 1990, and by year's end, the federal government had seized it."[9]

According to a former high-ranking employee, Arison had a vision but no business plan. He pursued acquisitions opportunistically and on an ad hoc basis. This is visible in his and his son's business practices.

In April 1997 Carnival Airlines merged with Pan Am; the merged company did not acknowledge the collective bargaining rights of Carnival's pilots.[11] The merger allowed Arison "to cut his losses and absolve himself of any personal exposure connected to investments in Carnival Airlines."[12] He made a $30 million capital investment in new Pan Am equity and guaranteed bank loans totaling $25 million, which Pan Am couldn't have gotten on its own. At the time of the merger, Arison was a 43 percent shareholder in Pan Am. His share decreased to 20 percent by the time Pan Am filed for bankruptcy protection in February 1998.[13] Carnival Airlines terminated operations April 3, 1998.

Quest to Be the Biggest

Carnival's first takeover target was Royal Caribbean Cruise Line (RCCL) in 1988. At that time P&O's Princess Cruises had just merged with Sitmar Cruises. Its 11,202 berths were more than Carnival or any other cruise ship operator had. Carnival had

8,448 berths, but would soon be put into third place when Royal Caribbean and Admiral Cruise Lines merged — the new company would have 9,034 berths.

Royal Caribbean had been established as a partnership involving three Norwegian companies: I.M. Skaugen, Anders Wilhelmsen & Co., and Gotaas-Larsen. Gotaas-Larsen also owned Admiral Cruise Line, which was created in 1986 by merging Eastern Cruise Line in Miami, Western Cruise Line operating out of Los Angeles,[14] and Stardancer Cruises, operator of the car-carrying *Stardancer*[15] sailing to Alaska and Mexico.

Plans were made in 1988 to merge Gotaas-Larsen's three-vessel Admiral Cruise Line with Royal Caribbean's four vessels, which included newly built *Sovereign of the Seas*. Before the merger could be completed, Carnival announced that it had agreed in principle to pay Gotaas-Larsen Shipping Corporation $275 million for its 36 percent stake in Royal Caribbean and Admiral Cruise Lines — $15 million more than offered two weeks earlier.[16] Carnival also agreed to purchase the 34 percent share held by I.M. Skaugen and its partners for an additional $275 million. Under terms of the agreements, Anders Wilhelmsen, who held a 28 percent stake, was given 40 days to match Carnival's bid.

With five days to spare, Wilhelmsen announced formation of a joint venture with the Pritzker family. The Pritzkers,[17] based in Chicago, controlled the Hyatt Hotel chain and the Marmon Group, an international association of 150 autonomous manufacturing and service companies, and held many other investments. Jay Pritzker, who ran the family's investments outside the Hyatt chain, negotiated the deal.[18] A third partner in the deal was Sammy Ofer, who was said to be very close to Jay Pritzker.

> When Pritzker, more by fate than design, found himself owning ships as a consequence of taking over other companies, he asked Ofer to manage them. And when the hotel entrepreneur got involved … with Norwegian Anders Wilhelmsen in the 50–50 ownership of Royal Admiral — later Royal Caribbean — Ofer as an old friend was invited to take a stake.[19]

It is believed that Ofer's stake today is 20 to 25 percent of the Pritzkers' 25 percent ownership of Royal Caribbean. Collectively, the partners put up $567 million for Admiral Cruise Line and Royal Caribbean.

Royal Caribbean's board of directors reflects the joint ownership of the company. The shareholders' agreement includes a provision that the board consist of four nominees of AndersWilhelmsen and four nominees of the Pritzker/Ofer holding company, Cruise Associates. By agreement, there are four additional members: the CEO, the majority shareholder of Celebrity Cruises before its takeover in 1997 by RCCL, and two others. Certain corporate actions require approval by at least one director nominated by each partner.[20]

Pritzker v. Pritzker

It appeared in 2002 that the Pritzkers were preparing to liquidate some holdings, including sale of their stake in Royal Caribbean (representing approximately 6 to 7 percent of the total Pritzker empire).[21] A lawsuit filed by Liesel and Matthew Pritzker claimed that their father, Robert, violated his fiduciary duty when he virtually emptied their trust funds in the mid-1990s during bitter post-divorce squabbles with his second ex-wife. The brother and sister claim that their father disapproved of Liesel's acting career and of the continuing relationship both had with their mother. They sought $5 billion in damages and return of the stock their father took from them.[22]

Robert Pritzker is the last surviving grandson of Nicholas Pritzker who arrived penniless in the US from Russia in the late 1800s, earned a law degree, and set up a successful law practice. Nicholas' sons also became lawyers and expanded into Chicago-area real estate deals. One of his sons, Abram, had four sons, including Robert. They bought into Hyatt Hotels and other businesses and shaped the estimated $15 billion empire that exists today.[23]

In 2005 three cousins, each a lawyer, preside over the Pritzker empire. Thomas, 55, is chair of Hyatt International and Hyatt Corporation. He serves on the boards of First Health Group, Royal Caribbean, and Bay City Capital. Nicholas, 59, is chair of the board and CEO of Hyatt Development Corporation, is CEO of Hyatt Equities, and directs Hyatt's casinos and timeshare operations. He is also chair of Eos Biotechnology and on the board of Bay City Capital. Penny, 46, heads Classic Residence by Hyatt and Pritzker Realty Group, and was former chair of Superior Bank. She is on the board of William Wrigley Jr. Company.

In September 2004 a Cook County (Illinois) judge ruled Pritzker v. Pritzker could proceed and a trial was scheduled for fall 2005. In January 2005 a settlement was reached and the lawsuit dropped. The Chicago Tribune reported that Liesel and Matthew would split $1 billion.[24] It is unclear whether this will impact the family's ownership of Royal Caribbean.

Royal Caribbean is Carnival's most ardent competitor. Their 2002/2003 fight for ownership of P&O Princess was not the first time the two companies have butted heads. Royal Caribbean shared Carnival's desire to take over Costa Cruises, and Carnival drove up the price to RCCL when it took over Celebrity Cruises in 1997.

An Alternative to "Fun Ships"

Less than two months after its unsuccessful takeover of Royal Caribbean, Carnival announced it was acquiring the travel and tourism businesses of Holland America Line for $625 million. The acquisition boosted Carnival's number of berths by 50 percent: Holland America Line had four ships and Windstar Cruises (part of Holland America Line) had three. The acquisition also included Westours.

Holland America Line had made its name in transatlantic passenger service since 1873. After 100 years it suspended transatlantic service, sold its cargo shipping service, and turned to cruises. The transition was not smooth. In 1973 it introduced its first purpose-built vessel, the 8,346-ton 452-passenger *Prinsendam*, and two second-hand vessels: *Brasil* and *Argentina* purchased from Moore McCormack and renamed the *Volendam* and *Veendam*. *Prinsendam* sank in the Gulf of Alaska in 1980,[25] *Statendam* was sold in 1982 because of reliability problems, and *Volendam* and *Veendam* were sold in 1983.[26]

As part of its shifting business plan, Holland America had taken over Westours in February 1971. Founded by Chuck West, the tour company was the largest and oldest cruise and tour operator in Alaska and Canada's Yukon and it relied on ships from other cruise lines for its summer operations in Alaska.[27] West was forced to sell the company after over-extending himself financially. Holland America was a willing buyer given that it had ships and the expertise to run them, and only needed a region to deploy them. Westours and Holland America became a single company in 1983 and Kirk Lanterman, who had joined Westours as controller in 1970 and was its current president, became president of the newly combined cruise and tour company, Holland America Line – Westours.

Holland America Line began a period of renewal in 1983. It added to the 1959-built *Rotterdam* (38,645 tons, 1,075 passengers) the newly built *Nieuw Amsterdam* and a year later its sister, *Noordam* (both 33,930 tons and 1,214 passengers). Holland America became profitable and in 1987 purchased 50 percent of Windstar Cruises— it purchased the other half a year later — which operated three ships. In 1988 it also purchased the two-ship fleet of Home Lines. It sold one (*Atlantic*) to Premier Cruises. The other, the 1986-built *Homeric*, was renamed *Westerdam*. At the *Westerdam*'s introductory events in November 1988, Ted Arison of Carnival was approached by Holland America Line Chairman Nico van der Vorm about selling Holland America to Carnival. Holland America presented a perfect opportunity for Carnival's plans to establish an upmarket operation of its own, called Project

New Minimum Wage: $33,315.40 an Hour

Kirk Lanterman retired from Holland America – Westours on November 30, 2004. He was 72 years old and had served as chair of the board and chief executive officer during the previous seven and a half years. On December 1, 2004, Mr. Lanterman began drawing from his retirement and consulting agreement with Carnival Corporation. In return for as many as five hours of consulting work per month Lanterman receives $1,998,924 annually — a minimum hourly wage of $33,315.40.[28] Under a separate consulting contract he receives an additional $788,000 in 2005 and 2006 for up to a maximum 1,000 hours.[29]

Tiffany.[30] The deal between Carnival and Holland America was finalized within weeks.[31]

Holland America has grown considerably under Carnival's ownership. The four ships inherited by Carnival when it took over Holland America Line have all been sold or retired.[32] In their place 12 new ships have been added to the former *Royal Viking Sun*, now named *Prinsendam*.[33] These 13 ships have more than 19,000 berths and reflect a fivefold increase in capacity between 1992 and 2006.

Through Westours, Holland America also owns and operates 14 Westmark Hotels in Alaska and the Yukon; more than 30 different tour programs to destinations in Alaska, the Yukon, and Washington; two luxury day boats offering tours to the glaciers of Alaska and the Yukon River; a fleet of over 300 motor coaches under the name "Gray Line" in Alaska, Washington, British Columbia, and the Yukon (including express motor coach service between downtown Seattle and the Seattle-Tacoma International Airport); and 13 private, domed rail cars, which are called "McKinley Explorers" and run on the Alaska Railroad between Anchorage and Fairbanks, stopping at Denali National Park.[34] Holland America is a big player in Alaska. Its largest competitors are Princess Tours — Princess Cruises' equivalent to Westours — and Royal Caribbean's Royal Celebrity Tours.

Looking for a Bargain

Carnival again looked to expand in 1991. It had just sold its 11 percent interest in Finnish shipbuilder Masa Yards to Kvaener Industries of Oslo. It had acquired the stake in October 1989 when it put up $10 million to help Masa Yards take over the operations of the bankrupt Wartsila Marine Industries to ensure that the Carnival ships on order would be delivered.[35] In April 1991 it announced plans to acquire Premier Cruises for $372 million.

Premier Cruises began in 1984 and was owned by Dial Corporation. Dial also owned Greyhound Leisure Services, which ran shops on cruise ships, and provided airport meet-and-greet for cruise passengers and other services to cruise lines. Premier had three ships (*StarShip Oceanic*,[36] 19,500 tons; *StarShip Majestic*,[37] 17,503 tons; *StarShip Atlantic*,[38] 19,337 tons) with a total capacity of almost 3,000 berths. However, Premier's attractiveness to Carnival was not its ships. Premier was the official carrier to Disney World and the only cruise line permitted to offer cruise packages that included the theme park. A high percentage of its business was derived from this association.

Carnival's deal with Premier was called off seven weeks later. Dial Corporation said negotiations had broken down because of disagreement over future earnings in the wake of the Gulf War.[39] Recession had also hit earnings. From Carnival's perspective, taking over Premier at the time would dilute its earnings.[40] A couple of months later, Carnival announced that it was negotiating a 50 percent stake in luxury vessel operator Seabourn Cruise Line.[41]

From K-Mart to Ultra Luxury

Seabourn Cruise Line was founded in 1987 by Norwegian industrialist Atle Brynestad. It operated two 200-passenger cruise ships catering to the ultra luxury sector of the cruise market, the first entering service in 1988 and the other following in 1989. Although the company had performed relatively well, the Gulf War reduced bookings. Though it believed it was rebounding, Seabourn saw that an association with Carnival would infuse cash and allow its fleet to expand. The takeover would give Carnival coverage across the full spectrum: from mass market Carnival to premium Holland America, to Windstar with its tall-masted sailing ships, to ultra-luxury Seabourn. They could target every segment of cruise consumer, and could encourage customers of one line to "graduate" to another.

Carnival's takeover of Seabourn began in February 1992. In return for sales and marketing support, Carnival took a 25 percent equity interest. Carnival also provided two secured 10-year loans: one for $15 million and one for $10 million. It could convert the $10 million note into an additional 25 percent stake at any time before maturity, which it did in December 1995.[42] In January 1996 Seabourn acquired *Queen Odyssey* from Royal Cruise Line and renamed her *Seabourn Legend*. The ship is a near-identical sister to the other two Seabourn ships.[43] Carnival took full control of Seabourn when it bought Cunard in April 1998.

Accessing Europe without Money

Carnival put up cash when it took over Holland America. It secured Seabourn through administrative support and loans. In September 1993 it acquired a 16.6 percent equity interest in Epirotiki Lines in exchange for the 1961-built *Mardi Gras*.

Epirotiki was a Greece-based operator of eight cruise ships with a total capacity of 5,200 passengers. It had recently experienced hard luck. After years without an accident, in October 1988 *Jupiter* collided with a car carrier and sank within 45 minutes. Two crew and two passengers lost their lives. In June 1991 *Pegasus* burned out after a fire broke out at her berth in Venice[44] — the vessel was the youngest in the Epirotiki fleet at 16 years old. Two months later *Oceanos* lost power and sank off a remote part of South Africa. No passengers or crew lost their lives, but the incident received international attention because senior crew members allegedly abandoned ship and left entertainment staff to evacuate the ship.[45]

Carnival's stake increased to 43 percent in March 1994 when the former *Carnivale*[46] was transferred to Epirotiki. Epirotiki's *Pallas Athena* had recently been destroyed by fire. Howard Frank, Carnival's chief financial officer, said Epirotiki needed Carnival for its expertise and modern management techniques; Carnival needed Epirotiki as a platform for it to expand into Europe at very low cost.[47] Pamela Conover, head of cruise shipping at Citibank, was brought in to manage Epirotiki.

Carnival expanded its ownership to 49 percent when Epirotiki was restructured in February 1995. Under the new shareholder agreement the Potamianos family, traditional owners of Epirotiki, retained 20 percent of the company. Paris Katsoufis, who also owned Dolphin Cruise Line, held all remaining stock in name. Katsoufis' participation allowed Epirotiki to claim it remained under Greek ownership, a prerequisite for its Greek flag cruise operation in the Aegean.[48]

Carnival's relationship with Epirotiki collapsed in April 1995 when George and Andreas Potamianos paid $25 million for Carnival's shares and those held by Paris Kotsoufis, an amount roughly equal to the combined value of the two ships Carnival gave to Epirotiki. Carnival had hoped to radically shake up Epirotiki's management practices and the company's fleet, but the Potamianos brothers reportedly felt they had relinquished power under duress and held decision-making in the company to a practical standstill.[49] Carnival's involvement with Epirotiki gave it useful knowledge and experience with the European market. It also divested two older vessels.[50]

Following its association with Carnival, Epirotiki merged with Sun Line Cruises in August 1995 to form Royal Olympic Cruises. The new company had five ships: *Triton, Olympic,* and *Odysseus* from Epirotiki and the Sun Line duo of *Stella Solaris* and *Stella Oceanis.*[51] In 1998 it raised $81 million in an initial public offering, largely to fuel expansion and growth.[52] Royal Olympic introduced *Olympic Voyager* in December 2000, and a year later *Olympic Explorer.* But the company was hit particularly hard by cancellations after the September 11 terrorist attacks. Compared with a slight profit in 2000, Royal Olympic posted a $25.5 million loss for 2001[53] and $26.7 million loss for 2002.[54] It filed for bankruptcy in early 2004 following the seizure of the *Voyager, Explorer,* and five of its other ships. The *Olympia Countess,*

Voyager, and *Explorer* were each sold in March; the remaining ships were allowed to continue to operate while the company reorganized.[55] Three were sold in April 2005; the company's future remains in question.

Keeping the Competition Afloat

Carnival was talking with British Airtours in 1995, but its plans for expanding into Europe were briefly sidetracked by its near-takeover of Kloster Cruises in late 1995. Kloster Cruises owned Norwegian Cruise Line (NCL) and despite selling Royal Viking Line to Cunard in 1994 and closing Royal Cruise Line (acquired in 1989) in 1996, still found itself $850 million in debt in October 1995.

With little or no growth in the North American market last year, after a decade and a half of buoyancy, Carnival has plainly concluded that this is no time to take chances with a clientele, both actual and potential, which is plainly less than whole-hearted at the moment in its desire to go cruising.

— Rationale behind Carnival's help for NCL, November 1995[57]

By early November 1995 Carnival had bought one-third of the bonds representing NCL's debt, in most cases paying between 70 and 75 percent of their par value.[56] Kloster's parent company, Vard, said it was in talks with Carnival, which could lead to joint ownership of NCL with Carnival taking a majority stake, but nothing materialized. Carnival kept NCL afloat by purchasing the remainder of its debt and offering close to 85 percent of par trading value, but it never entered into a shareholder agreement.

In February 1996 Carnival sold NCL an option to buy back $1.01 billion worth of its bonds, and made a small profit on the sale. Analysts at the time suggested Carnival was not really interested in owning NCL, operator of eight mostly modern cruise ships, given NCL's large debt. Instead, Carnival wanted to prevent the consumer backlash if NCL went out of business. The cruise industry was still struggling to fully rebound from the Gulf War and was working to cultivate consumer confidence, particularly as several companies were struggling. Carnival's assistance of NCL came a week before Regency Cruises announced bankruptcy.

By preventing the bankruptcy of NCL, Carnival avoided a major blow to the cruise industry, which relies largely on public confidence to promote demand. A year later, NCL was in vastly better financial condition and had announced plans for a public stock offering. It was soon talking of expansion through new ship construction.

Europe via England

Less than a year after collapse of its joint venture with Epirotiki, Carnival acquired a 29.5 percent equity interest in British Airtours in April 1996 for approximately $307 million.[58] Airtours provided Carnival an immediate foothold in Europe and opportunity to globalize its cruise business. Airtours was among the UK holiday industry's "big three," controlling 70 percent of the travel market.[59] It owned 770 retail travel agency locations in the UK and Scandinavia, a charter air fleet of 32 planes, 41 hotels in the Mediterranean, and two cruise ships — *Seawing* and *Carousel*.

During its association with Carnival, Airtours added two ships to its cruise line and bought Florida-based Travel Services International, a major distributor of leisure travel products (i.e., cruises, auto rental, alumni holidays, and hotel bookings) in the US. By 2000 the company was losing money and despite restructuring its North American operations[60] the losses were significant. Carnival's share was $43 million in 2001 and $41 million in 2000. It sold its interest on June 1, 2001, for $492 million. It claimed a net gain of $101 million. By this time it had established its presence in Europe through Costa and Cunard and no longer needed Airtours. Airtours' financial woes subsequently deteriorated further. Now known as MyTravel, the company offloaded its cruise business in 2004,[61] and continues on the financial brink.[62]

Asian Invasion

Carnival's expansion plans included Asia. In September 1996 it signed an agreement with Hyundai Merchant Marine to form a 50–50 joint venture to target the Asian cruise vacation market. Carnival and Hyundai each contributed $4.8 million and in November 1996 the joint venture bought Carnival Cruise Lines' *Tropicale* for $95.5 million cash. The vessel was chartered back to Carnival until it would be needed for cruise operations in the Asian market, likely the spring of 1998.

Carnival claimed irreconcilable differences and dissolved the joint venture a year later. According to Howard Frank, Carnival's vice chair, Carnival didn't share Hyundai's view of the Asian cruise market and the two "had very different views as to how the joint venture should be managed and the strategic direction it should take."[63] Carnival repurchased the *Tropicale* for $93 million and turned its focus back to Europe.

Invading Europe from the South

Rumors circulated in January 1996 that Royal Caribbean was close to taking over Costa Cruises. The Italian cruise group was valued at $350 million.[64] But the takeover never came to fruition. Instead, Carnival and Airtours signed a letter of intent in December 1996 to acquire Costa for approximately $300 million, with Carnival and

Airtours each contributing half. Costa sorely needed capital to expand so it could retain market share (70 percent of the Italian market, 55 percent of the French market, and a 20 percent of the Spanish market) and compete with the North American lines increasingly present in the Mediterranean.[65]

The takeover was completed in June 1997 and cost Carnival $141 million.[66] Costa at the time operated eight ships — five it owned and three it had on lease or charter — with aggregate capacity of about 8,500 passengers. The company had a net profit of $31 million in 1995 and $50 million in 1996.

Because Carnival was headquartered in the US, where laws prohibit US companies from doing business in Cuba, Costa had to divest its holdings in Cuba. It operated two cruise ships — *Costa Playa* and *Mermoz* under the Pacquet brand — and owned 50 percent of Silares Terminales Caribe, a joint venture with the Cuban government to operate three cruise ship terminals. Silares had just invested $5.8 million in a new terminal in Havana.[67]

On September 29, 2000, Carnival gained full control over Costa when it paid Airtours $510 million for its share. Micky Arison termed Carnival's purchase of Airtours' 50 percent as a strategic move: "Costa is the largest and most successful cruise operator in Europe and will serve as Carnival's primary platform for expanding our presence in this increasingly important market."[68] Since 2000 Costa has added six new ships: four newly built ships with 9,600 berths, and transfer from Carnival Cruise Line of the *Tropicale* (now the *Costa Tropicale*) and from Holland America Line the *Westerdam* (now *Costa Europa*). Costa grew from seven ships with a total of 7,710 berths in 1997 to ten ships with 14,490 berths before the *Costa Tropicale*'s transfer to P&O Australia. It has two 3,800-passenger ships on order: one for 2006 and another for 2007.

Spoiler or Brat?

Some questioned Carnival's intentions. In 1997 Royal Caribbean announced it was purchasing Celebrity Cruises for $500 million and assumption of $800 million in debt. Then in June 1997 Carnival offered $510 million, increased its offer a couple of days later to $525 million, and gave Celebrity's owners a choice between cash or stock — Royal Caribbean had offered a mix of cash and stock. Princess Cruises was rumored to also be preparing an offer.

John Chandris, who started Celebrity Cruises in 1990, partnered with Overseas Shipping Group (OSG) in 1992 to capitalize and expand the company. OSG was a bulk shipping company that a year earlier had talked with Knut Kloster about a similar investment in NCL. OSG received 49 percent of Celebrity Cruises for its $220 million investment.[69]

By 1997 Celebrity had renewed its fleet. The aging *Meridian* had been replaced with the third in a series of new ships giving it a fleet of five ships, all built since 1990, with 7,800 berths. It was viewed as a nice fit by Royal Caribbean. Celebrity offered an upscale product, which Royal Caribbean could use for its repeat passengers to graduate to, and the merger would produce savings from economies of scale.

Celebrity also fed into Royal Caribbean's need to compete with Carnival, which had 35 ships with 42,325 lower berths and 11 ships on order with an additional 20,484 berths. Royal Caribbean had ten ships with 19,550 berths and seven ships on order with an additional 15,600 berths. Royal Caribbean was losing ground.

Royal Caribbean purchased Celebrity in July 1997 for $515 million. It successfully marketed and grew Celebrity Cruises, doubling capacity with the addition of four 1,950-passenger ships between 2000 and 2002. In 2005 Celebrity had nine ships with 15,600 berths. It operates a tenth vessel, accommodating 100 passengers, under Celebrity Xpeditions.

Invading Europe from the West

Cunard Line was Carnival's next target. Cunard had been losing money and was purchased in May 1996 by Norwegian conglomerate Kvaener/ASA. The plan was to reposition the company, return it to profitability, and then sell it for a profit. Cunard's *Sagafjord* was chartered to Transocean Cruises and later sold to Saga Holidays, *Cunard Countess* was sold to Awani Cruises of Indonesia, and then its charter agreement for *Cunard Dynasty* was not renewed.[70] This left a five vessel fleet: *QE2*, *Vistafjord*, *Royal Viking Sun*, *Sea Goddess I*, and *Sea Goddess II*.

Rumors circulated that Cunard was for sale as early as November 1996. Kvaener was reportedly asking $600 million for the company, including $325 million for the fleet, a premium for the brand name, and a $240 to $250 million commitment to build a new ship at Kvaener's shipyard in Finland. By November 1997 Cunard was enjoying occupancy in the range of 90 percent compared with 60 or 70 percent a year earlier. It also had a serious suitor. Prudential Corporation had shown interest, but Kvaener's desire to retain a minority interest in the company was a sticking point.[71] Others were also interested in Cunard, but no deals were made.

On April 3, 1998, Carnival Corporation announced it was partnering with a group of Norwegian investors led by Chistiania Markets and acquiring Cunard Line for $500 million.[72] It also agreed to develop a new class of ships for Carnival Cruise Lines that would be built at the Kvaener Masa Yards in Finland.[73] Eighteen months later, in October 1999, Carnival acquired the remainder of Cunard from its minority partners for $203.5 million. According to Micky Arison, "Considering the strength of the Cunard brand and its plans to build the largest ocean liner in the world to complement the *Queen Elizabeth 2*, it simply makes sense for Carnival to own 100 percent of Cunard."[74]

Cunard gave Carnival further penetration into the European market and was a brand name with world recognition. According to Carnival, Cunard lacked the resources to develop further:

> What we bought was brand equity and a market niche, not ships ... Cunard sources half of its passengers outside the United States and dominates the transatlantic market with the *QE2*. There is no competition with any of the other companies in the Carnival Family. Plus, with Cunard, Carnival gains a leadership position in the luxury market.[75]

Cunard carried more than 100,000 passengers on its five ships in 1998.

Plans were well underway for *Queen Mary 2* when Carnival bought the remaining shares in Cunard. There were other changes. Cunard was left with two ships, the 1969-built *QE II* and 1973-built *Vistafjord*, now named *Caronia*. *Queen Mary 2* would be delivered in December 2003, and *Queen Victoria* in March 2005. The three other Cunard ships, *Sea Goddesses I*, *Sea Goddess II*, and *Royal Viking Sun*, were initially transferred to Seabourn. *Sea Goddess I* and *II* were subsequently sold to a partnership including Atle Byrnestad and Larry Pimentel, Seabourn's previous owner and its CEO, respectively, and sail as Seadream Yacht Club. *Royal Viking Sun* was transferred to Holland America Line and renamed *Prinsendam*.

Out of the Jaws of Victory

Less than two months after taking over Cunard, Carnival offered $1.7 billion for NCL. Officials at NCL said Carnival's offer of 30 Norwegian Crowns (NOK) a share and assumption of $800 million in debt was inadequate. It was rejected on December 2, 1999. NCL announced several days later that it was in talks with Star Cruises. NCL believed Star and Carnival would engage in a bidding war and drive up NCL's value to its current owners.

On December 15 NCL's board formally rejected Carnival's offer and a merger approach by Premier Cruises.[76] Star announced the next day that it held 39.3 percent of NCL's stock, but had no intention of making a takeover bid.[77] But a day later Star said its holdings were 50.2 percent of NCL and made a mandatory offer for all NCL shares at NOK35 per share.

Trygve Hegnar, a major shareholder in NCL who had been told that Star did not want to buy the company, characterized Star's tactic as a diversion to keep the share price down.[78] Star said it was moving to take over NCL because talks had failed: "Proposals were made by NCL, which Star did not feel were acceptable to it or provided a basis on which future discussions on intended cooperations were likely to succeed."[79]

The bidding war for NCL renewed in late January 2000 after NCL converted some debt to equity and reduced Star's holdings to approximately 47 percent. Carnival took advantage of the opportunity and on January 27 offered NOK40 per share (US$1.3 billion) in NCL.[80] This exceeded Star's offer by $200 million.

NCL's board recommended against Star's bid, but withheld advice on Carnival's offer. They disliked Star's offer, saying Star misled NCL by buying up shares when it said it would not. And they were irritated by Star's proclamation that Colin Veitch, a vice president with Princess Cruises, would be NCL's incoming chief executive.[81] They went as far as to attempt to deny votes to Star Cruises at the upcoming shareholders' meeting because under Norwegian law Star was required to notify the industry ministry when its stake in NCL passed one-third of the stock. Star claimed NCL was a shipping firm and therefore exempt from the notification requirement.[82]

The Oslo bourse (stock exchange) was to decide on the matter before the shareholders' meeting. But central people with NCL criticized the impartiality of Ole Lund, chair of Oslo's bourse, and called for his resignation after it was learned that Star had proposed him as board chair of NCL. Lund was a lawyer and also chair of Norway's state oil firm, Statoil.[83] In the midst of this, Star claimed it was supported by key stakeholders and institutions and had more than 50 percent of the votes it needed for the shareholders' meeting.

Star announced two days before the shareholder's meeting on February 2 that Carnival was withdrawing its bid. Star and Carnival would enter a 60/40 partnership with Star in the majority.[84] Star took control of NCL at the shareholder meeting on February 4, 2000, and appointed Ole Lund chair of the board. Six weeks later it canceled its joint venture agreement with Carnival saying it was not prepared to give more control to Carnival on NCL's future direction.[85]

NCL and Star were of similar size, each with nine ships. Combined, the new company was comparable in size with P&O Princess. But Star Cruises, launched by Malaysia-based Genting International in 1993 with a fleet of middle-aged ships, was relatively new to the scene of cruising. It quickly introduced ships it had designed and built — the first in 1998. The new ships replaced older ships that were then chartered or sold. One of its charters was to Hyundai Merchant Marine, which partnered with Star after its joint venture with Carnival failed.

In 2005 Star is smaller than it was when it took over NCL. In contrast to hopes in 1999 that it would operate 12 vessels with 18,000 berths,[86] it operates three ships with a total 4,000 berths on regular itineraries and two others under charter. Many of the new ships the company had planned and built have gone to NCL.

NCL was on a growth spurt when acquired by Star. After its brush with bankruptcy, the company expanded and returned to profitability. It acquired Orient Lines, which operated *Marco Polo*, and acquired Majesty Cruise Line and its two ships, which were renamed *Norwegian Majesty* and *Norwegian Dynasty*; stretched

Windward and *Dreamward* by 130 feet and added 500 berths to each; stretched *Norwegian Majesty* 108 feet and added 404 berths; and started Norwegian Capricorn Line in Australia. When acquired by Star, NCL operated three brand names and had nine vessels with about 13,000 berths. Since then NCL closed Norwegian Capricorn Line and began NCL America, a US-flagged line operating in Hawai'i (discussed in the next chapter). At the start of 2005 it operated 12 ships with over 20,000 berths and had an additional five ships due for delivery between June 2005 and fall 2007.

Invading Europe's Northern Flank and Australia

Carnival made its first public play for P&O Princess in August 1999 by attempting a buyout of the cruise line's parent company. But on August 22, its offer of £7 billion ($11.3 billion) was turned down by the British shipping group Peninsular and Oriental Steam Navigation Co. (P&O). It was speculated that Carnival intended to spin off P&O's ferries and ports business and keep the cruise business of P&O and Princess, valued at £4.5 billion.[87] This raised further speculation that a combination of the world's number one and number three cruise ship operators would raise the eyebrows of regulators.[88]

Carnival shifted to acquiring Cunard and attempting to buy NCL. As Carnival and Star were announcing their alliance to buy NCL, P&O announced plans to demerge its cruise division, estimated to be worth between $8.8 and $10.4 billion. Its logic was that the group's two businesses — cruising and logistics (i.e., ferries, cargo, and ports) — had become too big; with such different financial and operating characteristics, they should follow their own separate strategies. Demerger was a positive move for shareholders given the belief that the two resulting companies would have greater value individually than together.[89] P&O Princess became independent on October 23, 2000.

P&O Princess' Cruise Operations after Demerger, 2000

Cruise Line	# Ships	# Lower Berths
Princess (US)	11	19,920
P&O Cruises (UK)	4	7,170
Swan Hellenic (UK)	1	360
AIDA (Germany)	2	2,460
A'ROSA (Germany)	1	1,590
A'ROSA River Cruises	2	400
P&O Cruises (Australia)	1	1,200
TOTAL	**22**	**33,100**

Less than a year later, P&O Princess was in discussions with Royal Caribbean. On November 20, 2001, they announced a merger of equals. They had been holding secret negotiations the day of the terrorist attacks on the World Trade Center in New York and the Pentagon in Washington, after which "the deal made even more sense and we worked at it quickly."[90] Indeed, two cruise companies, Renaissance Cruises and American Classic Voyages with its four brands, filed for bankruptcy between September 11 and November 20.

Under the planned merger, RCCL and P&O Princess would continue to operate independently and have their separate legal identity, tax residence, and stock exchange listing, but the board of directors for the two companies would be identical and all shareholder decisions would involve shareholders in both Princess and Royal Caribbean. Princess would hold 50.7 percent of the new company; Royal Caribbean would hold 49.3 percent.[91] Two other critical elements in the merger agreement were a $62.5 million break-up fee and a joint venture.

Princess and Royal Caribbean agreed to equal ownership in a joint venture company targeting customers in southern Europe (primarily Italians, French, and Spaniards), in direct competition with Carnival's Costa Cruises. According to the Italian consumers' organization, Costa had practically uncontested dominance of the Italian market.[92] Each company would contribute two of its new ships currently under construction — one each in 2003 and one each in 2004. Once underway, the joint venture would cost $200 million to dissolve.[93] There was a single way out. The joint venture could be canceled in January 2003 "if certain commercial targets are not met ... [and] unless either party has been subject to change of control."[94] Regardless, analysts viewed the joint venture as a poison pill to deter Carnival from making a counter offer.[95]

Carnival was not deterred. On December 14, 2001, it bid $4.5 billion (£4.5 per share). Lord Sterling, Chair of P&O Princess, immediately rejected the offer, leaving Carnival (in its own words) "no choice" but to take its bid directly to the shareholders — a challenge, given that no single shareholder controlled more than 4 percent of the stock.

Carnival met with institutional shareholders and they called for an improved bid. Royal Caribbean's merger valued P&O Princess at £3.61 per share. Those pushing Carnival were looking for a bid of more than £5 per share[99] — 8 percent more than Carnival's first offer. P&O Princess would make Carnival a worldwide cruise company and, like Royal Caribbean, Carnival claimed that synergies and economies of scale would save the combined company $100 million per year.

On January 28, investors got their wish when Carnival offered £5, but shareholders rejected it and the bid increased to £5.15 per share. Carnival said that it was eager to spoil a marriage between Princess and Royal Caribbean, and that its latest bid was structured to avoid triggering any financial penalties or

If You Can't Win Fair and Square, Try Name Calling

Carnival's media campaign included an attack of Royal Caribbean's CEO, Richard Fain. A company press release on January 24, 2002,[96] in effect asked P&O Princess' shareholders if they wanted this man to run their cruise ship company.[97]

Carnival claimed Royal Caribbean's performance had been significantly weaker than Carnival's and offered statistics to make its point. Between 1995 and 2000, Carnival's average return on invested capital was 15 percent; Royal Caribbean's was 9.6 percent. As well, Carnival's earnings margin was 34.5 percent; Royal Caribbean's was 24.8 percent. Carnival's price-earnings ratio was 20.4; Royal Caribbean's was 16.2.

Royal Caribbean responded by claiming that Carnival's financial performance was a product of its market dominance and the Royal Carribean–P&O Princess merger threatened that dominance. It expressed total confidence that the Royal Caribbean–P&O Princess merger, with its larger scale and broader reach, would deliver significant operational and financial gains to its shareholders. Micky Arison scoffed at the claim: "It is not the size that creates superior operating margins; it is management talent and proven operating practices."[98]

"poison pills." Princess' board of directors said it would consider Carnival's latest offer,[100] but rejected it on February 8. Its chief concern was whether Carnival could obtain antitrust clearance for a merger with Princess. P&O Princess was also skeptical about Carnival's seriousness and questioned whether it was in the category of "nice to have if it is available." It feared that Carnival's sole goal was to disrupt the upcoming extraordinary general meeting (EGM) on February 14 scheduled to approve the Royal Caribbean–P&O Princess merger.[101]

The same day Princess rejected Carnival's offer, Richard Fain at Royal Caribbean warned that if the merger wasn't approved on February 14, there would be no deal. He elaborated:

> This observation is absolutely correct. There is no free option. I want my view to be very clear. If there is no approval of the P&O Princess/Royal Caribbean Cruises Ltd combination tomorrow, there will, for any number of reasons, be no deals — neither our combination nor the Carnival Corporation takeover.

Whilst we have yet to decide what specific actions we would take, it is clear that such an adjournment vote would strike at the heart of our transaction.[102]

P&O Princess' shareholders met, as scheduled, and following a 14-hour meeting, voted on a motion from HSBC Bank to adjourn to allow more time to consider Carnival's bid. Carnival's lobbying had been successful.[103]

Mergers Don't Come Cheaply

Expenses reported by each company for merger with P&O Princess

Carnival:	$60 million[104]
P&O Princess:	$55 million[105]
	$62.5 million break-up fee
RCCL:	$30 million[106]
TOTAL:	**$207.5 million**

With the viability of Carnival's offer relying on antitrust clearance, lobbying efforts moved to regulators. The Royal Caribbean–P&O Princess merger was not subject to review by the European Union's Competition Directorate, but because of its larger size Carnival's was. Carnival received a list of concerns in May; in June Micky Arison met with Mario Monti, the competition commissioner. Arison lobbied for approval of the Carnival–P&O Princess merger. Richard Fain met with Monti several weeks later and argued against Carnival's merger plans. Monti approved the Carnival–P&O Princess merger on July 24.

Speculation was plentiful regarding why the merger had been unconditionally approved, especially given early indications that it would not be approved and that divestitures would be required in the unlikely case approval were given. One factor frequently mentioned is that Monti was being overly cautious. The European Court of Justice had chastised him a month earlier for his office's rejection of a merger between First Choice Holidays and British Airtours. At least four other rulings had been appealed to the Court and were awaiting a hearing.[107]

The US Federal Trade Commission, on October 4, 2002, approved P&O Princess' merger with either Carnival or Royal Caribbean. This was the opening P&O Princess needed; until then it had been prohibited from talking to Carnival about a counteroffer. Carnival's offer had to be judged financially superior and deliverable and now it was. Carnival and P&O Princess held talks on October 12.

When Is a Monopoly Not a Monopoly?

The P&O Princess-Carnival merger redrew the landscape of the cruise industry. Before the merger, the industry had four key players: Carnival with 60,000 berths, Royal Caribbean with 50,000 berths, and P&O Princess and Star-NCL each with 30,000 berths. Post-merger, three cruise companies remain. The largest is twice the size of number 2, which itself is twice the size of number 3. Together, these companies control 95 percent of cruise tourism in the US; Carnival alone controls 53 percent.[108] How is such concentration not viewed as anticompetitive?[109]

A key consideration in the trade commission reports is the definition of "market" occupied by the cruise industry. Carnival argues cruise tourism comprises less than 4 percent of a larger travel and leisure vacation market that includes resorts, hotels, timeshares, and any number of other vacation options. As the Federal Trade Commission states in its report,

> Cruising has evolved from a minor offshoot of the oceanic passenger industry of the past into a broad-based vacation business .... Today's cruise ships, bearing a far stronger resemblance to floating luxury hotels or even amusement parks than to traditional ocean liners, offer their thousands of passengers amenities such as full-scale "Main Street"-style shopping districts, multiple restaurants, spas, basketball courts, and even ice skating rinks and rock-climbing walls.[110]

In this view, monopolistic behavior such as raising prices would only drive passengers to other vacation choices.

The other view is that cruise tourism is distinct from other vacation options. Richard Fain, CEO of Royal Caribbean, opines that under the broader market view, there could be a single cruise line in the world without causing harm to the consumer and without antitrust implications. Cruise tourism is, as such, a unique product and too much concentration will limit consumer choice and give a single company industry dominance. With 12 brand names, 68 ships, and more than 142,000 berths, Carnival is dominant. Two members of the Federal Trade Commission viewed Carnival's merger with Princess as anticompetitive.[111]

Two weeks later P&O Princess paid Royal Caribbean $62.5 million, signed a termination agreement, welcomed Carnival's proposal for a dual-listed company, and withdrew its recommendation for the Royal Caribbean combination. P&O Princess had until January 10 to recommend shareholders vote for a Carnival combination. This was after January 1. An earlier date would have triggered the costly Southern European joint venture poison pill.[112]

The P&O Princess board recommended the Carnival proposal on January 8, and on April 16, 2003, P&O Princess shareholders approved Carnival's takeover of Princess. The combined company had 66 ships with over 100,000 berths. P&O Princess also brought to Carnival Westours' key competitor in Alaska, Princess Tours, with its 3 hotels, 200 motor coaches, and 7 domed rail cars. By 2006 Carnival will have 83 ships holding 142,300 berths.[113]

Carnival Corporation Today

Carnival Corporation today operates 12 cruise lines and captures 53 percent of the North American market. At any one time, more than 150,000 passengers are cruising on ships owned by Carnival. The company has grown from a single ship in 1973 to a corporation earning a net profit of close to $2 billion in 2004.

What about Carnival Cruise Lines itself? The company grew slowly in the 1970s and 1980s and in the late 1980s expanded through new ship construction. Carnival Cruise Lines introduced 19 new ships with almost 46,000 lower berths between 1990 and 2005: eight Fantasy-class vessels with 2,052 lower berths, four Spirit-class vessels with 2,124 lower berths, and seven Destiny-class vessels with as many as 2,974 lower berths. Unlike its competitors who borrowed to fund expansion, Carnival's financial success allowed it to construct new ships and make acquisitions largely through operating revenue. It effectively drove the cruise industry's growth.

Carnival Cruise Lines remains the core of Carnival Corporation. Not only is it the largest cruise line, but it is also the most visible and best known. In addition it covers a different segment than the other Carnival brand names, catering to the mass market and to families. A Carnival cruise is not like the image of an ocean cruise on a stately liner, and it doesn't claim to be. Its competition, from the corporate perspective, is the resorts and hotels of Las Vegas, Atlantic City, and Branson, Missouri. And as "the fun ships," the fleet is more like a theme park than a sea cruise. The product sells, and there is no arguing with success.

Carnival Corporation continues to be successful. Early investors did particularly well: an investment in October 1987 would have had an annual rate of return over ten years of 23.5 percent if held through October 1996 — from $4 1/16 to $30 1/4.[114] The stock price fell in the early 2000s, but between April 2003 and April 2004 grew from $20 to well over $45.

Carnival Corporation Essentials

Cruise Lines: Carnival Cruise Lines, Holland America Line, Princess Cruises, Windstar Cruises, Seabourn Cruises, Cunard Line (UK), P&O Cruises (UK), Swan Hellenic (UK), Ocean Village (UK), Costa Cruises (Italy), Seetours/AIDA (Germany), P&O Cruises (Australia)

Other Holdings: Westours, Princess Tours, Miami Heat NBA Basketball team (owned by Micky Arison, but Carnival pays as much as $543,000 per year to sponsor), Carnival Airline (merged with Pan Am in April 1997; bankrupt), Crystal Palace Resort and Casino (sold November 1994), various banks and financial institutions (sold or seized by US Government)

Financials and Occupancy, 1990–2004

	1990	1991	1992	1993	1994	1995	1996	1997
Total revenue*	1,253	1,404	1,473	1,556	1,806	1,998	2,213	2,447
Net income*	206.2	85.0	276.6	318.2	381.8	451.1	566.3	666.1
Passenger cruise days (000)	5,565	6,365	6,766	7,003	8,102	9,201	10,583	11,908
Capacity (%)	106.6	105.7	105.3	105.3	104.0	105.0	107.6	108.3

	1998	1999	2000	2001	2002	2003	2004
Total revenue*	3,009	3,497	3,788	4,536	4,368	6,718	9,727
Net income*	835.9	1,027	965.5	926.2	1,016	1,194	1,854
Passenger cruise days (000)	13,008	14,952	16,746	21,657	22,550	34,442	44,998
Capacity (%)	106.3	104.3	105.4	104.7	105.2	103.4	104.5

*Millions of dollars. Source: Carnival Corporation.

The London Times provided interesting insights in a 2004 profile of Carnival Corporation.[115] The company rated relatively high on share performance (9/10); fat-cat quotient (8/10); future prospects (8/10); and strength of brand, innovation, and city star rating (all 7/10). But it rated relatively low on social responsibility (3/10) and its attitude to employees (4/10). Other parts of this book will address these last two areas in particular.

TABLE 2.2: REMUNERATION OF CARNIVAL'S TOP EXECUTIVES ($000's), 1998 – 2004

Executive	1998	1999	2000	2001	2002	2003	2004
Micky Arison chief executive officer Carnival Corporation	4,851	4,766	3,788	3,818	3,818	4,930	6,965
Howard Frank senior vice president Carnival Corporation	3,996	4,083	3,330	3,362	3,426	7,157	5,989
Robert Dickinson chief executive officer *Carnival Cruise Line*	2,858	3,468	2,295	3,050	2,797	7,443	3,780
Kirk Lanterman chief executive officer Holland America – Westours	3,303	3,323	3,829	3,451	2,639	1,894	2,566
Pier Foschi chief executive officer Costa Cruises	–	1,563	1,523	1,513	1,317	1,911	2,200
Peter Ratcliffe chief executive officer P&O Princess	–	–	–	–	1,648	2,256	3,368

Note: Amounts include salary, bonus, other annual compensation, and restricted stock awards.
Source: Carnival Corporation, Reports on Executive Compensation.

The "fat-cat quotient" is something that can be addressed now. *The Times* noted that Micky Arison had been paid 19 percent less in 2003 than was the norm for the CEO of a comparably sized, comparably performing Financial Times Stock Exchange (FTSE) 100 company and he hadn't received extra stock options in 2003; however, it is relevant that "Mr. Arison himself actually recommends the size of his bonus and there is 'no specific relationship' between that bonus and company performance."[116] His 2003 income was admittedly low, but Arison isn't hurting. He earned $40.5 million in 2001, including $36.7 million by exercising stock options acquired as past compensation. In 2004 he sold 11.9 million shares of Carnival for $551.6 million for "tax planning, estate planning, and diversification purposes."[117] Annual remuneration for Carnival Corporation's key executives is shown in Table 2.2.

Turning Water into Money

Carnival has been successful in building from a single cruise ship that ran aground on its maiden voyage to a multi-billion dollar corporation. Its growth has been achieved by building new ships and by acquisition of competitors. The corporation today controls more than 50 percent of the North American cruise market. It has even higher concentration in certain markets.

This chapter has described the growth of Carnival. The following chapters focus on how the corporation made the money it needed for expansion and how it saved money where it could. The use of foreign registration, both of corporations and of ships, is one way that Carnival and the industry generally has saved money. The next chapter explains why there are very few cruise lines registered in the US or operating ships registered in the US. It contrasts the use of foreign registries to avoid taxation with the cruise industry's cultivation of friends in federal, state, and local politics — a sort of representation without taxation.

3

Representation without Taxation

THE CRUISE INDUSTRY TOUTS ITS ECONOMIC IMPACT — more than $25 billion on the US economy in 2003.[1] Its expectation that this translates into special treatment from ports and governments is reasonable based on past experience. And yet the three cruise corporations comprising 95 percent of the US market pay virtually no income tax in the US. Carnival Corporation in 2003 paid a total of $29 million in taxes — just one-half of one percent of its $6.7 billion in revenues.[2] As a foreign-registered corporation its tax liability is limited to its US-based tour operations. Because cruise corporations pay no federal income tax, they also pay no corporate income tax to the state where they are headquartered.[3]

As foreign corporations, cruise companies don't pay taxes, but they are also prohibited from making contributions to political campaigns in the US. Regardless, the cruise industry has many friends in Washington, DC. In the 1990s it successfully lobbied against extending US labor laws to foreign-flagged vessels operating out of US ports, directly influenced the number of permits given for Glacier Bay National Park in Alaska, and received a $20 million a year savings after a senator inserted a single word in the federal budget bill that exempted the 17 cruise lines operating in the US from a $6 per passenger immigration fee to cover inspection costs for people arriving in US ports.[4]

In 2001 the industry had language inserted into an appropriations bill that allowed it to offer executives and other land-based workers more generous and secure pension benefits, previously barred by the tax code. The cost to the US treasury was $68 million.[5] On a smaller scale, Representative David Vitter inserted language into a Coast Guard Reauthorization bill in 2003 to relieve Carnival Corporation of $1.7 million in federal fines for two violations of the Coastwise Passenger Statute.[6] And in 2004 Senator Lisa Murkowski, backed by senators from Florida and Washington, added a provision to a corporate tax bill that saved the cruise industry $28 million. The amendment delayed for one year a requirement to pay taxes on income from air tickets, hotel rooms, and tours sold in the US.[7] This chapter looks at the source of the industry's political influence — its representation without taxation.

Why Pay Taxes If You Don't Have To?
The cruise industry, like the shipping industry, generally is largely foreign-registered. Even though corporate offices for most major cruise lines are in Florida,

and the clientele served is primarily North American, the three major corporations are registered in Panama (Carnival Corporation),[8] Liberia (Royal Caribbean Cruises Limited), and Bermuda (Star Cruises). The corporations derive many benefits, including avoidance of corporate taxes. The savings are significant. Estimates of lost tax revenues to the US from Carnival Corporation are about a half billion dollars; Florida loses more than $40 million.[9] UK-registered P&O Princess reportedly had a corporate tax rate in 2002 of 5 percent based on its worldwide income; 72 percent of its income is from North America so it is not taxed.[10]

Flags of Convenience

These foreign-registered corporations often register their ships in a country offering a "flag of convenience."[11] Most cruise ships in the 1990s were registered in the Bahamas, Panama, or Liberia.[12] The registries protect the companies from burdensome income taxes, US labor laws, and other regulations. The ship is governed by laws of the country where it is registered. The flag state is technically responsible for enforcement of international regulations and conventions, but flag-of -convenience registries often leave inspection and certification of safety equipment to the US Coast Guard (or similar authority in Europe and Australia). A ship may never be fully inspected unless it stops in a port where inspections are done.

Flags of convenience also severely limit recourse to US or other courts in disputes over wages or a workplace injury. A US court ruled in 2003 that claims related to a boiler explosion aboard NCL's *Norway*, which killed 8 workers and injured 20, had to be filed in the Philippines to comply with the employment contract that had been signed in the Philippines. This is not unusual. The employment contract of a worker on a Bahamian-registered ship states any dispute or claims "shall be governed and adjudicated pursuant to laws of the Bahamas, regardless of any other legal remedies that may be available."

The savings under a flag of convenience are significant. Citing a need to ensure competitiveness, Royal Caribbean has shifted all of its ships to Bahamian registry. It says the move to a single flag is a means to streamline the management process for all shipboard operations. But the real motive is economic. As it says, "should registration with Norway again become competitive, Royal Caribbean will revisit the flagging issue."[13]

Ship registry is big business. In 1995 Panama earned $47.5 million in ship registration fees and annual taxes — 5 percent of its federal budget — and another $50 million for maritime lawyers, agents, and inspectors. The government operates 56 maritime consulates around the world from which a registration can be purchased. The consul can offer discounts of up to 50 percent for transfer of multiple ships to Panamanian registry, and a complete waiver of fees for a year in some cases.

The consul receives a cash bonus based on the amount of business brought in.[14] Panama's share of ship registries has expanded significantly in the past decade.

Several countries have tried in recent years to prevent further loss of ship registries or to recover those previously lost. The UK successfully prevented Cunard's migration to another flag and regained much of the P&O and Princess fleets. After a 95 percent drop in the size of the UK-registered trading fleet and a 50-percent decline in the number of UK seafarers in just 20 years, the government pursued long-term strategies contained in the 1998 White Paper, *British Shipping: Charting a New Course*. Tonnage taxes were reduced from 13 to 5 percent, and reforms introduced in the Maritime Coastguard Agency. The size of the UK-registered fleet trebled between 1998 and 2004.[15] It apparently lost ground in late 2004 with Carnival's decision to shift its German-brand Seetour's AIDA ships from British to Italian registry.[16]

Italy has similarly worked to keep cruise ships under its flag. In the 1990s it offered subsidies to attract business to its shipbuilding yards and to its registry. A cruise line could receive a 30 percent construction subsidy for a new ship built and registered in Italy. This was on top of other grants used to attract business. Italy has more recently, like the UK, introduced reforms to make its flag more attractive to cruise lines.

New Ships 58 Percent Off Sticker Price

Most cruise ships built in the 1990s were significantly subsidized. None, however, was built in the US where commercial shipbuilding virtually collapsed after subsidies to shipbuilding yards were terminated in 1981. Shipyards in Europe, on the other hand, used subsidies to capture the burgeoning cruise ship business. The Italian government deliberately and effectively used subsidies to capture construction contracts for state-owned Fincantieri, which hadn't built a single cruise ship in 22 years. It secured a contract with Princess Cruises in 1988 and between 1990 and 2000 turned out more than two dozen ships. Other European shipyards — Chantiers de l'Atlantique in France, Kvaener in Norway, and Meyer Werft in Germany — also benefited from government subsidies.

Subsidies made it difficult for some shipyards to compete. Wartsila in Finland in the 1980s had been the world's premier builder of cruise ships; however, the government didn't provide enough subsidies for it to effectively compete. Its bankruptcy in the late 1980s is partly due to pressure to underprice ships it had contracted to build for Carnival. Three ships originally contracted for $200 million were renegotiated at costs of $225 million, $275 million, and $300 million, respectively[17] — in the case of the third ship a cost increase of 50 percent. Carnival also invested in Wartsila to keep it afloat long enough for delivery of the three ships.

The European Community ended shipbuilding subsidies for new ships in late 2000; subsidies continued for ships already under contract. Royal Caribbean

TABLE 3.1: FOREIGN SUBSIDIES FOR CRUISE SHIPS IN THE US TRADES

Cruise Line	Yard/Order Date	Ships (Delivery)	Price and Subsidy	Value of Subsidy
Holland America	Fincantieri '89	Statendam ('92) Maasdam ('93) Ryndam ('94)	$750m total.	$210m
Princess	Fincantieri '89	Crown Princess ('90) Regal Princess ('91)	$550m total; 20% grant; 30% Italian flag.	$319m
Princess	Fincantieri '93	Sun Princess ('95)	$300m; 9% grant; 30% Italian flag.	$117m
RCCL	Chantiers de l'Atlantique '87	Nordic Empress ('90)	$180m; 28% grant.	$50.4m
RCCL	Chantiers de l'Atlantique '88	Monarch of the Seas ('91)	$270m; 36.5% grant.	$98.7m
RCCL	Chantiers de l'Atlantique '89	Majesty of the Seas ('92)	$300m; 28% grant.	$84m
RCCL	Chantiers de l'Atlantique '93	Legend of the Seas ('95) Splendor of the Seas ('95)	314.1m each; Legend – 9% grant. Splendor – 20% grant;	$91.1m

TABLE 3.1: FOREIGN SUBSIDIES FOR CRUISE SHIPS IN THE US TRADES – continued:

Cruise Line	Yard/ Order Date	Ships (Delivery)	Price and Subsidy	Value of Subsidy
NCL	Chantiers de l'Atlantique '90	Dreamward ('92) Windward ('93)	$440m total; 40% grant.	$176m
Costa Crociere	Fincantieri '89	Costa Classica ('92) Costa Romantica ('93)	$540m total; 28% grant; 30% Italian flag.	$313.2m

Source: Statement of John J. Stocker to House of Representatives, *US Passenger Vessel Development and Tax: Hearings Before the Subcommittee on Merchant Marine of the Committee on Merchant Marine and Fisheries, House of Representatives, 103rd Congress, Second Session, on H.R. 3821 and H.R. 3822* (April 13, 1994), Government Printing Office, (Document Y 4.M 53:103-96).

International's *Jewel of the Seas*, for example, was delivered in June 2004 and had received German-government aid worth 7 percent of the shipbuilder's contract, approximately $25 million.

This subsidy is small in the context of ships built in the 1990s. While companies bragged about huge, new ships costing $300 million or more, they didn't thank the taxpayers in the country where the ship was built who had contributed as much as 58 percent of construction costs. Table 3.1 shows subsidies of close to $1.5 billion spread across 15 ships. Each ship presumably also received government-financing subsidies estimated to be worth another $10 to $20 million. Clearly, the cruise industry's growth was fueled in part by free money from European governments competing with one another.

Shipbuilders in the US complained about the unfair advantage given to European shipyards but unsuccessfully persuaded European governments to voluntarily stop subsidies. The Shipbuilding Trade Reform Act,[18] which passed the House of Representatives in May 1992, took a different approach. It removed the competitive advantage by requiring the owner of a cruise ship built or repaired at subsidized foreign shipyards to repay the subsidy, either to its own government or to the US Treasury, if the ship called at US ports.[19] The legislation, strongly opposed by the cruise industry, went to the Senate and died in the Finance Committee.

Portholes Yes, Loopholes No

We need to cut some of the ridiculous loopholes which exist today .... One glaring example is the law which exempts shipping companies incorporated in foreign countries from paying US income taxes .... It is totally unfair to let Carnival Cruise Lines pay nothing on profits just because it was incorporated in Panama .... Foreign flag lines are, in effect, getting an indirect subsidy from the US government that helps them keep US-flag companies out of the business.[20]

— Representative John Duncan (and his aide), 1993

With direct subsidies banned by the European Union, Chantiers de l'Atlantique has offered tax lease financing as a different incentive to attract new ship orders and to re-launch the French flag. Tax lease financing saves a cruise line as much as 20 percent of the cost of a vessel. Under the scheme, the ship is owned by a special-purpose company that then leases the ship to the cruise line for eight years with an early purchase option. The lease payments are used to pay back part of the debt for ship construction. Using accelerated depreciation and a capital gains exemption when the ship is sold leads to substantial savings, which are passed on to the cruise line.[21] The European Union is increasingly scrutinizing tax lease deals, with several cruise lines' use.

Are There Disadvantages to Foreign Flags?

The key disadvantage of a foreign flag is cabotage laws — the laws most countries have that prohibit a foreign-flagged vessel (seagoing or via air) from transporting passengers between two ports or places within that country. In the US this is contained in the Passenger Vessel Services Act (PVSA) of 1886. It was originally passed to protect US companies from competition by Canadian ferries that shuttled among resorts on the Great Lakes.

Key provisions of the PVSA have changed over time, but its core statement has not: "No foreign vessel shall transport passengers between ports or places in the United States, either directly or by way of a foreign port, under penalty of $2 for each passenger so transported and landed." The penalties increased to $200 in 1998 and to $300 in 2003.

Several provisions have become more clearly defined. In 1910 the Attorney General issued a legal opinion that allowed an around-the-world cruise to embark passengers in New York and disembark them in San Francisco. In 1968 the Customs and Border Patrol introduced a distant port exception, which allowed a foreign-flagged cruise ship to transport passengers between two US ports as long as a call is made at a distant foreign port. And in 1985 a regulation was introduced that allowed round-trip cruises from a US port to visit other US ports as long as the ship stopped at a nearby foreign port.[22]

Today, a foreign-flagged vessel may transport passengers between two US ports, with a distant foreign port in between, and it can transport passengers between a number of US ports as long as a nearby foreign port is included in the itinerary. This is a critical reason why Canadian ports are included in cruises of Alaska's Inside Passage — they provide the foreign port. The only thing a foreign-flagged vessel cannot do is to transport passengers between two US ports directly.[23] Norwegian Cruise Line's Hawai'i cruises on its foreign-flagged vessels must sail to the Republic of Kiribati; NCL America's US-registered ships are not required to make the detour. This yields an extra 31 daytime hours in port on a seven-day cruise.

Building a Merchant Marine

The Passenger Vessel Services Act is often confused with the Jones Act, officially the Merchant Marine Act of 1920. Passed shortly after World War I, it promotes the growth of a well-equipped and modern merchant marine available for use in the nation's defense and that would grow foreign and domestic commerce. It stipulates only ships built in the US are entitled to be registered in the US and thereby reinforced the PVSA by posing a strong barrier to foreign-registered cruise lines operating freely between US ports.

NCL required an exemption from the Jones Act in 2003 before it could operate NCL America. The company had purchased unfinished Project America ships (see following section) and through Hawai'i Senator Inouye's efforts was granted an exemption allowing it to operate three foreign-built cruise ships in Hawai'i. One ship was an already-operating foreign-built ship; the other two were the hulls of the Project America ships, which would be completed in Germany.

Cruise Industry Opposition

Segments of the cruise industry have lobbied for repeal or change in both the PVSA and the Jones Act, but without success. One reason could be that interest in loosening restrictions imposed by cabotage laws has largely been from four states — Alaska, Washington, Hawai'i, and California — and a select group of cruise lines. This issue has some advantages to the cruise industry, but not enough to justify spending much social capital.

A flurry of legislative activity between 1997 and 2000 was directed at loosening cabotage law restrictions. Four bills were introduced in 1997 and 1998.[33] None was successful. Senators McCain, Hutchison, Feinstein, and Murkowski tried again with S. 1510 introduced August 5, 1999. The legislation combined elements of previous bills. It allowed foreign-built vessels to be reflagged as US vessels and engage in domestic commerce. It also permitted limited employment of foreign-flag cruise ships in domestic commerce provided (1) all maintenance and repairs to these ships are done in the US and (2) there is a commitment to build replacement vessels in the US. These are essentially the conditions under which AMCV committed to the Project America ships and its reflagging of a foreign-built vessel. Like legislation before it, S. 1510 never reached a vote by the full Senate.

That these initiatives failed is not entirely surprising. Opposition was already well organized. In late 1995 a broad-based coalition called the Maritime Cabotage Task Force was formed of more than 400 American organizations and companies to support the Jones Act. The task force included US-flag ship operators; shipbuilding and ship repair yards; labor organizations; rail, trucking and airline groups; marine vendors and equipment manufacturers; and pro-defense coalitions. In 1997 the US House of Representatives passed a resolution of support for the Jones Act, and both Republican and Democratic Senate leaders declared their strong support for the Act. The cruise industry does not appear to have impacted the resolve of groups supporting key provisions of the Jones Act.

The cruise industry has also actively lobbied against efforts by the US government to increase its control over the industry. Several Congressional

When Foreign Built Vessels Aren't (Technically) Foreign Built

With great excitement American Classic Voyages (AMCV) announced its plans in March 1999 to build two 1,900-passenger vessels at Litton Industries' Ingalls Shipbuilding in the US. The two vessels, named Project America, were to be deployed in Hawai'i as part of American Hawai'i Cruises, a division of AMCV. Costing $1.4 billion, they would not only be the largest cruise ships ever built in the US, but the first large cruise ships in more than 40 years. Ingalls had delivered the last American-built large cruise ships, *Brasil* and *Argentina*, to Moore McCormack Lines in 1958.

Project America was born with the *US Flag Cruise Ship Pilot Project Statute*, an amendment tacked onto a Defense Department appropriations bill by Senator Inouye and passed by Congress in 1997.[24] It reached fruition in 1999, when the Maritime Administration committed up to $1.1 billion in loan guarantees. Construction of the ships began on July 3, 2000. But a year later, things were unraveling. Ingalls was reportedly as much as 18 months behind schedule.[25] And then in September 2001, AMCV filed for bankruptcy, leaving the US Government with Project America.

Almost a year after AMCV ceased operations, NCL met with Senator Inouye. NCL was already the only cruise line to offer inter-island cruises, but it diverted to Kiribati to satisfy the foreign port requirement. It now sought an exemption from the PVSA to operate inter-island cruises without a foreign port. According to NCL, its meetings with Senator Inouye in August 2002 were to gain an understanding of "his criteria for supporting a broadening of the cruise options available in Hawai'i."[26] An understanding was apparently reached because things began to move.

In the fall of 2002, NCL purchased Project America. It paid $29 million[27] for the partially completed hull of one ship and parts for the second ship. Then in January 2003 Senator Inouye tacked a provision onto the 2003 Omnibus Appropriations Bill allowing NCL to operate three US-flagged ships in Hawai'i.[28] The ships were the two Project America ships, which would be completed at Meyer Werft shipyard in Germany, and a current foreign-flagged ship. An argument used for the legislation was that by 2007, 3,000 jobs

continued:

When Foreign Built Vessels Aren't Foreign Built – continued:

would be created and $300 million in federal tax revenues generated. These benefits would more than recoup the estimated $185 million lost by the Maritime Administration on Project America. It falls short of the revised loss figure of $330 million released in April 2003.[29]

Senator John McCain opposed Inouye's amendment. He criticized the exemption saying it would "grant new life to an already failed shipbuilding project that has cost the American taxpayer over $185 million and give it to a foreign-owned corporation."[30] He further suggested that "by granting exclusive rights to one cruise line, there will be no competition and the people who want to cruise Hawai'i will pay much higher prices than for a commensurate cruise that people take out of the East Coast."[31] Other cruise lines also opposed the exemption, which they wanted broadened to include more cruise lines. Regardless, the amendment passed the Senate. A joint House–Senate conference added a provision that prohibits NCL from using the ships to transport passengers to ports in Alaska, the Gulf of Mexico, or the Caribbean Sea.[32] The president signed the legislation on February 24, 2003.

initiatives in 1991 stemmed from safety concerns by the Coast Guard and the National Transportation Safety Board, and the industry's avoidance of US taxes. There were the Gibbons Bill, which would force companies to repay shipbuilding subsidies; the Murphy Bill, which would bring seafarers on foreign ships regularly using US ports under the US labor laws; and the Taylor Bill, which would strip foreign-flagged vessels of the right to operate casinos unless they sailed on voyages of more than 36 hours or made a port call — this would prohibit "cruises to nowhere." None of these bills was successful, but they define the issues. The battle lines drawn have scarcely changed over the past decade.

The Cruise Industry and US Politics

The cruise industry actively participates in US politics. It works on many levels and involves politicians and their aides, senior government officials, the media, and nongovernmental organizations.

The Media as a Partner ... Sometimes

The cruise industry spends close to a billion dollars a year on advertising and promotion. This makes the media an important partner. And it isn't just print or other advertisements, although these can be significant as seen in Carnival Cruise Lines' $50 million campaign launched January 2005.[35] Carnival Cruise Lines is a co-sponsor of the *New York Times* Travel Show,[36] and a co-sponsor with the *Miami Herald* of the 5th Annual Mayor's Ball[37] and of the Miami Wine and Food Festival.[38] How much does spending on advertising and visible partnerships influence editorial decisions? Most journalists argue that it does not, but regular monitoring of newspapers across North America and Australia suggests that it must. There are clear differences in where stories appear in terms of countries and in terms of which markets within a country. Anecdotal comments by reporters reinforce this impression.

> Sooner or later the industry will have to get grips with Capitol Hill which no lesser person than Carnival's [President] Bob Dickinson has described as the greatest threat to the contemporary cruise industry.[34]

The cruise industry's relationship with the media is not passive. I learned in meetings with newspaper editorial boards that cruise industry executives and/or lobbyists were regular visitors. More than once I heard accounts describing industry efforts to shape the way issues were understood and how they should be presented. Editorial boards complained commonly that they were rarely exposed to the counterarguments against the industry. Those with counterarguments do not have lobbyists.

Staff at television and radio stations have told me of similar attempts to prevent my appearance or the airing of an interview. A personality with a major radio station in a large metropolitan area told me after an interview that her producer had been on the phone all morning with industry folks. First, they wanted my interview canceled. When that failed, they wanted to share the interview time — a head-to-head with me and the industry representative on the air at the same time. And when that failed, they demanded equal time and were granted an interview of identical length immediately after my interview. I don't know what was used to secure the final concession. An almost identical scenario played out a week earlier at a different radio station in a different city.

Not all media bow to industry pressure, but the media are pressured. We don't know when the industry is successful in closing access to critics or when it prevents news it considers negative from being aired.

Lobbyists Don't Come Cheap

A more direct effort to influence US policies and regulation is lobbyists — folks hired to chat up and to influence members of Congress and their aides, and senior executives in government departments. The International Council of Cruise Lines (ICCL) spends $1 million a year in lobbying activities.[39] NCL spent close to $1.5 million on lobbyists while it was securing approval for its US-flagged operations in Hawai'i. And Princess Cruises and Holland America Line each use lobbyists at more modest cost to influence, among other things, policies around granting permits for Glacier Bay National Park. The cruise industry spent close to $3 million on Washington lobbyists in 2003 alone (see Table 3.2).

ICCL is the cruise industry's primary advocate in Washington. Its mission is to participate in regulatory and policy development and to advocate industry positions to key domestic and international regulatory organizations, policy makers, and other industry partners. A sort of cruise industry cheerleader to the media, Congress, government departments and administrators, and other industries, ICCL promotes the cruise industry and presents it in positive light. In this sense, it is much like a trade organization. ICCL also works to prevent public criticism of the industry. We saw that in relation to the media. But it goes further. It unsuccessfully lobbied senior government officials to prevent my and others' participation on a panel at the White Water to Blue Water Conference in 2004.[40]

ICCL does its own lobbying and also employs the firm Alcalde and Fay. The two have an odd relationship in that the president of ICCL is a partner in Alcalde and Fay. The previous president, Cynthia Colenda, is Hector Alcalde's daughter and now serves as executive director of the Cruise Industry Charitable Foundation. The two organizations, ICCL and Alcalde and Fay, are inextricably linked. Curiously, the amount Alcalde and Fay claims as lobbying income from ICCL is greater than the amount ICCL says it spent on lobbying activities in recent years.

Cruise industry lobbying is not restricted to Washington, DC. Holland America Line spent almost $100,000 in 2002, in 2003, and in 2004 on lobbying activities in Washington state.[41] The amount more than doubled between 1999 and 2002 and has remained stable since. Campaign contributions in the state by Holland America have continued to increase. In contrast, the amount spent by the industry on lobbyists in Alaska has remained relatively constant, averaging approximately $360,000 per year. The way this money is used to influence state politics will be discussed later.

TABLE 3.2 CRUISE INDUSTRY SPENDING ON LOBBYISTS IN WASHINGTON, DC, 1997 – 2004

Cruise Line	1997	1998	1999	2000	2001	2002	2003	2004
Carnival	$126,000	$40,000	$80,000	$80,000		$10,000	$50,000	$40,000
RCCL						$10,000	$170,000	$20,000
NCL						$360,000	$1,140,000	$140,000
Princess		$50,000	$30,000	$120,000	$80,000	$90,000	$40,000	$40,000
Holland America		$50,000	$30,000	$120,000	$60,000	$70,000	$40,000	$20,000
ICCL	$420,000	$520,000	$420,000	$440,000	$1,000,000	$920,000	$1,040,000	$991,946
Total	**$546,000**	**$660,000**	**$560,000**	**$760,000**	**$1,140,000**	**$1,460,000**	**$2,960,000**	**$1,251,946**

Source: Secretary of the US Senate.

Alphabet Soup

Here's a list of the organizations and acronyms discussed in this chapter:

CICF	Cruise Industry Charitable Foundation
CLIA	Cruise Lines International Association
ECC	European Cruise Council
FCCA	Florida-Caribbean Cruise Association
ICCL	International Council of Cruise Lines
NWCA	Northwest Cruiseship Association
PSA	Passenger Shipping Association (UK)
PVSA	Passenger Vessel Services Act

Lobbyists by Another Name

Other organizations also promote or lobby on behalf of the cruise industry. Regional trade associations are the most active. They are similar to ICCL but focus on a geographic area. The Florida–Caribbean Cruise Association (FCCA), which represents 11 cruise lines operating almost 100 vessels in Florida, Caribbean, and Mexican waters, is a good example. Created in 1972, the FCCA's mandate is to provide a forum for discussion on legislation, tourism, development, port safety, security, and other cruise industry issues. It is the key player in the industry's relationship with Caribbean islands. Though it has initiatives to build positive relations with the people of the Caribbean, it often takes a political hard line on issues promoted by Caribbean states with which it disagrees. The most recent, a 2003 effort by the Caribbean Tourism Organization to institute a $20 levy on all passengers entering the Caribbean, is discussed in Chapter 7: The Art of Greenwashing.

> From what I have been told, it (the FCCA conference) was going to be something like — hotel people on one side, island representatives on another, cruise lines on another, step 10 paces back and fire.[42]
>
> **— Wylie Whisonaut, US Virgin Island tourism commissioner**

The Northwest Cruiseship Association (NWCA), based in Vancouver, is the west coast's equivalent of the FCCA. Established in 1986, it represents ten major cruise lines operating in the Pacific Northwest, Canada, Alaska, and Hawai'i. The NWCA was initially founded to provide security services to member lines, but its role grew to include government relations on legal and regulatory issues. It has lobbyists in Hawai'i, Alaska, and Canada, and acts in place of the ICCL in Alaska, Hawai'i, and Washington state.

The European Cruise Council (ECC), established in April 2004, is similar to the trade organizations in North America. But its beginning was not harmonious. The concept of an association to promote European cruising was first proposed by George Poulides, president of Festival Cruises, at Seatrade Europe Conventions in 1999 and 2000, but support was lukewarm. Then in October 2003, Pier Luigi Foschi, CEO of Costa Cruises, called for the creation of a European association to dialogue with EU regulators. He pledged Carnival Corporation's support for the idea and others quickly climbed on board. In a letter to *Seatrade Insider*, Poulides questions Foschi's belated concern and points out that the initiative "got off the ground when the largest European-owned cruise line, and the only company that has repeatedly called out for such a move, has been forced to stop sailing!"[43]

At the first meeting of the ECC, Foschi was elected chair and Patrick Ryan, managing director of Royal Caribbean International/Celebrity Cruises, was elected vice chair. The organization, whose founding members are dominated by Carnival Corporation and Royal Caribbean, is expected to "give the growing European cruise industry a distinct voice in Brussels as well as providing members with early notification of crucial EU initiatives such as taxation, health, the environment, safety, labor standards, and enlargement."[44] The industry hopes to impact European Community decision-making in its favor.

Closely related to trade organizations are cruise marketing associations. In the US there is Cruise Lines International Association (CLIA), in the UK the Passenger Shipping Association (PSA), and in Australia Cruise Council Australia, which also extends to Asia. Each organization performs similar functions. They promote cruising as a vacation choice and coordinate the collation and the publication of statistics related to the number of people who cruise and where they cruise. They also offer training and certification of travel agents specializing in cruise travel. They do not generally engage in direct lobbying, but are a key source for information about cruising and can have a major impact on cruising's image in the media and in local communities.

In addition there are examples of port marketing associations: Cruise Europe, Cruise Downunder, Cruise UK, the Atlantic Canada Cruise Association, and many more. These organizations market ports to the cruise industry, however, information flows both ways. The cruise industry can easily use the associations to lobby for improved port facilities, financial incentives for visits, reduced ports fees, and for other considerations that might facilitate a cruise ship's use of a port.

It is in many ways a perfect system: local nongovernmental organizations lobby on behalf of the cruise industry — a sort of representation by proxy. The marketing association spends its social capital to benefit the cruise industry while the industry saves its capital for use on other issues. For example, Cruise UK joined with the British Tourist Authority in August 2002 and called on the UK Department for Transport to reduce port usage fees to cruise ships. It argued, on behalf of the industry, that port usage fees were causing cruise operators to exclude the UK from itineraries in favor of continental competitors, and it presented restructuring options to benefit the cruise industry.[45] Fees were subsequently reduced.

Building Social Capital

Social capital is a critical element in political influence.[46] This amorphous concept refers to factors like reputation and image, the nature and number of linkages to others, and resources and skills. Corporations and individuals grow social capital through their image (often shaped by the media and advertising) and through social and political activity. The capital can then be "spent" to influence decisions in the social policy and political arenas. A couple of illustrations will clarify the concept.

Boards of Directors as Social Capital

Boards of directors provide critical links between corporations with common interests and concerns. A study of Fortune 500 companies found that overlaps between boards of directors produced 32 cliques, each comprised of between 5 and 14 companies.[47] These clique members often join forces for collective political or social action. This is demonstrated in a case study of the approval and construction of the Bay Area Rapid Transit system in San Francisco.[48] In that case, different corporate cliques lined up on opposite sides of the issue. The analysis demonstrates how social capital accrues from these overlapping boards of directors. While the cruise industry isn't much a part of corporate cliques, each company's board of directors provides linkages that are important for growing social capital.

Carnival Corporation's board of directors has traditionally been limited in its inclusion of "outsiders" — outsiders to the corporation and outsiders to a core of Arison family friends. This changed when Carnival merged with P&O Princess and several members of the P&O Princess board joined the board of Carnival. Presently, Carnival Corporation's 15-member board includes six corporate executives and nine nonexecutive members (see Appendix A). Two of the nonexecutive members are directly linked to the media: a former publisher of the *Miami Herald* and Vice Chair of Knight-Ridder Inc., and the CEO of Metromedia and board chair of Big City Radio. In addition, the Carnival board includes the president of Florida International University (reciprocated with the president of Carnival Cruise Lines serving on the board of the Florida International University Foundation) and has multiple connections to financial/investment groups and real estate companies. It also includes a member of the board of Lloyd's Register, the ship classification society used by many Carnival Corporation ships. Oddly, Carnival-owned Costa forced the chair of the Italian classification society, RINA, off the board of its archrival Festival Cruises claiming he was in a conflict of interest.[49] That view does not appear to apply in regard to Lloyd's and Carnival.

Two members of the Carnival board are on 14 other boards[50] though most are organizations with interests different from those of the cruise industry. One, Baroness Hogg, is noted as the busiest woman in Britain's FTSE 100. A former journalist and adviser to John Major she sits on four boards; on two she serves a senior role.[51] Even before its merger with P&O Princess, Carnival Corporation had a direct connection to the University of Miami. That connection has been maintained since the merger through the involvement of Carnival executives with the University's Rosenstiel School of Marine and Atmospheric Science.

Royal Caribbean's board of directors has similarities to Carnival's. It, too, has 15 members, but 11 are nonexecutive. Of those, eight are held (four each) by appointees of the company's two controlling owners: Norwegian shipping magnate Arne Wilhelmsen and Cruise Associates (the Pritzker family in partnership with the Ofer family). Members include a financial expert, an environmental expert, the former CEO of the world's largest Spanish language magazine publisher, and many linkages to financial and investment groups. Two board members in particular, Thomas Pritzker and William K. Reilly, are connected to an interesting array of companies (e.g., Hyatt Corporation, First Health Group, Dupont, Conoco, Eden Springs); financial institutions (e.g., Bay City Capital, Presido Trust); and nongovernmental organizations (e.g., University of Chicago, Art Institute of Chicago, National Geographic Society, World Wildlife Fund, Packard Foundation). Like Carnival, Royal Caribbean also has a board member in common with the board of Lloyds Register. Unlike Carnival, the RCCL board is more integrated with other corporate and nonprofit concerns. This is due, in part, to the Pritzker family's other business interests.

Foundations and Social Capital

It is not surprising that money is an effective source for social capital. Donations contribute to a positive image and if used strategically the benefits are significant. The cruise industry has several foundations.

Royal Caribbean's Ocean Fund is one. It distributed $4.6 million between 1997 and 2004. (The nature of the donations and benefits accrued are discussed in Chapter 7.) The Carnival Foundation is another example. It co-sponsors gala fundraisers (sometimes in tandem with Alcalde and Fay) and has reportedly made "more than $42 million in charitable donations, both through financial contributions through the Carnival Foundation, as well as in-kind donations to a wide range of local, national, and international charitable and arts-related organizations."[52] The in-kind donations include use of cruise ships for gala events — a large value for a relatively small expense and wonderful publicity.

The ICCL builds social capital through its Cruise Industry Charitable Foundation (CICF). Founded in 1998, the CICF "focuses its efforts on programs that are designed

TABLE 3.3: TOP 10 RECIPIENTS OF FUNDS FROM THE CRUISE INDUSTRY CHARITABLE FOUNDATION, 1998 – 2003

Recipient	Amount
Washington Workshops Foundation	$1,088,950
2001 Special Olympics, Anchorage	$250,000
Florida Governors Literacy Initiative	$150,000
Sertoma Center, Nashville, TN	$115,000
National Coalition of 100 Black Women	$105,000
Delta Education, Health and Cultural Center, Miami	$105,000
Celebrations for Children	$100,000
New York State NAACP	$100,000
Florida Prepaid College Program	$100,000
Presidential Classroom, NY & LA	$100,000

Source: Cruise Industry Charitable Foundation's IRS Form 990 <www.guidestar.org>

to improve the quality of life in the communities served by the cruise industry. CICF supports programs that enhance educational opportunities for youth, including those designed to improve literacy, teach basic life skills, and promote good citizenship. The Foundation also supports academic enrichment opportunities aimed at enhancing student proficiencies in reading, math, and science."[53]

How CICF has spent its money is a bit different. The foundation took in $4,173,137 between 1998 and 2003. It spent $596,862 (14.3 percent of receipts) on overhead and other operations and gave grants totaling $3,576,275. Table 3.3 shows the top ten grant recipients. They account for $2.2 million or 62 percent of all money granted by the CICF. Thirty-four recipients received $5,000 or less; their grants collectively totaled $153,525 — 4.3 percent of the total given in grants. Interestingly, the bottom 66 recipients (from a list of 95) collectively received the same amount as spent on overhead and other activities. A complete list of recipients and amounts is shown in Appendix B.

The single largest recipient of CICF funds is Washington Workshops Foundation, another client of Alcalde and Fay. It received $1,088,95954 — 30 percent of all money granted by CICF — to fund "at risk" youth from Houston, Miami, New Orleans, New York City, Duluth, Arizona, Alaska, Washington, and California. Washington Workshops is a seven-day program of seminars, workshops, and meetings that promotes interaction with senior government executives to provide students an opportunity to gain a greater understanding and appreciation of the US federal government and its day-to-day operations. The cruise industry's support clearly grows social capital. It benefits when members of Congress get positive press at home for welcoming a delegation of high school-age youth to Washington — the member of Congress feels good about the industry, as do the youth and their families. The media broadcast the positive impression further.

Some donations have political value. Support for Governor Bush's Family Literacy Campaign is an example that will be discussed later. Another example is Celebrations for Children. It has an attractive-sounding name, but its purpose may not be as clear. According to a complaint filed by Common Cause with the Internal Revenue Service, the organization is:

> a newly incorporated entity formed under the auspices, and by associates of Rep. Tom Delay (R-TX), the majority leader of the House of Representatives, who is closely associated with the organization. Celebrations for Children is purportedly organized for the purposes of raising funds to make donations to charitable groups that provide services on behalf of disadvantaged children …. Published reports indicate, however, that Celebrations for Children is instead being used as a vehicle to fund Rep. DeLay's political operations and to provide donor maintenance services.[55]

Regardless of the outcome of the complaint, Celebrations for Children was the ICCL's second largest beneficiary of funds in 2003.

Donations are often timed for maximal impact. Celebrity Cruises' *Zenith* was used before its inaugural cruise from Jacksonville's new cruise terminal to host a luncheon and special presentation on October 27, 2003. US Representatives Corrine Brown, Ander Crenshaw, and Cliff Stearns, and many members of the Florida legislature were present. "Highlighting the event was the presentation of a $55,000 donation from CICF to be shared by nine local charities."[56] The media gave positive coverage, with photos, for the politicians and the cruise industry.

A similar event was held in New York City on Celebrity Cruises' *Horizon* on June 9, 2001. In this case CICF donated $5,000 each to ten organizations[57] in the New York City Area. Representative Charles Rangel was in attendance, as were youth organization directors and children from the recipient organizations. The event received media attention and was used to promote "an industry known for creating lifetime memories for their passengers as well as many economic opportunities for the city of New York."[58] It accrued lots of social capital with relatively meager financial capital.

Barely one month earlier, on May 18, the CICF and Cruise Line Coalition invited business and community leaders to join Governor Jeb Bush and former First Lady

Barbara Bush for a charitable event held on Carnival's *Fascination* to benefit the "Fascination with Reading 2001" initiative. Carnival and ICCL were founding partners of the initiative and both contributed money. The event raised more than $1 million. One year later Carnival Corporation committed an additional $1.2 million over 6 years to the Governor's Family Literacy Initiative. The money would come from tax rebates Carnival received from the state's qualified target-industry tax refund program for its call center in Broward County.[59]

Another way CICF grows social capital is through sponsorship of events. The annual Capital Hill Oceans Week is an example. In 2003 CICF was a Gold Sponsor; in 2004 it was the Presenting Sponsor. This projects an image and impression and gives the ICCL's staff an opportunity "to work the room." Given the participation of legislators and policy makers, and management of the event by the National Marine Sanctuary Foundation, CICF's investment pays off.

Several environmental organizations have focused on the threat posed by cruise ships to the marine sanctuaries at Monterey Bay and Key West. They often feel their efforts are confounded by the conflicted allegiance of senior managers. The struggle in this age of scarce funds is whether to support the broader public interest or to adopt a pro-industry view and continue to have industry dollars funneled into the sanctuary's coffers.

Similar conflicted allegiance is found with the US Coast Guard, the agency charged with responsibility for ship safety, and enforcement of environmental regulations and other laws applying to the cruise industry. Yet retired officers from the Coast Guard are often hired by cruise lines to oversee corporate relations with the regulators.[60] The Coast Guard officer-become-cruise-line-employee is known to the regulators as a sort of insider who now as an outsider lobbies and cajoles those charged with protecting the public interest. But it doesn't stop there.

The ICCL and Carnival Foundation team up on an ICCL/Coast Guard Foundation dinner during ICCL's annual Leadership Forum in Miami. The event had 630 attendees and raised $300,000 in 2003; it had 750 attendees and raised $400,000 in 2004. NCL's CEO, Colin Veitch, commented at the 2003 event that NCL would soon introduce its US-flagged ships in Hawai'i and there are plenty of positions left for anyone about to retire from the Coast Guard. He also "talked about the 'great debt of gratitude' the cruise industry owes the Coast Guard. 'Consider the $300,000 a small down payment on that large debt.'"[62]

A similar event is held in Seattle. In fall 2003 it raised $115,000 with top money in the event's silent auction going to two items

> Ed Wenk, University of Washington professor and former presidential marine-safety adviser, sees a problem when a Coast Guard official goes into the private sector and then has dealings with his former subordinates.[61]

donated by Holland America Line: a Peter Max painting and two tickets for the inaugural cruise of the *Queen Mary 2*. Holland America's president, Stein Kruse, is on the board of the US Coast Guard Foundation and of ICCL.[63]

Philanthropy and Social Capital

Philanthropy is a powerful source of social capital. The industry also benefits from philanthropic acts by its key players. Ted Arison and his wife Lin founded the National Academy for Advancement in the Arts. In 1986 he gave $40 million in Carnival Corporation stock for establishment of a New World Symphony Foundation. The New World Symphony was established the following year.[64] Arison also donated $10 million to the Performing Arts Center of Greater Miami where the Carnival Symphony Hall is located.[65] In 2002 Carnival gave $1 million to name the Carnival Cruise Lines Science & Technology Building at St. Thomas University in Miami.[66] Carnival's president, Bob Dickinson, is on the board of trustees of the university. These donations are positive statements, but they also extend a positive image to Carnival Corporation. In the case of buildings, the investment pays off for decades.

The Pritzker family is similarly active in philanthropic causes — there is the Pritzker Military Library and, since 1968, the Pritzker School of Medicine at the University of Chicago.[67] In 1996 the family pledged $60 million to the Illinois Institute of Technology, another educational institution in the family's home state. In these cases the social capital resides with the Pritzkers and their primary business interests, not Royal Caribbean.

Lobbying Works Better If Combined with Money

The effectiveness of lobbying increases when combined with campaign contributions.[68] The cruise industry is an active contributor through US-based tour companies: Princess Tours and Royal Celebrity Tours, corporate executives and cruise line employees, political action committees (PACs), and various other funds and committees. Tracking is not always easy. ICCL has the Cruise Industry Community Fund, ICCL-PAC, and Community Pride Fund. In Florida there is the Florida Cruise Committee and Florida Leadership Cruise Committee. Of the more than $8 million in campaign contributions tracked to cruise industry sources from 1997 to 2004, 45 percent has gone to state campaigns, 34 percent to federal candidates for Congress or president, and 21 percent to national parties (see Table 3.4). The overwhelming majority of money contributed to state elections is through the state's Republican and/or Democratic Party.

The Cruise Industry and Federal Politics

Campaign contributions can be viewed by party or candidate. There is not a wide difference in support for the two national parties in these data. The Democratic

Party received slightly more than the Republican Party in 1998 and 2002; the reverse was true in 2000 and 2004. The differences — $20,000 to $30,000 — are small considering the major parties collected almost $750,000 over the election cycles.

The pattern of contributions to individual candidates is much more interesting. But it should first be noted that the Pritzker family introduces a wrinkle. The candidates they support are influenced by their other diverse business interests. Sometimes family members' contributions run counter to each other and sometimes counter to cruise industry interests. For example, the Pritzkers heavily supported Barak Obama and Richard Durbin, Illinois candidates for the US Senate, and Hillary Rodham Clinton's campaign in New York, though others in the cruise industry have given relatively little or nothing to these campaigns. They are not generally seen as the cruise industry's friends. Given that Pritzker family campaign contributions are not always in the interest of RCCL, the following discussion filters out contributions unique to the Pritzker family.

Table 3.5 and Table 3.6 show the industry's favorites — candidates receiving more than $15,000 between 1997 and 2004. The list of contributions is confusing on the surface. Some contributions make perfect sense, such as support for candidates from key cruise states such as Alaska, Washington, and Florida who collectively received $850,000 between 1997 and 2004.[69] Others on the list don't initially make sense: Why would senators from land-locked states such as Arizona, Nevada, and Montana be important to the cruise industry? There are similar apparent anomalies in industry support in the House of Representatives. These make sense if committee membership and other roles are considered for those whose campaigns are supported.

The US Senate

The list of top recipients of cruise industry money in the Senate between 1997 and 2004 includes many key people: the Democratic leader, Tom Daschle, and the party's whip, Harry Reid, eight members of the Appropriations committee[70] (including its chair Ted Stevens), and ten members of the Commerce, Science and Transportation Committee[71] (including its chair John McCain and ranking minority member Ernest Hollings).

The Appropriations Committee is important because it controls all spending bills. The industry's tax breaks originate in or pass through the committee. But secrecy keeps details in the dark. In 1998 an innocuous looking amendment to the Immigration Act eliminated as much as $20 million a year in fees to be collected from cruise lines to cover inspection costs for people arriving in US ports aboard cruise ships.[72] When Douglas Frantz of the *New York Times* attempted to find out who inserted the item, he was told by Ted Stevens' spokesperson that the committee chair knows who wrote the section and that he approved it, but he would not identify the senator.

TABLE 3.4: POLITICAL CAMPAIGN CONTRIBUTIONS BY CRUISE INDUSTRY, 1997 – 2004

	ELECTION CYCLE				
CONTRIBUTOR	1998	2000	2002	2004	TOTAL
Carnival Corporation	$	$	$	$	$
Federal Candidates	136,683	207,349	144,499	196,850	685,381
Federal Parties	99,149	352,850	162,250	126,400	740,649
Subtotal	235,832	560,199	306,749	323,250	1,426,030
Alaska	20,900	105,000	105,464	20,798	252,162
Florida	61,075	13,775	7,500	2,000	84,350
Washington	14,475	65,845	101,729	212,525	394,574
Other States	45,285	161,225	107,194	27,250	340,954
Carnival Total	377,567	906,044	628,636	585,823	2,498,070
Royal Caribbean					
Federal Candidates	49,550	53,100	64,150	128,750	295,550
Federal Parties	4,750	127,500	83,207	57,300	272,757
Subtotal	54,300	180,600	147,357	186,050	568,307
Alaska	9,600	31,500	60,635	16,380	118,115
Florida	21,425	61,100	88,900	1,500	172,925
RCCL Total	85,325	273,200	296,892	203,930	859,347
Princess Cruises					
Federal Candidates	55,750	9,600	9,600	9,600	84,550
Federal Parties	17,500	21,425	21,425	21,425	81,775
Subtotal	73,250	31,025	31,025	31,025	166,325
Alaska	27,399	21,606	64,648	6,450	120,103
Florida	12,000	30,000	6,500	0	48,500
Princess Total	112,649	82,631	102,173	37,475	334,928

TABLE 3.4: POLITICAL CAMPAIGN CONTRIBUTIONS BY CRUISE INDUSTRY, 1997 – 2004 – continued:

CONTRIBUTOR	ELECTION CYCLE				
	1998	2000	2002	2004	TOTAL
ICCL	$	$	$	$	$
Federal Candidates	186,904	150,634	187,605	167,238	692,381
Federal Parties	27,800	16,000	144,000	12,500	200,300
Subtotal	214,704	166,634	331,605	179,738	892,681
California	–	–	15,000	47,700	62,700
Florida	–	–	611,500	80,000	691,500
ICCL Total	214,704	166,634	958,105	307,438	1,646,881
Other Industry Players					
Federal Candidates	44,500	54,400	57,750	84,400	241,050
Federal Parties	500	36,250	1,100	600	38,450
Subtotal	45,000	90,650	58,850	85,000	279,500
State Elections					
Alaska	24,560	40,068	25,163	4,665	94,456
Florida	25,425	458,150	89,550	5,000	578,125
Other States	11,574	23,500	52,677	1,000	88,751
Others Total	106,559	612,368	226,240	95,665	1,040,832
Pritzker Family					
Federal Candidates	140,669	149,000	140,700	313,200	743,569
Federal Parties	43,500	72,500	17,500	205,250	338,750
State Elections	78,675	60,200	295,413	180,493	614,781
Family Total	262,844	281,700	453,613	698,943	1,697,100

Note: Each corporation or group includes corporate board members and executives, in-house political action committees, employees, and others associated with the company.

Sources: Federal Election Commission <www.fec.gov>, Common Cause <commoncause.org>, Follow the Money <followthemoney. org>, Open Secrets <opensecrets.org>, and the Office of Elections in California, Washington, Alaska, and Florida.

TABLE 3.5: LARGEST RECIPIENTS IN THE SENATE OF CAMAPAIGN CONTRIBUTIONS FROM THE CRUISE INDUSTRY, 1997 – 2004

RECIPIENT	ELECTION CYCLE				
	1998	*2000*	*2002*	*2004*	*TOTAL*
	$	$	$	$	$
Nelson, Bill (D-FL)	1,000	61,000	15,500	15,500	93,000
Murkowski, Frank/Lisa (R-AK)	15,250	3,000		45,500	63,750
McCain, John (R-AZ)	21,000	18,000	5,000	12,500	56,500
Boxer, Barbara (D-CA)	14,500	2,500	4,250	33,500	54,750
Clinton, Hillary (D-,NY)		41,500		3,000	44,500
Graham, Bill (D-FL)	21,750			18,250	40,000
Reid, Harry (D-NV)	16,000	2,000	9,000	11,000	38,000
Hollings, Ernest (D-SC)	21,000	4,000	10,000	1,500	36,500
Inouye, Daniel (D-HI)	9,000		3,000	24,100	36,100
Daschle, Tom (D-SD)	12,500	4,500	5,000	10,000	32,000
Stevens, Ted (R-AK)	1,000	10,000	16,100	3,000	30,100
Lott, Trent (R-MS)	14,200	5,000	5,500	5,000	29,700
Burns, Conrad (R-MT)	7,500	4,000	12,000	6,000	29,500
Pryor, Mark (D-AR)			26,000		26,000
Durbin, Richard (D-IL)	1,750	7,500	12,750		22,000
Cantwell, Maria (D-WA)		2,000	14,749	4,000	20,749
Murray, Patty (D-WA)	1,500		2,000	16,500	20,000
Baucus, Max (R-MT)	7,000	3,000	8,000		18,000
Shelby, Richard (R-AL)	13,000	1,000		4,000	18,000
Breaux, John (D-LA)	15,500	1,000	1,000		17,500
Specter, Arlen (R-PA)	1,250			15,249	16,499

Source: Federal Elections Commission <www.fec.gov>. Note that figures include contributions to a candidate's affiliated political action committee (PAC).

Congressman Gene Taylor was similarly stonewalled about the identity of an anonymous senator who three times in as many years singly blocked a measure approved in the House that would require foreign-registered vessels to stop at a foreign port,[73] thereby excluding foreign-flagged vessels from the lucrative cruise-to-nowhere market.

The Commerce, Science and Transportation Committee is no less important than Appropriations. It was assigned the Clean Cruise Ship Act of 2004[74] and consistently other legislation relating to the cruise industry. There are two relevant subcommittees: Oceans, Fisheries, and the Coast Guard; and Surface Transportation and Merchant Marine. The former has jurisdiction over the National Oceanic and Atmospheric Administration (including the National Marine Sanctuary Program), Coastal Zone Management, Fisheries and Marine Mammals, Oil Spill Liability, the US Ocean Commission, and the US Coast Guard. The subcommittee includes seven senators listed in Table 3.5.[75] The latter subcommittee is responsible for the merchant marine and has eight members (Table 3.5).[76] The Democratic Party's ranking member on the subcommittee in 2003–2004 was Daniel Inouye of Hawai'i.

The subcommittee was intimately involved in deliberations around the original Project America, and Inouye played a central role in resurrecting the project. His efforts appear to have been rewarded. NCL's CEO, Colin Veitch, contributed $15,000 to the Democratic Party of Hawai'i in the fall of 2002 after discussions between NCL and Inouye were begun. Veitch and NCL's CFO contributed $8,000 to Inouye's re-election campaign (an additional $3,000 followed in 2004 from NCL America's CEO) and $4,000 to Hawai'i's Congressperson Neil Abercrombie,[77] following approvals paving the way for NCL America to begin operations.

The House of Representatives

Compared with campaign contributions to senators, contributions to members of the House are spread across a larger number of recipients. Still, the pattern is like the Senate's. The industry's large contributions are concentrated on members of three committees: Transportation and Infrastructure, Ways and Means, and Energy and Commerce.

The Transportation and Infrastructure Committee is important because it includes the Coast Guard and Marine Transportation subcommittee. This committee was assigned the Clean Cruise Ship Act of 2004 and like the Commerce, Science and Transportation Committee in the Senate is generally referred all legislation related to the cruise industry. The committee's chair in 2003–2004 was Don Young from Alaska. The former Yukon tugboat captain is the largest recipient of contributions from cruise industry sources. Contributions are made to both his re-election campaign and his affiliated political action committee, Midnight Sun PAC. James Oberstar (number 9 on Table 3.6) was the ranking Democrat on the Committee. In sum the committee included eight members[78] listed on Table 3.6. Five others received lesser amounts.[79]

The ranking Democrat on two other committees with jurisdiction over issues of interest to the cruise industry also received significant campaign contributions from the cruise industry. Charles Rangel of New York was the ranking Democrat on the

TABLE 3.6: LARGEST RECIPIENTS IN THE HOUSE OF REPRESENTATIVES OF CAMPAIGN CONTRIBUTIONS FROM THE CRUISE INDUSTRY, 1997 – 2004

RECIPIENT	*ELECTION CYCLE*				
	1998	*2000*	*2002*	*2004*	*TOTAL*
	$	$	$	$	$
Young, Don (R-AK)	25,000	47,350	42,550	40,300	155,200
Rangel, Charles (D-NY)	2,500	34,000	5,000	11,000	52,500
Deutsch, Peter (D-FL)	8,500	2,500	6,500	25,000	42,500
Pelosi, Nancy (D-CA)	2,650	2,750	2,500	24,000	31,900
Brown, Corrine (D-FL)	6,000	6,750	7,500	10,500	30,750
Gephardt, Richard (D-MO)	4,000	5,000	6,000	13,500	28,500
Shaw, E Clay (R-FL)	6,635	8,500	9,000	3,500	27,635
Dingell, John (D-MI)		4,000	7,000	16,000	27,000
Oberstar, James (D-MN)	5,500	9,000	6,500	4,500	25,500
Shuster, Bill (R-PA)	14,850	10,500			25,350
Duncan, John (R-TN)	9,300	2,500	11,355	1,000	24,155
Meek, Corrine/Kendrick (D-FL)	5,500	5,000	4,500	7,000	22,000
Greenwood, James (R-TN)	4,000	4,000	5,000	8,000	21,000
McCollum, Bill (R,FL)	1,500	8,000		11,000	20,500
Hastings, Alcee (D-FL)	5,000	2,000	4,500	8,000	19,500
Abercrombie, Neil (D-HI)	6,000	2,400	2,400	8,400	19,200
Boehlert, Sherwood (R-NY)	5,000	11,180	2,000	1,000	19,180
Diaz-Balart, Lincoln (R-FL)	9,000	4,500	2,599	2,500	18,599
Davis, Jim (D-FL)	5,500	5,000	3,500	4,000	18,000
Coble, Howard (R-NC)	4,500	5,500	6,500	1,000	17,500
Frost, Martin (D-TX)		7,500	4,500	5,500	17,500
Ros-Lehtinen, Ileana (R-FL)	3,500	4,500	3,500	5,500	17,000
Mica, John (R-FL)	3,946	2,250	8,500	2,000	16,696
Crane, Phil (R-IL)	8,500	4,500	3,000		16,000
Hastert, Dennis (R-IL)		4,500	1,500	9,000	15,000

Source: Federal Elections Commission <www.fec.gov>. Note that the figures include contributions to a candidate's affiliated political action committee (PAC).

Ways and Means Committee in 2003–2004.[80] The committee has jurisdiction over the Internal Revenue Service tax code and for all customs and tariffs; the cruise industry's tax status is in the hands of this committee. John Dingell of Michigan is the ranking Democrat on the Energy and Commerce Committee.[81] This committee has jurisdiction over air quality and environmental health and is important because of the continuing focus on the cruise industry's environmental record and practices.

Major Support for Campaigns That Lose and That Win

There is one other pattern in campaign contributions. That is where an incumbent or a challenger is given generous support. The Pritzker family's support for Barak Obama's campaign for Senate, which approached $40,000, is one example. That scale of contribution undoubtedly builds social capital and yields influence.

ICCL has similarly contributed to campaigns, sometimes in concert with industry PACS and executives. The industry contributed $28,500 to Senator Alphonse D'Amato's campaign for re-election in 1998 from New York. D'Amato chaired the Senate's powerful Banking Committee; he lost the election to Charles Schumer. In 2000 the industry (mainly Holland America Line and Princess PAC) contributed $24,500 to Washington Senator Slade Gorton's losing bid for re-election. Maria Cantwell narrowly defeated him by 2,229 votes (48.73% vs. 48.63%). Senator Cantwell has quickly become a friend of the cruise industry; within the first two years of her six-year term she received $14,749. By the end of 2004 she had accumulated from cruise industry sources almost $20,000 toward her 2006 re-election campaign. The Cruise Industry Community Fund contributed $26,000 to Senator Mark Pryor's successful bid for re-election from Arkansas. The industry collectively contributed $19,000 to Senator Max Cleland's losing bid for re-election from Georgia.

How about a Free Cruise?

The industry has in past used more than campaign contributions to build social capital. In 1993 Representative Gene Taylor of Mississippi "rocked Capitol Hill with allegations that foreign-flagged passenger lines have engaged in 'subtle bribery' by providing free cruises to legislators and their families."[82] Though the industry denied it had given any free cruises since 1984, it did reveal that three groups of members of congress were granted free "fact-finding" cruises in 1983. The list included the former chair of the Merchant Marines and Fisheries Committee and the former chair of the Senate Ethics Committee.[83] Taylor eventually identified 15 legislators who had taken fact-finding cruises.[84] He became involved with the issue after being offered a free cruise on his way for the vote on legislation that would have prohibited foreign-flagged vessels from offering "cruises to nowhere."

The first time I went to pass that bill in the House, I will never forget what happened to me .... As I'm walking across the street to go handle the bill on the House floor, the chief lobbyist for the foreign cruise industry comes up and offers me and my family a free cruise if I withdraw my bill. He says, "It's just so that you get to know us." It sure sounded like a bribe to me.[85]

Hector Alcalde, the industry's lobbyist, gives a slightly different account to the *New York Times*.

It is true that I suggested he inspect the cruise ships. It is important that to take a position as a legislator, one must understand the industries that they are attempting to regulate. It is true that I suggested that they are an excellent vacation, especially for families. Never did I offer Taylor any favor or incentive, and I am truly sorry that he misunderstood me.[86]

While offering a free cruise would not have been against US laws, acceptance by a member of Congress could constitute a violation of ethics rules.

There have been no further claims of free cruises for members of Congress, but that doesn't mean that free cruises are not still given. In 1994 a scandal erupted over allegations that foreign-flagged cruise vessels had routinely granted free and discounted cruises to families and friends of US Immigration and Naturalization Service officers responsible for inspecting the lines' vessels.[87] During confrontations between environmentalists and the cruise industry in the late 1990s and early 2000s a significant number of "activists" were offered free cruises and some accepted the offer. Anecdotal evidence indicates free or discounted cruises are sometimes given to port officials, local government officials, and a significant number of reporters and writers.

Recurring Critical Issues

Several recurring issues are worth considering given that they illustrate how the cruise industry plays US politics.

Labor

Congress has tried several times to extend US labor laws to foreign-flagged cruise ships. The most concerted effort was over a four-year period by William Clay who at the time chaired the Labor Management Subcommittee of the Education and Labor Committee in House of Representatives.

In 1989 Clay introduced HR 3238, which would extend collective bargaining rights and protection under labor standards (including payment of minimum wage) to seafarers on most foreign-flagged cruise ships operating from US ports.[88] The committee was told at hearings of seafarers working 100 hours a week with no days off, many without an employment contract, and some earning as little as 53 cents an hour. The subcommittee approved the bill in the summer of 1990, though it went no further.

The legislation was reintroduced by Clay in 1991 as HR 1126. Claiborne Pell of Rhode Island introduced a similar version of the bill in the Senate. The House Education and Labor subcommittee heard testimony of seafarers "being required to work 18–20 hours a day for less than $1 an hour; of living conditions so unsanitary as to threaten life; of sailors being forced to provide kickbacks to labor contractors; [and] of sailors being abandoned in foreign ports and blackmailed from the industry for seeking to improve intolerable and inhuman conditions."[89] Despite the grave conditions, the act stalled in committee. It lacked support from the Bush Administration and was actively opposed by the cruise industry.

Representative Clay tried again after Bush left office. He introduced HR 1517 in 1993. No new information came from hearings except that the ICCL threatened the House of Representatives that it would relocate to non-US ports if legislation passed.[90] The legislation made its way to the floor of the House but again failed to be heard. Some attribute the industry's threat as a factor in it becoming stalled; others suggest its demise was a result of the measure's lack of sponsorship in the Senate — Senator Pell had not reintroduced his bill — and that the Clinton Administration had not extended its support for the legislation. Despite all of the attention in the 1990s and early 2000s to the conditions of workers on cruise ships, the matter has remained legislatively dormant since 1993.

Glacier Bay National Park

Glacier Bay is an important destination for cruise ships and there is great competition for the limited number of permits issued each year.[91] Senator Frank Murkowski unsuccessfully tried in 1993 to legislate an increase in the number of permits given to cruise ships. He soon tried again. Following the 1994 elections, which gave the Republicans a majority in both the House and Senate, Senator Murkowski and Representative Young called on Interior Secretary Bruce Babbitt to order that the National Park Service increase the number of permits for cruise ships entering Glacier Bay from 107 to 184, a 72 percent increase. Their influence resided in the fact that when Congress reconvened in January 1995, each would assume the chair of a committee having jurisdiction over most Interior Department agencies and programs.[92]

Interior Secretary Babbitt[93] responded by directing the National Park Service to endorse 184 visits per year — a number corresponding to an average of two visits a day during the 92-day season.[94] The increased number of permits was opposed by environmentalists and by the Park Service's own experts. In its effort to deal with the pressure from Secretary Babbitt, the Park Service solicited public comments on the plan to increase the number of permits. Eighty-five percent favored a reduction rather than an increase.

With pressure from the Department of the Interior on one side and from environmentalists on the other, the Park Service struck a compromise. It agreed to increase the number of permits to Glacier Bay to 139 (rather than 184)[95] on the condition that the Park Service receive authority to impose higher antipollution standards if found to be warranted by later studies. The impasse was resolved until the compromise was published in the Federal Register. Senator Murkowski responded by adding a last minute amendment to the 1996 Parks Bill taking away the Park Service's authority to increase pollution controls, a change that came at the urging of the cruise industry whose lobbyists had argued that it was unfair to hold their ships to a higher standard than other vessels.[96]

With the compromise solution broken, the National Parks Conservation Association challenged the increase and sued the Park Service in 1997. In February 2001 the Ninth US Circuit Court of Appeals found the Park Service erred when it responded to industry appeals by allowing a 30 percent increase in summer cruise ship traffic in Glacier Bay without doing a full study of the environmental impact of the additional ships. The government appealed, but the decision was upheld in August 2001 and the judge ordered an immediate reduction to the pre-1995 limit of 107.

Senator Stevens sought to override the court decision with a rider to the appropriations bill for the Department of the Interior. The rider instructed the National Park Service to freeze cruise ship entries at the current level of 139 ships until it completes an environmental impact statement (EIS) as ordered by the court in February.[97] The rider passed the Senate in August, but didn't pass the House early enough to take effect in 2001. It took effect in 2002 and remains in effect until the EIS has been completed and approved.

Senator Stevens' actions coincide with a federal judge's ruling in June 2001 that struck down major sections of Alaska's campaign finance law and which legalized soft money contributions. Within a month, Holland America Line, Princess Cruises, and Royal Caribbean International had each contributed $25,000 to the Alaska Republican Party.[98]

Representative Young has also provided favors to the cruise industry. In the fall of 1996 he inserted an amendment into a Coast Guard authorization bill that prevented the State of Alaska from banning gambling on cruise ships, except when the ship is docked or within three miles of a port of call. The amendment was sought by the cruise industry and applied only to large cruise ships.[99] In October 1998 Young preserved the monopoly foreign-flagged cruise lines hold on entry permits to Glacier Bay National Park by inserting an amendment, on the day a bill was being passed, excluding Glacier Bay from parks where open competition would be used for granting entry permits. As a result, current permit holders retained their preference through 2009.[100] And in 2003, Young added a paragraph to a Coast Guard bill defining the 300 gross ton cruise ship *Empress of the North* as under 100 gross tons in so far as its qualification for a permit to Glacier Bay National Park. At the smaller size, the ship was classified as a tour boat and would not have to compete with cruise ships for a permit.[101]

Liability

Cruise line liability was addressed by Congress in a tort reform measure attached to the Coast Guard Reauthorization bill passed on May 9, 1995. The amendment, for the most part written by the ICCL, was introduced by Representative Young. He referred to it as a "noncontroversial manager's amendment."[102] It passed the House by a vote of 406 to 12. Only afterwards did people read the final print.

For one thing, the amendment limited the rights of foreign seafarers to sue in US courts for grievances against foreign cruise lines.[103] This went against the stream of court cases taken up by the US government several years earlier. In 1991 the US Equal Employment Opportunity Commission (EEOC) won two cases against foreign flag cruise vessels. In one the court enjoined a foreign cruise line from discriminating on the basis of sex against any actual or potential job applicant. In the other NCL was charged with sex discrimination by an assistant cruise director who alleged she lost her job after becoming pregnant, and with discrimination by race and national origin by a bar manager who says he was forced to resign. NCL disregarded two subpoenas, claiming the EEOC lacked jurisdiction. It won in the US District Court in Miami but the decision was reversed by the US Court of Appeals in Atlanta, which affirmed the EEOC's jurisdiction.[104] This was a dangerous precedent for the cruise industry and Young's amendment gave them an out.

The amendment included two other provisions. One was designed to protect ship owners from unlimited liability in suits brought by passengers or crew members who were harmed by medical malpractice at a shore-side facility. It limited liability to that set by the laws of the state in which the medical provider is located. Currently cruise line liability for shore-side treatment is unlimited.

The other provision, directed at mounting claims from injuries and sexual assaults, limited liability to passengers and crew for "infliction of emotional distress, mental suffering or psychological injury" unless negligence or an intentional act can be proven. The American Trial Lawyers Association characterized the amendments as "dangerous legislation" that "jeopardized the safety of women on cruise ships." Opposition also came from the Women's Defense Fund, the National Organization for Women's Legal Defense Fund, the Maritime Committee of the AFL-CIO, and rape treatment centers.[105]

The amendment languished for more than a year waiting to go to a House–Senate conference where lawmakers would resolve the House and Senate versions of the Coast Guard Reauthorization Bill. Lobbying by the industry continued, including a delegation of cruise line executives led by Micky Arison, in March 1996. He and Celebrity Cruise's president Richard Sasso met with Senator Larry Pressler and separately with other members of the Senate Committee on Commerce, Science, and Transportation. Pressler chaired the committee and would serve on the conference committee charged with reconciling the House and Senate versions.[106]

By October 1, 1996, a compromise had been negotiated. Ernest Hollings, from the Senate's Commerce, Science, and Transportation Committee, observed before the Conference Committee that no one knew if the cruise ship people had enough votes to push the amendments through, but the cruise industry figured they were 50 percent there and didn't have much to lose.[107] When the Conference Committee convened, he threatened to kill the entire reauthorization bill if ICCL's amendments remained. In the end he capitulated after amended language was adopted for two of the provisions.

In the final version, ship owners were prohibited from limiting their liability in cases involving sexual harassment, sexual misbehavior, assault, or rape in cases where the victim is physically injured. Limitations were allowed in all other situations; a cruise line sued by one of its workers in regard of treatment at a US health facility or doctor's office can invoke an award cap allowed medical practitioners under the laws of the state in which the care is provided. The provision limiting a seafarer's use of US courts was scuttled and replaced with a provision that seafarer employment contracts can block the worker from seeking legal remedies in US courts.[108]

This last issue is one that remains cloudy. The families of crew members who lost their lives when Windjammer Barefoot Cruises' *Fantome* sank off Honduras during hurricane Mitch in October 1998 were initially denied the right to sue the cruise line in US courts by the District Court in Miami. But that decision was overturned by the 11th Circuit Court of Appeals in January 2003. The court justified the decision by citing the extent of the company's operations in the US.[109]

Families of survivors of a May 2003 boiler blast on NCL's *Norway* in which eight crew members died and about 20 others were seriously burned were similarly denied the right to use US courts even though the accident occurred while the ship was docked at Miami. The US District Court in Miami ruled workers' claims must be resolved in the Philippines to comply with the terms of contracts that workers and recruiters for the cruise ship in Manila signed with the Philippine government. The most they can expect to receive in the Philippines is $50,000. The 11th Circuit Court of Appeals in Atlanta upheld the district court's decision.[110]

Another issue on which there is debate regarding US jurisdiction is medical malpractice on board a cruise ship. Cruise lines have traditionally argued that physicians and other medical personnel are independent contractors for whom they are not liable. The argument has generally been accepted, but in August 2003 was rejected by the 3rd District Court of Appeals in a case involving malpractice on a Carnival ship. The court ruled that ship doctors are legal agents of cruise companies and the cruise line is liable.[111] A week earlier, the same court ruled in a case involving medical malpractice on a Royal Caribbean ship that a doctor may not use a ship's foreign registry as a shield against claims of malpractice in the death of a passenger's newborn.[112] The case involving Carnival was appealed to the Florida Supreme Court. So was a case in which the Appeals Court ruled it had jurisdiction based on the Florida constitution, which sets the state boundary to the edge of the Gulf Stream or three miles out, whichever is the greater distance. In that case NCL's ship was 14 miles off the Florida coast but had not reached the Gulf Stream.

Cases involving liability will continue in the courts. The issue is likely to surface also in Congress and in state legislatures. What the industry is unable to achieve in the courts it often accomplishes through legislation on the federal or the state level.

The Cruise Industry and State Politics

The cruise industry actively seeks to influence decisions in key cruise states such as Florida, Alaska, Washington, California, and Hawai'i. It uses campaign contributions and lobbyists, and also builds on its social capital. The situation is a bit different in each state. The industry appears to spread contributions to as many legislators as possible in Alaska, Washington, and Florida where few individuals stand out as receiving more. Contributions in California and Hawai'i appear more strategic.

Florida

The cruise industry is headquartered in Florida, and the majority of its passengers depart from Florida ports. It not surprisingly participates in the Florida political system. Between 1998 and 2004 the cruise industry contributed $500,000 to federal politicians from the state and more than $1.5 million to state elections. Less than 10 percent of this went to individual candidates; the remainder was to the state's political parties, mainly the Republican Party.

The industry contributed over $100,000 across 138 candidates for state office. Most received relatively small amounts. The ten receiving the most were led by the lieutenant governor and included the governor, attorney general, and chairs of the Appropriations Committee and of the Economic Opportunities and Consumer Services Committee in the Senate, and chair of the Finance and Tax Committee in the state House.

Contributions to the state political parties are more interesting. Between 1998 and 2004, the Florida Democratic Party received close to $200,000 from cruise industry sources; the Republican Party of Florida received more than $1.17 million. In 2002 alone the Republican Party of Florida received $640,000: $515,000 from ICCL's Cruise Industry Community Fund; $50,000 from its Community Pride Fund; and $75,000 from cruise lines and their executives.

The timing of contributions is interesting. On December 6, 2001, Florida was the first state to sign a memorandum of understanding (MOU) with the cruise industry for dealing with environmental protection[113] — Hawai'i followed a year later. The signing ceremony was held at the Florida Ocean Alliance[114] Conference on Carnival Cruise Lines' *Fantasy* while it was in port at Port Canaveral. In addition to signing of the MOU by the State of Florida and the ICCL a check for $50,000 was presented from CICF to the University of Miami's Rosenstiel School of Marine and Atmospheric Science. The local media covered the event and cast the industry in positive light.

The cruise industry showed its appreciation for the MOU, and also for Governor Bush who single-handedly squashed a plan to tax Miami cruises to pay for a new Florida Marlins stadium, an issue on which the industry's lobbyist, John LaCapra, reportedly spent $836,676 in 2000,[115] the largest amount spent by any lobbyist in Tallahassee that year.[116] In June it gave the Republican Party of Florida $515,000 toward Jeb Bush's re-election campaign. An additional $50,000 followed in August. The fundraiser for the Governor's Family Literacy Campaign (discussed previously) fell between these donations.

Alaska

More than 900,000 people visited Alaska's Inside Passage via cruise ship in 2005. Ketchikan, the southernmost port on Alaska's side of the Inside Passage, expects passenger numbers to increase another 350,000 (or more) in the next eight years. Alaska is an important summer destination for the North American cruise industry. It spends significant sums to influence Alaska state politics and thereby protect its interests.

The largest beneficiary of cruise industry campaign contributions in Alaska is Frank Murkowski. He stepped down as Senator to run for Governor in 2002 and when elected appointed his daughter Lisa to fill the remainder of his term in the Senate. Not only does Murkowski have a history of being a friend to the industry, but his Attorney General Gregg Renkes[117] is a member of ICCL's CICF,[118] and Ernesta Ballard, his commissioner of the Department of Environmental Conservation, previously served as a lobbyist for the Northwest Cruiseship Association.[119] Her department oversees the state's cruise ship monitoring and certification project. Table 3.7 shows that the cruise industry spends, on average, more than $350,000 a year on lobbyists in Alaska.

TABLE 3.7: CRUISE INDUSTRY SPENDING ON LOBBYISTS IN ALASKA, 2000 – 2004

Cruise Line/ Association	2000 $	2001 $	2002 $	2003 $	2004 $
Princess	79,289	86,740	74,628	80,134	78,542
RCCL	74,628	69,646	60,000	60,999	71,000
Holland America			76,107	85,080	73,782
Northwest Cruise Ship Association	158,720	191,087	185,578	142,771	139,223
United States Cruise Ship Association	15,269	37,827	–	–	–
Alaska Small Cruise Vessel Association	–	–	–	–	42,095
Year Totals:	327,906	347,473	396,313	368,984	404,642

Source: Alaska Public Offices Commission.

Unlike Florida, a small proportion of campaign contributions in Alaska go to the state political parties. Of the $585,000 given to Alaska state campaigns between 1998 and 2004, individual candidates received half, political parties one-third (80 percent to the Republicans; 20 percent to the Democrats), and the remainder went to ballot initiatives. Royal Caribbean, Holland America, and Princess collectively gave $25,000 in 2000 to the Alaskans United Against the Cap Committee, an initiative to defeat a statewide property tax cap; Holland America gave $10,000 in 2000 to "No on 5," a committee opposed to a proposition that would legalize marijuana; and Holland America gave $25,000 to the "Vote Yes!" committee in 1999, an initiative to allow the government to use $4 billion in dividends from the state's Permanent Fund. The initiative was opposed by than 83 percent of Alaska's voters. The industry has contributed modest sums to other local community initiatives.

The top individual candidates receiving funds from the cruise industry include candidates of both parties for Governor. The top recipients among legislators in the 2003–2004 senate were the Senate President, chair of the Senate Rules Committee, both co-chairs of the Senate Finance Committee, and co-chair of the Senate Transportation Committee; and in the 2003–2004 house: the Speaker of the House, chair of the Rules Committee, and co-chair of the Finance Committee.

Members of committees important to the cruise industry received more in campaign contributions from the cruise industry than did other members of the Alaska legislature. For example, the average amount received from the cruise industry by a member of the Senate Judiciary Committee is $2,050. In contrast, the average received by a member of the Senate Finance Committee is $3,000, of the Rules Committee is $4,266, and of the Transportation Committee is $4,557.

As in federal politics campaign contributions usually pay off, but not always. Alaska Governor Tony Knowles introduced Alaska's Cruise Ship Initiative in March 2001. Despite industry opposition, the legislation passed Alaska's House of Representatives, but got held up in the Senate's Transportation Committee where the chair (who had previously blocked legislation opposed by the cruise industry when he was in the house) warned that it would not pass his committee before the session was adjourned. The governor called a special session of the legislature and kept them in session until the bill was passed. This is one of the few times the cruise industry did not get its way.

The case of State Representative Eldon Mulder gives a different picture of the cruise industry and state politics.[120] In 2001 a subcommittee of the Select Committee on Legislated Ethics recommended that Mulder and his staff attend ethics training "in an effort to avoid action that may result in the filing of additional ethics complaints."[121] Mulder had been investigated by the Committee after shepherding a bill through the Legislature that exempted the cruise industry from state environmental regulations. This was at the same time that other legislators were considering tougher regulations on cruise ships. The problem wasn't that Mulder introduced the bill, or that it was referred to the Finance Committee where he was co-chair, but that his wife was paid $85,000 as an office manager for Joe Hayes, the NWCA's chief lobbyist in Juneau. Mulder did not stand for re-election in the 2002 general elections.

Washington State

The cruise industry's involvement in Washington state politics mainly involves Carnival Corporation's Holland America Line-Westours, which is headquartered in Seattle. Between 1998 and 2004, the company contributed over $380,000 to political campaigns in the state. The largest contributions were to advocacy groups such as Washington Leadership Council, Harry Truman Fund, Roosevelt Fund, and Speakers Roundtable; they collectively received $95,000 between 2002 and 2004. The company gave $10,000 to "Taxpayers for R-51," a 2002 referendum that would raise money through a 9-cent gas tax increase over two years, a 1 percent surcharge on vehicle purchases, and a fee increase for heavy trucks. Holland America's contributions to political parties in the state are modest — the Republican Party received $59,000, the Democratic Party received $31,000.

The pattern of donations to elected officials in Washington is as interesting as in Florida or Alaska. The most generously supported campaigns are for governor. The next largest recipient was Seattle Port Commissioner Claire Nordquist. Five other port commissioners received $1,000 or more from Holland America between 1998 and 2004; three sit on the Port Commission in 2004–2005: Pat Davis, Bob Edwards, and Paige Miller. Alec Fisken replaced Claire Nordquist in 2003. In 2001 Jack Block (another recipient of Holland America contributions) lost his seat to Lawrence Molloy.[122] Holland America has also supported candidates and incumbents on the Seattle City Council, the King County Council, and the Mercer Island Council.

In the state Senate the top recipients of contributions include the majority leader, the chair and vice chair of the Ways and Means Committee, and the vice chair of the Highway and Transportation Committee, the Natural Resources Committee and the Commerce and Trade Committee. In the House the list includes the chair of the Rules Committee.

A recent case in the Washington House of Representatives is an interesting illustration. In January 2004 Representative Mary Lou Dickerson introduced legislation that would have imposed $25,000-a-day penalties against cruise ships discharging untreated sewage and oily liquid from bilges and would have allowed state inspectors onto ships. Introduction of the legislation coincided with the state nearing agreement on a MOU with the industry to deal with environmental concerns.

The industry lobbied against Dickerson's bill and the legislation died because it couldn't get enough votes to make it out of the House Fisheries, Ecology and Parks Committee.[123] At the time, six members of the nine-person committee had received campaign contributions totaling $2,875 from Holland America. Six months after Dickerson's bill died, all nine committee members had received contributions from Holland America; they now collectively totaled $5,675.

California

The cruise industry's participation in California state politics is relatively recent. ICCL has a lobbyist in Sacramento and has actively promoted its position on environmental legislation when the state took a legislative route to deal with environmental issues. The cruise industry successfully blocked some legislation in 2003; similar attempts failed in 2004 (see Chapter 7).

The cruise industry is selective in its contributions. The ICCL's Community Pride Fund gave $10,000 to Governor Gray Davis' 2002 re-election campaign and $5,000 to the "No Recall" campaign the following year. In 2004 it gave $1,600 to State Senator Michael Machado. He serves as chair of the Agriculture and Water Resources Committee and is a member of the Appropriations Committee, which is where the environmental legislation was held up in 2003.

The Community Pride Fund also gave $1,000 to both State Assemblyman Alan Lowenthal and State Assemblywoman Jenny Oropeza in 2004. Each is from Long Beach, though their Committee assignment is probably more important than Carnival Corporation's ownership of the cruise terminal in their district. During 2003–2004, Lowenthal served on the Assembly's Select Committee on California Ports and the Environmental Safety and Toxic Materials Committee. Oropeza served on the Appropriations Committee and chaired the Assembly's Transportation Committee.

California's lieutenant governor, Cruz Bustamante, has been treated generously by the cruise industry. In 2003 Royal Celebrity Tours and Holland America contributed $40,000 to "Bustamante Against 54," a racial privacy initiative prohibiting the state from classifying an individual by race, ethnicity, color, or national origin. It had no apparent relevance to the cruise lines.

Also in 2003 the Community Pride Fund contributed $21,200 to Bustamante's campaign for governor (following the successful recall of Governor Davis) and $31,500 toward Bustamante's re-election campaign for lieutenant governor. The lieutenant governor is important because he is one of three members on the California State Lands Commission (the others are the state controller and the state's director of finance). The Lands Commission has authority for the Ballast Water Program, the Marine Facilities Division, and the Environmental Planning and Management Division. Each has direct interface with the cruise industry.

Hawai'i

Campaign contributions in Hawai'i are mainly directed to candidates. NCL made contributions to the state's Democratic Party following the exemption given NCL, and there were other small donations. There are few to the state Republican Party.

As in other states, the industry's contributions are strategic. Among the largest recipients is Ben Cayetano, the governor who signed the MOU. His successor, Linda Lingle, former head of Hawai'i's Republican Party, is similarly among the highest beneficiaries — she renewed the MOU after its first year. Three members of the legislature received $2,000 or more in the 2002 elections: the vice chair of the House Transportation Committee, chair of the Senate Transportation Committee, and a member of the House Legislative Management Committee. Lesser but still significant amounts were received by a member of the Senate Energy and Environment Committee, and in the House the chair of the Transportation Committee and one member each on the Energy and Environmental Protection Committee, and Tourism and Culture Committee.

The value of these contributions is evident in how legislation to regulate wastewater discharge from cruise ships was handled in February 2003. The legislation introduced by Senator J. Kalani English stalled in both the House and the

Senate. The House measure passed two committees and was then referred jointly to the Transportation and Tourism Committee. The chair of that committee stated very simply that he didn't think the measure was necessary, and that was that. The chair of the Senate committee, Cal Kawamoto, similarly refused to bring the bill forward; he refused to give reasons for his decision when asked by the bill's sponsor.[124] In 2004 English's legislation passed the senate but not the house.

Interestingly, in 2004 Kawamoto was assessed the second largest penalty ever by the state Campaign Spending Commission. He had been caught not reporting, among other things, dozens of campaign contributions. Critics referred to him as a poster boy for bad behavior; he said he was just doing his job.[125] In any case the cruise industry's contributions, whatever they were, paid off like a jackpot on a slot machine. Kawamoto was not re-elected in 2004. He was the largest recipient of cruise industry funds among Hawai'i's legislators.

Social Capital Is Cheaper Than Paying Taxes

Representative Gene Taylor seemed to capture the idea well when he told ICCL's president during hearings in the merchant marine subcommittee: "You are using all the benefits of being American but you do not want to pay the cost."[126] That is one angle — the issue of taxation. The other is the degree of influence the cruise industry has in federal and state politics. No doubt Congressman Taylor would also have much to say on this topic given that he has come up against the industry many times — and has usually lost.

This chapter has looked at campaign contributions and lobbying as two elements used by the cruise industry to influence political decision-making. While the value of campaign contributions and lobbying shouldn't be underestimated, the concept of social capital gives a better sense of how the industry's influence operates. Social capital involves more than simply giving some dollars and making personal contact. It recognizes the value and importance of constructing a positive image and reputation, and of social, economic, and political linkages. Each is a critical element. As we have seen, the ICCL through its foundation, political action committee, Community Pride Fund, and other arms is an illustrative case example of how social capital accrues, how it is used, and how the dividends pay off.

Part Two
Cruise Ship Squeeze

4

Cruising Cash Cows

According to the US Maritime Administration, Office of Statistics and Economic Analysis, 73.2 percent of cruises from US ports in the first six months of 2003 were to the Caribbean or the Bahamas. In 2004 almost 50 percent of the bed days sold by the North American cruise industry were to the Caribbean. With all the money being made by cruise lines, one would imagine that Caribbean islands are raking in huge amounts of money. But a 2004 study by the World Travel and Tourism Council (WTTC) concludes "the economic contribution of cruise tourism to Caribbean economies is arguably negligible."[1]

Why does cruise tourism make scads of money for cruise lines, but apparently does not favorably impact the islands on which it depends? Perhaps the WTTC study didn't know what it was talking about — that's what some critics might claim. Rather than get into that debate, let's look at some reasons why income from cruise tourism may not be as much as imagined.

Every Port City's Dream

"Everyone is very excited …. To be selected as a port of call is a real honor and it creates a rather glamorous side to our community."[2] This view expressed by a town councillor of Campbell River, British Columbia, reflects a sentiment commonly found in port cities wanting to attract cruise ships. The folks in Campbell River so strongly believe that having a cruise ship, any cruise ship, will have a major economic impact on the aboriginal community and the region in general that they spent CDN$4.2[3] (US$2.8) million to build a cruise ship dock half a mile from downtown.[3] With the terminal built, the question is how many ships will come.

Prince Rupert, just up the British Columbia coast, opened a new CDN$9 (US$6) million terminal in 2004 with expectations that cruise ships would flock there. The city anticipated more than CDN$30 (US$20) million in revenue from the cruise ships: projections said each passenger would spend CDN$80 (US$55) and each crew member would spend CDN$14 (US$9).[4] Thirty-five stops had been scheduled for 2004; then Celebrity Cruises announced the first week of the 2004 Alaska cruise season that *Mercury* would shorten its 13 stops from a six-hour port call to a one hour "technical call" to comply with the Passenger Vessel Service Act.[5] Passengers would not disembark. So much for revenue expectations.

Mercury is one of two ships visiting Nanaimo in 2005. Just south of Campbell River, Nanaimo is poised to spend CDN$13 (US$10) million to upgrade its wharf.[6]

Time will tell whether the expenditure can be justified, particularly given that Port Alberni, its neighbor up the coast, is also working to attract cruise ships.[7]

Expectation gave way to disappointment in Saint John, New Brunswick on Canada's Atlantic coast. It learned in August 2004 that one-third of its cruise ship passengers would be lost in 2005 because the Royal Caribbean's *Voyager of the Seas* will replace Saint John with Bermuda.[8] Compared to 59 cruise ship calls with 143,000 passengers in 2004, the city expected only 37 calls with 88,000 passengers in 2005. It slowed construction of a CDN$12 (US$9) million cruise terminal, specially built to accommodate *Voyager of the Seas*.[9]

Port cities collectively spend billions of dollars to attract cruise ships and to keep them coming back. Expenditures are justified with a belief that cruise ships leave tons of money in their wake. The belief knows no limits.

Nunavut, a Canadian territory in the Arctic, is spending considerable energy on developing cruise tourism in the region. In 2004 its tourism agency published a handbook to instruct communities on how to attract and how to orchestrate cruise ship visits,[10] and is working directly to attract cruise ships even though visits are erratic and often canceled.[11]

On the other end of the hemisphere, Punta Arenas, Chile is under pressure to lower the fees it charges cruise ships to be more competitive with nearby Ushuaia, Argentina.[12] The season is short, the number of ships is limited, and the two ports compete for the same, finite business. This competition between nearby ports is not unique. It is common in the Caribbean and elsewhere and works to the cruise line's advantage.

Hey Big Spender

"Just off the cruise ship, the American tourist got in line at the automatic banking machine, but he had a question before he put in his card. 'This give dollars? He asked. 'I just tried another machine, and it only gave out their money.' 'They,' I quickly assumed were Mexicans, and 'their money' was pesos. But it took me a bit longer to figure out why this guy came all the way to Mexico and needed only dollars. He either didn't plan on spending money during his morning-to-evening stay on the island .... Or he didn't plan on spending any money in the mom-and-pop shops that don't take dollars."[14]

Ports spend money on the premise that a cruise ship is a cash cow. This perception may have been accurate 15 or 20 years ago, but is not so true today.

Average Per Passenger Spending at Ports of Call in 2000

Antigua	$86.81
Aruba	$82.02
Bahamas	$77.90
Cayman Islands	$79.42
Cozumel, Mexico	$141.40
Montego Bay, Jamaica	$71.53
Ocho Rios, Jamaica	$74.77
San Juan, Puerto Rico	$53.84
St. Kitts and Nevis	$56.22
St. Thomas, USVI	$173.24

Source: PricewaterhouseCoopers, *Economic Contribution of the F-CCA Member Lines to the Caribbean and Florida* (Florida-Caribbean Cruise Association, July 27, 2001).

Regardless, ports are quick to claim that each cruise passenger spends $100 (or more) during a port call. They then extrapolate that a 3,000-passenger ship generates $300,000. But these figures are suspect, and are estimates at best. Take the words of Robert Giangrisostomi, vice president of business development for the Canaveral Port Authority: "It's not an exact science, but we figure these people spend $90 per person per day when ships come here as a port of call ... and to have two megaships in on the same day is a win–win situation for our county and Central Florida. That's $450,000 pumped into our area for the day."[13]

The belief that ships are a cash cow is based in part on the level of passenger spending common in the 1980s and early 1990s. Then, ships were smaller, onboard shops offered limited selections of merchandise, and they did not directly compete with stores onshore. As well, because a cruise cost relatively more then than today, the typical cruise passenger was more affluent. Rather than a vacation reserved for the upper-middle and upper class, cruises today are accessible to almost everyone.

On average, cruise passengers today have less disposable income than those who cruised in the early 1990s. A 1994 study commissioned by the Florida-Caribbean Cruise Association (FCCA) found passengers on average spent $372 on the island of St. Thomas.[15] The average for the Caribbean region was $154 per passenger per port. Key West was at the bottom of the list with average spending of $53 per passenger. Spending on St. Thomas had fallen to $173 per passenger six years later,[16] and the overall average in the region decreased to $89.72 per passenger per port.[17] San Juan,

Puerto Rico, was lowest at $53.84 (Key West was not included in the latter study). Despite these significant decreases, perceptions haven't changed. Cruise passengers are seen as big spenders.

Our Research Proves It

When its tax status came under scrutiny by the US Congress in the early 1990s, the cruise industry responded that it contributed significantly to the US economy despite its tax exempt status. John Estes, president of the ICCL, reminded Congress in May 1993 that "ICCL member lines last year accounted for 450,166 jobs, more than $14.5 billion was paid in wages to US employees, and the industry generated $6.3 billion in federal, state, and local taxes."[18]

The numbers are impressive, though it is difficult to know their basis, especially if compared with comparable data for 2003. The cruise industry in North America almost doubled in the number of passengers carried (from 4.14 million to 8.2 million) between 1992 and 2003, but the economic impact reduced instead of increased. According to a report issued by the ICCL in August 2004, the North American cruise industry in 2003 generated (directly and indirectly) 295,000 jobs that collectively paid more than $11.6 billion in wages. It also paid approximately $200 million towards employer contributions to Social Security and sales and property taxes.[19] One explanation for the decrease is that the cruise industry has exported jobs and purchases over the ten-year period. Carnival Cruise Lines took to out-sourcing their booking call centers overseas but says the Philippine center was experimental and intended to handle reservation overflow only.[20]

The 2003 data raise other questions. In 2003 the cruise industry claims it generated in the State of Washington $530 million in direct purchases, employment for 14,869 people, and wages in excess of $588 million. A study prepared for the Port of Seattle, covering the same year and the same area, reports significantly lower figures: the industry spent $124 million in direct purchases (accounting for $39 million in local wages and salaries), created directly and indirectly 1,072 jobs, and through purchases from local businesses generated $3.8 million in state and local taxes.[21]

There are similar problems with numbers for Florida. ICCL says, "An estimated 195,000 passengers visited Florida ports of call. These passengers spent an average of $45 per visit, resulting in total expenditures of $8.8 million. Finally, crew spent an average of $35 on each call to a Florida port."[22] The numbers overlook Key West, Florida, which had close to 1 million passengers in 2003. It is unclear why these passengers aren't included, but this and other "errors" make it difficult to extrapolate from the industry's numbers.

But Our Passengers Spend Lots

Studies of passenger spending are used to support the industry's claim that passengers leave lots of money on shore. These studies are suspect for a number of reasons. Often they are based on a small number of passengers who volunteer to be interviewed or who agree to mail back a survey when they return home. These responses are generalized to all passengers on board the ship, and the ship's total impact is extrapolated from that. A port's expectations may not be realized if other passengers don't do as the respondents. Estimates can be further inflated given that not all passengers disembark. The Port Authority of Jamaica estimates 15 percent of cruise passengers stay on board when a ship is in port.[23]

The assertion that cruise passengers on average spend $100 per port cannot be factually disputed. But averages can be deceptive. In St. Thomas in the eastern Caribbean passengers spend an average of $173; average spending in Cozumel in the western Caribbean is $141. At the other extreme are San Juan, Key West, and St. Kitts and Nevis where spending is approximately $55 per passenger per day. Ports in the middle are lucky.[24]

Studies of what passengers buy are in some ways more interesting and instructive. There are similarities across different regions and ports. A study of cruise passenger spending in Alaska found that: "[m]ost spending is on shore excursions (such as motor coach tours, wildlife viewing, flightseeing, and sportfishing), gifts and souvenirs, and food and beverages."[25] Similar patterns are reported by Canadian ports: passengers in St. John's, Newfoundland, most frequently purchased (excluding shore excursions) souvenirs (56%), food or beverages (35%), local handmade crafts and clothing (35%), liquor (23%), and taxis (19%). Passengers in Halifax spent $50 on gifts and souvenirs, $33 on taxis and tours, $14 on meals and beverages, $13 on other shopping, and $7 on recreational activities.[26]

With duty-free jewelry and inexpensive booze, spending patterns in the Caribbean are expectedly a bit different. A FCCA study reports that port of call passengers in the Caribbean typically spent "...$39 on watches and jewelry, $13 on clothing and $12 on souvenirs, as well as smaller amounts in other categories."[27] Though the numbers appear small per passenger, considering that Cozumel receives 2.7 million cruise passengers a year, and both the Cayman Islands and St. Thomas receive 1.8 million,[28] cumulative spending is significant. But local folks in ports do not appear to be getting rich.

The Port as Cash Cow for the Ship

Cruise tourism depends on ports, which provide critical sources of income for cruise ships. One is shore excursions — land-based tours sold by the cruise ship. Almost one-third of Royal Caribbean's profit in 2002–2003 was derived from shore excursions.[29]

There's no interchange. The people who come in the cruise ships aren't interested in that .... Before, people had a lot of friendships because of these interchanges.

— Paloma Cazares, Cozumel's subdirector of tourism[32]

Shore excursions are convenient for passengers and often sold as safer than independent sightseeing.[30] The 50–80 percent of passengers who buy an excursion in any particular port pay a premium for the convenience. As little as one-half to one-third of the cost goes to the shore excursion provider. A shore excursion costing a passenger $60 may yield the in-port provider $20 or less.[31] While the cruise line and its shore excursion concessionaire take a hefty cut, passengers expect a product worth $60 and will blame the port, not the cruise ship, if dissatisfied.

North American-based cruise lines generally use one of three companies to plan and run their shore excursion program: International Voyager Media, Onboard Media, or the PPI Group. These companies arrange excursions, hire port lecturers, and handle shore excursion sales. Tours are provided by local companies in most locations. The model is different in Alaska where the major cruise lines own the tour companies and the associated infrastructure. Carnival Corporation, through Westours and Princess Tours, operates more than 500 motor coaches and 20 domed railway cars in Alaska. Royal Caribbean, on a much smaller scale, has Royal Celebrity Tours. NCL appears to building a similar set up for itself in Hawai'i with its purchase in late 2004 of the state's second largest tour bus company.[33]

The companies selling shore excursions also provide port lecture and port shopping programs where passengers receive a map marked with preferred stores. They are told the recommended stores will give the best prices and the cruise line will guarantee what they buy. As the small print on some maps says, merchants pay referral fees to be listed. The amount can be significant. A retailer in Nassau reported in 1995 that he "pays more than $100,000 a year in such fees to one cruise line alone ... but if you don't pay it, the cruise line will recommend someone else."[34] The vice president of Royal Caribbean defended these charges saying, "this is just a regular part of doing business."[35] These onboard promotions have evolved into a mini industry with the cruise line capturing significant income.

"What used to happen is that the tour directors on a major line would earn a quarter of a million dollars a year in royalties from port merchants."[36]

These arrangements are not unique to any region or set of ports. They are as common in the Caribbean as in Alaska, and slowly develop in each new port. This should not be surprising given that several companies operate jewelry stores across

Caribbean islands. These same companies operate in Alaska and one, Colombian Emeralds, even has a store on a NCL ship. The cost associated with referral programs is usually low at first, but increase as cruise tourism and merchants' income grows. In 2004 the PPI Group expanded its referral program to Seattle, a city where cruise tourism began in 2000. "It costs $3,000 to be on the company's shopping map for passengers aboard four ships. It costs more to be included in the lecture or in television commercials."[37] If the pattern in other ports holds, these fees will increase quickly and significantly.

Some of the larger lines were made aware of the coming water crunch, particularly in the Caribbean. One of the larger players bought a water plant just outside the cruise dock area in Mexico. The water is well sourced. The more the lines pump out the less is available for the locals, the more salinity is introduced, and name that tune to who gets screwed and who makes off with the moola.[38]

Cost of Being a Port

Between the take by cruise lines of shore excursion receipts and the referral fees charged to stores, ports are squeezed and left with a fraction of the income generated. At the same time they deal with costs and problems associated with cruise tourism. Cruise passengers come with a price.

It could be as simple as the port costing more to run than the revenue it generates: the Port of Seattle lost between $150,000 and $200,000 in 2003 and barely broke even in 2004.[39] After all, cruise terminals cost money; Seattle has built two in a very short time and is looking to build a third. A new terminal costing around $30 million (excluding dredging costs) to handle 300,000 passengers per year would need to gross $5 m a year, or around $17 per passenger."[40] Seattle's fees, like those in most other ports, are a fraction of that amount.[41]

All We Want Is Our Fair Share

Prime Minister Owen Arthur of Barbados states it well:

> As the industry grows, investments in bigger ships placed parallel requirements on destinations and governments to make major investments in upgraded ports facilities. 'Much of these investments in expanded facilities cannot be recovered from the existing revenue rates. It is also equally clear, that the highly centralized purchasing and warehousing systems cruise companies must maintain, in the interest of promoting their own efficiency, makes it difficult for small Caribbean suppliers to participate in a meaningful manner that would assure us a greater domestic value-added from the growth

Are There Limits to Carnival's Greed?

In November 2002 *Carnival Conquest* began homeporting at New Orleans. The city was excited given its competition with nearby Galveston and Gulfport, something Carnival appeared ready to exploit. The company began threatening to pull *Carnival Conquest* from New Orleans before it even arrived. The problem was that the ship was too tall to safely fit under power lines stretching across the Mississippi and Carnival wanted the problem corrected. At the ship's inaugural activities, "an exasperated Carnival President Bob Dickinson told reporters that if the problem isn't solved within 60 days, Conquest is moving to Gulfport."[44] Not only did Carnival want the problem resolved immediately, but it expected the $17 million price tag to be paid by Entergy Louisiana (the power company) and passed on to its Louisiana customers.

The situation was not corrected on Carnival's timeline and in March 2003 *Carnival Conquest* relocated to Gulfport, Mississippi, for 18 weeks because "rising waters of the Mississippi made it too dangerous to sail the mammoth vessel under a set of Entergy power lines straddling the river."[45] A year later, in March 2004, Carnival and Entergy were in court. Carnival was suing Entergy for $3 million in expenses it incurred in moving the ship to Mississippi. It claimed Entergy had failed "to comply with the Army Corps permit that granted Entergy the right to stretch the power lines across the river so long as it could raise them when ships needed to pass."[46] Entergy responded "that any losses suffered by Carnival occurred as a result of the cruise ship company's own decisions, and ... that Carnival was never ordered by any maritime official to relocate the ship."[47]

of the industry .... The role of countries in the region should be that of partners of the cruise industry and not just mere facilitators.'[42]

The cost to ports goes beyond construction and maintenance of terminals and piers. A typical cruise destination spends money to market itself; it incurs costs associated with port security and with increased police presence on days that cruise passengers are in town; and it absorbs costs associated with wear and tear on infrastructure, use of city services, and demands on the health care system for passengers needing emergency medical attention.[43] Many of these costs are hidden

— there is no way to measure the wear and tear on roads and streets or on sewer systems with the presence of several hundred thousand cruise passengers. The impact of any one cruise is negligible, but the cumulative cost may be significant.

Take Peggy's Cove, Nova Scotia (population 120) for example. It is a popular tourist spot for cruise passengers on shore excursions.[48] Between 2001 and 2004, the number of individuals making day trips increased by 49,000 people, an increase attributed mainly to cruise passengers. The 50 buses a day bring congestion and pollution and compete with pedestrians on the village's roads.[49] Eliza Manuel, co-chairwomen of the Peggy's Cove Preservation Society says, "The buses are just too big, and they don't fit .... So we have to work something out."[50] The province intervened by hiring a consultant to come up with a plan to manage the tourist traffic while maintaining the integrity of the village. The costs of the consultant and any construction or other changes are hidden costs of cruise tourism. But what will be the cost to the town?

The cost of cruise tourism to Yakutat, Alaska, is similarly a mix of economic and noneconomic impacts. The town of 800 is located en route to Disenchantment Bay and Hubbard Glacier[51] and is frequently used for medical emergencies from cruise ships. Having just one ambulance, local residents were concerned that emergency services may not be available when needed, especially if the ambulance is responding to a cruise ship. Ecological impacts were also a concern.

Disenchantment Bay is a prime birthing area for seals, a subsistence food for some residents, and there was fear that ships were scaring the pups from the safety of the ice floes. The Yakutat Tlingit Tribe wanted ships to stay roughly four miles away from the glacier during pupping season. The cruise industry said that was too far, but promised instead to keep a half mile from the glacier and 500 yards from ice floes bearing seals. Unable to resolve the matter, the Yakutat city council followed through in May 2001 with plans to impose a $1.50 per passenger tax on every cruise passenger passing by the city even though the ships didn't stop there.[52] The effort was undermined by an amendment to the Maritime Security Act of 2002 sponsored by Representative Don Young.

Cruise Tourism and Quality of Life

Both Yakutat and Peggy's Cove bring into focus the issues of people pollution and quality of life.

Anyone living or visiting a cruise destination knows the crowding and congestion in Peggy's Cove is not unique. Some would say Peggy's Cove has it easy compared to towns along Alaska's Inside Passage, many having as many as 12,000 cruise passengers a day. On some days, there are ten times more cruise passengers in Skagway, Alaska than local residents. Local residents develop a love–hate relationship with cruise passengers. They realize that cruise ships are a source of

If We Can't Win by Negotiation

The people of Yakutat thought they were being reasonable. A $1.50 charge for passengers on cruise ships passing by their town on their way to Hubbard Glacier in Disenchantment Bay. After all, their only ambulance was often used for cruise ship emergencies and was unavailable for local emergencies, and cruise passengers offloaded placed a drain on Yakutat's medical care system. An even a bigger concern was the impact of cruise ships on Disenchantment Bay and the seal population. One local resident reported: "I was up there when several ships were blasting their horns to try and make the glacier calf .... It was quite a racket." The noise also frightened mothers away from pups and chased seals from the safety of the bay. According to another resident, "One time last summer I saw five or six pods of killer whales feeding on little seal pups .... Without the protection of the ice floe they were prime targets."[53]

The town approved the $1.50 tax in January 2001. The tax would generate $300,000 a year in income to be used for the town's clinic and emergency medical services and toward monitoring pollution and disruption of seal habitat. The cruise industry opposed the head tax, calling it "strange" because ships never dock and passengers never step ashore. Negotiations were held but failed because agreement couldn't be reached on a safe distance for ships to remain from the glacier and ice floes.

In January 2002 Yakutat sent a bill to seven cruise lines for the $1.50 per passenger tax; collectively $382,833 for the 155 ships that passed by the town. The town said it was willing to go to court over the matter, the cruise industry said it would rather negotiate an alternative to the tax because of concern that paying the levy would leave it vulnerable to similar taxes by other cities, and the two agreed to meet.[54] The cruise lines still rejected the tribe's request that ships stay four miles away from Hubbard Glacier. They said they would stay 500 yards from ice floes bearing seals and agreed to help fund a study being done by the National Marine Sanctuaries Service. Individual cruise lines began talking with local fishers about buying halibut and salmon.[55]

continued:

The issue of the head tax became moot in November 2002 when Representative Don Young inserted an amendment into the Maritime Security Act. The law prohibits nonfederal entities from levying "taxes, tolls, operating charges, fees or any other impositions whatsoever" on vessels in navigable waters subject to US authority, but exempts "reasonable fees charged on a fair and equitable basis."5[6] Even though Young says the law does not pose a problem for Yakutat, his spokesperson, Steve Hansen, admits the amendment was spurred by the Yakutat tax. He defends the amendment by arguing, "If every coastal community passed a tax on cruise ships that simply passed by the community, it would be catastrophic to the state tourism industry .... What would be next? Are they going to start taxing airplanes passing by just because they could make emergency landings?"[57]

income but resent losing their quiet town and lifestyle — something as simple as being able to walk down the street and go out for a quiet meal. This was not an option during the summer high season.

Some ports in the Caribbean report similar numbers. St. Thomas and St. Maarten in the eastern Caribbean have 12,000 or more passengers a day. Cozumel in the western Caribbean had close to 40,000 cruise visitors on December 26, 2002, though this is not the norm.

It isn't only that the number of cruise ships is increasing, but the number of passengers carried is also increasing. Three megaships can disembark more than 10,000 passengers in a port. In the 1970s it would have taken 10 or 12 ships to disembark that number of passengers. When Carnival's Project Pinnacle comes to fruition it will take only two.

Cruise tourism takes its toll on local residents. Crowds disrupt usual routines and the activities associated with cruise tourism can themselves be a problem. People living in Juneau, Alaska, complain of the constant sound of helicopters ferrying cruise passengers to glaciers or other

The United Nations Committee on Sustainable Tourism notes that when the social carrying capacity of an island is surpassed, cost of living increases along with overcrowding, traffic congestion, and noise pollution. A lower standard of living results for a significant segment of the population and an attitude shift occurs whereby the tourist is blamed for the majority of social problems.[58]

sights. Residents in Victoria, British Columbia, complain about sail-away parties and horn toots after midnight when ships sail through a residential area as they leave the port. Lobster fishers in Prince Edward Island complain that ships pass over buoys and sever lines to which traps are attached, causing them to drift, with captive lobsters inside — a loss of the $100 trap and lobsters. Because there is still bait in the trap other lobsters will be caught and die because they can't get out.[59] Norfolk's Elizabeth River Run, which celebrated its 25th anniversary in 2003, was canceled in 2004 because it conflicted with a cruise ship visit.[60] A benefit walk for multiple sclerosis in San Diego had to be relocated because of traffic concerns stemming from the arrival of a cruise ship.[61] And pier expansion plans in Maui would have ended outrigger canoe racing, regattas, and other paddling events in Kahului Harbor and severely impacted traffic congestion had the government not backed off under staunch public pressure.[62] These are impacts on quality of life.

Pirates of the Caribbean in Ketchikan

Ketchikan, Alaska, with a population of less than 8,000, had 43 jewelry stores downtown in 2004; a decade earlier there were only a handful.[63] "Locals call the migrants who own and run these jewelry and curio shops taking over downtown the 'Pirates of the Caribbean,' since they follow the wake of the ships"[64] and because many of these stores are owned by the same companies that own the stores on Caribbean islands.

Cruise tourism can affect the overall tourist appeal of a location. Cruise passenger numbers rose in Key West, Florida, from 375,000 in 1995 to close to 1 million in 2004. Many living on the two- by four-mile island say the million cruise passengers a year is a major reason for the "getting ugly" label assigned by *National Geographic Traveler's* "2004 Destination Scorecard." Key West scored 43 out of 100. Another cruise port, St. Thomas, scored not much better with 45.

Concerns in Key West extend beyond the congestion at tourist attractions, the kitschy shops that have sprung up around the port, and the disruption caused by Conch Trains running cruise passengers around the town. A greater concern, particularly among restaurant and hotel owners, is that cruise tourism displaces the traditional market. People who stay at a hotel for a week spend money in restaurants and bars and shop in the stores are being driven away by changes in the city. The president of the Lodging Association of the Florida Keys and Key West says cruise passengers change the nature of a destination.

Our whole advertising and marketing program is around Key West being an easy-going, laid-back, relaxed destination with interesting shops and stores and great cultural and historical resources .... Put yourself in the position of a visitor who comes for the first time, checks into one our fine hotels, and then decides to take a stroll down this town's main drag — Duval Street — and encounters crowds more reminiscent of Times Square.[65]

The problem of people pollution hit its peak in March 2004. Local residents were already sensitive to the number of cruise passengers arriving in Key West, but then it was learned that the city had been violating a 1993 resolution that placed a limit of seven cruise ships visits per week at Pier B, a privately owned dock adjacent to the Hilton Hotel. At about the same time *National Geographic Traveler* dubbed the city as a victim of crowding, poor planning, and greed. "Key West was heavily criticized for its influx of cruise day-trippers, coral reef die-offs, spring-break-like atmosphere, and an overriding sense that the city's character was lost."[66]

In response, and to focus attention on the severity of the problem, Livable Oldtown called for a protest by Key West residents on March 11, 2004, when there would be five ships visiting the city. They encouraged residents to drive up and down Duval Street between 11 AM and noon. Though cruise passengers barely noticed the added congestion, the point was well made with city residents and city councilors by the 100 or so protestors.[67] The issue so polarized segments of the community that the event's organizer received a bomb threat (from a downtown merchant) the day of the action. A flurry of newspaper editorials and guest columns followed.

The issues confronted in Key West are not unique. The problem is not cruise tourism; it is the question of how many cruise passengers a town or an island can comfortably accommodate. At what point does the number of cruise tourists change the attraction such that it is no longer what it was that made it an attraction?

Risks Associated with Dependence

While ports make money from cruise tourism, they risk becoming overdependent. Between 85 and 90 percent of tourist arrivals in Cozumel and Cayman Islands are cruise passengers. St. Thomas, St. Maarten, and Belize are not far behind: cruise tourists account for close to 75 percent of their tourist arrivals.[72] This dependence has its costs. Though anecdotal, it is interesting that in the early 1990s when cruise tourism was a smaller proportion of tourists Cayman took a lead in enforcing environmental regulations. It is less vigilant today and was among the first to break ranks with other Caribbean Tourism Organization members on a Caribbean passenger levy.

Growth in cruise tourism has been particularly significant for some. Belize had a 1,600 percent increase in cruise tourists in just four years — from 34,000 passengers

Who Needs Who?

Tom Oosterhoudt, a flamboyant Key West city commissioner, captured the essence of the issue:

> Cruise ships have changed the dynamic; it's budget, budget, budget and volume, volume, volume .... There was a time when we all thought of cruise ship customers as high rollers. Today that is not necessarily so .... We need to evaluate where we are going with the extreme increase we are seeing each year with the number of cruise ships .... We need to stand back and evaluate where we are at and make sure we are controlling the cruise ships and they aren't controlling us.[68]

Citizens in Key West seriously confronted problems with cruise tourism in 2003. It isn't that concerns had not been voiced earlier, but the sudden growth in numbers sharpened the issue and in some ways polarized the town. A key turning point was a panel discussion in January 2003 hosted by the community organization Last Stand. Entitled "Keys in Balance," the panel debate looked at the good, the bad, and the ugly of cruise ships in Key West. While acknowledged that cruise ships generate approximately $2.5 million in disembarkation and docking fees for the city's yearly budget, there were questions about the impact of cruise ships on the fragile marine environment surrounding the lower keys, the risk of dependence on cruise ship dollars, and the social impact of thousands of cruise passengers pouring into town each day. The overarching question was stress on Key West's 27,000 residents from the daily influx of cruise ship passengers.[69]

Hoteliers and restaurateurs unsuccessfully pressured the city to limit cruise ship visits. But under pressure from Last Stand and a well-orchestrated public education campaign by Livable Oldtown, the city went ahead with a quality of life study promised three years earlier to settle legal action by Last Stand. Concern about a potential conflict of interest was raised when it was announced the study would be overseen by Florida International University. The university's president is on the board of Carnival Corporation, the

continued:

president of Carnival Cruise Lines is on the board of the Florida International University Foundation, and both Carnival and Royal Caribbean are large donors to the university. In addition, the city's cruise ship consultant is married to a person associated with the group contracted to do the quality of life study.[70] The concerns were dismissed on the basis that "many large businesses contribute to the university" and "there's a firewall between the academic professors and the contributors."[71]

The quality of life study proceeded, but the city has remained under pressure. Last Stand and Livable Oldtown have continued their education campaign and have kept the issues on the agenda. Part of their success is the skill of those leading the organizations, part is that there is an independently owned and open-minded press in the city, and part is use of old-fashioned social activism.

in 1999 to 575,000 in 2003. Growth has brought increasing concern about dependence on cruise tourism dollars and displacement of land-based tourists by the numbers of cruise tourists. "Cruise passengers by the hundreds and thousands will overrun the popular destinations, diminishing the premium you can charge, destroying the exclusivity of Belize and after a few good years, Belize would lose its cruise industry charm, and with the loss would be the loss of a steadily growing overnight sector."[73]

Some new purpose-built ports are entirely dependent on cruise ships. Icy Straits is a day port at Hoonah, Alaska. It was built using public funds[74] and then turned over to the local aboriginal community and leased for a nominal fee to the partnership that developed the port. In return for the several cruise ship visits a week, the port has agreed to refrain from ever implementing any tariffs, head taxes, tonnage, or similar user fees or charges for the use of the dock facility.[75] It is a money maker for the local community,[76] so long as cruise ships continue to come and local merchants are allowed to keep the money paid them by cruise passengers.

Hoonah is an alternative to Alaska's other already-congested ports. It also reminds those considering port charges that alternatives exist. Whittier, Alaska, repealed a $1 passenger head tax in April 2003 after Princess Cruises issued an ultimatum that it would not return to Whittier as long as there was a head tax or the potential for a head tax. Ships had shifted from Whittier to Seward when the head tax was introduced ten years earlier. When the tax was dropped (and an exemption from a seasonal sales tax and a passenger transport fee paid by smaller day-cruise

TABLE 4.1: CRUISE PASSENGER ARRIVALS
AT CARIBBEAN PORTS

Port of Call	Passenger Arrivals, 2003	Percent ± from 1999
Antigua	385,686	+17
Aruba	542,327	+88
Bahamas	2,970,174	+50
Barbados	559,122	+29
Belize	575,196	+1,591
Bermuda	226,097	+17
Cayman Islands	1,818,979	+76
Cozumel	2,708,913	+108
Curaçao	279,378	+26
Dominica	177,044	-13
Dominican Republic	398,263	+41
Grenada	146,925	-40
Jamaica	1,132,596	+48
Martinique	268,542	-20
Puerto Rico	1,234,992	+8
St. Lucia	393,240	+12
St. Maarten	1,171,734	+ 90
St. Vincent & Grenadines	64,965	+36
Trinidad and Tobago	55,532	-2
US Virgin Islands	1,773,948	+26

Source: Caribbean Tourism Organization.

operators), Princess Cruises returned to Whittier.[77] Juneau's $5 head tax introduced in 1999 is the only head tax charged by a port in Alaska.[78]

Opportunity Costs of Cruise Tourism

One of the costs of cruise tourism is opportunity costs. These are the projects or expenditures forgone to permit investment in cruise tourism. It may be city services, capital improvements, or health services. Considerable publicity was given when Saint John, New Brunswick's mayor cut $40,000 from the city budget for lifeguard services at area beaches but spent $25,000 on pins to be given to all male cruise ship passengers. The city council subsequently reversed the mayor's decision after it had been mocked and ridiculed in the national media.[79]

Many ports have invested huge amounts in cruise terminals. Vancouver spent $49 million on redevelopment of the Ballantyne Cruise Terminal and then $79 million to construct a third cruise berth at Canada Place. The new berth at Canada Place was ready for the 2002 cruise season. Its construction was encouraged. In 1997 Royal Caribbean Cruise Line's Vice President of Corporate Planning stated, "...you will not see us taking off any time soon and moving to Seattle."[80] Others made similar commitments.

In April 2001 the chairperson of the Vancouver Port Authority said the third berth secured the port's position in the cruise industry and allowed for future growth and prosperity.[81] Optimism was not justified. After 20 years of growth, Vancouver's passenger numbers and cruise ship stops decline significantly in 2003 and 2004: cruise ship calls decreased 18 percent; passenger numbers decreased 13.5 percent. The shift is mainly because ships relocated to Seattle and that Seattle is cheaper.[82]

Again, the question is whether there are opportunity costs: are other projects foregone so a $100 million can be spent on upgrading or building a cruise terminal? Ketchikan, Alaska, is in the middle of a $100-million project; New York City has committed $200 million to modernize the West Side Passenger Ship Terminal and to build a new cruise terminal in Brooklyn;[83] and San Francisco has a $246-million project that includes a new cruise terminal, shopping center, and 22-story condominium tower.[84] There are smaller projects: Port Everglades is spending $80 million on infrastructure improvements to keep up with cruise industry growth;[85] Miami will open two $60-million terminals in September 2005;[86] Norfolk, Virginia, is spending $41 million with hopes that its new terminal will be used as a homeport — two of the four cruise lines homeporting there announced in April 2005 that they were withdrawing their ships in 2006;[87] Mobile spent $20 million on a terminal that opened in 2004 — the terminal's owner, Retirement Systems of Alabama, spent $17 million to renovate the Riverview Plaza Hotel as part of a push to make the city more attractive to cruise passengers.[88] Seattle spent $38 million on one cruise terminal that opened in 2000[89] and another $17 million on a terminal that began operating in 2003 to accommodate the overflow from the Bell Street terminal.[90] In the Caribbean, Antigua spent $22 million as part of a cruise expansion investment;[91] over time, St. Maarten invested more than $60 million.[92]

Portland, Maine, on the other hand, scaled back its plan for a $40 million cruise terminal to a more modest facility costing $16.5 million. With cruise ship calls falling from 53 in 2001 to 26 in 2005, there was concern about the success of the investment.[93] Baltimore went further. It put its plans for a $50-million cruise terminal on hold. The city faced a fiscal crisis in its schools, the legislature was struggling to pay the state Medicaid tab, and it was politically impossible to get the support needed.[94] This illustrates opportunity costs perfectly. There was a basic choice between education and health versus a cruise terminal. What have other cities given up in their quest for cruise tourism?

The Return of Cruise Passengers

One selling point made to ports about cruise tourism is that passengers return for longer visits. Not surprisingly, surveys done by ports that ask whether passengers enjoyed their stay and whether they would return always yield very favorable results. Commonly 98 percent of passengers are "completely satisfied" or "mostly satisfied" with their visit, and 75 percent would "definitely" or "probably" return. This says nothing about whether cruise passengers actually return. Although 70 percent of cruise passengers visiting Cozumel said they would like to come back, and despite handing out 2 million brochures, the local hotel association can only count two passengers who actually returned.[95] Carnival Corporation's experience with its Crystal Palace Resort and Casino similarly contradicted the proposition that cruise passengers return as land-based tourists.

There is no evidence that cruise tourism's explosion has carried over to spur any growth in overnight tourism.[96]

— **Hon. Mark Epsat, Belize minister of Economic Development, Investment, Tourism and Culture.
September 2004**

Results of an American Express-sponsored study of visitors to the Caribbean are more encouraging. It found 20 percent of first-time land-based tourists previously visited that Caribbean island on a cruise.[97] Given a typical cruise stops at three or four ports, the actual return rate for any particular destination will be considerably lower — if distributed evenly, the average per port is 5 percent.[98] Realistically, more popular ports will see a larger return rate than others.

The American Express study contradicts the cruise industry's mantra at the annual Seatrade Cruise Shipping Convention in Miami Beach: cruise passengers convert into land-based vacationers. Ports want to believe this is the case and are encouraged to spend on activities to lure cruise passengers back. This all makes sense on the surface, but as Peter Ilchuk, president of the Lodging Association of the Florida Keys and Key West, points out, "A passenger paying $99 a night all inclusive is not a likely candidate to return."[99]

This is a sobering thought. Ports need to balance claims of returning cruise passengers with the financial ability of cruise passengers to return. What islands or beach destinations can compete with a cruise ship offering an all-inclusive product for less than $100 per person per day, including transportation from Miami? Comparably priced options are limited and nonexistent at many island destinations.

The Lure of Homeporting

Homeporting — a destination from which cruises begin and end — is another lure. Some figures suggest homeporting is big business. New York City reports that 60 percent of cruise passengers leaving from the port stayed in the city an average 2.1 nights and spent $355.[100] Other figures give little reason for enthusiasm. In Florida ports, passenger spending is rarely much more than the cost of cab fare from the airport to the port: $12.34 in Fort Lauderdale and $17.07 in Miami. Pre- or post-hotel stays contribute modest amounts.

Average Per Passenger Spending at Homeport

Homeport	Arrive day of cruise	Pre/post stay	Average # nights
Ft. Lauderdale	$ 12.34	$ 69.19	1.4
Miami	17.07	74.00	1.2
San Juan, PR	11.18	104.58	1.4

Source: PricewaterhouseCoopers, *Economic Contribution of the F-CCA Member Lines to the Caribbean and Florida* (Florida-Caribbean Cruise Association, July 27, 2001).

Findings in Seattle may be more typical. Approximately 73 percent of passengers spend a night or more in the city (average 1.6 nights). They spend on average $63 per night per person in local hotels. For those passengers making local purchases on specific items — not all passengers buy items in all categories — each passenger spends $27 in restaurants, $26 on retail purchases, $34 on local trans-portation and rental cars, and $30 on entertainment and landside tours.[101]

Seattle's study also says crew members spend $120 per call at Seattle, the majority on restaurant and retail purchases. The amount seems a bit high. If figures for crew spending in Victoria and Alaska are added to those for Seattle, each crew member spends $800 a month in ports. That is more than many workers earn in a month.

Homeporting brings in additional money, but it is difficult to know how much. A larger concern, however, is whether homeporting is an overall benefit. It is ideal for a location with excess hotel rooms and excess airlift (or easy road access). It is not a good choice when hotel rooms and/or airlift are limited given that land-based vacationers are likely to be displaced and they spend twice as much per day as those visiting by cruise ship.[102]

The main attraction of homeporting is that cruise passengers occupy hotel rooms, dine at restaurants, and spend money in stores. This works until vacationers spending a week or more are displaced. It could be that rooms are not available the night before the ship departs and the night it returns. Airline seats may similarly be limited on certain days. Vancouver's lack of airlift (airline seats) typically required many cruise passengers to fly into Seattle and be bussed to the ship. This reduces overnight stays before and after the cruise and is another factor in cruise ship migration from Vancouver to Seattle.

These tradeoffs were made abundantly clear in a presentation at the 2003 Caribbean Hotel Industry Conference by Fernando Garcia Zalvidea of the Cancun-based Best Day Group.[103] In discussing the implications of Carnival Corporation's plans for a homeport at Xcaret (near Cancun),[104] Zalvidea pointed out that Cancun already is underserviced by airlines — if every seat were filled every day, hotels in the region could at best achieve 50 percent occupancy. Loss of seats to cruise passengers would directly and negatively impact hotels. He also presented figures that indicated home-ported passengers spend less time in the city (an average 1.9 nights for home-ported cruise passengers vs. an average 5.62 nights for land-based tourists), spend less money in the city (an average US$117.31 per day for home-ported cruise passengers vs. US$218.66 per day for land-based tourists), and given their relatively small numbers in comparison with land-based tourists, have a smaller economic impact. He suggested Cancun should put money toward advertising and facilitating land-based tourists, not to subsidizing cruise passengers who have relatively small economic impact.

Keeping the Myth Alive

This chapter contrasted cruise industry claims about its economic benefits with their actual impact on ports. It has not only considered the size of economic impact and other ways in which cruise tourism affects a port and the surrounding area. Ports and governments need to look carefully at the costs of cruise tourism, as well as the opportunity costs of diverting resources to the construction and maintenance of facilities required by the cruise industry, but for which the industry is generally unwilling to pay its fair share.

5

A Game of Divide and Conquer

Our margins may go down, but they (our competitors) will go out of business.[1]
— Bob Dickinson, president Carnival Cruise Lines

THE SAME CUT-THROAT ATTITUDE IS REFLECTED in the cruise industry's relationship with ports. Each competes for the same finite dollars — money made by ports is lost income to the cruise line.

One area of struggle is port charges — the head taxes charged for arrival of each passenger. Cruise lines work to keep them as low as possible and price their fares as high as the market will bear. The less charged for passengers in port fees, the more left in the cruise company's coffers.

The amounts fought over can be relatively small, as in the case of Princess' ultimatum to get Whittier, Alaska, to drop its $1 head tax. There are other cases. Carnival Cruise Lines began a boycott of Grenada in November 1999 over a $1.50 per-passenger charge the island is required to collect under a World Bank–sponsored loan for a region-wide garbage reception capability. The project is part of a wider plan to have on-land garbage reception facilities sufficient for the Caribbean's designation as a "special area" for environmental protection under international maritime pollution protocols.[2] Ironically, Carnival pays the fee in other ports. Grenada apparently is a reminder to others thinking of raising port charges.

The threat works. Airport taxes at Caribbean islands are as high as US$25 or $30 but departure taxes for cruise passengers are as low as $1.15. Those that raise cruise passenger taxes are often pressured to roll them back. Antigua and Barbuda was immediately threatened with a boycott by the Florida-Caribbean Cruise Associations' 12 members when it raised its charges by $2.50 per passenger in December 2004. Though there was concern that cruise ships might follow through on their threat to boycott, the government of Antigua and Barbuda viewed the increased tax as necessary given increased security costs following the 9/11 terrorist attacks.[3] It subsequently backed down from the increase.

How Much Are We Worth?

A port raising passenger fees is commonly pressured to offer incentives that reduce charges to their original level or lower. The Puerto Rico Tourism Company in San Juan rebates $3 per passenger for every 120,000-passenger arrivals in a year.[4] Bahamas has a $15 per passenger head tax, but offers incentives that drop the cost to

$7.50 per person; it waives the head tax if a company brings in half-million people per year.[5] Jamaica as well charges $15 per passenger, but has contracts with individual companies that cut the rate in half.[6] The passenger fee in St. Maarten is $5.00; in Miami, $5.50; in Seattle, between $5.50 and $6.00; in Boston, $8.50; and in Key West, $10.60.[7] Bermuda charges $60, the highest in the western hemisphere.

Mexico's Head Tax Dead in the Water

Mexico's Chamber of Deputies defeated a $10 per cruise passenger tax in November 2004. The tax, proposed by Mexico's secretary of tourism and the secretary of ports and communication, would have generated $60 million per year. Commenting on its defeat, Michelle Paige, FCCA president, said, "It was because of the private sector of Mexico's commitment to the cruise industry that the growth of the industry has been assured by the defeat of this tax .... It is good to have the cruise industry planning as part of the country's overall tourism plan."[8] Paige credited the defeat to people who do business with cruise lines and who spoke out.

Panama has a different strategy for growing cruise tourism. In 2000 it began offering a bounty of as much as $12 for passengers landed at a Panamanian port. It shifted from receiving no port calls to dozens a year or two later. Its first cruise ship call at Colón on November 6, 2000, was followed with commitments from Princess Cruise Line, Carnival Cruise Lines, P&O Cruises, Fred Olsen Cruise Line, Sun Cruises, Celebrity Cruises, and Holland America Line. Within a year Colon was welcoming at least one cruise ship per week.[9]

Rebates and bounties are a potential windfall for cruise lines. They presumably base passenger charges for "port fees, taxes, and other charges" on the port fee before the rebate or bounty. The rebate is pure profit for the companies.[10]

There's Nothing Like Ownership

Ownership or management of cruise terminals can further squeeze a destination. Belize is an example. Royal Caribbean invested $18 million for co-ownership of the Fort Street Tourism Village. Opened in November 2001 Tourism Village is where all cruise passengers are tendered from cruise ships. The port charge is $5 per passenger, 80 percent of which goes to Tourism Village. Receiving $4 for every cruise passenger landed, Royal Caribbean will recoup its investment in six or seven years.

Carnival's Heaven Is Belize's Hell

Though kept secret for the longest while, an agreement between Carnival Corporation and the Government of Belize became public in October 2004.[12] Following are critical terms of the contract for a US$50 million cruise terminal and option to build a 50-room hotel and casino.

- Except for the Carnival passenger fees (80 percent of which are rebated to Carnival), no fees of any kind shall be imposed (i) on the Belize Cruise Terminal, Carnival, or Belize Ports Limited; or (ii) on any cruise ships of any of the Carnival Lines calling at any port located within Belize.
- There will be no limit (other than those already in place) on the number of cruise passengers arriving on Carnival lines.
- Carnival is not required to employ Belizean entities, nationals, or government agencies for navigation or docking, and in respect to the Project and/or any of its business operations.
- The contract is for 20 years and automatically renews for another 10 years.
- Passenger head taxes may increase to $7 in May 2005, but no further increase is permitted until 2010. Thereafter, increases cannot exceed 3 percent per year for the next 24 years.
- The terminal is entitled to all tax exemptions and other benefits available to a free-zone business under the Commercial Free Zone Act. Carnival avoids taxes and red tape. The government procures annually a license for cruise ships to each of the Carnival lines.
- Carnival will explore opportunities to develop additional ports and commercial facilities throughout Belize, including Commercial Bight and Punta Gorda in the southeast of Belize.

Source: Agreement executed April 29, 2004 between Government of Belize, Carnival Corporation, Belize Ports Limited, and Belize Cruise Terminal Limited.

Thereafter the net cost to Royal Caribbean will be $1 per passenger, giving its ships a competitive advantage.

Belize planned in 2004 to raise port fees to $7 and to use the extra income to protect coral reefs and jungles, but under pressure from the cruise lines it agreed to a five-year moratorium on any increases.[11] Residents' hopes that income would be generated from tendering passengers between cruise ships and the port were quickly dashed. A television journalist in Belize City reported that Royal Caribbean wanted tenders with larger capacity than available in Belize City. Principals in Royal Caribbean started a new company to provide the service.

A second cruise terminal was announced for Belize City in September 2003. The $50 million project is a joint-business venture of Belize Ports Ltd. and Carnival Corporation and is expected to open in late 2005; an option was also granted for a 50-room hotel and casino adjacent to the terminal.

The Carnival-owned terminal will accommodate two ships and include a welcome center with 200 spaces for gift shops, restaurants, and other stores and a transport hub for hundreds of buses and taxis[13] — not the sleepy Belize City I visited on a 600-passenger cruise ship in 1994. Under terms of its contract with the Belize government Royal Caribbean receives $4 for every passenger landed at Carnival's new terminal. But Carnival's contract doesn't require it to pay the fee — like Royal Caribbean it is rebated $4 for every passenger landed at its new terminal.

As a result the Government of Belize is on the hook for the 500,000 passengers Carnival brings each year and is required to pay Royal Caribbean US$2 million. The money will likely come from the country's general tax fund, meaning Belize citizens will be generously subsidizing cruise tourism in the country.[14] When Carnival's terminal is completed, the daily cap on cruise passengers will double from 8,000 to 16,000. Curiously, the 8,000-passenger cap was imposed after Belize realized that up to 13,000 cruise tourists were arriving daily.[15] Tourism groups challenged the contract between the Government of Belize and Carnival in Belize's Supreme Court.[16] The court's decision had not been handed down by the spring 2005.

At the same time that the Belize terminal is scheduled to open, Carnival Corporation will unveil the first terminal on Turks and Caicos. The financial arrangement for this $35-million terminal was not publicly reported, but it is a safe assumption that it is similar to Carnival's arrangement in Belize and elsewhere.

In August 2001 Carnival Corporation announced plans to invest $8.5 million to upgrade San Juan, Puerto Rico's Pier Four, making it practical for the 3,400-passenger Destiny-class vessels to be homeported in San Juan. In return Carnival has preferential berthing at the pier for 20 years and recoups its investment by retaining a portion of the port charges paid by passengers. A similar arrangement was made between St. Thomas and a Carnival-Royal Caribbean Partnership, but was quashed at the last minute by Virgin Island's Governor Charles W. Turnbull (see Sidebar).

Here's a Good Scheme

In November 1999 the US Virgin Islands announced it planned to raise head taxes on passengers 33 percent to $9.50. Opposition from merchants and from cruise lines forced the hike to be canceled and the government began exploring alternatives with the FCCA. In August 2001 an agreement was announced.[17] The cruise lines agreed to increase the number of passengers brought to the US Virgin Islands during the off-season between May and September — over five years, a 15 percent annual increase on St. Croix and a 10 percent annual increase on St. Thomas. In return, the government agreed to allow Carnival Corporation and Royal Caribbean to jointly develop port facilities at St. Thomas's Crown Bay.

The two companies agreed to invest $31 million to enlarge the two-berth pier so it could accommodate each line's newest megaships. They also planned to improve 7.5 acres of adjacent land into an area offering taxis and tour dispatch, and to include 90,000 square feet of retail, restaurant, and amphitheatre space. Overall, 5,000 square feet would be reserved for local vendors and include an attraction themed on the islands' sugar cane heritage, a rum distillery, and a terminal to accommodate homeporting of smaller ships.[18]

In return for their investment, Carnival and RCCL would enjoy priority berthing for 30 years, retain 75 percent of the head tax charged passengers,[19] and receive a percentage of revenue from the retail operations. Passenger port charges would pay for the investment needed for the project, and profit would generate from retail operations at the terminal.[20]

The project was approved by the legislature, despite opposition. It appeared on track until March 13, 2002, when the Governor announced the agreement was canceled. He stated that although the agreement "has many merits, I believe it is important that the Virgin Islands maintain full control of its harbor and harbor development."[21] It is hard to know whether this is why ports from Barbados to St. Maarten had rejected similar arrangements.[22]

The Crown Bay project continued without the cruise lines, after the Port Authority reimbursed them $900,000 in preliminary costs.

continued:

Although the cruise lines say it is because of "isolated criminal incidents," virtually all cruise ships stopped visiting St. Croix following collapse of the Crown Bay deal.[23] There were 2,000 cruise passengers in all of 2004, and in 2005 an expected total of 10,000 — a 1,500-passenger ship had seven scheduled stops.[24] These numbers do not include Royal Caribbean's announcement in November 2004 that ships visiting St. Thomas will dock in St. Croix for a six-hour overnight refueling stop from the HOVENSA oil refinery.[25] In contrast, St. Croix welcomed 154 ships carrying approximately 230,000 passengers in 2000.

Ownership and investment in terminals are not limited to the Caribbean. Carnival owns the terminal in Long Beach, California; Costa paid one-third of the construction cost for a terminal in Savona, Italy, in return for a 22-year operating lease; a Carnival/Costa-Royal Caribbean partnership holds the concession for the cruise terminal at Civitavecchia (Rome); and Royal Caribbean opportunistically invested $25 million in the terminal at Kusadasi, Turkey, in return for a 30-year concession.[26] Royal Caribbean's investment in ports "is based on a variety of circumstances: high volume utilization; inadequate facilities; ports' inability to perform; opportunities for privatization; strategic or competitive advantage; and operating cost control."[27] The incentives are usually economic and focus on the cruise line's bottom line, not benefits to the port.

Avoiding Port Charges

Cruise lines can avoid passenger head taxes in some ports. Most intermediate ports in the US have no charge or only a nominal fee. For example many ports in Hawai'i charge $2 per passenger but Honolulu charges nothing; most ports in Alaska charge nothing, except Juneau has a $5 per person head tax.

Juneau was the first intermediate port in a US state to impose a passenger tax. The cruise industry threatened to challenge its legality in court,[28] but the threat never materialized. However, Holland America retaliated by announcing it would withdraw much of its support to local charities. Al Parrish, a company vice president reportedly said, "If the community doesn't really want us there, if that's really truly what they're telling us, then we need to reassess what we're doing."[29] Royal Caribbean withdrew its support to charities in the spring of 2002 saying that 2001 had been a bad year.[30]

Some of the same issues that gave rise to Juneau's $5 tax were relevant in a petition campaign that has placed on Alaska's 2006 primary ballot an initiative to levy a $50 passenger fee for every cruise passenger visiting the state. The cruise industry actively opposes the fee. Industry representatives actively interfered with the collection of signatures during the petition campaign. After the petition was certified by the state's lieutenant governor and recertified by the state's director of elections, the Northwest Cruiseship Association hired a former Secret Service agent to search for forgery among the more than 23,000 signatures submitted and several days later launched a lawsuit to challenge the signatures and the legality of the tax.[31]

One way to avoid the uncertainty that port charges will increase is to either enter into a long-term agreement with a port, like those between cruise lines and Jamaica, or to establish ports for which there are no port charges. Hoonah is an excellent example. So was the port of Xcaret near Playa del Carmen and Cancun, Mexico, until the mayor of Playa del Carmen announced there would be a $30 head tax when the port opened.

Carnival had searched for nine years for the perfect purpose-built homeport from which to operate three- and four-day cruises in the western Caribbean. In 2001 it settled on a homeport between Playa del Carmen and Cancun. The $80 million port would be built beside Parque Xcaret's (its partner in the project) nature park located several miles from the core of hotels in Cancun[32] and accommodate four homeported cruise ships per week plus 24 other ships visiting as a port of call — approximately 800,000 visitors a year.

Despite opposition from environmentalists concerned about the cumulative risks posed to the 220-mile coral reef[33] and from hoteliers concerned about further loss of business to the cruise lines, all levels of the Mexican government, except the mayor of Playa del Carmen, approved the project. He agreed to permit construction of the homeport subject to a number of conditions.

> All [conditions] were accepted at the time, although Carnival and Xcaret did indicate there could be some problem with the mayor's demand that the investors agree to pay a head tax for each passenger disembarking at the homeport …. However the investors thought the head tax would be a nominal amount, certainly no more than approximately $2.50 per passenger.[34]

But the mayor surprised everyone when he announced a non-negotiable port fee of $30 per head.

The project's developers argued the tax was illegal, but the mayor responded that the necessary tax legislation would be in place by the time the first passenger was ready to board a Carnival cruise ship at the Xcaret homeport. The planned development was put on hold, according to the president of the Xcaret group, "until there is a change of attitude on the part of local authorities,"[35] which is likely in two years when the mayor's term of office ends. In the interim the mayor of Cancun revealed plans to build a cruise homeport near the commercial center of Cancun, but those plans have not moved forward.[36]

Not far away, Carnival owns the cruise terminal at Cozumel. It bought the terminal from the developers of the terminal at Costa Maya on the Yucatan's southeastern shore. Costa Maya opened in 2001 and welcomed its one-millionth passenger in 2004. It has a 70,000-square-foot shopping center and was expanded from two to five piers in 2005. Despite some cautioning about the dangers of unbridled growth in Costa Maya, the port gets high marks from those in the industry. "For a new destination, they're definitely the one who are doing the best job .... They've listened. Every time we've had an issue, they've taken care of it. Plus, their location helps, too."[37]

Playing Ports Off Against One Another

There is potential for competition between Cancun, Playa del Carmen, Costa Maya, and Cozumel, but this is not unique. Ports compete with one another every day. And cruise lines take great advantage of — even encourage — the competition. As businesses, they'd be foolish not to.

> We need to keep in mind that the cruise industry made Haines a destination .... The reality is, if we're not nice to the cruise industry, they will leave. And they did.[38]
>
> — **Former tourism director, Haines, Alaska**

Competition between ports changed after the 9/11 terrorist attacks. The cruise industry was reminded of its dependence on the air transportation system and grappled with increased fear among Americans to fly or to visit a "foreign country." The solution was what NCL advertised as "Homeland Cruising," described by some as "drive-to cruising." By 2004 Carnival Cruise Lines had ships in 17 homeports in the US and 2 in Canada. Other cruise lines did the same and quickly there were cruises to Alaska from Vancouver, Seattle, and San Francisco; to Mexico from Los Angeles, Long Beach, and San Diego; to New England and Canada from Boston, Bayonne's Cape Liberty, and New York City; to Bermuda and the Caribbean from Boston, New York, Philadelphia, Baltimore, Norfolk, Charleston, Jacksonville, Port Canaveral, Port Everglades (Fort Lauderdale), and Miami; and to the Gulf of Mexico from Houston, Galveston, New Orleans, Gulfport, Mobile, and Tampa.

One benefit of expansion is that cruises are more accessible to a wider clientele, both physically and because the out-of-pocket cost is lowered. A person in the tri-state area around New York City, for example, doesn't have to fly to Miami for a cruise, but can drive, take a bus, or take a commuter train or taxi to the ship and reduce the vacation cost by a couple of hundred dollars per person. In addition travel time is significantly reduced and the hassle of having to get to the ship via an air connection is eliminated. The cruise line benefits because its ship is not dependent on the air transportation system.

The disadvantage for ports is that close proximity makes them interchangeable, leaving one to compete with the other. Royal Caribbean's Cape Liberty at Bayonne, NJ, was established because the New York City Port Authority was not responding to cruise industry needs and Bayonne was willing to cut a favorable deal. New York City reacted to Royal Caribbean's migration by agreeing to a $200 million project to upgrade its own terminals.[39] Pressure on Baltimore to build a new terminal similarly increased in August 2004 after three cruise lines announced they wouldn't return in 2005 — favoring other ports instead.[40] With many choices for departures along the eastern seaboard, cruise lines clearly tell a port what they want.

The same goes on the west coast where there is fierce competition between Vancouver and Seattle and between Long Beach and the Port of Los Angeles. The $700 million waterfront overhaul of the Port of Los Angeles became more urgent after Carnival built its competing cruise terminal in nearby Long Beach. Carnival Cruise Lines had been a mainstay client.[41]

Destinations also compete. In addition to everything else, they may provide direct incentives. Free or discounted water is common. Bayonne, like many ports, has a water shortage but sells water to the cruise lines at below-market rates.[43] Other incentives are hard to know. The bottom line is that "when taxes are proposed at one port, cruise operators talk about shifting to another where costs are lower."[44]

Caribbean states are susceptible to the continued threats of a pull out by a cruise line if they do not get what they want. Case in point … was Barbados' recent request from cruise lines that all passengers had a passport. This was met by a threat to pull out by a particular cruise line.[42]

— Noel Lynch, tourism minister, Barbados, October 2004

Divide and Conquer

Competition makes ports concerned about their neighbors. The Bahamas is uneasy about the impact of Carnival's terminal at Turks and Caicos.[51] Halifax, Nova Scotia, and Saint John, New Brunswick, compete for many of the same ships, as do British Columbia ports en route to Alaska's Inside Passage. And ports of the Caribbean are in continual competition, each trying to attract or maintain business that might go elsewhere. Solidarity among Caribbean countries is undermined and collective action difficult. This was demonstrated in 2003 when the Caribbean Tourism Organization (CTO) announced plans for a $20 passenger levy.

Better Watch It — We'll Take Our Toys and Play Somewhere Else

San Juan, Puerto Rico, between 2000 and 2002 illustrates a cruise line's pressure on a port. During difficult negotiations around construction of a mega-cruise ship terminal in 2000, Royal Caribbean's John Tercek, vice president of commercial development, reminded the territorial government that "if we feel like it, we can take our fleet elsewhere."[45] The terminal was eventually built.

In 2002 the FCCA alleged "that in comparison to other Caribbean destinations, Puerto Rico has ignored the cruise industry for more than a decade and that has made it hard for them to do business on the island."[46] John Tercek complained that, "Puerto Rico's government puts more emphasis on hotels than cruise business .... Developers who want to build hotels are given incentives. We ask for infrastructure and receive nothing."[47] Tercek ignores incentives already provided, but the complaints worked. The Puerto Rico Tourism Company spent $141,000 on a "Young at Heart" program designed to make Old San Juan livelier and more attractive to cruise passengers.[48] Its Lelolai program focused on improving San Juan's ambiance and grabbing cruise passengers' attention; it included new trolleys and new garbage trucks, all suggestions made by cruise line executives.

Also in 2002 Royal Caribbean complained it was having trouble finding major hotels in Puerto Rico that want to block-book rooms at inexpensive rates for pre- and post-cruise passengers.

> "Of course we [Royal Caribbean] don't expect to find $60 room rates in San Juan, but we don't expect to pay $300 a night for a room either, especially when we buy in bulk," ... [we seek] to get pricing from local hotels no higher than the 150 dollar range.
>
> In response, Rick Newman, president of the Puerto Rico Hotel and Tourism Association, says there is a large inventory of hotels in San Juan that are able to provide a variety of rates, but to find low rates, cruise lines should be approaching hotels off the beach that are willing to take that kind of business.[49]

continued:

> Royal Caribbean International's brochure at the time offered hotel rooms in San Juan starting (in low season) from between $209 and $379 per night (for a required two-night stay). They receive $5 per room per night from the Puerto Rico Tourism Company.[50]

In early 2003 the CTO discussed a $20 passenger levy on every cruise ticket sold to the Caribbean. The money would go into a "Sustainable Fund" and be used for regional security, environmental management, product development and marketing, human resource development on the islands, and lobbying activities in Washington. Island governments would share any excess.

Details of the levy leaked to the cruise industry before the plan had been circulated to all CTO members. The FCCA lobbied against it and made rounds in the Caribbean. It aggressively argued its position to governments and private sector suppliers, which had the effect, as pointed out by the CTO's secretary general, of short-circuiting and undermining a full discussion of the plan by CTO members.

> While we accept that every person or agency with a vested interest in any matter, is expected to argue their case, certain tactics would be regarded as unacceptable by reasonable men. We have heard, for example, that a representative of the cruise lines telephoned a Caribbean prime minister in hospital the night before he was to undergo a major operation, to dissuade him from supporting the levy. Statements attributed to the FCCA and not so far denied, have named particular governments, and even particular heads of government, as being not in support of a levy which is still under discussion by Caribbean governments. This seems to show great disrespect for those countries and for their leaders. There have been stories, allegedly spread by the cruise lines, of countries which are considering giving up their membership in CTO because they disagree with the levy. There have also been reports of port authorities and other Caribbean suppliers, including taxi operators, being mobilized against their own governments by what is a foreign consolidated oligopoly. All this, if true, seems to be an abuse of market dominance which falls in the category of practices not allowed under the General Agreement in Trade in Services now being negotiated and which was the fundamental reason for the failure of recent WTO talks in Cancun.[52]

Despite lots of media attention and publicity, the passenger levy did not succeed. An editorial in a Bahamian newspaper observed:

The cruise line officials' opposition to the levy tax, their scare tactics, empty pretensions and vain posturing, suggest that in their dealings with the Caribbean they are operating with an unsophisticated colonialist mentality. Their thinking seems rooted in the premise that Caribbean countries are here to serve metropolitan needs and that the islands exist primarily to provide a market for them to extract wealth and repatriate the profits, while they contribute very little to the regional development.[53]

The FCCA's success was based on exploiting divisions in the Caribbean and demonstrating the adage "divide and conquer," not on its artful use of persuasion.

If the cruise industry had been patient, the passenger levy would have died on its own. Divisions existed over where the money would go, how it would be used, and how it would be distributed — a number of governments saw the plan increasing the size of the CTO, but not having enough direct benefit to the individual islands. There was general agreement on a passenger levy, but not in the form proposed.

Cruise Lines Don't Have a Monopoly on Insensitivity

A store owner on the island of Hawai'i told me about an NCL cruise passenger asking for a *kama 'aina* (child of the land) discount. Passengers are instructed on board that this is a local's discount and told to ask for it. The store owner was upset because she didn't offer discounts to anyone and was indignant that a tourist would ask for a discount in a language they neither spoke nor understood.

In Papua, New Guinea, where Cunard's *QE II* was in port, locals found a tourist's postcard and handed it to the country's local newspaper. The card read: "Tues 2/24 Lae, New Guinea. Hard to find postcards in this primitive village. Thousands of natives came out of the mountains to see the white people who came on the big ship .... Very uncomfortable in the village — (they) stare at us like wild — there are still cannibals in the hills so we don't want to end up in the soup."[54]

An effort to mend the rift between the CTO and FCCA was announced in May 2004. Together with the Caribbean Hotel Association (CHA), they established the Caribbean Tourism Facilitation Committee (CTFC), a tripartite committee for cooperation in regional tourism development.[55] The success of CTFC depends in part on FCCA's approach. If its demeanor is arrogant, then little progress may be made.

Success depends on the industry understanding and directly addressing issues underlying perceived need for a passenger levy. But success may not be the industry's goal as long as solidarity can be so easily broken.

Paternalism or Social Capital

Social capital accrues from a range of sources. Donations to local charities and participation in local initiatives are two techniques, even if contingent on cooperating with the cruise industry. But there is a thin line between building social capital and paternalism, as shown when cruise lines withdrew support for local charities in Juneau.

Donations to Local Causes

Similar to ICCL's Cruise Industry Charitable Foundation, FCCA has its Foundation for the Caribbean. The FCCA Website says the foundation has given "almost $2 million in funding to causes and charities throughout the region" in nine years — an average $220,000 per year.[56] But it is unclear how much money has been given to whom.

Recipients of grants from FCCA are varied. They include the Cayman Islands Football Association, Boys & Girls Club of Key West, Caribbean Special Olympics, Red Cross in Aruba and St. Maarten, and the Barbados Association for the Blind & Deaf. Grants are often presented to a prominent person in a public forum and photographed. The photo of a 2001 donation for the Association for Battered Women in Aruba shows a check being presented to the governor's wife. A 2001 donation for the Bahamas National Disaster Fund is pictured with a check being given to the country's minister of tourism.

That donations and grants are not given quietly or anonymously suggests they are more than simple philanthropy. A dual purpose is seen in other FCCA activities. For example its annual Children's Essay Contest is open to children in the Caribbean, and offers cash prizes of $2,500, $1,500, and $1,000 for the top three essays, respectively, in each of two age divisions. A matching prize is given to the winner's school, so the contest costs the FCCA $20,000.

The investment is small for the value derived. The topic in 2000 was "Cruise Passengers Return as Land-Based Vacationers" (What is my country doing and should do to encourage cruise passengers to return to my destination for future visits?).[57] The list of winners included noteworthy tips from students on how destinations can encourage repeat guests. Suggestions include: improve pier and port facilities, survey guests to find out their level of satisfaction, encourage hotels to offer passengers use of their facilities, and keep taxes/costs low. Each suggestion benefits the cruise lines without helping a tourist destination reduce its dependence on cruise tourism.[58]

Getting to Parents through Children

The Caribbean isn't the only place where children are used to shape public opinion about the cruise industry. Several communities in Alaska offer a curriculum to fifth graders that culminates with a tour of a cruise ship and includes a group photo taken by the ship's photographer and "lunch in grand style — such as pizza, hot dogs, burgers ... or occasionally a visit to the Buffet in one of the ship's restaurants .... Each Community has a box of curricular materials, sample menus and daily newsletters from a ship, writing extensions, math extensions, and a selection of literature with nautical or sea-ocean themes. Children can examine careers on board, science as applied to pollution control, and national origin — as many ships have over 60 different nations represented in their crew."[59] The industry teaches that they have pollution systems that are environmentally friendly; but they don't teach that these systems degrade the environment.

Topics in other years are similar. In 2003 the question was, "What steps can/has my country taken towards improving the cruise passenger experience while in my country?" While the idea of an essay contest is positive, one that focuses students on how they can better serve cruise passengers does not benefit small island states of the Caribbean. Future leaders should be encouraged to think about what their country can do for its own development. Tourism may be part, and cruise tourism a subpart, but the contest stifles creative thought that may move the country beyond the dominance of the cruise industry. There is something inherently wrong when a student suggests that hotels should offer cruise passengers use of their facilities. This strategy benefits the cruise line and the cruise passenger, but displaces and compromises the experience of the person paying to stay at an island resort for a week or two.

FCCA's Foundation for the Caribbean also has held an annual Environmental Poster Competition since 1998. This, too, is in two grade divisions, though prizes are more modest. Topics appear less biased than those in the essay contest, though ironically this industry promotes environmental responsibility and environmental thinking among youth while showing insensitivity to islands' environmental concerns.

There is similar irony in FCCA's participation in beach cleaning days. This should be complimented, but is offset by islanders' complaints that a significant amount of

Cruise Tourism versus Land-Based Tourism

The tradeoffs between cruise tourism and land-based tourism were stated clearly at a public hearing at Crane Garden Bay, British Virgin Islands (BVI) in February 2004. Residents talked about crowding on beaches, traffic, and not enough restrooms; cruise passengers conflicting with yachting and long-term visitors; cruise passengers conflicting with the community as a result of topless sunbathing near school; and lack of local input or control of "visitor invasion."

The public hearing was told the average overnight visitor contributes $485 per day compared with $25 per day from cruise tourists. Annual revenues in BVI were $141 million for overnight hotel visitors, $100 million for yacht visitors, and $9.6 million from day-visitor tourism.[60] Cruise tourism in this case appears to have a negative impact and expansion will likely undermine the income being generated from other forms of tourism. Is anyone listening?

---

the garbage washing ashore is from cruise ships. Though the cruise industry denies anything is tossed overboard, evidence suggests otherwise. A passenger on board *Norwegian Wind* in February 2003 took photographs as crew members tossed overboard whole beer bottles, whole wine bottles, beer and pop cans, corks, plastic plates, plastic utensils, plastic cups, and organic material from the back of the ship. The ship was between Hawai'i and the island of Kiribati. In another case I learned of garbage from a passing cruise ship washing ashore on the Cayman Islands.[61] The refuse included milk cartons from a US dairy. A government official contacted the dairy and a short time later received a call from a cruise line. It did not admit that the garbage came from its ship, but it agreed to pay for the clean up.

Buying Goodwill

The industry has other mechanisms for buying goodwill. Donations for relief following hurricanes not only are the right thing to do but contribute to public image. Cruise corporation sponsorship of golf tournaments and other sporting events gets their name out and projects a positive impression. Royal Caribbean spent $5 million to be the sole sponsor of the half-time show at the 1998 Super Bowl and from 1990 through 2004 sponsored the Professional Golfers' Association's (PGA) Royal Caribbean Classic — a tab estimated at $2 million a year. Carnival Corporation sponsors the Carnival Charity Golf Classic[62] and the Miami Heat (through its CEO), and offers its ships for fundraising events. Further, it benefits from the Carnival

Let Us Refer You to Our Consultants

Consultants play a role in the relationship between cruise destinations and the industry. Take for example Bermello, Ajamil & Partners (B&A),[63] a Miami-based consulting firm. It has given advice to almost every major Canadian port and many ports in the US.

B&A's recommendations often include increased marketing that may achieve unprecedented growth — essentially what a port that sees the cruise industry as a cash cow wants to hear — and suggestions for a new terminal (plans for which it can provide). In the case of Saint John and Halifax, B&A's advice put the neighboring ports in competition with each other. They both were spending money to attract the exact same ships.

Potential conflicts of interest were discussed in a 1999 series of newspaper articles looking at advice to the City of Key West from B&A. One issue was that B&A was advising the city while maintaining both Carnival and Royal Caribbean as major clients,[64] a relationship not visibly acknowledged by B&A in its proposal to work for Key West. B&A claimed its involvement with the cruise lines was not a conflict of interest because the services were not in North America.[65] The City of Key West no longer uses B&A.

B&A's advice reinforced the appearance of a conflict of interest. Two clauses were included in the final report that had not been publicly vetted. One provided that, "...all revenues received at the Port [will] be used exclusively to fund operations and improvements at the cruise port, without any benefits being directed toward any other city need."[66] This clause meant taxes would need to be raised to make up for revenues previously covered by cruise ship income. The other clause required that the city maintain and expand existing port facilities. Both clauses were dropped.

The report was also questioned because it recommended that the city not raise its per-passenger port charge — the recommendation was based on data that excluded ports with high port charges such as the Bahamas ($15) and Bermuda ($60). It included ports that collectively supported Key West's port charge remaining at $6.50, such as Melbourne, Australia; Copenhagen, Denmark; Osaka, Japan; Haifa, Israel; and Vancouver, British Columbia.[67]

continued:

B&A suggests that its relationship with the cruise industry is positive because it shows how well they understand the industry. In fact, its events at Seatrade Cruise Shipping Conventions have been called a highlight of the social calendars at Seatrade conventions during the past decade by *Seatrade Insider*. B&A, like others, thrives on having excellent connections to the cruise industry.

Cruise Lines Science and Technology Building at St. Thomas University and the Carnival Symphony Hall at the Performing Arts Center of Greater Miami.

These comments shouldn't detract from the positive value of contributions. It focuses on the dual purpose served. A similar duality is seen with the consultants that many ports use for advice around development and expansion. Their advice is expert, but some question whose interests they serve (see previous sidebar).

Let's Throw a Party and Have the Ports Pay

The cruise industry's largest trade show is the Seatrade Cruise Shipping Convention held annually in March in Miami Beach. There are also Seatrade Conventions in the Mediterranean, Middle East, and Europe, but the one in Miami is by far the largest. It attracts over 9,000 people from 100 countries and has a trade floor with more than 950 exhibiting companies. They include every imaginable company that sells or wants to sell product to the cruise industry such as shipbuilders; purveyors of food; talent management companies; and manufacturers of wastewater treatment systems, propulsion systems, and power plants. Probably the single largest group of exhibitors is ports. There are ports from Australia, Asia, Europe, Africa, and from across the Western Hemisphere. There is a Caribbean Village, a Canadian Pavilion, a French Pavilion, an Australian Pavilion, and on and on.

Seatrade Cruise Shipping Convention is a wonderful event for the cruise industry as long as ports foot a significant portion of the cost through booth rentals, registration, and other fees. Many ports attend in hopes that a cruise executive (anyone with a card that has a logo with a cruise line) will grace their booth with a visit and encourage them that they too will cash in on cruise tourism. It is sad to watch ports giving away "goodies" to lure executives to its booth. Some even schedule evening receptions or sit-down dinners hoping to meet someone higher in the corporate structure.

The industry also uses the convention as a media event. It offers complimentary press passes to journalists and other media professionals with hopes that stories about the event will follow. But only the "good media"[68] — those who write positively about the cruise industry — are permitted to attend. The "bad media" — writers who criticize the industry — are excluded. I had a press pass for three consecutive years. Following publication of *Cruise Ship Blues* I was denied press credentials for 2004. I could pay the full registration fee if I wanted to attend the convention but I was barred from the press room or press conferences. While the event sponsors proudly told of the media that were in attendance — correspondents from CNN, Reuters, the Associated Press and Agence France Presse, to name just a few — it said nothing about those barred from the event.

My experience in 2002 was quite different. I was not only given a press pass, but invited to several private events. One was an annual event sponsored by Carnival and called "Pause for Claws." It was held at Joe's Stone Crabs in Miami Beach and included a couple dozen media professionals and presidents and vice presidents of Carnival Corporation and its cruise lines. I also attended a tour and lunch on Windstar Cruise's recently acquired *Wind Surf*. The conversation at lunch, at one point, turned to cruising. One journalist told of calling a cruise line's director of public relations in January — this was in March — and telling him that he was sick of the snow and the cold and to get him on a ship, anywhere, as soon as possible. He was on a ship in the Caribbean a couple of days later. He said this was not unusual — it was a common request that was always fulfilled. The journalist writes positively about cruising.

Others at the table had similar accounts, though there was variation in how quickly a request was filled. But all received free trips. Some journalists acknowledge these gifts, others do not. Some refuse free trips and clearly state this in their articles.

Anything to Turn a Profit

This chapter has looked at ways the cruise industry maximizes profit for itself, often at the detriment of ports. Part of the strategy relies on pitting ports against each other for the same cruise ships and passengers. The industry is simply taking advantage of what classic economic theory and laws of supply and demand tell us would be the case. By encouraging more and more ports to compete, cruise lines can pick and choose the ones they want. Choices often depend on one port either underselling another or providing greater incentives. The industry orchestrates, supports, and directly benefits from this classic buyer's market.

6

Squeezing to the Last Drop

C RUISE PRICING TEMPTS PEOPLE TO SAIL. Why wouldn't it? They can spend relatively little and enjoy what is sold as a luxury, all-inclusive vacation. But, as conventional wisdom dictates, if something appears too good to be true, it usually is. The catch with a cruise is that the extra costs can exceed the cruise fare.[1]

The squeeze comes from two sides. First, passengers are squeezed on board for every last dime. Then, as passengers spend more on board, they have less to spend ashore. In this way cruise ships and ports directly compete for passenger spending.

The increased competition between onboard and onshore spending is recent. Cruise ships built in the late-1990s and early 2000s are larger and devote considerably more space to income generators such as shops, cafes, activities, casinos, and bars. Onboard revenue has also developed out of need as the cruise industry has been forced to lower fares in order to fill ships.

The cruise industry actively promotes onboard spending. Products and services are directly marketed, and sometimes individually tailored to the passenger. The onboard account of purchases records the passenger's spending pattern on this and potentially all other cruises. Companies are beginning to exploit these data and take onboard revenue generation to a new level.

Monitoring is not limited to regular purchases. NCL installed a system in its casinos that uses a cashless ticket in/ticket out technology. It permits NCL to follow player activity individually to identify high rollers for comps and other incentive offers. The system can also award player points and rewards for customers going to different destinations on different vessels. All of these steps lead to increased income.[2]

Cruise Passengers as Captive Spenders

We are accustomed to stores advertising loss leaders — products a store sells for less than it pays assuming consumers buying that product will buy others priced at the normal profit margin. Thus, a store may lose money on one item but makes up its loss plus makes a profit overall. Cruises today are sold in much the same way. The cruise fare is the "loss leader" while onboard revenue generates sizable profits.

The increasing number of onboard revenue sources has raised concern among some in the industry. They see an eventual unbundling of the cruise product: Cruise ships would be sold much like a hotel room, pay-as-you-go. This would revolutionize cruise tourism and boost the economic bottom line.[3]

Unbundling began in full with easyCruise. The brainchild of Stelios Haji-Ioannou, founder and owner of easyJet, easyCruise provides a minimalist floating hotel that visits the same ports as other cruise lines but for a fraction of the cost.

> On an easyCruise rooms will cost $50, and include a minimum of expectations. Housekeeping will be an optional extra … and don't expect too much entertainment onboard …. Gone are the exclusive spectacles, candlelight dinners, ice skating and simulated rock-climbing walls found on some ships.[4]

Passengers can purchase meals and beverages and shore excursions, but otherwise are on their own. EasyCruise began in early 2005 with one ship carrying 172 passengers and 53 crew members.

Generating Onboard Revenue

A cruise ship can generate onboard revenue in many ways. The bars buy ingredients at duty-free prices and charge the same as at a five-star hotel onshore for beverages — a hefty profit. Bar purchases are maximized by prohibiting passengers from bringing beverages on board when they embark or reboard at ports. Some maximize casino play by allowing passengers to charge their onboard account or credit card; many have ATMs.[5] And then there are art auctions. Single pieces of art cost can cost tens of thousands of dollars — and people buy.[6] The cruise industry has a formula that works for separating passengers from their money.

There are also new sources of onboard revenue and changes in the old sources. New sources include activities and enrichment programs, in-room mini-bars, in-room entertainment systems that include gambling, Internet connections, cell phone connections, virtual reality games, lessons from golf professionals, charges for transportation from the pier to center city in port, admission fees for shows and entertainment, and much more. Many amenities and activities previously provided at no cost now have a fee or are no longer offered.

Income can be maximized in many ways. Onboard spas push the limit by pricing services the same or more as major hotels. Some onboard shops guarantee not to be undersold onshore — a sign is clearly posted telling passengers that if the same product is found ashore at a cheaper price, the ship's shop will match that price. And one of the newest waves is extra-tariff restaurants — onboard restaurants at which passengers pay for their meal the same as at an onshore restaurant. Steakhouses became particularly popular in the early 2000s: Carnival's Supper Club, Royal Caribbean's Chops Grille, Princess Cruises' Sterling Steakhouse, and NCL's Cagney's.[7]

The concept of extra-tariff restaurants is not new. In 1990 the *Royal Viking Sun* introduced The Royal Grill, which charged a flat fee of $45 per person. Paul Bocuse, a Michelin three-star chef in Lyon, France, developed menus for the upscale restaurant. But the idea failed. Passengers were not willing to pay extra for what they believed was already part of the all-inclusive cost of a cruise.

A decade later extra-tariff restaurants were the norm. Purpose-built ships for NCL's "Freestyle Cruising" have as many as nine or ten restaurants with half or more charging a fee. Some have a flat fee, sometimes nominal; others are fully a la carte and can cost $30 or $40 for food only. The *Queen Mary 2*, a ship that has been described as "luxury for the masses," has a restaurant with celebrity chef Todd English's name on it. Lunch sells for $20; dinner for $30. The cruise line claims that competition for seats was so great without the charge that some passengers stole reservation cards left for other passengers. The charge reduces demand. Royal Caribbean International used a similar rationale when introducing charges at the Johnny Rockets on board its ships. A $3.95 per-person service charge was introduced in October 2004 after being tested in the spring and summer. The charge "helped the line 'better manage guest volume' at the restaurant."[8]

Saving Money and Making Money at the Same Time

Cruise ships are innovative in generating income. For example theme nights were found to increase beverage purchases. One company capitalized on the popularity of line dancing and replaced the traditional midnight tropical fruit buffet with a country and western theme buffet. Passengers who had previously come to the buffet to look briefly or sample some foods began staying longer and either participated in or observed the line dancing. Bar revenue increased by $1.10 per passenger — a quarter of a million dollars a year on a 2,000-passenger ship. In addition the cruise ship saved $50,000 a year because of lower food cost for the western-themed buffet.[9]

Private islands similarly save and make money for cruise lines. NCL introduced the concept. A private island, an alternative to landing passengers in already congested ports, was initially used on Sundays when shore side shops were closed, and saved the expense of port charges.

Private islands have other economic benefits. Most notably, passengers are a captive market. The cruise line runs all beverage sales and concessions, such as tours, water activities, souvenirs, and convenience shops. It has no competition, so all money spent contributes to its revenue and profit. An added advantage is that passengers tend to enjoy the experience, which indirectly leads to increased revenue in the form of future passenger referrals.[10]

The location of private islands also saves cruise lines money. Ships save fuel by cruising at a slower speed between two primary ports. Rather than sailing non-stop from St. Thomas to Miami, a ship may reduce speed between the two ports with its scheduled stop at the private island. The ship saves money on fuel and the island increases passenger satisfaction.

It Isn't Just Ports Getting Squeezed

The cruise industry, which has long said that travel agents are its friends, has done much to keep them as supporters. The importance of travel agents is clear. Direct bookings with cruise lines by passengers via the Internet or the telephone constitute between 5 and just over 15 percent of all reservations.[11] Travel agents account for the rest.

Commission rates between 12 and 18 percent, higher than any other travel product, have helped to keep travel agents onside with cruise lines. Promotions for travel agents further reinforce goodwill. Crystal Cruises, for example, gave two prizes worth $25,380 each to travel agents entered in their travel agent sweepstakes — travel agents received five entries for each stateroom they booked in 2000 for a cruise in 2001.[12] Holland America Line gave agents a chance to win a Grand Alaska Journey CruiseTour — for every Alaska Cruise Tour booked between January 1 and February 28 they received one chance to win. Other cruise lines had similar promotions.

Tension surfaced between the cruise industry and travel agents in September 2001 when most major cruise lines, led by Carnival, halved commissions (from 10 to 5 percent) for air travel booked through the cruise line. Travel agents responded angrily and some diverted passengers from a line that was cutting commissions to one that was not.[13] This was before the terrorist attacks of September 11. After the attacks the cruise lines were begging for business. While none reversed the reduction in commissions, Carnival announced "Operation Jump Start." It offered $100 in extra commission for every three cruises booked, including three-day cruises that cost $199 per person.

As business returned to normal and cruise ships were again sailing full, the industry took it to travel agents. In July 2003 Carnival announced an end to the preferential pricing it gives to large Internet agencies for consumers' cruise bookings, a policy called "price neutrality across the different channels of distribution."[14] Royal Caribbean followed suit. One travel agent believed Carnival but learned later that inequities remained. She had called for a fare on a cruise to nowhere from New York City and was mistakenly quoted an AAA rate that was $20 cheaper than the regular rate. As she said, "I've seen the ad [that says] it's not treating me any different than these bigwigs. But it is."[15]

Another travel agent reported the price she could offer for a Royal Caribbean cruise was undersold on the Web by $400. The cruise line defended the differential saying the lower-priced seller was one of the line's key accounts and was offered prices that RCCL's top sellers sometimes get. So much for a level playing field with standardized pricing.[16]

Royal Caribbean went even further a couple of weeks later. On July 31, 2003, it sent a letter from the line's president to travel agents saying that effective October 15, special fares based on age, state of residence, or other criteria[17] would now require passengers to prove their eligibility for the fare when they board the ship. If they are booked on a fare for which they are not technically eligible, they must either rebook the cruise at the lowest rate available on the day of embarkation or they will be denied boarding.

The industry announced another new policy in the summer of 2004. Responding to complaints from smaller traditional travel agencies that were finding it difficult to compete with discounts offered by larger agencies, both Carnival and Royal Caribbean said they would reduce sales commissions of any travel agent advertising prices lower than the line's published rate and in some cases put a "stop sell" on an agency that advertises nonapproved rates and promotions.[18] Carnival appeared willing to accept that agencies would continue to provide discounts, but only if directly asked by a customer and as long as the price was not advertised. Royal Caribbean was less flexible. It not only prohibited any form of rebate, even if not publicized, but warned it wouldn't support retailers that included gifts that could be converted into currency, such as onboard credit or gift certificates.[19] Bon voyage gifts and amenities available in its online "Gift and Gear" catalog were permitted.

In these cases, for its benefit, the cruise industry set ports in competition with one another; and prevented competition between travel agents. This appears contrary to free enterprise.

Where are things headed? A report by UBS Warburg in August 2004 says travel agent commissions are an area in which cruise lines could save considerable costs. Travel agent commissions are one of the highest expenses as a percentage of sales.[20] Clearly cruise lines have an incentive to combine direct sales and marketing with a reduction in travel agent commissions. Time will tell what the industry will do about commission rates.

Charging Passengers for Labor Costs

Unlike a hotel, which includes labor costs in room charges, the cruise industry charges separately for onboard service. At one time these charges were called gratuities or tips. A cruise line recommended an amount to be paid, per person per day, to the room steward, dining room waiter, waiter's assistant, assistant maitre d' and maitre d'. There were sometimes recommendations for the butler and/or chief steward. The daily charge typically totaled $10–$15 per person per day.

In the early 2000s cruise ships began automatically placing gratuities on passenger onboard accounts. A passenger on a seven-day cruise would be charged an additional $70 for the week — a sort of surcharge for having someone clean their room and serve food. This isn't much different from easyCruise, except in that case passengers explicitly choose services for which there is an additional charge.

Some cruise lines held on to the idea that payments to shipboard staff are gratuities. Holland America Line, for the longest while, had a policy of "tipping not required." Passengers were told:

> Our "tipping not required" policy ensures that the professional and gracious service you receive on board is truly sincere; that we are dedicated to providing the most relaxed cruise vacation, not simply providing service in return for tips. You are free, however, to extend monetary recognition if you wish; it's entirely up to you. (Company policy prohibits us from suggesting how much.)[21]

Under this policy, most service staff who would have received tips on other cruise lines were paid a higher salary per month ($300 vs. $50), but after tips generally earned less than workers on these other ships.

Holland America dropped the "tipping not required" policy in 2004 and joined the crowd. Not only do they recommend the amount of gratuity, but automatically charge passenger onboard accounts. A passenger can adjust the amount upward or downward, but if they do nothing the charge goes through. Imagine staying at a hotel and having a separate charge added for the labor cost for the cleaning staff.

Aside from the debate of whether these charges are a gratuity, the main relevance here is that cruise ships take first dibs on passengers' expendable income by automatically charging these amounts on their credit card. Norwegian Cruise Line and NCL America have substituted the quasi-voluntary charges with a mandatory service fee of $10 per passenger per day. Other companies will surely follow suit. Passengers have less to spend onshore and again, the cruise ship benefits while ports suffer.

Piracy in Action

This part of the book has looked at three separate but related issues dealing with the cruise industry's piracy. Chapter 4 looked at how the industry projects itself as a cash cow for ports. Believing that cruise ships bring in real income, ports work to attract or maintain cruise ships. Chapter 5 follows with how the cruise industry plays ports against one another, and how this financially benefits the industry at the expense of ports. Finally this chapter looks at how onboard charges and revenue sources squeeze passengers' disposable income. This undoubtedly negatively impacts on spending in ports and the income generated onshore.

Part Three
Purveyors of Trust

7

The Art of Greenwashing

IMAGINE AN INDUSTRY COMPRISING A GROUP OF CONVICTED FELONS. Their crime is a long period of habitually dumping into the world's oceans everything from hazardous chemicals such as perchlorethylene (dry-cleaning fluids) and silver nitrate (photofinishing chemicals) to oily bilge and plastic bags filled with garbage. That is the cruise industry in the 1990s and early 2000s. But it is not the image most hold. To the contrary, many see the cruise industry as environmentally sensitive. It promotes itself as a leader in environmental responsibility. How can an industry with such a poor record so easily project such a positive image? The answer, in one word, is greenwashing.

We Visit Some of the Most Pristine Places

When confronted with past practices and challenged to do better, the cruise industry's response is something like, "We visit some of the most pristine areas of the world and it is in our self-interest to keep them clean." How true! It begs the question, why don't they act in their own self-interest? Perhaps economic self-interest takes precedence over environmental responsibility.

The issue of discharges from cruise ships made a splash in world media in June 1998 when Royal Caribbean International paid a $9 million fine in San Juan and Miami for discharges of oily bilge. The Coast Guard investigation revealed that, "at various US ports, mariners allegedly removed the ejector pump bypass system's rubber hose, then closed off the connection between the clean and oily bilge systems with a metal plate to conceal the existence and use of the hose to bypass the oily water separator."[1] Oily bilge water could be discharged directly into the ocean without filtering required by international regulations.

The 1998 plea followed two incidents in 1994: a discharge off Bermuda by the *Nordic Empress* and a discharge from the *Sovereign of the Seas* while en route to San Juan. The company admitted the discharges, but argued the US government lacked authority to bring charges against a foreign-registered cruise line. It also began a public relations campaign, announcing in 1996 that it had taken immediate and decisive action to increase monitoring and enforcement procedures. These included:

> the creation of the position of senior vice president for quality assurance (filled by an ex-US Coast Guard captain) and environmental enforcement officers on each of the firm's 11 ships, upgrading pollution control equipment,

installing new computer monitoring equipment, and re-checking its environmental program. The firm said: 'Of particular significance is Royal Caribbean's recent recognition by Det Norke Veritas in naming the company as the first and only cruise line to be awarded its Safety and Environmental Protection Certificate. This certification recognizes the company enhancement of safety and environmental practices, which exceed those required by law and regulation. This certification and all the company's environmental efforts are clear evidence that the employees and management of Royal Caribbean are committed to protecting the environment well beyond legal requirements.'[2]

Despite the company's best efforts, a formal indictment was filed in December 1996.[3] RCCL was not charged for dumping — it had occurred in waters beyond US jurisdiction. It was charged with making false statements to the Coast Guard.

Royal Caribbean responded. It asked the governments of Norway and of Liberia to intervene as the flag state for the ships involved and to take over the matter. On March 12, 1997, a delegation from the Norwegian embassy in Washington delivered a diplomatic note to the US State Department seeking jurisdiction in the case because one of the ships involved flew the Norwegian flag.[4] Given that the Norwegian government had already looked into the case and decided that no action was necessary, the US Government declined Norway's request.

On the eve of trials in Miami and San Juan, Royal Caribbean agreed to admit to polluting the sea by dumping waste oil from nearly half of its fleet and to pay a $1 million criminal fine for the Miami phase of the case and an $8 million fine for eight felony counts in Puerto Rico. In total "the settlement covers 11 charges accusing the cruise line of systematically discharging waste oil from five of its ships, lying to US law enforcement investigators, falsifying records, tampering with witnesses, and destroying evidence."[5] Royal Caribbean was placed on probation for five years, "during which the conduct of the company will be closely monitored, with periodic reports to the Court and government detailing the company's environmental compliance and including the results of independent audits."[6]

Dumping Is the Norm

Royal Caribbean was not the only cruise line in the news for environmental violations. The US began stricter enforcement for pollution offences in 1993 following a number of unsuccessful attempts to have the problem addressed by the state where offending ships were registered.[7] Between 1993 and 1998 the federal government confirmed 87 illegal discharges from cruise ships (81 cases involving oil, 6 involving garbage or plastic). Seventeen "other alleged incidents" were referred to the countries where the cruise ships were registered.[8] Some of these incidents

Cruise Ship Waste

Ships today can carry upwards to 5,000 passengers and crew. The volumes of waste produced are significant:[9]

- 30,000+ gallons (114,000 liters) of sewage per day:
  Vacuum toilets keep volumes to 6 gallons (22.5 liters) or less per person per day.

- 450,000 gallons (1.7 million liters) of gray water per day:
  Water from sinks and showers, the galley, the laundry, etc., contains detergents, cleaners, grease, and much more.

- 19 tons (17,237 kilograms) of garbage and solid waste per day:
  Food waste, bottles, cans, plastic, cardboard, and the full range of packaging materials for products used on board.

- 15 gallons (57 liters) of hazardous waste every day:
  Dry-cleaning sludge, photofinishing chemicals, paints and, solvents, print shop waste, fluorescent lamps, batteries, etc.

- Diesel exhaust equivalent to 12,240 automobiles every day:
  Some ships have reduced this with gas turbine engines, but most use inexpensive bunker fuels.

- 7,000 gallons (26,500 liters) of oily bilge water every day.
  Contains fuel, oil, wastewater from engines, and possibly rags, metal shavings, paint, glass, and cleaning agents.

- Up to 1,000 metric tons of ballast water per release.
  Of concern because ballast water introduces non-native species — bio-invaders as they are sometimes called — to areas of discharge

received media attention: a half-million-dollar fine after crew members on Princess Cruises' *Regal Princess* were photographed by passengers as they threw overboard plastic bags of garbage while off the Florida Keys, and a $250,000 fine after passengers and a musician on Regency Cruises reported the same behavior.

Royal Caribbean used our nation's waters as its dumping ground, even as it promoted itself as an environmentally 'green' company...[and] to make matters worse, the company routinely falsified the ships' logs — so much so that its own employees referred to the logs with a Norwegian term meaning fairy tale book...[T]his case will sound like a foghorn throughout the maritime industry.[12]

— **Attorney General Janet Reno**
July 21, 1999

But it was Royal Caribbean's 1998 plea agreement, followed a month later by an announcement of another case involving Royal Caribbean that propelled the topic of cruise industry environmental practices onto front pages. The new case was reported to the company by crew members and Royal Caribbean in turn reported it to the US Government.[10] In July 1999 the company pleaded guilty to 21 counts of dumping oil and hazardous chemicals and lying to the US Coast Guard; it agreed to pay an $18 million fine.[11] Because it violated probation — twice convicted of a felony — the company was debarred: it could not enter into legal contracts with the US government. This meant it could not contract for permits to Glacier Bay or any other national park.

The violations covered by the 1999 plea agreement included oil, dry-cleaning fluids, photographic chemicals, and solvents from the print shop. They applied to Miami, New York City, Los Angeles, Anchorage, St. Thomas, and San Juan. The State of Alaska also filed suit in August 1999 charging Royal Caribbean with seven counts of violating laws governing oil and hazardous waste disposal. The company paid a fine of $3.5 million in January 2000.[13]

In the midst of this, Holland America Line paid a $1-million fine and $1 million in restitution in October 1998 for a 1995 incident in which it pumped overboard oily bilge water in Alaska's Inside Passage. The assistant engineer reporting the incident received a reward of $500,000 — one-half of the company's fine.[14]

Alaska Leads the Way

Alaskans had seen oil spills in and around Glacier Bay, sometimes from accidents at sea; however, the public outcry had been limited. But the cases involving Holland America Line and Royal Caribbean International caught their attention. It tipped public support in favor of Juneau's head tax initiative and spurred a move by the state toward monitoring and regulating cruise ships. The State Department of Environmental Conservation (DEC) with the US Coast Guard launched a cruise ship initiative in December 1999.

The initiative began with meetings between the State, US Coast Guard, Environmental Protection Agency (EPA), cruise industry, and environmental groups. The goal was to discuss the activities and operations of cruise ships to assess possible environmental issues. When the workgroups realized there was little technical data, they developed a plan for sampling wastewater from cruise ships and for monitoring air emissions. Participation in monitoring was voluntary. Thirteen of 24 ships refused to participate. They chose to go beyond three miles from shore to dump raw sewage without monitoring and without limitations.

The results of monitoring during the summer of 2000 were, in the words of Alaska's governor, "disgusting and disgraceful." Seventy-nine of 80 ships' effluent had levels of fecal coliform or total suspended solids that would be illegal on land — up to 100,000 times the federal standard. This was true of both black water and gray water.[15] As well, all samples indicated that "conventional pollutants" were part of the wastewater. According to the Juneau port commander for the Coast Guard, the results were so extreme that it might be necessary to consider possible design flaws and capacity issues with the Coast Guard–approved treatment systems that were currently in use.[16]

Air emission monitoring also gave reason for concern. The EPA had cited six cruise ship companies (involving 13 ships) for air pollution violations in the 1999 season. The situation had not improved. In August 2000 state investigators charged seven companies with 15 violations of state smoke-opacity standards in Juneau between mid-July and mid-August.

Monitoring results had three direct effects. First, in a bid to repair its image, Princess Cruises announced in late September 2000 that its ships would plug into Juneau's power supply while in port instead of running their polluting engines in port to generate electricity. The initiative, which required an investment of $4.5 million by the cruise line and $300,000 by the city, began in July 2001.

Second, Alaska's Senator Murkowski introduced legislation to regulate the dumping of raw sewage in "donut holes" that had been previously treated as outside federal waters and where such disposal was common.[17] The legislation set standards for treated sewage, banned discharges while ships were within one mile of shore, and empowered the State of Alaska to regulate black water (sewage) discharged into state waters.[18]

Third, the Alaska Cruise Ship Initiative was born. Based on the monitoring results, Alaska Governor Tony Knowles introduced in March 2001 legislation designed to strengthen state monitoring of the cruise industry's waste disposal practices and enforce state clean air and water standards for cruise ships. Monitoring and enforcement would be funded by a $1 per passenger fee charged to cruise ships. The act passed Alaska's House of Representatives on May 3 and Alaska's Senate on June 20; it took effect on July 1, 2001.

The law was not more stringent than current US law regarding the disposal of sewage or pollution from smokestack emissions, but represents the first time a state held cruise ships accountable to environmental standards. A ship with advanced wastewater treatment systems (AWTS) was permitted to discharge within state waters (within three miles of the coast) if the system was certified by the state. Inspections could lead to decertification if it didn't meet standards: 4 of 18 ships certified in 2003 were subsequently decertified and later recertified.[19]

Alaska's Cruise Ship Initiative has had positive effects. Air emission violations reduced from 39 between 1999 through 2001, to 1 in both 2002 and 2003. Violations of wastewater discharge standards are almost nil compared with four in the first two months of the Initiative. And AWTS are properly maintained so they operate as specified.

The Same Old, Same Old — We Are Stewards of the Ocean

Six days after Royal Caribbean's 1999 plea agreement, the ICCL issued a press release affirming the cruise industry's commitment to maintaining a clean environment and keeping the oceans clean.

> Regrettably, there have been violations of environmental laws involving cruise lines in the past few years. These incidents have served as an important wake-up call, causing our industry to redouble its efforts to improve its environmental performance.[20]

Most would assume the industry had gotten the message and was cleaning up its act. But that was not the case. A continuing stream of new incidents quickly eroded the credibility of ICCL's public relations campaign.

Responsibility Isn't Cheap

It isn't cheap to be environmentally responsible. Royal Caribbean's *Vision of the Seas* is a moderate-sized ship carrying 2,000 passengers. It operated two three-day and two four-day cruises from Seattle between May 19 and June 2, 2002. The cost of pumping out sewage and gray water, rather than discharging within Puget Sound or Canadian coastal waters, is estimated at $540,595 for the five port calls in Seattle. That's an incentive for some to use the ocean as a ship's toilet.[21]

Royal Caribbean–owned Celebrity Cruises' *Mercury* allegedly released perchlorethylene (PERC) in San Francisco Bay several months following the ICCL's statement. A couple reported what they saw to the EPA, was given a runaround, and then turned to Bluewater Network, a San Francicsco-based non-profit organization concerned with cruise ship pollution. The company denied the allegation[22] and a subsequent criminal investigation by the EPA did not lead to charges. However, according to Bluewater Network, Celebrity Cruises had admitted to discharging a deck cleanser that included arsenic, cadmium, and lead. These elements were apparently in small enough quantities that the EPA chose not to press charges, though Bluewater Network advised that passengers were liable to come into direct physical contact with the cleansers through their bare feet and that their use should be discontinued. They further advised that Celebrity was violating California's Proposition 65, which requires that people be warned when in the presence of toxic chemicals.

The Benefits of Self-Reporting

In 2000 the Justice Department subpoenaed records from NCL after its parent company, Star Cruises, reported it had uncovered questionable practices before its ownership of the company.[23] The Coast Guard was already pursuing its own investigation.[24] A former officer on NCL's *Norway* had gone to the EPA in 1999 with piping diagrams and videotaped evidence of oil dumping by the ship. The EPA began an investigation.

> Months into it, senior Norwegian officials were faxed an anonymous letter warning that the former officer had tipped off the EPA .... Agents already had come across other disturbing information: The Norway had few of the legally required records for its wastes and had apparently routinely dumped sewage and hazardous waste into the ocean for years.[25]

In July 2002 NCL signed an agreement with the US Department of Justice pleading guilty to discharge of oily bilge water between May 1997 and May 2000, and to falsifying discharge logs.[26] The company was fined $1 million and ordered to pay $500,000 toward environmental service projects in South Florida.[27] Federal prosecutors described the sentence as lenient.[28]

Like Royal Caribbean, NCL didn't appear to learn from its mistakes. In February 2003 passengers aboard the *Norwegian Wind* photographed crew members throwing garbage and plastic overboard while the ship was en route from Hawai'i to the Fanning Islands.[29] And then in May 2003, the *Norwegian Sun* was cited by the State of Washington for an illegal discharge of 16,000 gallons (40 tons) of raw sewage into the Strait of Juan de Fuca. The strait is known to be habitat for orca whales. NCL didn't deny the discharge, but argued the state lacked jurisdiction over the discharge. The state dropped its case.

A Small Price to Pay

Carnival Corporation was also subpoenaed in 2000 for records relating to the environmental practices of ships with each of its six cruise lines.[30] In April 2002 Carnival pleaded guilty to six counts of falsifying records in relation to oil discharges. It admitted to dumping oily waste from five ships operated by Carnival Cruise Lines and that employees made false entries in record books from 1998 to 2001. In return, the Department of Justice agreed not to pursue further investigation of other Carnival Corporation brands. This was an important inducement given that Holland America Line was already on probation for its 1998 felony conviction and would be debarred if convicted of another felony while on probation.

Under the plea agreement Carnival Corporation paid a $9-million fine and agreed to contribute $9 million to environmental projects over five years. It also agreed to five years of court supervision and pledged to hire new managers and to put in place an executive-level environmental standards program.[31]

Carnival Corporation was like its competitors. Four months after paying the fine Holland America Line's *Ryndam* was charged with releasing more than 40,000 gallons (151,416 liters) of partially treated sewage into Juneau Harbor.[32] The case went to a grand jury in Anchorage and after more than two years the company agreed to plead guilty to a single misdemeanor count of negligently discharging 20,000 gallons (75,708 liters) of untreated sewage into Juneau Harbor. It apologized and agreed to three years' probation, to spend $1.3 million to improve its ships' handling of waste, to pay a $200,000 fine, and to pay $500,000 in restitution to the National Forest Foundation to reduce the amount of pollutants that enter the watersheds and coast of Southeast Alaska.[33]

And there was more. In January 2003 Carnival Cruise Lines reported an incidental discharge of 60 gallons (227 liters) of gray water while anchored one-half mile from land while in Avalon Bay (Catalina Island, California).[34] In October 2003 it paid a $200,000 administrative fee to settle with the California State Lands Commission over noncompliance with state ballast water law.[35]

In between, Carnival found itself back in the Federal court in Miami in July 2003. They were summoned by a judge after the company's probation officer reported to the court that Holland America Line employees falsified information in 12 audits provided to an independent consultant, and that it failed to "develop, implement and enforce" the terms of the environmental compliance program required by its 2002 plea agreement.[36] The probation officer petitioned the court to require Carnival to pay another community-service fine. A month later, Carnival signed a settlement with the court and avoided any further fines. It said it had fired the three environmental-compliance employees responsible for the false audit reports and agreed to hire four additional auditors to oversee the compliance program and provide additional training for staff. The company explicitly did not admit to any wrongdoing in the settlement pact.[37]

And still, the company couldn't get it right. On March 5, 2004, Holland America Line notified the US and Netherlands governmental authorities that one of its chief engineers had admitted to improperly processing bilge water on *Noordam*. A subsequent internal investigation determined that the improper operation may have begun in January 2004 and continued sporadically through March 4, 2004. The matter had also been raised by Coast Guard officials in San Juan, Puerto Rico, to their counterparts in Tampa following a report to them of the incidents. It isn't clear whether Holland America's self-report predates the report made by the Coast Guard. Holland America Line and three shipboard engineers received grand jury subpoenas from the Office of the US Attorney at the ship's homeport, Tampa, Florida.[38]

And then in June 2004, Holland America Line's former vice president responsible for the company's environmental compliance, Richard Softye, pleaded guilty to confirming environmental audits that were never performed. He was fined $10,000 and ordered to perform 450 hours of community service.[39] An industry insider suggests that Softye was a convenient scapegoat — that he wouldn't have done anything without the approval of higher-ups. This view appears reasonable in light of disclosures in the whistle-blower case filed by Carnival Cruise Lines' former vice president of environment, health and safety, James Walsh. Walsh was fired after Carnival paid the $18 million fine in 2002. According to his complaint, he had been instructed more than once to ignore, overlook, or otherwise keep quiet about environmental and safety violations at Carnival Cruise Lines and at Holland America Line.[40]

Don't Look at What We Do, Listen to What We Say

With violations and investigations continuing, ICCL again went on the offensive. On June 10, 2001 it released *Cruise Industry Waste Management Practices and Procedures*. The report was originally planned for release on June 11, but the date was advanced after Alaska's senate cleared the way for final approval of the Alaska Cruise Initiative.[41] ICCL claims it was not influenced by these events but its timing is anything but random. The largest cruise corporation, Carnival, was under investigation by the US government, as was NCL. And a pattern of environmental disregard continued, including three environmental violations in Alaska waters between May 5 and June 6, 2001. A fourth violation occurred on June 18, 2001.

According to ICCL, compliance with environmental standards is a condition for membership — therefore compliance is mandatory. As a public relations statement, it sounds good. But what the ICCL means by "mandatory" came into question as violations continued and there were no apparent sanctions by ICCL. On June 18 Royal Caribbean International's *Rhapsody of the Seas* illegally discharged 200 gallons

It's Beginning to Sound Familiar

These incidents have served as an important wake-up call, causing our industry to redouble its efforts to improve its environmental performance.

— ICCL Press Release, July 27, 1999

The International Council of Cruise Lines (ICCL) today released a statement that outlines the industry's plans to enhance and strengthen environmental standards for the cruise industry in the area of waste disposal and onboard waste management.

— ICCL Press Release, October 4, 1999

Our member cruise lines are committed to protecting and preserving the environment. The industry will continue to work diligently with lawmakers, regulators and stakeholders to ensure that our joint efforts continue to reflect that commitment.

— ICCL Letter to the Editor, *St. Petersburg Times*, April 28, 2000

Regrettably, there have been violations of environmental laws involving cruise lines in the past few years. These incidents served as a wake-up call.

— ICCL President Michael Crye, quoted by *Associated Press*, June 10, 2001

The International Council of Cruise Lines (ICCL) announced today that its members have unanimously adopted mandatory environmental standards for all of their cruise ships. The adoption of these standards marks the first time an association of international passenger vessel operators has adopted mandatory waste management practices and procedures.

— ICCL Press Release, June 11, 2001

(757 liters) of gray water into Juneau's harbor when wastewater was being transferred to a holding tank. Wastewater was discharged through an overboard discharge valve when the holding tank exceeded its capacity. According to Nancy Wheatley, a senior vice president for Royal Caribbean, "they were using too many pumps, pumping it too fast, and they didn't shut the pumps off quite fast enough.

They got essentially a splash of gray water out the air vent …. It should not have happened and we're sorry it did."[42] The discharge violated ICCL's mandatory standards, but no action was taken

Given the apparent inconsistency between what ICCL says and what it does, I consulted a dictionary to see whether I misunderstood the meaning of mandatory. According to the *Oxford English Dictionary*, mandatory is defined as "required by law or mandate; compulsory." The *Cambridge International Dictionary of English* has a similar definition: "something which must be done, or which is demanded by law." It would seem, given these definitions, that if membership in ICCL requires compliance with the mandatory standards, then the organization's membership list should be getting fairly thin. But that is not the case. So how do they define what is meant by mandatory?

The ICCL claims the environmental regulations are mandatory because each member line will integrate "industry standards into its internationally mandated Safety Management System (SMS), which ensures compliance through internal and third-party audits. Failure to comply with SMS procedures could prevent a ship from operating from US ports."[43] In other words, a cruise line must have written policies that are consistent with the mandatory standards. If these written policies are violated, then it is the responsibility of the ship's flag state, or of the US or other port state, to deal with it. All the ICCL is ensuring is that something in writing says the right thing.

Unfortunately, that which is written does not always follow in practice. The CEO of Royal Caribbean issued a form letter on September 24, 2003, responding to letters he received as part of Oceana's campaign to get Royal Caribbean to commit to a timetable for installing advanced wastewater treatments systems on its ships. The letter clearly states that Royal Caribbean discharges its black water (wastes from toilets) and its gray water (wastewater from sinks and the galley) "only when we are 12 or more miles from the shore and moving at least 6 knots." It proudly promotes the company's policies and procedures for exceeding Coast Guard requirements and as stricter than US law. It's an impressive claim, but contradicted with a report in December 2003 that the company had 12 times violated a memorandum of understanding signed with the State of Hawai'i, which prohibits discharges within four miles of the coast.[44] Royal Caribbean's letter was not announcing a new policy; the policy of not discharging within 12 miles was ongoing, but apparently not in practice.

Selling a Green Image
Since the early 1990s the cruise industry has promoted itself as environmentally responsible. Princess Cruises was promoting Planet Princess when it was caught throwing garbage-filled plastic bags overboard; Royal Caribbean's crew members

proudly wore pins with the company's slogan, "Save the Waves," while hazardous chemicals and oily bilge were dumped into coastal waterways; and Holland America Line had trash bins with "SEA: Seagoing Environmental Awareness" around the ship as part of its demonstration of environmental stewardship when its vice president of environmental compliance pleaded guilty to confirming environmental audits never performed.

The public relations campaign using creative expressions goes beyond the ship. Cruise line executives and ICCL make the rounds to ports and try to minimize environmental concerns. Royal Caribbean's president visited Alaska ports to apologize to local communities and talk about how the line had learned its lesson. His words were not always viewed as sincere or as adequately appreciative of the damage done. But they provided positive media and were politically wise.

Visits are also used to influence public opinion on legislation impacting the industry and on construction of new terminals. In October 2004 Royal Caribbean sent its director of environmental programs, Richard Pruitt, to Norfolk to ease the minds of activists and officials worried about damage that cruise ships could inflict on local waterways. He assured the local audience that, "the cruise industry has learned its lesson, is making environmental strides and no longer is behaving badly." And he went into the industry's all-too-often heard mantra: "We take people to beautiful places ... so why would we want to foul those places? It makes no business sense. People don't want to see soiled beaches and damaged coral reefs."[45] The tone is as sincere as the company's statement eight years earlier that it had taken immediate and decisive action to increase its monitoring and enforcement procedures.

Re-Framing the Issue

Cruise line brochures promote environmental initiatives and each company's exceedingly high standards of responsibility. They yell out, "Look at what we say, not at what we do." When confronted with apparent contradictions, the industry usually makes one of two arguments.

The first is that cruise ships comprise a small proportion of ocean-going vessels, so it is unfair to focus on them. It is a compelling point, but passenger vessels are different from other vessels. A cruise ship's 5,000 inhabitants produce the full range of garbage, sewage, dirty wastewater, and hazardous chemicals that come with photo processing, dry cleaning, and print shops. It is a hotel at sea and the volumes are overwhelming. These are in addition to wastes produced by all ocean-going vessels: air emissions, oily bilge, ballast water with bio-invaders, and residues from painting activities and other ship operations.

The second focuses on the industry's use of cutting-edge technology in wastewater treatment. They specifically point to adoption and use of advanced

One of the Top Ten Greenwashers of 2003

Royal Caribbean understands that its customers would be shocked and disappointed by the facts about cruise pollution. Thus it paints a pretty picture colored by various tones of green.

The company's "Get Out There" advertisements depict passengers trekking across glaciers and swimming with stingrays. Launched in 2000 and created by marketing firm Arnold Worldwide of Boston, "Get Out There" has piggybacked on consumers' fondness for nature and raised brand preference for Royal Caribbean by 26 percent.

Since no reputable environmental organization would bestow environmental honors upon Royal Caribbean, in December the company awarded its own ship, *Adventure of the Seas*, with the Fourth Annual Best Environmental Innovation of the Year award. The ship pioneered such advances as "recycling programs that included clothes hangers, and the reuse of empty laundry soap and chlorine pails."

Source: Geoff Johnson, *Don't Be Fooled: The Ten Worst Greenwashers of 2003* (The Green Life. April 2004), <www.thegreen life.org/dontbefooled.html>, Accessed April 5, 2004.

wastewater treatment systems (AWTS). These systems have generally been installed only on ships sailing Alaska's Inside Passage where there is an incentive for their use. Ships certified to have properly operating AWTS are permitted to discharge within Alaska's coastal waters; those without must sail beyond the three-mile limit and outside the Alexander Archipelago before discharging waste. About one-third of the ships visiting Alaska do not have AWTS.

The industry's commitment to new technology has historically appeared weak. Royal Caribbean resisted for more than a year Oceana's call that it commit to AWTS on all its ships. Only after introduction of the Clean Cruise Ship Act of 2004 in Congress on April 1, 2004, did it reverse its position, issuing a statement in May 2004

> Referring to cruise ships' wastewater treatment systems:
> "I've seen their bright shiny equipment and it looks good to me."
>
> — **Mayor of a medium-sized port,**
> **October 2003**

that it would have AWTS on all of its ships by 2008. At the time only three of the line's ships had such systems.[46] Royal Caribbean's timing is interesting given that the Clean Cruise Ship Act provided incentives for early adopters of AWTS. It gave no acknowledgment for Oceana's influence in its decision.

How Advanced Is Advanced?

Despite their many advantages, a key problem with AWTS is they ineffectively deal with nutrient loading.[47] They can produce between 40 and 120 tons of concentrated sewage sludge per day — the same problem in concentrated form. The sludge is either dumped at sea or incinerated. The incineration of sludge generates harmful emissions of arsenic, beryllium, cadmium, chromium, lead, mercury, and nickel.[48]

Buying a Green Image

There is a limit to how effectively environmental responsibility can be projected simply by advertising and public pronouncements. Words go further when reinforced with the appearance of environmental concern and supported by social capital. Entities such as Royal Caribbean's Ocean Fund and ICCL's and Conservation International's Ocean Conservation and Tourism Alliance do both: reinforce a perception of environmental concern and grow significant social capital. They are also a divisive force in the environmental movement.

Royal Caribbean's Ocean Fund

Royal Caribbean established its Ocean Fund in 1996, about the time it was indicted for its 1994 discharges of oily bilge. The Fund's mission is "to support efforts to restore and maintain a healthy marine environment, minimize the impact of human activity on this environment, and promote awareness of ocean and coastal issues and respect for marine life."[49] Its purpose is to cast a green image on Royal Caribbean.

Between 1996 and 2004 the Ocean Fund awarded over $4.6 million to 41 separate organizations. Sixteen organizations received $100,000 or more and collectively account for 77 percent of all money granted (see Table 7.1). The pattern of awards provides some interesting insights.

When the Ocean Fund was announced in October 1996 at a press briefing at the Seamen's Church Institute in New York City, Royal Caribbean's CEO, Richard Fain, committed contributions totaling $1 million over the next three years. The Fund's first grant went to the Center for Marine Conservation (CMC). As he presented the $50,000 grant to CMC's president, Fain said:

TABLE 7.1: TOP RECIPIENTS OF OCEAN FUND GRANTS,
1997 – 2004*

Recipient	Total
World Wildlife Fund	$700,000
Center for Marine Conservation (Ocean Conservancy)	$575,000
National Audubon Society	$500,000
Alaska Sea Life Center	$200,000
National Marine Sanctuary Foundation	$200,000
Harbor Branch Oceanographic Institution, Florida	$165,000
Conservation Fund, Alaska	$150,000
University of Florida, Carr Centre for Sea Turtle Research	$150,000
Cabrillo Marine Aquarium (San Pedro, CA)	$145,000
Rosenstiel School, University of Miami	$140,000
Bermuda Underwater Exploration Institute	$118,000
Bahamas Reef Environment Education Fund	$100,000
Clean Islands International (USVI)	$100,000
Earthwatch Institute (Maynard, MA)	$100,000
International Seakeepers Society	$100,000
Tongass Coast Aquarium (Ketchikan, AK)	$100,000

* See the Appendix for a complete list of grants by the Ocean Fund.

The oceans are very important to us. We think that this fund can make a contribution to the oceans that support us. We're pleased to have the Center for Marine Conservation be our first recipient. We look forward to hearing the results of work supported by the fund and sharing them with others in the cruise and shipping industries and the public at large.[50]

In 1998 CMC received another $75,000 to support the 1999 International Beach Cleanup and Model Communities Project on waste reduction in San Juan Bay. Two years later it received $450,000 ($150,000 a year for three years) to expand its Model Communities program to the Bahamas, Bermuda, and the US Virgin Islands.

While pursuing these projects, CMC commissioned a study of how cruise ships affect the marine environment. After some delays, a report titled *Cruise Control*,[51] was released May 2002. Purportedly, an advance copy was given to Royal Caribbean and the cruise line attempted, unsuccessfully, to prevent its release. Royal Caribbean formally expressed its displeasure shortly after the report came out. In a letter dated

June 12, 2002, from Jack Williams, president and COO of Royal Caribbean to Roger Rufe, president of The Ocean Conservancy — the CMC had changed its name — the company expressed its "disappointment and dismay." It also suggested future installments of the grant from the Ocean Fund would not be forthcoming. The message was clear that criticism of the industry would not be tolerated from organizations taking money.[52]

The largest beneficiary of the Ocean Fund is World Wildlife Fund. In 1998 it received $50,000 to conduct a biodiversity assessment of the 620 mile (1,000 kilometer) Mesoamerican Reef and to conduct an eco-regional planning workshop in Belize. In 2000 it received a $450,000 grant over three years to certify sustainable fisheries and create eco-labeling of seafood products by the Marine Stewardship Council (which itself was given $50,000 in 2004 for a similar project). In 2003 it received $200,000 for a two-year pilot project in the Gulf of California aimed at reducing global bycatch of cetaceans — whales, dolphins, and porpoises — by focusing on the endangered vaquita marina porpoise. That's a total of $700,000, and like the Ocean Fund's other projects has very little to do with improving the impact on the environment of cruise tourism, or with gaining knowledge about how to build and operate "green" cruise ships.

The money to World Wildlife Fund (WWF) is also curious because William K. Reilly, chair of the board of the WWF-US, is a member of Royal Caribbean's board of directors and paid $300,000 a year as an environmental consultant to the cruise line. He was in the position when WWF received both the $450,000 grant and the subsequent grant of $200,000.

A grant to the National Marine Sanctuary Foundation gives another clear sense of how the Ocean Fund is used for positive imaging and to grow social capital. Announced in January 2004, the money is for the Nancy Foster Florida Keys Eco-Discovery Centre being built in Key West, Florida. City officials had heard in advance to expect a "six figure" contribution, but the numbers bantered around were generally higher than the $200,000 actually given. A plaque in the visitor's centre will visibly acknowledge Royal Caribbean's contribution. This played a key role in its decision to donate the money,[53] given that the centre will be included in shore excursions from cruise ships stopping at Key West. The advertising and goodwill value of the plaque far exceed the size of the donation.[54]

The Best Money Can Buy

In December 2003 ICCL announced a joint initiative with Conservation International (CI) "to protect biodiversity in top cruise destinations and promote industry practices that minimize the cruise industry's environmental impact."[55] They established the Ocean Conservation and Tourism Alliance (OCTA) with a commitment of $850,000 from ICCL and $250,000 from CI. In January 2004 Royal

Caribbean's Ocean Fund gave CI $50,000 to develop and analyze data on threats to marine species in the Caribbean Basin and create a network of marine-protected areas. On the surface these initiatives are laudable. Scratching below the surface reveals a different picture.

The connection between ICCL and CI began in 2001, but first became visible in March 2003 at the Seatrade Cruise Shipping Convention. ICCL convened a panel on "Cruising, Voyage to Environmental Stewardship: Miles Traveled" at the World Cruise Tourism Summit. The panel was moderated by the executive vice president of ICCL and included presentations by John Hansen, president of the Northwest Cruiseship Association (NWCA); Ernesta Ballard, former lobbyist for the NWCA and recently appointed commissioner of Alaska's Department of Environmental Conservation; Richard Softye, the Holland America vice president who pleaded guilty the following year to confirming environmental audits that were never performed; Craig Vogt, a deputy director with the EPA; and the authors of a newly released "interim summary report" from Conservation International's Center for Environmental Leadership in Business — the center is a partnership between CI and Ford Motor Company. The interim report was the first item and everything that followed, except comments from Mr. Vogt, constituted a cheerleading session about how great the cruise industry is doing.

The report is interesting on several counts. First, it is based almost exclusively on data provided by the cruise industry. Industry critics were not included in the process, and only one person affiliated with an environmental organization was asked to comment on a draft. Her comments had no apparent impact.

Second, the report begins from a pro-cruise industry position. In the foreword the executive director of the Center for Environmental Leadership in Business states:

> What we have found is that the cruise industry's environmental programs and specific actions are more extensive than might be expected given the headlines of the past few years. Many of the major cruise lines have instituted environmental programs and policies that, in some cases, go beyond prevailing regulations and shipping practices.[56]

Sounds good, but the statement is glaringly in opposition to Oceana's launch the following day of a campaign to get Royal Caribbean to stop dumping sewage into the ocean.[57] It was also inconsistent with Mr. Vogt's recommendations that the EPA revise standards for discharge of black water, that it clarify regulations applying to landing of hazardous waste, and that it seek legislative review of both black water and gray water standards. In each the need was to apply more stringent regulations to cruise ships.

Greenwashing Machine for Sale or Rent

Many organizations have names suggesting a warm, fuzzy environmental group: Citizens for the Environment, Evergreen Foundation, the Environmental Conservation Organization, and the National Wetlands Coalition are just a few. But "those aren't green groups. They're lobbying organizations that represent developers, utilities and mining companies that generally want to, ahem, 'free up' public lands."[60] As stated by Jane Feldman of the Las Vegas Sierra Club: "These big groups have resources that us little people in the street — who are really concerned about the environment — don't have …. So they can market this stuff as being environmentally friendly when it's really not."[61] George Monbiot puts it a bit differently when he states, "Environmentalism, like almost everything else, is in danger of being swallowed by the corporate leviathan. If this happens, it will disappear without a trace. No one threatens its survival as much as the greens who have taken the company shilling."[62]

Some add Conservation International to this list. According to the Mexican Center for Political Analysis and Social Economic Research, "Conservation International is 'the Trojan Horse of major transnational corporations and the US government …. CI's strategy is to gather information and buy large tracts of land with high bio-prospecting potential, which allows it to administer natural and/or strategic resources and place them at the disposal of major transnationals.'"[63] New Zealand–based researcher and writer Aziz Choudry is no less critical: "CI's track record suggests a motivation to conserve biodiversity as a resource for bio-prospecting for its private sector partners rather than any concern for the rights of the peoples who have lived with and protected these ecosystems for so long."[64]

Established in 1987, Conservation International's mission is to conserve the Earth's living natural heritage, our global biodiversity, and to demonstrate that human societies are able to live harmoniously with nature. Corporate funders read like a who's who from The Green Life's worst greenwashers: Ford Motor Company, British Petroleum, Starbucks Coffee, and Exxon Mobil. Other supporters include Citigroup, Chiquita, Gap, J P Morgan Chase and

continued:

Co., McDonald's, Sony, United Airlines, Walt Disney, and now Royal Caribbean and the ICCL. The organization will not run short of money. It received a donation of $261 million from Gordon Moore, founder of Intel Corporation in 2001 — dubbed by the media as the biggest ever grant to an environmental organization. Moore chairs CI's executive committee. In 2003/2004 the committee's vice chair was Nicholas Pritzker, whose family's holdings include controlling interest of Royal Caribbean.

What is so bad about an organization that is so well endowed and that projects itself as an environmental leader? The answer depends on perspective. If one believes that business is more concerned with people than profit, and more concerned about the environment than money, then Conservation International is an exemplar to be followed. However, those resistant to blindly trusting large corporations, especially when profit appears to take precedence over social and environmental responsibility, will be skeptical of CI. The issue isn't the stated mission or goals of the organization. It is how the organization works to achieve its goals. It favors voluntary industry-led initiatives that governments should encourage and support.[65] According to Choudry:

> CI claims to work with local communities on conservation alternatives to logging and other environmentally destructive activities — ecotourism and small enterprises to grow and market coffee, exotic foods, chemicals and medicines from the rainforest. Playing the role of an environmental NGO, CI participates in the plunder of the global South. Meanwhile, it willingly collaborates with, and fails to condemn, some of the world's most ecologically destructive corporations and institutions devastating the planet.[66]

In CI's case, with a quarter-billion dollars in net assets, financial capital is closely allied with social capital.

CI's report ends on a high and complimentary note. The oral presentation was even more positive. It concluded that the industry (1) is responding to environmental challenges; (2) should continue its leading practices; (3) should ensure that industry demand doesn't overwhelm the environment; and (4) should establish partnerships for development of a sustainable model for tourism and shipping. The presenters granted media interviews to further tout the industry's positives following the presentation.

By the next Seatrade Convention in March 2004 the ICCL–CI partnership had been cemented and the Ocean Conservation and Tourism Alliance (OCTA) was well underway. The interim report had been further reframed. Michael Crye, ICCL's president, said, "the study found that environmental and waste management protocols of cruise lines go beyond prevailing regulations and, for that reason, encouraged the cruise industry to take a leadership role in promoting sustainable tourism."[58] This is the same industry that had more than 40 environment violations, some exceedingly serious, in the two years leading up to the interim report.[59]

OCTA is focused on four priority areas: apply best practices for wastewater management, establish destination partnerships, promote environmental education, and promote vendor environmental education. A fifth element of the alliance is ICCL piggy-backing on Conservation International's other projects and activities for the "green" transference to the cruise industry. The priorities dissuade attention from what the cruise industry does by focusing on things that project a purely green image — it is excellent public relations. Let us look at each priority in turn.

Best Practices for Wastewater Management
The stated goal, to "improve shipboard technology, specifically accelerate and adopt advanced wastewater purification systems," is laudable. The industry opposed calls from Bluewater Network and Oceana for a commitment to adopt AWTS and it opposed the Clean Cruise Ship Act 2004, which mandates use of these systems. But under OCTA it appointed an independent science panel charged with recommending AWTS (now renamed advanced wastewater purification systems). The panel was announced at the 2004 Seatrade Cruise Shipping Convention in Miami Beach. At least three of the eight panel members are not independent.

The chair of the panel is well-known marine biologist Sylvia Earle. In theory it is an excellent choice. However, she has been the executive director of Conservation International's Marine Programs Division[67] and part of CI's "headquarters leadership since January 2002." The board of directors of which Nicholas Pritzker is vice chair at CI ultimately oversees her work.

Dr. Earle is also notably an Explorer-in-Residence at the National Geographic Society where William K. Reilly of Royal Caribbean is on the board of directors. Mr. Reilly (as EPA administrator) and Dr. Earle (as Chief Scientist at NOAA) both served in George Bush's administration and likely worked together. Whether these connections influence independence is impossible to know.[68]

ALPHABET SOUP

AWTS	Advance Wastewater Treatment Systems
CCSA	Clean Cruise Ship Act of 2004
CELB	CI's Center for Environmental Leadership in Business
CHA	Caribbean Hotel Association
CI	Conservation International
CTO	Caribbean Tourism Organization
EPA	Environmental Protection Agency
FCCA	Florida-Caribbean Cruise Association
ICCL	International Council of Cruise Lines
NOAA	National Oceanic and Atmospheric Administration
NWCA	Northwest Cruiseship Association
OCTA	CI/ICCL's Ocean Conservation and Tourism Alliance

Dr. Earle is joined on the Science Panel by Thomas Lacher, executive director of CI's Center for Environmental Leadership in Business (CELB). CELB issued the interim report in 2003 and houses OCTA. With one-fourth of the science panel employed by CI, the concept of independence does not come readily to mind.

A third member's independence is also not self-evident. Dr. Ellen Prager has worked under contract for Royal Caribbean, served as assistant dean of the Rosenstiel School of Marine and Atmospheric Science and was involved with the School in its partnership with Royal Caribbean, and has represented the cruise industry's position at press conferences. I was present when she attempted to derail Oceana's press conference to announce its cruise ship campaign at the Seatrade Cruise Shipping Convention in 2003.

Establish Destination Partnerships

A second priority of OCTA is to work with local governments and communities to maintain high-quality travel experiences by protecting the natural and cultural assets of cruise destinations. This places expectations on cruise destinations to enhance the experience of cruise passengers landed — a clear benefit to the cruise industry — but the cruise industry's practices are not expected to change. It subverts focus from

There are "several dangers when companies and NGOs get into bed with each other. NGOs risk jeopardizing their legitimacy. Businesses risk wasting resources. But there are also risks to the partnership — that the business simply reaps the reputational reward without making serious efforts to achieve progress."[69]

what the cruise industry does to what cruise destinations can do to serve the cruise industry. Even the tone is paternalistic — the industry will partner to help ports do what they are presumably unable to do on their own, and in the process no attention is given to the garbage, sewage, oily bilge, and other wastes dumped along the destination's coastal waters.

Promote Environmental Education

The priority is again focused away from what the cruise industry does. The goal is to raise guest and crew awareness of and support for critical conservation issues. From the industry's perspective, because cruising contributes a miniscule amount of pollution to the world's oceans, Americans should be more concerned about the runoff from farms in the Midwest that makes its way into the Gulf of Mexico via rivers and tributaries feeding into the Mississippi River. Activities will be designed for children so they can engage in environmental activism at home and work to ensure that local businesses, corporations, factories, and farms are more responsible.[70] The cruise industry isn't discussed because it is viewed as a minor contributor, and a leader in environmental practices and standards. The shell game reframes the problems and the solutions.

Promote Vendor Environmental Education

Just as with the other priorities, promoting vendor environmental education benefits the cruise industry; it focuses on what others do. The explicit goal is to lessen the environmental impact of suppliers not to make cruise ships or cruise corporations more environmentally green through changes in their practices. In fact the only practice of relevance to cruise ships covered by the four priorities is advanced wastewater purification systems.

Green by Association

One advantage to ICCL of OCTA is its instant association with CI's other initiatives, including hotels and resorts and its integration with "green" organizations. Riding CI's coat tails ICCL is directly included in many forums; in others it participates indirectly through CI as its proxy. CI also gives ICCL access to conferences, as was the case with a 2004 conference at Stanford University sponsored by the Center on Ecotourism and Sustainable Development. The Center is a joint program of Stanford University and the Institute for Policy Studies and is housed with The International Ecotourism Society (TIES). TIES and ICCL are linked through the director of Travel and Leisure at CI's CELB, who is directly involved in OCTA and a board member of TIES. With its relatively small financial contribution for co-sponsorship, ICCL gained a platform to present its agenda. The Center on Ecotourism and Sustainable Development website[74] quotes I. F. Stone, Marxist and political activist: "An institute

Clean Cruise Ship Act of 2004

The Clean Cruise Ship Act (CCSA) was introduced in Congress on April 1, 2004. Authored by a coalition of environmentally concerned organizations in cooperation with Senator Richard Durbin and Representative Sam Farr, the act was quickly criticized by the cruise industry for being unnecessary. The ICCL pointed to the industry's leadership in environmental practices and argued that if critics were correct about its behavior, "the pollution produced would represent a fraction of one percent of the coastal water quality issues"[71] and that 80 percent of coastal water problems are from land-based sources. In a form letter to members of Congress, Michael Crye characterizes the Clean Cruise Ship Act of 2004 as "an enormously costly solution in search of a problem."[72]

What does the CCSA say that poses such a threat to the cruise industry? The eight main provisions focus exclusively on pollution from wastewater and oily bilge. Drawing key provisions from legislation in Alaska and the Clean Water Act, the CCSA would:

- prohibit discharges of sewage, gray water, and bilge water within 12 miles of the US shore;
- establish interim discharge standards for treated sewage and gray water discharge outside of 12 miles, and subsequently requires the Coast Guard and EPA to issue final standards taking into account the best available technology, with the goal of zero pollutant discharge by 2015. Certain treatment systems in Alaska would be "grandfathered," due to the investments already undertaken;
- provide for inspection, sampling, and testing;
- require the Coast Guard to establish a three-year program in which independent observers would be placed onboard cruise vessels to monitor compliance of cruise vessels;
- direct the NOAA to help develop and foster commercialization of alternative technologies that would allow for monitoring of cruise ship compliance;
- empower citizens to commence a civil action against anyone in violation of the act; and

continued:

> • authorize appropriations and establish a Cruise Vessel
> Pollution Control Fund.
>
> Bluewater Network responded to ICCL's form letter to members
> of Congress: "Overall, cruise ship pollution is a problem. The fact
> that water pollution generated on land is also significant does not
> remove responsibility for other ocean polluters to change their
> practices. In fact, it increases responsibility, particularly with a leisure
> industry that profits handsomely from clean coastal water and that
> can easily prevent and reduce its contribution to water pollution. To
> quote a recent report by the US Commission on Ocean Policy, 'the
> existence of other sources does not diminish the importance of
> finding better ways to reduce vessel pollution.'"[73]
>
> Note: The act is available online at <thomas.loc.gov>. In the 108th
> Congress see S 2271 and HR 4101.

for the rest of us." I doubt Stone's "the rest of us" includes the ICCL, its membership of convicted felons, and its greenwashing machine.

What Happens to All Those Fines?

It seems perverse, but the cruise industry may benefit from fines for environmental violations. Restitution and community service required by the courts potentially grows further a green image. Three corporations, between 1998 and 2002, were ordered to pay over $20 million toward community service payments for designated environmental service projects, mostly in South Florida.

Among large recipients of restitution and community service are the Fish and Wildlife Foundation, the National Parks Foundation, and NOAA. Because many recipients are not publicly identified, there is potential confusion about when a cruise line is being generous versus giving money because it has to. In an odd way, Holland America got positive press when $20,000 of a $50,000 restitution payment went to the basketball program run by a partnership between the Amateur Athletic Foundation and Watts-Willowbrook and Wilmington Boys Club in Los Angeles.[75] The fine gave free advertising and goodwill.

Payments make their way to organizations by other means. Carnival agreed to contribute $30,000 to a Surfrider–Algalita Research Foundation and $30,000 to a Surfrider-Aquarium of the Pacific wetland project to settle a lawsuit challenging Carnival's inadequate Environmental Impact Report for their Long Beach cruise terminal.[76] Princess Cruises, Holland America Line, and Royal Caribbean vowed to follow California's state-mandated ballasting program and to spend a total $75,000 to research alternative ballast water management methods and technologies to settle a lawsuit brought by the Environmental Law Foundation, Bluewater Network, San Diego BayKeeper, and the Surfrider Foundation. Carnival refused to settle out of court and was subsequently ordered to stop its illegal dumping and to pay civil penalties totaling $200,000. Other examples can be dredged up. The point is that while the cruise industry brags about its support for the environment and environmental causes, often courts, lawsuits, and local governments that stand up to protect the environment dictate this good behavior.

Shaping Public Opinion

The cruise industry's use of the political system and of the media was discussed in Chapter 3. It lobbies legislators and media professionals, contributes to political campaigns, influences media, and uses financial capital to grow its social capital. The industry finds its way onto boards of directors of "green" organizations and funds those that share its viewpoint. It also has moderate success in stacking panels at scientific and industry conferences and conventions with speakers who support the industry. Critics are often invisible or not present at all. How does the cruise industry influence the environmental movement and how does it promote "science"?

Silencing Critics

Royal Caribbean's response to The Ocean Conservancy when it published *Cruise Control* is only one example of saying, in effect, "industry critics do not receive industry money." One other Ocean Fund recipient reports being told its stance would undermine any future funding. Subsequent applications have all failed. Vancouver-based Oceans Blue Foundation (OBF) also learned criticism is not tolerated.

OBF was established in 1996 through a cooperative effort involving the Vancouver Port Authority, Tourism Vancouver, Tourism British Columbia, the Canadian Tourism Commission, private foundations, and business leaders in British Columbia. Its "Cruise Ship Stewardship Initiative" was a key project. The Initiative's goal was that the cruise industry would voluntarily adopt standards of environmentally responsible

"Whenever you visit someone's house, you ask permission from the people who live there. We're asking for cruise lines' cooperation not only based on the law, but also in line with the spirit of aloha and the best interests of all parties, especially the cruise lines hoping to establish a long-term partnership with Moloka'i."

— Walter Ritte, Jr., Hui Spokesperson
January 14, 2002

Moloka'i Gives Greenwashers a Lesson

In October 2002, members of *Hui Hoopakela Aina* ("Rescue the Land") raised concerns about the potential adverse impact on the ocean and reefs off Kuanakaki Harbor when Holland America Line's *Statendam* visits December 28. It would be the first large cruise ship to stop at Moloka'i. In addition to very specific concerns, the community complained about the absence of a proper environmental review. According to Walter Ritte: "There was no process to even ask questions .... It took us six years to move just a traditional fish pond stone, and these guys can drive up to our reef with a floating city with no process at all."[77]

With Holland America remaining steadfast with its plans, Earthjustice represented *Hui Hoopakela Aina* and went to court. It claimed the state had failed to require an environmental review before granting access to Moloka'i. The state and cruise lines said no such review was needed. Earthjustice also asked for a temporary injunction because of the environmental impact. The judge agreed to hear the matter, but not until after the *Statendam* had made its first visit.

On December 28, 2002, *Statendam* dropped anchor off Moloka'i, with more than 100 demonstrators lining the harbor, and many media people watching from beyond. It was a wonderful photo opportunity and one that was well exploited by *Hui Hoopakela Aina*. After a short while *Statendam* sailed on claiming rough water and windy conditions prevented safe use of tenders for transfer of passengers to shore. The *Statendam's* next visit on January 22 was also canceled because the ship was asked by the Coast Guard to assist three people aboard a sinking sailboat.

The Earthjustice lawsuits did not succeed. But there have been no visits to Moloka'i by large cruise ships since.

tourism. In turn OBF would develop an eco-certification program that would identify and reward those lines that took meaningful and positive steps. The initiative began with a series of meetings between the cruise industry and OBF, and included the NWCA, which like OBF was located in Vancouver. These meetings ultimately led to a March 2002 roundtable involving representatives of the cruise industry and environmental organizations. But there was a critical turning point before the roundtable occurred.

In preparation for the roundtable, OBF convened environmental groups and organizations for a discussion of strategy and cooperation. One of the invited groups was Vancouver-based David Suzuki Foundation. The foundation's president came to the meeting with a member of the organization's board of directors. Given the sensitivity of the meeting, her guest was asked whether he had ever been employed by the cruise industry or held a contract with the cruise industry. He responded that his firm, James Hoggan and Associates, was the public relations firm for the NWCA; he also represented the David Suzuki Foundation. Though he said he had much to offer to the meeting, he was told that only environmental nongovernmental (ENGOs) were invited and he would have to leave.[78]

The relationship between OBF and the cruise industry changed shortly thereafter. OBF, previously viewed as a potential partner, was now perceived with caution and suspicion. One of Hoggan's associates apparently undertook a risk assessment of the ENGOs participating in the meeting. He contacted them by telephone; some perceived his boss's association with David Suzuki was used to gain confidence.[79] The associate reportedly led a strategy session with industry people before the joint roundtable with OBF.[80]

The roundtable's potential was limited by a growing distrust of OBF and did not live up to either side's expectations. The positive working relationship of the past had become strained and was further deteriorating. There was posturing, cloaked threats, and other forms of political gamesmanship. With the potential slipping away for industry cooperation on a plan for eco-certification and commitment to greater environmental responsibility, OBF became more confrontational, culminating in an October 2002 report that likened the cruise industry to "Enron of the Seas."[81]

OBF lost most of its funding in retribution. Tourism Vancouver criticized the report and said that "there are better ways of being able to encourage that kind of discussion and debate," that the matter would be raised with the Canadian Tourism Commission (CTC), and that Tourism Vancouver would consider ending support for OBF. A CTC official was also critical, suggesting that "the CTC supports a balanced approach between environmental protection and economic development."[82] OBF closed its doors a year later. The fact that Tourism Vancouver, Tourism British Columbia, the Port of Vancouver, and the NWCA are industry partners, and that the executive vice president of Princess Cruises was a board member of Tourism Vancouver should not go unnoticed. A follow-up to Ocean Blue's October 2002 report, completed in September 2003, was never published.

It was unable to prevent a lecture I gave in Monterey, California, in January 2003, but the cruise industry was present and did try to undermine it. The lecture was held at Monterey Institute of International Studies and co-sponsored by three local organizations.[83] The audience of approximately 100 included Joe Valenti, vice president of marine operations at Crystal Cruises, who was there on behalf of ICCL. When permitted to ask questions he attempted to derail the presentation and was finally asked to sit down to allow others to pose questions. He complied, but not quietly.

Valenti remained in the hall after the lecture and talked with those who would listen. A couple of days later the lecture's sponsors received a four-page single-spaced letter attempting to discredit my presentation and which misrepresented and misquoted what I said. The letter's distribution included the sponsoring organizations, local media, and the harbormaster.[84]

Prefacing his first question, Valenti proudly claimed the industry's high degree of environmental responsibility and pointed to his company, Crystal Cruises, as going beyond the others. While he said this, unbeknownst to the audience, he was aware Crystal had violated a written promise he signed that the *Crystal Harmony* would not discharge anything while in the Monterey Bay Marine Sanctuary — the largest marine sanctuary in the world.

In late February the city of Monterey learned the ship had discharged 36,000 gallons (136,275 liters) of sewage, gray water, and oily bilge the previous October while in the sanctuary. Valenti defended his silence by saying his company had only broken agreements, not laws.[85] ICCL President Michael Crye also dismissed the violation, telling a news reporter the ship's discharge occurred 14 miles from the coast so it wasn't illegal.[86]

The people of Monterey showed their displeasure with Crystal's behavior. They barred Crystal Cruises from entering the port of Monterey for 15 years; the *Crystal Harmony* is barred forever.[87]

Dilution Is the Solution

Some believe the oceans are so vast that a small amount of sewage, oil, or other pollutant is bound to be quickly diluted and have no effect. It is a compelling thought until one considers the volume of waste produced and discharged by a cruise ship. Each of Carnival Corporation's 150,000 passengers per day produce, per day, approximately 48 gallons (180 liters) of accommodation wastewater, 24 gallons (90 liters) of galley and waste treatment plant wastewater, 20 gallons (75 liters) of wastewater from the laundry, and 5 gallons (20 liters) of raw sewage. That's more than 97 gallons (365 liters) per day per person.[88] Not counting crew members, Carnival Corporation ships collectively produce more than 14.5 million gallons (55 million liters) of wastewater every day.

The issue isn't just volume. The constituents of a ship's discharge are also a concern. Alaska's monitoring demonstrated that traditional marine sanitation devices were unreliable in effectively reducing fecal coliform and total suspended solids from sewage, and were ineffective with many conventional pollutants that make their way into a cruise ship's waste stream. That is one reason why Alaska encouraged installation of AWTS on ships in its coastal waters.

There is no debate that AWTS are better than the old-style marine sanitation devices, but there is still a lack of scientific evidence about these systems' effectiveness. Manufacturers admit the AWTS ineffectively deals with nutrient loading, an important consideration given the risk to reefs in warm water locations that are nutrient poor. Nutrient loading is associated with disease and death of reefs. But it isn't the only problem. Alaska's monitoring found the effluent from AWTS fails to meet Alaska Water Quality standards with regard to ammonia, copper, nickel, and zinc.[89] ICCL's executive vice president, Ted Thompson, admits there is no "objective science about what are the real issues and problems. We can't make decisions without that information."[90]

The cruise industry brushes aside these pollutants and problems posed by traditional marine sanitation devices claiming that studies have proven that effluents from cruise ships quickly disperse and pose little to no risk to the marine environment. It is a wonderful and reassuring claim if it were true; however, there is reason for skepticism. According to Craig Vogt of the EPA, an often-cited study found that following discharge of effluent the plumes trailing a ship stay together and are visible for three to five hours as they travel with the Gulf Stream.[91]

In August 2001 the EPA studied dye dispersion behind four large cruise ships off the coast of Miami. The study's goal was to measure the dispersion of the dye and to extrapolate how quickly sewage and other shipboard effluent would become diluted. The study hypothesized specific mixing values and three of the four ships approximated these. The fourth ship, the only one with an Azipod propulsion[92] system, had results that were anomalous. Rather than repeat the study, the results for the fourth ship were ignored and a model was constructed based on how the dye should have dispersed rather than how it actually dispersed. Some scientists would be interested in explaining outliers — the exceptions — rather than excluding them.

The EPA study is the foundation for a subsequent report from the Alaska Department of Environmental Conservation, which asserts that cruise ships pose no risk to Alaska's waters.[93] Based on the report, the industry extrapolates that if dilution is a solution in Alaska's waters, it must be a solution everywhere else. This leap may not be justified for several reasons. Most importantly, the Alaska science panel did not undertake original research. Their study was theoretical — there was no direct analysis of the water quality or biota. Consequently, it is not a study of impacts, as claimed, but instead an academic exercise.

Another problem is that the cruise industry uses the study to justify claims that risks are low given the rate of dilution. But the study itself raises caution given its assumption of a certain level of dilution, which depends upon depth, topography, flushing, salinity, temperature, stratification, etc. If the assumptions are incorrect, then the conclusions are unreliable. What is true for Florida is probably not true for Alaska, and what is true for Alaska is likely not true for Hawai'i, and on and on.

Another serious problem is that the Alaska study does not consider the impact of multiple ships discharging in the same places along the same sea lanes. More than two dozen ships traverse Alaska's and British Columbia's Inside Passage between early May to late September. The cumulative impact and the closed nature of the passage are both relevant considerations.

Is dilution the solution? At this point there are enough reasons to proceed cautiously. A range of factors need consideration, including something as simple as the influence of differential water temperatures of effluent from a ship and the ocean where it is being discharged. The cruise industry wants people to think the OCTA Science Panel will provide all of the answers, but the industry chose the scientists on the panel, and no industry critics are included. But the industry has another mantra: "trust us."

Trust Is Not a Sound Environment Policy

Governments have used two distinct approaches to manage cruise ship wastes. Alaska, Maine, and California have passed legislation. The US Government was headed in that direction with the Clean Cruise Ship Act of 2004, but the bill died in committee. Florida, Hawai'i, and Washington have used memoranda of understanding (MOUs), an approach that relies on voluntary compliance. Canada took a similar approach when it issued quietly and without public announcement in January 2004 guidelines it hopes the industry will respect.[94]

The key element distinguishing the two approaches — legislation versus a MOU — is "trust." California Assemblyman Joe Simitian's warns it might be too late for trust.

Trust Us ... Nudge, Nudge, Wink, Wink

The cruise industry would not dispute that its environmental record in the 1990s was miserable. It says it has learned its lesson, has been hit with a wake-up call, has redoubled their efforts, but violations continued. They may be less habitual, but they still happen and the industry continues to deny, minimize, hide, or make excuses — discharges are "accidental" or "technically legal." When a discharge occurs, they don't measure themselves against what they say they do — such as a claim to not discharge any wastewater within 12 miles of the coast — but fall back to international protocols that permit discharge of raw sewage beyond three miles of the coast and discharge of gray water virtually anywhere. It is easy to

> *Regrettably, cruise lines have a history of violating their agreements and gaming the system. 'Trust us' is no longer an effective environmental policy.*[95]
>
> **— Joe Simitian, California Assemby member, August 2003**

claim "we meet or exceed all international regulations" when official regulations are more lax than company policies, but not more lax than practice.

It is within the context of "accidents" and "mistakes" that the cruise industry asks to be trusted. A MOU is based entirely on trust. The cruise industry promises, as long as government doesn't pass legislation, that it will follow laws and regulations presently in effect. This sort of arrangement has two problems.

First, if the industry is agreeing to follow laws, then a MOU isn't needed. If something is already illegal, it is redundant to promise not to do it. With the exception of Hawai'i, which sets a four-mile limit for wastewater discharge rather than three, none of the MOUs exceeds current US law. The only party appearing to benefit from the MOU is the cruise industry because the state government has not taken the legislative route to regulation and control.

A second problem with an MOU is how to know the party is complying. The MOU is a voluntary statement. There is no monitoring or observing behavior, and there are no penalties (other than those that already exist under state law) to the cruise line for non-compliance. It is not that cruise ships are necessarily violating their word — it is a question of how to know they are keeping their word.

The voluntary nature of a MOU, not surprisingly, maintains the status quo. A 2003 report from the Paris-based Organization for Economic Co-operation and Development (OECD) questions the environmental effectiveness and economic efficiency of voluntary approaches. Focusing specifically on environmental policy, it notes few cases where voluntary approaches have improved the environment beyond a business-as-usual baseline.[96]

Florida's First

The State of Florida was the first to adopt a MOU. The signing ceremony was on December 6, 2001, at a Florida Ocean Alliance Conference on Carnival Cruise Lines' *Fantasy* while it was in port at Port Canaveral. The MOU committed the cruise industry to follow the mandatory guidelines issued by the ICCL six months earlier. It did not go beyond ICCL's guidelines and did not provide for monitoring, enforcement, or penalties.

Hawai'i Follows

Hawai'i was the next to adopt a MOU. In October 2002 the governor signed an agreement with NWCA as the cruise industry's representative. Hawai'i's MOU was identical to Florida's except that Hawai'i required ships to be four miles from the coastline for discharge of treated sewage and wastewater; ships with AWTS are exempt from this requirement. Despite reports of 16 violations of the MOU in the first year, it was renewed in October 2003.

There is a strong movement in Hawai'i to replace the MOU with legislation. Key players include KAHEA (the Hawaiian Environmental Alliance, which works with many groups across the islands) and Sierra Club. Like everywhere else, it is an uphill battle. The cruise industry has lobbyists, and uses campaign contributions and both economic capital and social capital.

In addition to broader issues, KAHEA receives more-than-occasional local reports of visible pollution trailing a cruise ship and frequent complaints of illness that appears associated with cruise ships. Everywhere I spoke during a lecture tour in October 2003 I heard from swimmers and surfers who reported eye and ear infections, sore throats, and gastroenteritis in areas they have used for years for swimming. Illness coincides with a concentration of cruise ship traffic. The cruise industry insists it is not responsible.

Swimming in E. Coli

The Oregon Department of Human Services monitors water quality at 19 beaches along the coast for *Enterococcus* bacteria, a microorganism that has been shown to have a greater correlation in marine water with swimming-associated illnesses than other bacterial organisms. On September 29, 2004, test results for pristine Cannon Beach and Oswald West State Park beach indicated unacceptable levels of the bacteria and an advisory was issued — the first time since monitoring began in late 2003 that the beach had been closed.[97] Follow-up tests on October 4 indicated that levels had dropped from 185 and 213 organisms per100 milliliters of marine water to 10 and 63 at Cannon Beach and 10 and 20 at Oswald.[98] The elevated levels coincided with cruise ships passing by the Oregon coast as they relocated from their summer market in Alaska.

Washington Caves In

The State of Washington signed a MOU with NWCA in April 2004.[99] The route getting to that point was not smooth. Despite assurances given by the cruise industry to the Port of Seattle that Alaska standards would be followed by cruise ships in Washington state waters, *Norwegian Sun* on May 3, 2003, was cited for the illegal discharge of 16,000 gallons (60,567 liters) of raw sewage into the Strait of Juan de Fuca. A couple of months later it was disclosed, contrary to assurances, that ships using the new cruise pier at Terminal 30 were not using low sulfur fuels while in port. The Port of Seattle claimed the requirement was voluntary, but it had previously twice given assurances that use of low sulfur fuels would be a condition for ships docking at Terminal 30. On January 8, 2003, the port assured the Army Corps of Engineers:

> In order to make sure that all applicable air quality standards are met, diesel-powered cruise vessels using T-30 as a homeport will use on-road diesel fuel, or a similar fuel with less than 0.05 per cent sulfur. Turbine-powered cruise vessels will use fuel with no more than 0.5 per cent sulfur while home porting at T-30.[100]

The Port of Seattle is in a conflicted position around these issues because it has dual roles. It develops the cruise terminal and is also the lead agency in regard to environmental issues. Normally different parties would assume these roles because positions on environmental issues can be easily swayed by a developer's self-interested economic considerations.

While cruise lines knew the conditions when they committed to using Terminal 30, they subsequently argued they couldn't use low sulfur fuels. "Tom Dow, vice president of Princess Tours, said his company plans to remedy the problem [in 2004] by substituting two cruise ships with cleaner burning engines for the single vessel calling"[101] but didn't address the current year. He also minimized the impact of Princess' ships stating that his ship would be in Seattle only 18 days, and only for part of those days. "That's a tiny fraction of the parade of ships that enters and exits Puget Sound," he claimed.[102]

These statements get at the core of the problem. A promise was made with regard to fuels used when ships agreed to shift from Vancouver to Seattle, but the promise didn't correspond with practice. There are also promises to do better in future, but without monitoring there is no way to know whether word translates to behavior.

Support for monitoring is found in how it became public that low sulfur fuels were not being used in Seattle. The California legislature was considering a bill that would require use of low sulfur fuel in California state waters. At the last minute cruise industry lobbyists claimed that it wasn't technically possible for a ship to shift to low sulfur fuel.[103] Bluewater Network, being aware of the commitments made to Seattle and of Seattle's requirements, contacted the Port of Seattle and asked: "Aren't the cruise ships using low sulfur fuel there?" The answer: "Well, no they're not. Not any more."[104]

The Legislative Route

The basic issue posed by an MOU versus legislation is whether monitoring and enforcement are necessary. Experience may be the best answer. In jurisdictions where regulations have been legislated and enforced, behavior has changed. Initial violations appear to "test" the resolve to enforce the law, but in time there is compliance. This has been the case in Alaska, was the case with discharge of ballast water in California waters, and was also the experience of Cayman Islands and Bermuda when they began enforcing environmental regulations in the early 1990s.[105]

There is variation in the legislation passed in different jurisdictions. Alaska's 2001 legislation focuses on wastewater (black water and gray water) and air emissions measured by air opacity. Maine's law, passed in March 2004, focuses on wastewater as well. The law was more progressive when introduced to the state legislature, but was compromised as a result of intense lobbying by the cruise industry. The law's weakness may be made up by the strictness of regulations it authorized.[106]

California Takes the Lead

Three pieces of legislation directed at environmental regulation of the cruise industry and introduced in the California state legislature in 2003 (1) prohibited cruise ships from dumping sewage sludge or oily bilge into state waters and sought federal support to extend the bans to marine sanctuaries along the California coast; (2) prohibited ships from using onboard waste incinerators while within 20 miles of the coast and would eventually require ships within 25 miles of the California coast to use low-sulfur diesel fuel; and (3) prohibited the discharge of hazardous waste in state waters and sought federal support to extend the ban to marine sanctuaries along the California coast. The bills were supported by an August 2003 report prepared by the state Environmental Protection Agency and the state Water Resources Control Board, which concluded:

> Many vessels are not complying with international, state or federal standards in regards to handling hazardous materials, garbage, and discharges or treatment of gray water or sewage …. The report said it found "particularly troubling" the discharging of sludge 12 miles out to sea, and the lack of monitoring of shipboard treatment plants and gray water, which had higher fecal coliform counts than treated sewage.[107]

The industry's intense lobbying blocked the bill dealing with low sulphur fuel, and gutted the bill dealing with sewage sludge and oily bilge. The bill dealing with hazardous waste went through with minor change. Key factors that produced changes in the bills, aside from direct political pressure, were concern in the appropriations committee about the economic bottom line rather than the environment; two committee members were facing tough elections in 2004 and didn't wish to be perceived as "too green"; and some suggest a committee staffer unduly influenced the process.

In 2004 the California legislature again considered three pieces of legislation.[108] Each bill captured elements lost in the 2003 legislation, and in some cases was more stringent than provisions a year earlier. All three bills passed despite the cruise industry's strong opposition:

- AB 2093: Prohibits cruise ships from discharging gray water from kitchens, laundries, and showers into state waters. Gray water was previously unregulated and could be discharged anywhere, including ports and harbors.
- AB2672: Prohibits cruise ships from dumping sewage (treated or untreated) into state waters, including effluent from AWTS. Cruise ships could previously dump treated sewage anywhere, including into ports and harbors. Untreated sewage could be dumped just outside state waters.
- AB471: Prohibits cruise ships from burning garbage, paper, sludge, and any other materials in onboard incinerators while operating within three miles of the California coast.

Despite direct lobbying by the cruise industry, Governor Schwarzenegger signed all three bills in September 2004.[109] They are the strictest regulations legislated by a US state.

Federal Government Follows

The Clean Cruise Ship Act of 2004 is a step toward universal regulation of the cruise industry across the US. As already discussed, its focus is limited to wastewater treatment and oily bilge. While some may argue the legislation doesn't go far enough, especially with regard to pollutants and waste streams other than oily bilge and wastewater, it is a beginning. As has become obvious, the cruise industry is not going to adopt or abide by practices of good environmental stewardship without being forced. This makes the legislation, which failed to get out of Committee in 2004, critical for passage in the 109th Session of Congress.

Close to Drinking Water Quality

The cruise industry assures governments and the public that effluent from cruise ships with AWTS is close to drinking water quality. Sounds good, but this is different from the impression given by a vice president in Carnival Corporation who confessed, "Some people drink the water to prove it is clean, but I wouldn't touch the stuff." He went on to say that in his mind the effluent was still sewage and not fit to drink. I agreed. But it is apparently fit for consumption by the environment, sea life, and who knows whom else. Even if the systems worked as claimed, relatively few ships have them — most still have marine sanitation devices that have been demonstrated to be unreliable. And then there are all of the other waste streams from a cruise ship.

The cruise industry would lead us to believe that cruise ships are environmentally neutral. The industry projects this image through its lobbyists, public relations campaigns, infiltration of environmental organizations, and advertising, but it is inconsistent with its pattern of behavior. Saying "trust us, we've changed" is like the child who warned the sky is falling. The cruise industry needs to devote more effort to changing its behavior and less to isolating and attacking those who watch what it does and who call public attention to contradictions between what it says and what it does.

8

Paradise Lost at Sea

PROBLEMS ON CRUISE SHIPS MAY NOT BE FREQUENT, but they happen. The following (among other more minor things) occurred in three weeks while writing this book:

- On September 8, 2004, seven crew members from the *Empress of the Seas* were seriously injured after a lifeboat plunged 60 feet from the deck of the ship during a training exercise when it was docked in Bermuda. All miraculously survived, but four were still in hospital a week after the accident including one who had been airlifted to the US immediately after the accident and who remained in intensive care. The ship's agent assured local media in Bermuda that the ship had adequate lifeboat space despite loss of the one involved in the accident.[1] While it undoubtedly did, that may not always be the case.[2]

- On September 20 and 21, 2004, Princess Cruises reported health outbreaks on both coasts of Canada. On the west coast *Sun Princess* had two weeks in a row with norovirus outbreaks that made 265 passengers and crew sick. In the east *Regal Princess* reported an increased number of passengers (47 of 1,537 or 3.06 percent) with gastrointestinal illness. A year before *Regal Princess* arrived in New York City two days early from a transatlantic cruise to be thoroughly sanitized. Over 300 passengers and 45 crew members reported illness.

- On September 26, 2004, the 500-passenger *Van Gogh* collided with an oil tanker in foggy conditions off the southern coast of Spain. There were no injuries. Five years earlier the 1,800-passenger *Norwegian Dream* collided with a cargo ship, *Ever Decent*, in clear conditions in the English Channel. There were no injuries but each cruise ship required major repairs.

- On September 28, 2004, Holland America Line's *Rotterdam* was greeted by ambulances when it arrived in Halifax after the ship encountered monster waves generated by hurricane Karl in the North Atlantic. About a dozen passengers were taken to hospital with suspected fractures and severe bruising. In total, 90 people (including five crew members) reported minor injury. The encounter was made worse because the engines were shut off when engineers noticed sediment was accumulating in lubricating filters; this meant the ship lost momentum and stabilizers became ineffective. The ship was dead in the water for almost three hours.[3]

Cruise ships are very complicated. The ship lost power for three hours. I was evacuated from my hotel in Washington three times recently because of false fire alarms and I didn't see any stories about it. But relatively insignificant [cruise] events make world wide news.[4]

— **Micky Arison, CEO Carnival Corporation, October 2000**

Each of these incidents reminds us that things go wrong on cruise ships. These ships may not be prone to any greater calamity than other modes of transportation or other resort vacation spots, but they do present unique problems and concerns.

Cruising Is Safe

According to ICCL the US Coast Guard says the cruise industry is the safest form of transportation.[5] The cruise industry has to its credit increased passenger safety in many ways. Many changes have been responses to negative public attention or required by international conventions or regulatory bodies. ICCL's commitment in November 2000 to install local sounding smoke alarms is an example. The cruise industry opposed a National Transportation Safety Board (NTSB) recommendation following three cruise ship fires in 1996. One of these fires was on the *Universe Explorer*, in which five crew members died and 67 crew and two passengers were injured.[6] The industry dropped opposition to the NTSB, issued a press release, and garnered positive media attention, but left unstated a timetable for when the commitment would be fulfilled.

ICCL issued two statements on July 27, 1999. One was a commitment to redouble efforts to improve its environmental performance. The other was a "zero tolerance policy for crimes committed onboard ships"[7] — more specifically, a zero tolerance for sexual assaults.

The industry was under a microscope by the *New York Times* and other media for a range of problems.[8] The issue of sexual assaults hit front-page headlines in July 1999 during discovery in a case where a nurse on board a Carnival ship was reportedly raped by the chief engineer. Carnival Cruise Lines and Royal Caribbean International together disclosed receiving 166 reports of sexual assault between August 1994 and August 1998. Only a handful of cases had ever been reported in the media. None of the 166 reports involved passenger-on-passenger assaults.[9]

Despite the zero-tolerance policy, assaults appear to continue. FOX News at 10 (Los Angeles) aired a story on February 21, 2005 saying that Royal Caribbean had logged 173 sexual assault complaints between 1998 and 2002. There is no single pattern among these or among the six sexual assaults reported in the media between June 1 and December 31, 2004. Some involve children, some involve two passengers; in others it is only crew, and some involve crew and passenger. Other cases are undoubtedly reported to lawyers or go entirely unreported. Under a zero tolerance policy, one assumes none of this is going on. Unfortunately, there are still victims whose complaints about their cases are not handled satisfactorily.

Stowaways Beware

O'Neil Persaud somehow got past the security system and boarded RCI's *Adventure of the Seas* when it was in St. Maarten on July 19, 2002. The 31-year-old Canadian was discovered after the ship set sail for St. Thomas. He was taken to a holding cell. The ship docked at St. Thomas early the next day and notified port personnel there was a stowaway aboard. About noon, a call was placed to the 9-1-1 emergency hotline to report a death on board the ship. Five security guards had accidentally smothered Mr. Persaud to death.[10]

What was known was that Mr. Persaud died after being tranquilized. But what wasn't clear was whether he was alive when the ship docked, and whether he was tranquilized before or after the ship arrived in St. Thomas. Local authorities investigated but did not pursue the case. Many questions remain for Mr. Persaud's family.

Limited Solace with SOLAS

The Convention for Safety of Life at Sea (SOLAS) is an international treaty that sets minimum standards for shipboard safety, including fire safety, construction guidelines, and recommendations for life-saving equipment. Each of the 138 nations subscribing to the International Maritime Organization (IMO) is responsible to ensure that vessels sailing under their flags comply with the treaty's requirements.

Despite SOLAS problems remain. Cunard was probably as surprised as anyone when the British Marine and Coastguard Agency ordered the *Queen Mary 2* in June 2004 to fit extra sprinklers in the ship's 1,300 passenger cabins. A BBC investigation revealed material used in the ships' bathroom units did not meet international fire safety regulations. A short-term remedy was fitting all cabins with an extra smoke detector, but the ship must also add extra sprinklers in bathrooms. The ship is estimated to contain 140,000 pounds (63,503 kilograms) of the material causing concern.[11]

Speaking about NCL's **Norway,** *May 2001:*

The Coast Guard said more than 100 leaks had sprung in the main pipe feeding the giant ship's fire sprinkler system. The leaks, located where welds in the pipe are, were patched with temporary "soft patches" of rubber .... A fire could melt the rubber patches, and the compromised pipe's loss of pressure would threaten the entire sprinkler system.[14]

Sprinklers were also a problem on Holland America Line's *Zaandam* shortly after it began sailing. In May 2001 a crew member noticed a sprinkler head missing from a passenger cabin and upon investigation found that a branch of the sprinkler system did not connect to the main water supply. The problem was corrected.[12]

At that same time NCL's *Norway* was prevented from sailing after US Coast Guard inspectors found more than 100 leaks in the ship's fire safety system. NCL said in its press statement that passenger safety is its first priority. But had a previous passenger not reported to the Coast Guard what he had seen, the ship would have sailed. The ship was out of service for a week to undergo full repairs.[13]

No less serious were problems experienced by *Marco Polo* and *Pacific Sky*. In February 2003 Orient Lines' *Marco Polo* (owned by Star through NCL) hastily returned to Ushuaia after being blown into shallow waters while in the South Shetland Islands. It was found upon inspection to have three cracks (13, 10, and 5.5 feet [4, 3, and 1.7 meters] long by 0.75-inches [2 centimeters] wide). The ship had a double-hull bottom, so water was impeded from entering. The head of the Coast Guard station at Ushuaia said the ship was never at risk, "but it wasn't in condition to continue sailing."[15] Three-inch-thick plates were welded over the cracks at Ushuaia and the cruise continued.

A month later P&O's *Pacific Sky*[16] made an emergency return to Auckland after taking on water. The 46,000-ton ship was carrying 1,470 passengers on what was to have been an 11-day cruise to Tonga, Samoa, Fiji, and back to Auckland, but it turned around after sailing 310 miles. Passengers weren't immediately told they were heading home, but many suspected things weren't right.[17] Ironically an inspector from Lloyd's Register was on board to ensure that a leak found when the ship sailed from Sydney to Auckland had been properly repaired. The *Pacific Sky* struggled back to port with 165 tons (65,000 gallons) of water leaked into an internal tank.[18] The company said the ship was in no danger, but passengers claimed the cinema was closed because of water. In a different incident in November 2004, a P&O spokesperson commented, "60 tons is a lot of water." That gives perspective to 165 tons.

Pacific Sky periodically returns in the news. Up to 200 passengers were sickened by Norwalk-like virus on its Christmas cruise in 2003. The cruise before was marked by a rowdy bunch of high school graduates who, by passenger accounts, were drunk and disorderly, harassed and disregarded the staff, threw deck chairs overboard, and called "man overboard" the night before arriving in Sydney. The captain stopped the ship, ordered a headcount, and sent a boat down to the water, only to discover that it was a hoax. The cruise after, the New Years Follies cruise, had 60 passengers report gastrointestinal illness. There were also two outbreaks of gastrointestinal illness in May 2004.

Pacific Sky returned to the news in November 2004 when it turned back to Brisbane from a 12-day South Pacific cruise with scheduled stops at New Caledonia, Fiji, and Vanuatu. The ship developed engine problems and couldn't operate at full speed. Its departure had been delayed because of a faulty boiler, and further delayed to repair a damaged gearbox in the starboard engine. A problem with the starboard engine was the reason given for the cruise being aborted. Passengers arranged deck chairs to spell out SOS when *Pacific Sky* limped back into Brisbane's harbor. They complained that parents back home knew more than they did about what was happening.[19] Nine days later the ship was delayed at Brisbane for 15 hours after jellyfish clogged the engine's water intake.[20]

We're Concerned for Your Health

Though not required by international maritime law, all modern cruise ships maintain an infirmary and usually have at least one physician and one nurse on board, neither of whom is technically a cruise line employee. They work under contract and the cruise line claims limited to no liability for their services. The exact limit of cruise line liability continues to be tested in court.

Under pressure from the American Medical Association, which at the time had called on the US Congress for the development of medical standards for cruise ships, ICCL adopted industry guidelines for medical facilities and personnel on cruise ships in 1996. They were updated November 1997. The AMA also called for greater passenger awareness about shipboard medical facilities. It wasn't a matter that medical facilities were inadequate, notwithstanding concerns raised by *New York Times* reporter Douglas Frantz.[21] The problem is many passengers assume greater medical capability on board than is practically available. The result is that expectations or need for medical care exceeds capability. A cruise ship infirmary is more akin to a neighborhood clinic than it is to a hospital emergency room.

The nature of a cruise ship presents a health challenge no matter what medical facilities are on board. Though not normally problematic, the ship's confined nature and the tendency for passengers to constantly socialize make it the perfect incubator when illness is present. The risk is exponentially magnified when weather is poor and passengers spend more time indoors. Consequently outbreaks of influenzas and colds are not uncommon. These closed situations also make for easy transmission of

Don't Let the Bedbugs Bite

There has been much recent attention to the return of bedbugs in hotels. The American Hotel and Lodging Association obviously downplays the bedbug threat. But exterminator Orkin Inc. says there's been a steady increase in cases nationwide: from zero in 2000, to 390 in 33 states in 2003. Cruise ships are not immune.

In 2002 I heard from a cruise ship passenger on a major North American cruise line. She told of at least three rooms on the ship infested with bedbugs. The passenger had complained before she and her parter realized what the problem actually was, and their room was cleaned and sprayed with insecticides. After insisting, they were moved to another room the following day. It was only then that they learned that their former neighbors had the same problem and their rooms had been extensively cleaned. But they had not officially been told about bedbugs.

Incidents such as these are difficult to track because passengers are often compensated and sign confidentiality agreements that require silence. However two cases were widely reported in April 2005. One involved an infestation on Royal Caribbean's *Jewel of the Seas*. The other was on Carnival Cruise Lines' *Carnival Victory*.[22] These remind consumers to always be on guard, no matter where you choose to stay.

---

illnesses. It is one factor in the rash of outbreaks of gastrointestinal disease attributed to Norwalk-like virus.

The Barf Boat

There have always been health outbreaks on cruise ships. Several times there have been multiple outbreaks on the same ship — *Royal Odyssey* in March 1997 and *Regal Princess* in 1998; both had three successive cruises with illness traced to a Norwalk-like virus.

You know it is a bad year for gastrointestinal illness onboard cruise ships when a ship is nicknamed "the barf boat."[23]

The number of cases was relatively stable — 6 or 7 outbreaks per year — until 2002 when the figures exploded.[24] In four months, between September and the end of the year, cruise ships reported 22 outbreaks affecting 1,350 passengers and 218 crew members. Incidents where large numbers of people became ill received the most attention.

- Holland America Line's *Amsterdam* had outbreaks on four successive cruises (October 1–November 21). In sum 464 passengers and 56 crew members reported their illness to the ship's infirmary.

- *Disney Magic* had outbreaks on two successive cruises (November 16–30) affecting 439 passengers and 23 crew members.

- P&O's *Aurora* was denied permission to dock at Philipsburg, St. Maarten (December 10) because 269 passengers and 24 crew members had contracted a stomach illness. The incident came a day after four people working in St. Lucia's tourism industry reported stomach illness, after meeting cruise visitors when the ship docked there two days before.[25]

- Carnival Cruise Lines had two cruises affected. *Fascination* reported 190 passengers and 13 crew members ill on December 2; 224 passengers and 39 crew members became ill on the *Carnival Conquest's* cruise ending December 15.

With so much negative attention in such a short time, the cruise industry reacted predictably with a focused and concerted public relations campaign. To fully appreciate what the cruise corporations were able to do, it is helpful to have some understanding about norovirus.

"Bug Ship" Shunned[26]

Spain shut its border with the British colony of Gibraltar for the first time in two decades on November 3, 2003, when P&O's *Aurora* with more than 550 passengers sickened by norovirus arrived in Gibraltar's harbor. Those who were judged to be healthy were allowed to disembark in Gibraltar, but the frontier to Spain was closed and their travel severely restricted. Three days before, the same passengers were forced to stay on board while the ship took on supplies at Piraeus (Athens). Local authorities would not allow passengers to disembark. P&O Cruises said the infection was believed to have been brought on board by a passenger.

It All Began in Norwalk, Ohio

Norovirus refers to a family of unclassified, small, round-structured viruses, often called Norwalk-like virus (NLV). It is named after Norwalk, Ohio, where the first outbreak was documented in a school cafeteria. Today at least 101 viruses are known within the norovirus family; 99 of these affect humans.[27]

Norovirus causes nausea, vomiting, diarrhea, and abdominal pain, and sometimes a headache and low-grade fever. The disease develops 24–48 hours after contaminated food or water is consumed and lasts for 24–60 hours. A person, even when asymptomatic, continues to shed the virus for as long as two weeks. For this reason, and because the virus follows a fecal-oral route, conscientious and correct hand washing is essential on cruise ships, as anywhere else. The concept is simple, but not always practiced. More than 30 percent of travelers using public restrooms at airports don't wash their hands;[28] these same travelers end up on cruise ships.

Norovirus can be transmitted through water or through food prepared or served by an infected food handler — this was the norm in the 1980s and 1990s. Forty-two percent of outbreaks in one Centers for Disease Control (CDC) study were attributed to water or food; only 12 percent were linked to person-to-person contact.[29] Food and water contamination have clearly been reduced as a result of the Vessel Sanitation Program's twice-yearly inspections, but the scores indicate cleanliness and not the risk for illness from norovirus.[30]

Norovirus is also transmitted person-to-person through direct physical contact or from contact with a surface that was previously touched by someone who had the virus on his hands — recall that it follows a fecal-oral route. This makes it as nasty a challenge for a cruise ship as it is for institutional settings such as nursing homes, hospitals, schools, and camps. Once the virus "goes public," the immediate goal is containment. The actual source of the virus may never be determined.[31]

The Centers for Disease Control Weighs In

With increased media attention to the "cruise ship virus," as it became labeled in late fall 2002, the CDC increased its flow of information including two telebriefings. The first, on November 27,[33] supported the cruise industry's view. Blame for the illness was placed on passengers coming aboard; its spread was explained by person-to-person contact, and the media was reassured that the CDC had figures that showed that the rates of infection were actually going down. When challenged to supply numbers, none was provided, but an article was soon published supporting the claims made. The research, however, covered 1990 to 2000 and said nothing about the recent rash of illness.[34]

The second telebriefing was on December 12 and also supported the cruise industry's view but gave some insights into a recently released study. The study reported on five outbreaks of norovirus on cruise ships in 2002. Person-to-person

Repeat after Me: "Passengers Bring It with Them"

I received an e-mail from a passenger on board the *Regal Princess* telling about an outbreak of norovirus during the transatlantic crossing from Copenhagen to New York City. This was August 29, 2003, and the ship had just canceled its stop in St. John's, Newfoundland, to arrive early in New York City for two days of intensive cleaning and sanitization. More than 300 passengers and 45 crew members had reported to the infirmary that they were ill on the transatlantic cruise.

The cruise line used the industry's mantra saying it believed one or two passengers brought the illness aboard in Copenhagen.[32] But a passenger disembarking the ship in Copenhagen e-mailed me and said, "During our trip, several days of overflowing toilets in the public restrooms, as well as in the passengers' cabins occurred. Carpets were changed; plastic over carpet in several areas seemed the norm. Several crew members fell ill including our assistant waiter who was quarantined for days."

transmission appeared likely in four outbreaks, but the common element for those who became ill in the fifth outbreak was lunch served at the embarkation buffet — the illness was likely food-borne.[35] The study mentioned disincentives for crew members to present to the infirmary with illness because they are likely to be quarantined and lose pay during the time they are ill. CDC researchers found "that when we surveyed all of the crews, that there were a significant number who had not reported to the infirmary, although they were required to by virtue of being employed by the vessels."[36]

A key conclusion of the CDC's study represents a view that is rarely acknowledged by the cruise industry:

> Cruise ship outbreaks demonstrate how easily noroviruses can be transmitted from person to person in a closed environment, resulting in large outbreaks. The continuation of these outbreaks on consecutive cruises with new passengers and the resurgence of outbreaks caused by the same virus strains during previous cruises on the same ship, or even on different ships of the same company, suggests that environmental contamination and infected crew members can serve as reservoirs of infection for passengers.[37]

The cruise industry's public relations campaign deflects attention away from the ship and its crew.

The Cruise Industry Goes on the Offensive

The ICCL laid out its strategy at the 2003 World Cruise Tourism Summit on March 3, 2003. An almost-inspirational video was shown about the situation in which the industry found itself and the way that it successfully responded on the public relations front.

> *The ship is not sick. There are sick people getting on the ship.*[38]
>
> — **Rose Abello, vice president of Public Relations, Holland America Line**
> **November 12, 2002**

At the start, the industry was depicted as receiving an inordinate amount of attention for a series of norovirus outbreaks on cruise ships. Illness on cruise ships had been the topic of stories on mainstream television: Inside Edition, CNN, NBC, and many others. The industry had even become the brunt of jokes on late night television — Jay Leno and David Letterman among others. Evening news with increasing frequency showed people who had become sick on board ships.

But there is also misinformation. Peter Greenberg on the 8 AM segment of NBC's *Today Show* on November 22, 2002, really messed up. He inflated the number of passengers reporting ill on *Amsterdam*; incorrectly assumed that two affected ships operated from the same port; contradicted the CDC's conclusions, which ruled out food or water as a source; and suggested that terrorism could not be ruled out. Greenberg's misinformation was a source of humor and a turning point in the video. This is when the industry began its offensive.

The industry's media strategy had three elements: provide talking points to cruise executives and others in a position to present the industry's position, arrange as many media interviews as possible, and flood the media with positive information about the cruise industry. It proactively distributed pictures and video footage showing ships being disinfected, and engaged in positive messaging. Carnival Cruise Lines' president, Bob Dickinson, framed the problem as part of a national epidemic and said there was no cause-and-effect with regard to norovirus on cruise ships. Colin Veitch, NCL's CEO, pointed to the incidence of norovirus in the general population to minimize the problem as unique to cruise ships. The industry also enlisted the help of third parties in its campaign, most significantly the Centers for Disease Control. It helped promote the idea that people get sick on airplanes too, but they don't experience symptoms until they get home so they don't associate it with air travel.

Cruise Ships with Three or More Gastrointestinal Outbreaks, 2002–2004

Ship Name	Cruise Line	# Outbreaks
Amsterdam	Holland America Line	7*
Nantucket Clipper	Clipper Cruises	7
Norwegian Dream	Norwegian Cruise Line	5
Ryndam	Holland America Line	4
Norwegian Crown	Norwegian Cruise Line	4
Pacific Sky	P&O Australia	4
Sun Princess	Princess Cruises	4
Disney Magic	Disney Cruise Line	3
Veendam	Holland America Line	3

* Includes one outbreak caused by E. coli brought aboard with bunkered water. **Source:** <www.cruisejunkie.com>

ICCL's video concluded with "Smooth Seas Ahead." The industry successfully fought off the negative media attention and reframed the issue. Its message was two-pronged: cruises are a great vacation at a good price, and why worry about norovirus — it is as common as the common cold. You can't argue with that. The media became desensitized to the issue and most of the 79 outbreaks affecting 6,630 people in 2003 and 2004 went unnoticed.[39]

Is It as Simple as "Passengers Bring It with Them"?

The assertion that passengers bring norovirus with them implies that the cruise industry is as much a "victim" as the passenger. While it proudly says that containment is within its control, the idea that passengers bring it on board and spread it around, places the problem beyond its control. This resists assignment of blame, presumably including liability for the outbreaks. As the cruise industry might say, "We're doing everything humanly possible, so don't penalize us."

The underlying assumption is that outbreaks are random. But that is not the case. Certain ships and certain cruise lines appear more prone to outbreaks than others. There is no ready explanation, but it presents an interesting area for study: is it a ship's design, the nature of the passengers, the mix of crew members, or something else?

Another area given inadequate attention is the role of crew members as reservoirs for the illness. Even if a worker is quarantined, she or he returns to work after 48 to 72 hours of being symptom-free; however, the virus continues to be shed for as long as two weeks. It can easily be reintroduced and/or carried over from one cruise to another. Crew members as much as passengers can be the source of person-to-person contact. The frequent number of outbreaks that carry from one cruise to another supports their role in the spread of disease.

Four or More Reported Health Outbreaks by Cruise Line, 2002–2004

Cruise Line	# Outbreaks
Holland America Line	21
Princess Cruises	13
Norwegian Cruise Line	12
Carnival Cruise Lines	10
P&O	8
Royal Caribbean International	7
Celebrity Cruises	6
Clipper Cruise Line	5
Cunard Line	4
Disney Cruise Line	4
Others	22
TOTAL	112

See Appendix E for a complete breakdown by cruise line and by ship.

The cruise industry argues that this position is not supported by the relatively small number of reported illness among crew members as compared to that of passengers. The fact is that crew members as far back as the 1980s and 1990s reported illness at levels lower than did passengers. Perhaps they are less susceptible to gastrointestinal attacks, are stoic when they suffer, or are responding to disincentives to reporting illness. If they depend on tips, they are not paid when they don't work. With the likelihood that ill passengers will be confined to their cabins for 48 hours or more, there are increasing anecdotal reports that passengers are not reporting illness either.

Another interesting element to add to the mix is not all people can be infected by norovirus. Research reported in 2003 found that 29 percent of a study population lacked the gene required for norovirus binding and did not become infected after receiving a dose of the virus.[40] Because there is not a vaccine for norovirus, and because resistance does not accrue from infection (getting it once does not provide antibodies to resist subsequent infection), knowledge that some people are naturally immune is interesting. Its implications are hard to anticipate.

It's a Matter of Trust

Other things go wrong on cruise ships, but few are routine. There is the 95-year-old legally blind man and his 82-year-old traveling companion who were involuntarily disembarked from *Zaandam* in Ketchikan, Alaska, in summer 2003 after the younger man reported his usual gastrointestinal sensitivities (for which he took medication) to the infirmary during a norovirus outbreak. They were taken by taxi from the ship to a hotel and left to carry their luggage up several flights of stairs and around the hotel. There were no porters. Assurances on board that a cruise line representative would assist the men in Ketchikan and upon their return to their home airport were not realized. The men got home safely, though one reinjured his back from handling baggage.

On a more mundane level, a fellow arrived in his suite and found the thermostat broken. He reported it and asked for another suite if it could not be fixed immediately. They offered another suite nearby, which he took. It was also warm so he again called for a technician who installed another thermostat and promised that it would eventually cool the suite. The guest told the technician, as he was leaving, about the broken thermostat in the other suite. Not long after, there was a knock at his door:

> When I answered my door knock, I was shocked to find the technician along with several senior officers and security officers at the door. The senior officer told me that the technician reported that I was breaking the air conditioners and that he would have to disembark us before the ship left port.[41]

The guest was able to explain the situation and stay on board.

A guest on NCL's *Norwegian Star* was not as convincing in February 2004. She and her husband were detained and forced to disembark at the next port when the cruise line claimed that she was working as an undercover agent for her employer, a New York City law firm that was pursuing a class action suit for NCL workers regarding a pay dispute. The detained employee worked as a paralegal in the firm's bankruptcy department. She launched her own lawsuit for being detained and disembarked.[42]

Other problems are equally as individual.[43] For example, an 82-year-old man participated in "Who Wants to Be a Cunard Zillionaire?" aboard the *Queen Mary 2* in February 2004 and is now suing the company for $1 million. The publicity for the contest allegedly included the representation that the winner would receive up to

$1 million in cash, so when Owen Schwam answered the final question correctly he expected to be paid. That decision will ultimately be made by a Florida Circuit Court.[44] I another case, a 68-year-old German pensioner sued a travel company after a cruise ship steward threw his dentures into a bin. He claimed the action left him speechless and barely able to eat for two weeks, but the court turned down his claim.

Some problems are more routine. Overbooking is one of them. Just like airlines, cruise lines overbook their ships and offer passengers incentives to give up their room on one cruise to sail on another, or to upgrade to free space someplace else on the ship. But some are also displaced. The problem hit the news with a splash in Baltimore in late summer 2004. "Hundreds of people were bumped from eight oversold cruises on the 2,121-passenger _Carnival Miracle_ in September and October."[45] Unlike the airlines, there are no federal guidelines for the cruise industry to follow when they find themselves overbooked.

Two additional areas stand out from letters I receive: itinerary changes and the application of the Americans with Disabilities Act.

I Thought We Were Going to Helsinki

Many people complain of altered itineraries. Sometimes changes are made for weather, other times due to a mechanical problem. In either case, there's not much you can do other than grin and bear it. Despite protestations and disappointments when one Caribbean port is substituted for another it isn't all that bad, especially considering the alternatives. But imagine arriving for the start of a cruise and learning you were going to Amsterdam instead of St. Petersburg, Russia.

Passengers were not only angry about the change in itinerary but that the decision had been made two days before the ship departed on April 28, 2003, and it had not been communicated to passengers. As late as April 25 those who called NCL to inquire were told the itinerary was a go. The cruise began in Dover but instead of sailing to St. Petersburg, Helsinki, and Talinn, Estonia, the itinerary was changed at the last minute to include Amsterdam, Norway, and Germany. Ironically, some passengers flew to London from their home in Amsterdam to take the cruise. Despite passenger discontent, the company refused all requests for refund, including those who would have chosen not to take the cruise.

A group of passengers pursued a class action suit, but it fell through.[47] The leaders of the petition encouraged passengers to

---

"We were really looking forward to it but it's not to be."

Passenger John Miller after announcement that the 103-day voyage of P&O's _Aurora_ was canceled. Passengers had spent the previous ten days on board the ship waiting to see whether the propulsion system could be fixed.[46]

file small claims actions in their home states, which many did. NCL called most to settle before trial.

NCL's original offer was usually for 50 percent of the amount of the suit paid as vouchers to use on future cruises. Very few accepted the vouchers — almost all vowed they would not sail on NCL again and would tell everyone they knew not to sail on NCL — and most received checks. Some passengers negotiated up from the 50 percent initial offer by citing special circumstances (e.g., meeting friends in Helsinki, celebrating a 50th wedding anniversary). Interestingly some passengers included the airfare, value of frequent flyer mileage, and other expenses and some did not; NCL settled for 50 to 70 percent of the amount of the suit, not the amount of the cruise fare.

NCL attended trials for a few passengers. Passengers filing in the small claims courts in Miami-Dade County did not receive a settlement offer. In two cases, the passengers lost; the other case is pending.

NCL attended two small claims hearings in California, though settled with other passengers in California. One case was thrown out because the cruise had been purchased through an online travel agency operating out of state. The court ruled it had no jurisdiction. The other case was brought by Emily Frankel, one of the leaders in the original petition for the class action suit. In her case the judge stated in open court that NCL should have advised the passengers before the sailing that the itinerary had been changed, and he ruled for Frankel. The judge asked Frankel for the value of the substitute cruise, and Frankel said one-half. The judge gave her what she asked for — $1,119.48

The legal issue in this case was not whether NCL or any other cruise line has the right to change an itinerary under adverse weather conditions. The issue is that NCL had knowledge before embarkation in Dover that the itinerary would be drastically different and it waited until embarkation day to tell passengers. Refusing refunds further eliminated options to travel to the itinerary that was marketed and sold by NCL.

Leave Your Wheelchair at the Door

The cruise industry's compliance with the Americans with Disabilities Act (ADA) continues to be an issue and is a source of frustration and inconvenience for many using a wheelchair or other aid to assist with mobility.

Concern for whether the ADA applies to foreign-flagged cruise ships surfaced in 1992, soon after the 1990 Act became law. It was openly discussed after a 1996 report by the Volpe National Transportation Systems Center, which concluded that all passenger-ship newbuildings should comply with the ADA, and emphasized "that owners and operators of existing passenger ships in most cases also could be, and should be, required to comply with the act by retrofitting their vessels."[49] While the

Clinton Administration stated its commitment to full implementation of the Americans with Disabilities Act, the foreign-flagged cruise industry emphatically insisted the ADA did not apply to its ships.

The standoff brought lawsuits. In a 1998 suit, Carnival allegedly discriminated against disabled passengers because shipboard amenities do not provide adequate access or require the aid of an assistant.[50] A settlement was reached in April 2001. Carnival Cruise Lines agreed to make up to 25 cabins on each ship handicapped-accessible, which included widening doorways to 31 inches and having roll-in showers in bathrooms. The renovations are to be completed by 2007.[51] Two other Carnival Corporation lines, Holland America and Costa, were reportedly settling suits with similar commitments.

In the meantime the US Justice Department intervened in 1999 in a case thrown out by a Florida court. A woman was assured before embarkation that her wheelchair could be accommodated on board, but when she embarked she found the bathroom was not wheelchair accessible — she was given two buckets to use instead — and was shut out of excursions. She sued Premier Cruises, but a Florida court ruled that the ADA did not apply to foreign-flagged ships. When the case was appealed, the Justice Department stated in a friend-of-the-court brief that the ADA does in fact apply. In June 2000 the appeals court ruled that cruise ships registered abroad must comply with the ADA.[52]

Before the ruling the ICCL maintained that "members are striving to make their ships accessible, but they don't believe they are legally bound by the ADA at this time because no access rules have been issued."[53] After the ruling it stated that there were no ADA regulations specific to the passenger vessel industry for accessibility, but it would willingly comply with whatever ADA regulations were established.[54] In the meantime cruise companies were left to do as they wished.

Other cruise lines were also targets. NCL settled a suit filed in January 2001 by a passenger turned away at the dock after *Norwegian Sea*'s doctor told him he might injure himself while on board because he was blind and traveling without an assistant.[55] After the Justice Department received two other identical complaints, NCL settled by changing its policy.

Through all of this, the question of whether the ADA applies to foreign-flagged cruise ships remains in the air. A California court threw out a case against Crystal Cruises in March 2004 saying that the ADA did not apply. A woman with spina bifida learned upon embarkation that *Crystal Harmony* was not handicapped-accessible, contrary to assurances from the cruise line.

> 'It is incredibly disappointing to spend all of that money on a cruise only to find as soon as you leave port that the ship fails to provide basic access to its common areas .... For example, there was a threshold that was really hard to

get over to get to the most important deck of the ship, where the buffet, bar and grill, pool and hot tub, and the best viewing areas were located.' Crew members kept removing portable ramps that would've provided access through this threshold, and her complaints to the ship's concierge were in vain. At one point, she fell over in her wheelchair trying to traverse the entryway.[56]

Donald Spector, a real estate broker who uses a wheelchair because of a tumor on his spinal cord, had a similar experience on an NCL ship. "He couldn't use the ship's public toilets, eat in the acclaimed top-deck restaurant or swim in the pool because they weren't accessible to someone who couldn't walk up steps."[57] He sued and like others the case was thrown out. He continued to appeal and in September 2004 the US Supreme Court agreed to hear the case. The ICCL said it welcomed a US Supreme Court ruling, but cautioned that, "in the absence of any guidelines from the federal government, there is no standard to adhere to."[58]

The US Access Board in late November 2004 released draft guidelines in advance of a public hearing planned for January 10, 2005, with a comment deadline of March 28. The cruise industry through ICCL commented, "After taking seven to eight years to come up with recommendations, that period of seven weeks over a major holiday is insufficient to analyze and present salient comment .... It's a little over the top to expect the industry to come up with solutions in seven weeks if the board can't come up with them over seven years."[59] This response gives good reason to monitor what happens and to ensure that proper protections are maintained.

Like Any Travel Product

The cruise industry, like other modes of travel and resorts, faces challenges when it comes to safety, health, and delivery of the product promised. And like others, it is doing what it can to address problems, many times only after mandated to do so. At the same time it projects an image that belies what it is actually doing. This is perhaps not unique to the cruise industry — it may be how corporations behave generally. However, the cruise industry appears to stand out as being particularly arrogant and nonresponsive to what some would consider reasonable expectations or concerns.

Are cruise ships safe? Undoubtedly they are, however, they are not without problems and consumers should be as aware traveling by ship as they are when traveling by other modes and when staying at hotels and resorts. The same precautions are in order.

Part 4
Looking at the Future

9

Prospects for Positive Change

THE US-BASED CORPORATIONS OPERATING FOREIGN-REGISTERED CRUISE LINES have done well. Profits from the Caribbean, Central America, and Alaska are impressive. They have fueled growth and expansion and funded commitments for newer, bigger and better ships. With the approach of each new point of saturation the industry has expanded further and targeted a wider clientele. Carnival's acquisitions and mergers have positioned it as the dominant player in North America, Europe and the Mediterranean, and Australia. Expansion generates income and provides places to deploy ships no longer attractive to the US market. Australia knows this best being served by Princess and Carnival/Costa hand-me-downs. Canival's plans for Asia are still being developed though are likely to focus on some specific national markets[1] and involve deployment of older ships.

Do Pirates Have to Win?

As cruising expands, so does the number of calls at existing ports and the call for ports to be newer, bigger, and better. And ports cooperate. Some are like addicts. They mainline cruise passengers, never getting enough, and only realize their dependence when it is too late. Port "wanna-bes" see benefits but not costs, and they will do almost anything to attract cruise ships. They go in with unrealistic expectations and come out with mixed impressions. The benefits keep them coming back, but increasing costs raise public interest and involvement and sometimes political action. The 2006 ballot initiative in Alaska for a $50 passenger tax is a good example.[2]

The cruise industry takes advantage of workers much the same as it does the ports of small island states and developing countries from which they come. While worker incomes are impressive by standards at home — in 1997, the average per-capita income in the Philippines was less than $1,000 a year; an elementary school teacher in Romania earned just $70 a month — they are paid poorly by the standards of the developed world. The International Labor Organization's minimum wage for an able-bodied seafarer in 2005 is $500 a month. Assistants and trainees are paid less. Most cruise ship workers who depend on tips take home between $1,000 and $1,500 a month, though they also have debts and other expenses related to acquiring their job. Many pay a recruiting agent $1,500 or more to secure their job. For this, they work 14 or more hours a day, every day of the week, for as long as 10 or 12 months.[3]

The workers who built Carnival's ships earned an average monthly wage of less than {euro}1,000 ($1,160) in 2003 and demonstrated for improved pay and working conditions at delivery ceremonies for Carnival's newest ship, Carnival Glory. In an unprepared aside Micky Arison warned, "without cooperation with management, union members would be 'marching out in the yard like in France and Finland and Germany' ... If workers wanted to maintain order books, 'this will require cooperation.'"[4]

Can Things Change?

The cruise industry presented in this book is not what many readers expected when they started. Some will complain I have been too lenient with an industry comprised of a bunch of convicted felons. Others will say I have been unforgiving and at times harsh. In my view, I have presented an industry that takes advantage of available tax loopholes, influences policy and decision makers to its advantage and benefit, engages in public relations campaigns that effectively reframe and redefine issues, and projects a positive image overall. It is an excellent exemplar of US-style free enterprise.

So why focus on the cruise industry? On an academic level, the cruise industry is interesting as a model (on a small scale) of how corporations behave and how they wield influence. As corporations and industries get larger they are more difficult to track and analyze than the cruise industry.

On a practical level, the cruise industry is chosen because it is still small enough to be both vulnerable and sensitive to public opinion. Political and social action related to four issues can have real and meaningful impact on this industry.

Economic Issues

Equitable distribution of income from cruise industry operations is a critical issue. Governments of small island states and ports in the Caribbean say they are not getting a fair share. Their attempts to deal with the cruise industry in the 1990s and early 2000s had unsatisfactory outcomes. Most ports want more than the relatively small economic benefits derived from use of the port as a cruise destination. They want cruise tourism to provide real jobs and opportunities for local residents and income that will fund health, education, and social services. Simply, like everywhere else, there is a desire to improve the quality of life of people living in the country. One way this can be achieved is by spending more money in local economies and employing more local workers.

A second economic issue is taxes. The US Congress needs to close loopholes for the US-based, foreign-owned cruise industry. Other governments should do the same. The cruise industry, like other corporations, influences legislation and the rules under which it operates through lobbyists, campaign contributions, effective use of social capital, and many other means. Like these other corporations it should pay taxes. It should also pay its fair share to ports, to merchants and vendors in ports, and to cities/towns for ameliorating the negative impacts of cruise tourism.

"The major cruise lines are all doing well — RCCL, Princess, HAL, Carnival. Look at the increases shown in the Carnival annual report. I am assuming those increases came out of someone's hide."

Social Issues[6]

— **Kirk Lantarman, CEO, Holland America Line-Westours**[5]

There are three social issues. First is the opportunity cost of pursuing cruise tourism. What does a community forego by spending money on a $100-million cruise terminal rather than something else? Even small expenses can have implications, as in Saint John, New Brunswick, where the mayor tried to cut funding for lifeguards to keep funding for pins to be given to cruise passengers. The large-scale tradeoffs are much greater.

Tradeoffs can mean compromising quality of life. It can be minor, as in Juneau where, for the convenience of cruise passengers, youth are prohibited from skateboarding in the area of the pier during cruise season. Many similar examples have a cumulative impact. In question is the point at which cruise tourism compromises a local community's or an island's quality of life. It may be difficult to get around the community because of crowds, the volume of visitors may generate noise, cruise passengers may leave refuse behind, or local residents may be displaced from their own beaches.

A second quality of life issue is the effect on local folk, some living on the margin, being faced daily with the opulence and arrogance exhibited by some middle- and upper-class cruise passengers. How sustainable is tourism that reminds people of their relative lot in life without visible means for improvement? When does goodwill turn to resentment?

Worker issues are the third social issue. There is plenty written elsewhere about the "sweatship" nature of cruise ships.[7] Stated simply, cruise ships' workers deserve better overall treatment, better access to independent arbiters to ensure they are treated as the company says they are, and better incomes. While the fat-cat owners of the cruise lines saw the value of their stock more than double between March and October 2003 and continued to receive dividends, workers' pay remained the same as it has been for years. Stock prices continued to rise through 2004 and Carnival increased its dividends. Carnival and other companies are in a position to significantly improve work conditions and remuneration.

Environmental Issues

The environmental issues are many. The key question is whether environmental standards need to be legislated. Notably, the cruise industry behaves responsibly in Alaska where there are inspections, monitoring, and audits. It is a safe assumption that they would behave the same in other places where practices are legislated and enforced.

Areas needing attention include sewage, wastewater, and oily bilge treatment and discharge; air emissions from cruise ship incinerators and from engines; safe disposal of incinerator ash; safe release of ballast water; proper disposal of solid waste; and the elimination of plastic into the waste stream. In addition, the number of ship collisions with whales suggests the value of electronic sensors to detect whales and small craft. It is time for the industry's behavior to match its rhetoric. This is not something it can be trusted to do voluntarily.

Policy Issues

The main policy issue is legislation. The State of Alaska clearly demonstrated the benefits of legislation that includes monitoring, certification, and enforcement of environmental regulations. The State of California has further demonstrated the state's power to deal with cruise ship discharges. Similar efforts are underway in other states and on other issues.

Whether in the US, Canada, Australia, UK, Ireland, or any number of small island states or countries with cruise ports, an overriding issue is that the interests and concerns of taxpayers and local residents should take precedence over those of an industry that does not contribute its fair share to the welfare of a country. The American Revolution had a rallying cry, "No taxation without representation." A reasonable corollary is "No representation without taxation."

Arenas for Action

Successfully influencing the cruise industry depends on coordination, collaboration, and cooperation. People must support one another toward a common goal. When this works the results are impressive, however, it doesn't always work. And that is what the industry depends on.

It isn't that individual or small-scale action isn't possible or productive. The folks in Yakutat, despite federal legislation, demonstrated the power of local action. So did the citizens of Juneau in passing a $5 head tax on cruise passengers, and the residents of Key West in their influence over city planning around cruise tourism. Some individuals have successfully used Websites to extract resolution of a grievance with a cruise line; others such as those who put up "Carnival Sucks" or "NCL Sucks" were unsuccessful, but their stories were online for all to read. I maintain a "Boycott Carlson Companies" message at my Website. While I don't expect it to significantly impact Carlson's business, I gain a sense of satisfaction knowing that corporate staff and lawyers regularly visit the site. They are spending more on monitoring what I do than it would have "cost" to have handled the original complaint properly — the solution was not monetary. However, my potential for impact is severely limited as long as I am acting alone. Having a real effect requires working with others or participating in the political process.

Support and Oppose Legislation

As we have seen, the cruise industry benefits from its friends in Congress. So far it has been relatively successful in preventing legislation counter to its interests, and in promoting legislation consistent with them. It is successful, in part, because it is largely unopposed. Few voices speak out about the industry's windfalls. Perhaps it is naive, but it is reasonable to believe that members of Congress are as sensitive to letters from constituents as they are to cruise industry lobbyists.

Loud public support will be critical to the success of the Clean Cruise Ship Act, which was reintroduced in the 109th Congress in April 2005. Congressional committees must be pressured to hold hearings, the hearings must be fair and represent all views and interests, and members of both houses of Congress need to be pressured. Individuals can write letters to members of Congress, letters to the editor of newspapers, guest editorials, and other public venues that present the issue. The goal is to counterbalance what the cruise industry does behind the scenes through its lobbyists, campaign contributions, and social capital. The industry also has alternative legislation that it would hope replaces the more stringent Clean Cruise Ship Act.

Another bill introduced in 2004 that may reappear in the 109th Congress is the Pay Back America Act of 2004 introduced by New York Congressman Gregory W. Meek.[8] Its intention was to charge a $3 per passenger tax on cruise ships with the money going into a Caribbean Fund and a Wildlife Fund. Money in the Caribbean Fund would be distributed to Caribbean governments; money in the Wildlife Fund would be directed toward marine environmental protection. The legislation's goal was similar to the CTO's $20 passenger levy.

It is equally as important to become involved in state legislative initiatives. The value and importance of public support are more visible locally than on the national level. Legislation in Maine in 2004 was watered down at the last minute as a result of cruise industry lobbying; no doubt Friends of Casco Bay <www.cascobay.org> and its partners could have better inoculated against such changes with greater support for its efforts from both inside and outside the state. The same may be true of the 2003 legislation in California cosponsored by Bluewater Network <www.bluewater network.org>. Industry pressure on the Senate Appropriations Committee may have been countered if greater pressure were put on legislators by non-cruise industry sources. Most of what was lost in 2003 was regained in the 2004 legislation. Support from outside the state may also be critical in efforts by KAHEA — the Hawaiian-Environmental Alliance <www.kahea.org> (with the Sierra Club) — to replace Hawai'i's MOU with meaningful legislation and to protect the North West Hawaiian Islands.

In 2006 the big electoral fight will be in Alaska between the cruise industry and a group of citizens that successfully put together a petition campaign for a $50 tax on all cruise passengers. The tax will undoubtedly be played out in the media and in the state legislature — maybe even in Congress. Organizers of the campaign work on a shoestring and like any grassroots social action campaign welcome financial, moral, and political support.

Many of us devalue the importance of letters of support and of public attention through the media and other forums. They do make a difference to politicians and can have an impact. The cruise industry's success is due in part to the fact that much of what it does is unopposed and is often kept secret. When its actions are made transparent, they are easier to confront and contain.

Educate Local Policy and Decision Makers

Closely related to supporting and opposing legislation is educating policy makers and decision makers. They often lack information, particularly information that is contrary to the cruise industry's interests. As I heard more than once from newspaper editorial boards in my travels around the US, "Why don't we hear more about this side of the cruise industry?" While critical information is out there, the cruise industry effectively promotes its view, places positive news stories about the industry, and sells the idea that cruise ships are green — environmentally and economically. Decision and policy makers need to be reminded about the impacts of cruise tourism: social and economic costs; the risks posed by out-of-control growth to other more lucrative, profitable, and secure forms of tourism; and the environmental impact. Cruise tourism should have clear and direct economic and social benefits to port communities, and should have no environmental impact. It's that simple.

Though few organizations take on the full set of issues, there are some good examples of education campaigns. KAHEA produced an excellent video capturing key environmental risks posed by cruise ships and the industry's record of contradicting in action what it says it does. The 2004 video was distributed on DVDs to legislators, community and port leaders, environmental groups, and community groups affiliated with KAHEA, and to people in the state and beyond who were interested. The cost of production is small compared with its educational and political value.

Livable Oldtown <www.livableoldtown.com> in Key West, in association with Last Stand, undertook an educational campaign taken out of Saul Alinsky's strategy book.[9] They developed a series of "Did you know?" spots for the newspaper. The issues ranged from pollution to crowding to the industry's tax-free status. The technique kept the industry in the public eye, helped Last Stand keep city government accountable, and maintained a high degree of community interest. As effective as they have been, it has been done with little involvement or support from outside. The Ocean Conservancy's local staff is actively involved in the efforts, as are other local organizations. But Last Stand's and Livable Old Town's strength would increase if city government knew people outside Key West were watching and ready to speak out. "Outsiders" provide essential support to local efforts.

The work of Counterpart International <www.counterpart.org> through its Caribbean Media Exchange for Sustainable Tourism (CMEx) is another example of educating policy and decision makers, in this case by educating the media. CMEx <www.mediaexchange.info> brings together 60 or so media professionals from across the Caribbean to discuss with experts and politicians issues critical to the Caribbean, including cruise tourism. In addition to providing a supportive environment and building solidarity across the Caribbean, CMEx is an opportunity to share information. There are many similar venues, including large events such as the multinational White Water to Blue Water Partnership Conference in March 2004 in Miami. But Counterpart International's efforts are different because they bring together folks from small island states and Central America, free of outside influence, with a focus first on common local issues and concerns and, second, on the cruise industry and other "outsiders." The perspective would be different if the cruise industry or other outsiders influenced the agenda.

Education can take many forms. The previous examples are representative of several efforts by organizations. Individually one can help to educate others — letter writing and chatting with others, for example. There are also opportunities to join in or help organize a local campaign.

Participate in and Support Local Campaigns

Those living in or near a cruise port may be able to participate in local campaigns or efforts. Many of these have been successful: the work of Save Our Shores, Friends of the Sea Otter, the Ocean Conservancy, and their partners in protecting Monterey Bay and the Monterey Bay Marine Sanctuary; the efforts of the residents of Moloka'i to resist the "invasion" of cruise tourism, both through the courts with the help of Earthjustice and through direct social action; and the work of Bluewater Network and San Franciscans for a Healthy Waterfront to ensure environmental risks associated with the new cruise terminal in San Francisco are effectively ameliorated. The campaign in San Francisco included other organizations and experts in their efforts and used demonstrations at the San Francisco Cruise Ship Terminal to protest cruise ship pollution.

Some are fortunate to be able to participate in these actions. The best others can do is to follow the actions through the news or the organizations' Website and send our support from a distance. Letters of support to the organization and letters to the media are both helpful.

Some may ask, "Why engage in a demonstration or some other collective action?" The reason is simply that the cruise industry is not prepared for a grassroots groundswell. They are not prepared for a significant threat. And it wouldn't take much. I watched in March 2003 from the Press Room at the Seatrade Cruise Shipping Convention as *Oceana's* planned rally and press conference to launch its campaign against Royal Caribbean was preceded by full-page newspaper ads in the *Miami Herald* and *Fort Lauderdale Sun-Sentinel*. The stage was set for "an event." Cruise industry executives knew about *Oceana's* midday press conference and their concern was visibly heightened by the ads that morning. But their concern quickly deflated when they walked across the street at noontime to see that *Oceana's* rally and press conference consisted of about 15 people — more media than demonstrators. Their relief was only exceeded by their smiles. The event missed its mark and lost a golden opportunity.

Though the outcome isn't what was ideally desired, the case is instructive. The cruise industry was clearly concerned about the threat posed by *Oceana*. Imagine the outcome if the industry executives' fears and concerns had been supported by the rally and press conference, and if the media event had exceeded their expectations. The outcome would have been considerably different. They were not prepared for a grassroots groundswell then, and are equally as vulnerable today.

Be Selective in Support for National Organizations

The most many can do is to financially support local and national organizations. Our time is limited, but we have resources that we gladly share for the right causes and the right organizations. In doing this, we should be knowledgeable about the organizations we support: their primary sources of funding, linkages maintained through board of directors, and grants received that might compromise objectivity on issues that concern you. You must research this on your own because it is usually not readily advertised.

For example, despite all of its good work, *Oceana's* funding comes almost entirely from the Pew Charitable Trusts. It is relevant to consider.[10] When I first learned of this connection in 2002 I did an Internet search — I didn't know then that the Pew family fortune derived from Sun Oil of Pennsylvania — and was surprised to find that Pew Charitable Trust's Washington lobbyists belonged to the same firm used by the cruise industry, Alcalde and Fay. Pew was subsequently dropped from Alcalde and

Fay's Web-posted client list. I later heard positives and negatives about Pew's work in British Columbia and Washington state with regard to old-growth forests and logging — some felt the grassroots western wilderness environmental movement was being smothered.[11] Interestingly, the strategies Pew used there are not unlike those used in relation to grassroots groups working on cruise ship issues. Funding is more difficult for others to get because the funds are going to Oceana and the issue is viewed as within Oceana's domain. When funds are given often implicit strings are attached.[12] While I support Oceana's efforts, I recognize its political connections.

In recent years organizations have used cruise ships to generate income. On the surface, it is a great idea. After all, the lefty-imaged *The Nation* magazine earns between $50,000 and a couple of hundred thousand dollars from each of its cruise seminars at sea.[13] While trashing the conservative agenda and discussing topics that include exploitation of the world labor market, the magazine walks away with a profit. And its readers leave the ship without it being pointed out that all of this is taking place on a "sweatship." But *The Nation* is in good company. The *National Review*, the Freedom Alliance, National Rifle Association, and *Yoga Journal* each have cruise ship events that generate income. The *New Republic* had planned to join the crowd in 2003, but canceled because of lack of support from its readers.

With all of this said, consider becoming involved on a local or national level. Some national organizations do wonderful work locally and these efforts need the support of those nearby. San Francisco-based Bluewater Network/Friends of the Earth, as one example, is involved in local efforts in the Bay area, in statewide initiatives in California, and in national initiatives (such as its petitions to the Environmental Protection Agency with regard discharges from cruise ships). All forms of support are helpful and contribute to its success. There are plenty of other national regional and local organizations. No matter where you live there is one that no doubt can use your help. Choose carefully and wisely.

Prognosis for the Future of the Cruise Industry

The cruise industry continues on a trajectory of growth. Though the speed of growth has slowed, new ships continue to be built and announcements continue for future delivery. The industry's continued growth depends on several factors.

Firstly, the economy needs to grow and be healthy. As long as people have disposable income or credit, the cruise industry will continue to be healthy. People are going to take vacations and cruise lines have effectively priced their product to be accessible to a broad segment of the population. Even if there is war, cruise lines remain largely unaffected because cruise ships can easily redeploy to ports where passengers feel safe and secure.

Secondly, continued growth assumes there will be no terrorist attack on a cruise ship. Thus far, this topic has been visibly avoided. It isn't that it is not a risk, but there is no value in being alarmist or in fear-mongering. The cruise lines and ports are doing all they can do to maintain safety and we need to trust their efforts. Still, should an attack occur, the cruise industry will likely experience a dive in business and short-term, if not long-term, economic uncertainty. This sort of event is considered unlikely.

The third assumption underlying the industry's continued growth is that it maintains economic advantages with regard to taxes and port relationships. Any changes in these will increase the cost of the cruise and reduce demand. No doubt the cruise industry will work hard to maintain the status quo. Local activists will work equally as hard. Increases in cost are likely to be initially covered by increased corporate efficiency and there would not be an increase in total operational costs. I am confident that the cruise industry will always find a way to fill its ships and to turn a profit.

In addition to continued expansion and growth, four other projections will be advanced.

- Carnival Corporation will replicate in Europe, the Mediterranean, Australia and New Zealand the market and political dominance it has within the industry in North America, and also replicate the industry's relationship with governments. This is already happening in Europe. It would appear that Star Cruises will maintain its dominance in Asia, but Carnival will expand into that market. These other markets and a segment of small players will continue to absorb excess and older tonnage.

- Cruise ship deployments in the Caribbean, Alaska, and elsewhere will increasingly be defined by cost considerations more than by consumer demand. Ports will continue to be pressured for economic and other concessions and played against one another when that benefits the cruise lines. While there will be winners as well as losers among ports, there will only be winners among the cruise lines.

- Governments in the Caribbean will continue to work for some form of regional fee or revenue from cruise tourism, not unlike the $20-passenger levy discussed in 2003, and the cruise industry will continue to lobby against it. Through the mix, solidarity among Caribbean ports will remain elusive. As well, other governments will enter into agreements such as those between Carnival and Belize and Carnival and Turks and Caicos. These arrangements further compromise the potential for Caribbean-wide support for a tax or passenger fee.

• The effect of growth on the two extremes of the cruise industry is hard to anticipate. On the one hand are ships such as *The World of ResidenSea* that operate as a condominium, or Four Season's Hotels and Resorts' and Canyon Ranch's plans for cruise ships under their respective names. The cruise ship as hotel or condominium may take hold. On the other extreme, but not dissimilar, is easyCruise and other lines that unbundle the cruise product. The mainstream cruise lines, in an effort to compete, will likely increase the services and amenities for which there are onboard charges. This will change the texture of cruising, and can potentially have wide ranging effects.

The cruise industry is obviously here to stay. The goal of this book is simple: to advocate for an industry that is socially, economically, and environmentally sustainable and responsible. While it would be nice to assume cruise lines would do this voluntarily, history tells us that is not the case.

. Consumers and citizens need to do what they can to ensure that cruise ships are held accountable and that they behave in the ways the company claims. Boycotts are always a potent option to directly influence behavior. As well, consumers and citizens need to help communities and ports resist pressure from the cruise industry, and to advocate the value of alternative forms of tourism. Until clear laws govern the cruise industry, with monitoring and enforcement, the only way to protect ourselves, our communities, and others from the negative impacts of cruise tourism is through direct action. Piracy can be contained.

Glossary and Guide to Abbreviations

ADA: Americans with Disabilities Act.

AWP: Advanced Waste Water Purification (see AWTS).

AWTS: Advanced Wastewater Treatment Systems. Effluent from these systems is usually referred to as "near drinking water quality." Several different technologies are used for treatment. While all are significant improvements over traditional shipboard marine sanitation, devices they still have their limitations.

Azipod propulsion: Azipod (short for *azimuthing podded*) propulsion systems are mounted on the underside of the ship's hull (rather than inside the hull) and have 360-degree maneuverability. The systems are also known as mermaid propulsion systems.

Ballast: A ship uses ballast water for stability. It will take on sea water to offset the weight of fuel that has been consumed and for stability during voyages. This water is released when the ship enters ports, each release can be up to 1,000 metric tons of ballast water: literally millions of gallons. Ballast water is a concern because it introduces non-native species to areas of discharge.

Bilge: Bilge is a combination of water that collects in the hull of the ship from condensation, water-lubricated shaft seals, propulsion system cooling, and other engine sources. It contains fuel, oil, and wastewater from engines, and may include rags, metal shavings, paint, glass, and cleaning agents. If filtered to 10–15 parts per million of oil, the water can be legally discharged into the ocean.

Black water: The waste that goes down toilets; sewage.

CCSA: Clean Cruise Ship Act of 2004. Introduced in the Senate and House on April 1, 2004, but failed to make it out of committee. It was reintroduced in the 109th Congress in April 2005.

CELB: Center for Environmental Leadership in Business <www.celb.org> is a partnership between Conservation International and Ford Motor Company.

CHA: Caribbean Hotel Association < www.caribbeanhotels.org>.

CI: Conservation International <www.conservation.org>.

CICF: Cruise Industry Charitable Foundation <iccl.org/foundation/history.cfm>.

CLIA: Cruise Lines International Association <cruising.org>.

CTO: Caribbean Tourism Organization < www.onecaribbean.org>.

ECC: European Cruise Council.

EPA: US Environmental Protection Agency <www.epa.gov>.

Flag of convenience: A situation in which the beneficial ownership of a ship is in a country different from where it is registered; where the owner of a ship is a US-based corporation but the ship is registered someplace else, often a country in the developing world such as Panama, Liberia, or Bahamas.

FCCA: Florida-Caribbean Cruise Association <f-cca.com>.

Gray water: The wastewater that goes down the sink and showers, from the galley and from the spa and beauty parlor.

ICCL: International Council of Cruise Lines <iccl.org>.

IMO: International Maritime Organization <www.imo.org> is a United Nations agency concerned with maritime safety, environmental protection, and all other maritime issues.

Jones Act: Also known as the Merchant Marine Act of 1920, this act limits access to the US flag to ships built in the US.

MARPOL: International Convention for the Prevention of Pollution from Ships <www.imo.org/Conventions/contents.asp?doc_id=678&topic_id=258>.

NCL: Originally Norwegian Caribbean Line, which was later renamed Norwegian Cruise Line.

NOAA: US National Oceanic and Atmospheric Administration <www.noaa.gov>.

NWCA: Northwest Cruiseship Association <nwcruiseship.org>.

OBF: Oceans Blue Foundation.

OCTA: Ocean Conservation Tourism Alliance established in 2004 by ICCL and CI and housed in the CELB.

PSA: Passenger Shipping Association in the UK <www.psa-psara.org>.

PVSA: Passenger Vessel Services Act of 1886 limited transportation of passengers between two points in the US to US-flagged vessels. This cabotage law also applies to airlines and air travel; thus only US-flagged airlines are permitted to fly passengers between two cities in the US.

RCCL: Royal Caribbean Cruise Line until the company bought Celebrity Cruises and became Royal Caribbean Cruises Limited. The cruise line was renamed RCI.

RCI: Royal Caribbean International (previously Royal Caribbean Cruise Line).

Social capital: An amorphous concept that sees individuals, organizations, and/or groups as able to grow "social capital" through reputation and image; the nature and number of linkages to others; social, economic, and political resources; and social and political skills.

SOLAS: International Convention for the Safety of Life at Sea <www.imo.org/Conventions/contents.asp?topic_id=257&doc_id=647>.

Appendix A

Board of Directors of Carnival Corporation & Royal Caribbean Cruises Limited

1. Carnival Corporation Board of Directors, 2004

Senior Management
Micky Arison, chair of the board and CEO, Carnival Corporation & plc
Robert H. Dickinson, president and CEO, Carnival Cruise Lines
Pier Luigi Foschi, chair of the board and CEO, Costa Crociere, S.p.A.
Howard S. Frank, vice chair of the board and COO, Carnival Corporation & plc
A. Kirk Lanterman, chair of the board and CEO, Holland America Line Inc.
Peter Ratcliffe, CEO, P&O Princess Cruises International Ltd.

Nonexecutive Directors
See Table A-1 on page 206–7.

Directors Leaving with P&O Merger
See Table A-2 on page 208.

2. Royal Caribbean Cruises Limited Board of Directors, 2004

Senior Management
Richard D. Fain, chairman and CEO
Jack L. Williams, president & COO, Royal Caribbean International and Celebrity Cruises
Adam M. Goldstein, executive vice president
Luis E. Leon, executive vice president and CFO

Nonexecutive Directors
See Table A-3 on page 209–10.

Directors Recently Leaving Board
See Table A-4 on page 211.

TABLE A. 1: Carnival Corporation Nonexecutive Directors, 2004

Director Year Appointed	Present and Recent Professional Appointments	Boards of Directors and Other Relevant Links
Richard G. Capen, Jr. 1994	US ambassador to Spain, 1992–1993; vice chair, Knight-Ridder, Inc, 1989–1991; chair & publisher, *Miami Herald*, 1983–1989.	• Fixed Income Funds, Capital Group • New Economy Fund • Smallcap World Fund
Arnold W. Donald 2001	Chair & CEO, Merisant Company (maker of Equal); senior vice president of Monsanto Company, 1998–2000	• Belden, Inc. • Crown Cork & Seal Company, Inc. • The Laclede Group • GenAmerica Insurance Company • Oil-Dri Corporation of America • The Scotts Company
Richard J. Glasier 2004	President and CEO, Argosy Gaming Company. Previously, executive vice president and CFO, RCCL	• Aztar Corporation
Baroness Hogg 2000	Head of the Prime Minister's Policy Unit (Adviser to John Major), 1990–1995.	• Chair, GKN plc • Chair, 3i Group plc • Chair, Frontier Economics Ltd.

TABLE A. 1: Carnival Corporation Nonexecutive Directors, 2004 – continued

Modesto A. Maidique 1994	President, Florida International University.	• Ivax Corporation • National Semiconductor, Inc.
John P. McNulty 2000	Chief financial officer, Biodelivery Sciences Inc; chief financial officer, Hopkins Capital Group; former managing director, Goldman Sachs & Co.	
Sir John Parker 2000	Chairman, National Grid Transco plc & RMC Group plc,	• Chair, Lattice Group plc • GKN plc • BG Group plc • Firth Rixson plc • Lloyds Register
Stuart Subotnick 1994	General partner & executive vice president, Metromedia.	• Board chair, Big City Radio • Metromedia Fiber Network, Inc. • Metromedia International Group, Inc.
Uzi Zucker 1987	Senior managing director, Bear, Stearns & Co., 1986–2002.	

TABLE A-2: Carnival Corporation Board of Directors Leaving with P&O Merger

Director Years Served	Present and Recent Professional Appointments	Boards of Directors and Other Relevant Links
Shari Arison 1987–1993; 1995–2003	Chair, Arison Holdings, Ltd	• Bank Hapoalim • Ted Arison Family Foundation
Maks L. Birnbach 1990–2003	Chair of Board, Forcutt Manufacturers	• Diamond Manufacturers & Importers Association • Vice chair, American Committee of the Weizmann Institute for Science, Israel
James M. Dubin 1995–2003	Partner, Paul, Weiss, Rifkind, Wharton & Garrison	• Conair Corporation • Change Technology Partners • European Capital Ventures plc
Sherwood Weiser 1978–2003	Chair and CEO, Continental Companies; Chair and CEO, CRC Holdings (d/b/a Carnival Resorts & Casinos), 1998–2001; Chair & CEO, CHC International, 1994–1998.	• Mellon United National Bank • Wyndham International, Inc. • Interstate Hotels Corporation • Trustee, University of Miami
Meshulam Zonis 1987–2003	Senior VP, Carnival Cruise Lines, 1979–2000	

TABLE A-3: Royal Caribbean Cruises Limited Nonexecutive Directors, 2004

Director *Year appointed*	*Present and Recent Professional* *Appointments*	*Boards of Directors and Other* *Relevant Links*
Bernard W. Aronson 1993	Managing Partner, ACON Investments, LLC & Newbridge Andean Partners, LP; From June 1989 to July 1993, Assistant Secretary of State for Inter-American Affairs.	• Liz Claiborne, Inc. • Hyatt International, Inc.
John D. Chandris 1997	Chair, Chandris (UK) Limited; Before 1997, Chair, Celebrity Cruises.	• Leathbond Limited • Lloyd's Register (classification society)
Arvid Grundekjoen 2000	President & CEO, Anders Wilhelmsen & Co.; Previously Chair & CEO of Awilco ASA.	• Chair of the supervisory boards of Listow AS & Creati AS
William L. Kimsey (financial expert) 2003	Previously CEO of Ernst & Young Global; Deputy Chair & COO, Ernst & Young.	• Western Digital Corporation • Parsons Corporation • Accenture
Laura Laviada 1997	Founder, *Area Editores* (publishing company); Before 2000, Chair & CEO, Editorial Televisa (world's largest Spanish magazine publisher);	
Gert W. Munthe 2002	Managing Partner, Ferd Private Equity; Previously, a Director of Alpharma, Inc., & CEO of NetCom.	• Anders Wilhelmsen & Co. AS
Eyal Ofer 1991	Chair, Carlyle M.G. Limited; Chair, Associated Bulk Carriers.	

TABLE A-3: Royal Caribbean Cruises Limited Nonexecutive Directors, 2004

Director Year appointed	Present and Recent Professional Appointments	Boards of Directors and Other Relevant Links
Thomas J. Pritzker 1999	Chair & CEO, The Pritzker Organization & Hyatt Corporation; Chair, Hyatt International; Partner in law firm of Pritzker & Pritzker.	• Board of Trustees, University of Chicago • Board of Trustees, Art Institute of Chicago • Bay City Capital • First Health Group Corp
William K. Reilly 1998	CEO, Aqua International Partners; From 1989 to 1993, administrator of the US Environmental Protection Agency; Paid $300,000 pa by RCCL as an environmental consultant.	• Board Chair, World Wildlife Fund • Trustee, American Academy in Rome • National Geographic Society • Packard Foundation • Presidio Trust • DuPont • Conoco • Ionics • Eden Springs • Evergreen Holdings • Yale University Corporation
Bernt Reitan 2004	Vice President, Alcoa Inc.; Group President, Alcoa Primary Products.	
Arne A. Wilhelmsen 2003	Executive Vice President, Anders Wilhelmsen & Co.	• A. Wilhelmsen AS

TABLE A-4: Royal Caribbean Cruises Limited Directors Recently Leaving the Board

Director Years Served	*Present and Recent Professional Appointments*	*Boards of Directors and Other Relevant Links*
Tor B. Arneberg 1988	Senior Advisor/Executive Vice President, Nightingale & Associates, since 1982.	• Executive Trustee & VP, American Scandinavian Foundation • Precision Contract Manufacturing
Kaspar K. Keilland 1993–1999	Chairman, Kvaener AS.	• A. Wilhelmsen & Co. AS
Peter Lorange 1993–1999	President, IMD – International Institute for Business Development; Until 1993, President, Norwegian School of Management.	• Chairman, Citibank Norway AS • Citibank International PLC • ISS AS
Jannik Lindbaek 1999–2000	Executive VP, International Finance Corp., World Bank Group, 1994–1999; President & CEO, Nordic Investment Bank, 1986–1994.	• Vital Life Insurance Co. • Anders Wilhelmsen & Co. • Board chair, Den norske Bank • The Chubb Corporation • East African Development Bank
Edwin Stephan 1996–2002	President or General Manager, RCCL, 1968–1995.	
Arne Wilhelmsen 1968–2003	Chair, Anders Wilhelmsen & Co. AS.	

Appendix B

Donations from Cruise Industry Charitable Foundation, 1998–2003

Beneficiary	1998	1999	2000	2001	2002	2003	Total
Africare, Washington, DC						5,000	5,000
Allianza Dominicana Youth Program, NYC				5,000			5,000
ALS Association – Race Against ALS						5,000	5,000
American Association of Port Authorities					3,000		3,000
American Red Cross of Southeast Virginia						15,000	15,000
Arlington Free Clinic, Arlington, VA						3,000	3,000
Art of Leadership Foundation, Birmingham, MI						25,000	25,000
Big Brother and Big Sisters, Anchorage, AK					25,000		25,000
Black Women United for Action, Miami & VA	15,000	15,000		10,000			40,000
Booker T Washington Learning Center – NYC				5,000			5,000
Boy Scouts of America, Florida				10,000	10,000		20,000
Carrie Meek Foundation, Miami, FL						25,000	25,000
Celebrations for Children, Washington, DC						100,000	100,000
Chantilly Mews Boys Athletic Program, Springfield, VA						9,300	9,300
Children's Home of Jacksonville, FL						10,000	10,000
Children's Home Society of Florida					25,000		25,000
Community Association of Progressive Dominicans, NYC				5,000			5,000
Communities on Schools of Putnam County, FL						15,000	15,000

Beneficiary	1998	1999	2000	2001	2002	2003	Total
Community Rehabilitation Center, Jacksonville, FL						5,000	5,000
Congressional Award Foundation			25,000	25,000	15,000	15,000	80,000
Congressional Black Caucus Foundation		5,000	20,000	1,000	2,500	35,000	63,500
Congressional Hispanic Caucus Institute				25,000		35,000	60,000
Crisis Center of Tampa Bay, FL					25,000		25,000
Crisis Services of Brevard County, FL				5,000			5,000
Delta Education, Health, and Cultural Center, Miami		60,000		45,000			105,000
Dominican American National Roundtable, NYC					25,000		25,000
Doyon Foundation, Fairbanks, AK	50,000						50,000
East Harlem Council for Community Improvement, NYC				5,000			5,000
Edgewood Children's Ranch, Orlando, FL			15,000				15,000
Edward Waters College, Jacksonville, FL						5,000	5,000
Fairbanks Community Food Bank, AK						25,000	25,000
First Coast African American Chamber of Commerce, Jacksonville, FL						5,000	5,000
Florida Conference of Black Legislators						5,000	5,000
Florida Governor's Literacy Initiative				150,000			150,000
Florida Prepaid College Program					100,000		100,000
Florida State Society, Washington, DC					250		250
George Mason University Law Foundation, VA					25,000		25,000
George Miller Youth Fund, Los Angeles, CA			300				300
GWU/MPA Mobile Mammography Program, DC				5,000		10,000	15,000
Harlem Knights Football League, NYC				5,000			5,000
Harlem Little League, NYC				5,000			5,000

Appendix B: Donations from Cruise Industry Charitable Foudation, 1998–2003 – continued:

Beneficiary	1998	1999	2000	2001	2002	2003	Total
Hillsborough Community College, Tampa, FL			3,500	7,000			10,500
Hillsborough Head Start Community Foundation, Tampa, FL						20,000	20,000
Hispanic Designs Foundation, Washington, DC				3,500			3,500
Hispanics United, Miami, FL					5,000		5,000
I.M. Sulbacher Center for the Homeless, Jacksonville, FL						10,000	10,000
International Kids Fund, Miami, FL					10,000		10,000
Inwood Community Services, NYC				5,000			5,000
Jacksonville Council for the Blind, FL						5,000	5,000
James Scott Community Association, Miami, FL				10,000		10,000	20,000
Johnson Family YMCA, Jacksonville, FL						5,000	5,000
Kids in Distressed Situations, NYC						10,000	10,000
Leadership Broward Foundation, FL						10,000	10,000
League Against Cancer, Miami, FL						25,000	25,000
Leukemia & Lymphoma Society, Washington, DC				34,000	10,000	10,000	54,000
Life with Cancer, Fairfax, VA					3,000	5,000	8,000
Lupus Foundation, Florida Chapter						10,000	10,000
March of Dimes, Washington, DC				15,000	15,000	15,000	45,000
Marketplace of Ideas, Mandan, ND						10,000	10,000
Mary McLeod Bethune Community Center, Daytona Beach, FL						5,000	5,000
Meeting Street Center, Rhode Island			5,000				5,000
Mercy Ships, Washington, DC					10,000		10,000

Beneficiary	1998	1999	2000	2001	2002	2003	Total
HMiami Children's Museum, FL						50,000	50,000
Martin Luther Wilson Boys and Girls Club, NYC				5,000			5,000
Mobile Area Chamber Foundation, AK				3,975			3,975
Museum of America, Muse Academy, VA					5,000		5,000
National Capital Area Council, Washington, DC				5,000			5,000
National Coalition of 100 Black Women, NY	60,000			45,000			105,000
National Foundation of Women Legislators, Washington, DC					3,000	1,500	4,500
National Marine Sanctuary Program					10,000	10,000	20,000
North Carolina Rural Center			5,000				5,000
New York State NAACP				100,000			100,000
Open Door Mission, Houston, TX		20,000					20,000
Operation Warm Heart, Yuba City, CA						7,500	7,500
Overton Youth Center, Miami, FL					10,000	10,000	20,000
Preservation Society of Newport County, Rhode Island						10,000	10,000
Presidential Classroom, Los Angeles and NYC				100,000			100,000
Publix Supermarkets - Turkeys for Needy, Florida					2,500	2,500	5,000
Range Cultural Foundation, Miami, FL		5,000	10,000				15,000
Roar Foundation, California				40,000			40,000
Robert F. Kennedy Memorial, DC				15,000			15,000
Salvation Army, Tampa, FL		10,000	-10,000				0
SCAN – LaGuardia, NYC				5,000			5,000
Sertoma Center, Nashville, TN		35,000	25,000	25,000	15,000	15,000	115,000
The 60 Plus Program, Arlington, VA						10,000	10,000

Appendix B: Donations from Cruise Industry Charitable Foudation, 1998–2003 – continued:

Beneficiary	1998	1999	2000	2001	2002	2003	Total
Space Coast Early Intervention Center, Melbourne, FL						25,000	25,000
Special Olympics 2001, Anchorage, AK			84,000	166,000			250,000
Special Olympics of Jacksonville						5,000	5,000
Stop Hunger, Miami, FL					3,000	3,000	6,000
University Medical Center Candlelighters, MS				10,000	2,500	2,500	15,000
University of Central Florida, Orlando, FL						10,000	10,000
University of Montana Foundation, Missoula, MT						25,000	25,000
University of Tampa, FL					25,000	25,000	50,000
The Valley, (Tasa Program), NYC				5,000			5,000
Washington Workshops: (AK, AZ, CA, DC, NY, TX, WA, Duluth, Houston, Miami, Los Angeles, New Orleans, NYC)		291,812	200,000	250,000	193,000	154,138	1,088,950
YMCA of Greater Miami, FL						25,000	25,000
Total of Donations	**75,000**	**491,812**	**382,800**	**1,155,475**	**577,750**	**893,438**	**3,576,275**
Overhead and Expenses	**21,034**	**119,714**	**126,387**	**138,963**	**131,356**	**59,408**	**596,862**
Total	**96,034**	**611,526**	**509,187**	**1,294,438**	**709,106**	**952,846**	**4,173,137**
Overhead as % of Total	**21.9%**	**19.6%**	**24.8%**	**10.7%**	**18.5%**	**6.2%**	**14.3%**

Source: IRS Form 990 (accessed through <www.guidestar.org>

Appendix C

Federal Candidates Receiving $4,000+ in Campaign Contributions Funds From Cruise Industry, 1997–2004

Candidate	Party-State	1998 $	2000 $	2002 $	2004 $	Total $
			Election Cycle			
Abercrombie, N	D-HI	6,000	2,400	2,400	8,400	19,200
Alben, A	D-WA				4,000	4,000
Ashcroft, J	R-MO		5,000			5,000
Baucus, M	D-MT	7,000	3,000	8,000		18,000
Bayh, E	D-IN			2,000	3700	5,700
Bean, M	D-IL			500	4,000	4,500
Berkley, S	D-NV	2,250	3,500	4,000	2,000	11,750
Bilbray, B	R-CA	9,000	1,750			10,750
Bilirakis, M	R-FL	500	1,000	2,500	1,500	5,500
Bloom, E	D-FL		4,250			4,250
Boehlert, S	R-NY	5,000	11,180	2,000	1,000	19,180
Bond, C	R-MO	5,250			2,000	7,250
Boxer, B	D-CA	14,500	2,500	4,250	33,500	54,750
Boyd, F	D-FL				4,000	4,000
Bradley, B	D-NJ	2,000	10,000			12,000
Braun, C	D-IL	9,000			1,000	10,000
Breaux, J	D-LA	15,500	1,000	1,000		17,500
Brown, C	D-FL	6,000	6,750	7,500	10,500	30,750
Burns, C	R-MT	7,500	4,000	12,000	6,000	29,500
Bush, GW	R		26,499		36,500	62,999
Byrd, J	R-FL				6,000	6,000
Cantwell, M	D-WA		2,000	14,749	4,000	20,749
Carnahan, J	D-MO			7,100		7,100
Castor, B	D-FL				13,500	13,500
Chico, G	D-IL			1,000	6,000	7,000
Clark, W	D				5,000	5,000
Cleland, M	D-GA			19,000		19,000
Clement, B	D-TN	6,000	2,250			8,250
Clinton, H	D-NY		41,500		3,000	44,500
Coble, J	R-NC	4,500	5,500	6,500	1,000	17,500
Coles, M	D-GA	7,000				7,000

Candidate	Party-State	Election Cycle				
		1998 $	2000 $	2002 $	2004 $	Total $
Crane, P	R-IL	8,500	4,500	3,000		16,000
Cubin, B	R-WY				4,000	4,000
D'Amato, A	R-NY	28,500				28,500
Daschle, T	D-SD	12,500	4,500	5,000	10,000	32,000
Davis, G	D-CA			10,000		10,000
Davis, J	D-FL	5,500	5,000	3,500	4,000	18,000
Davis, T	R-VA	1,500		1,000	5,000	7,500
Dean, H	D				5,000	5,000
Defazio, P	D-OR		5,000	500		5,500
Deutsch, P	D-FL	8,500	2,500	6,500	25,000	42,500
Diaz-Balart, L	R-FL	9,000	4,500	2,599	2,500	18,599
Diaz-Balart, M	R-FL			8,000	4,000	12,000
Dicks, N	D-WA	2,000	1,500	2,000	6,500	12,000
Didrickson, L	R-IL	3,000	3,000			6,000
Dingell, J	D-MI		4,000	7,000	16,000	27,000
Dodd, C	D-CT	1,500	500	2,000	2,000	6,000
Dorgan, B	D-ND	2,500		500	9,000	12,000
Duncan, J	R-TN	9,300	2,500	11,355	1,000	24,155
Durbin, R	D-IL	1,750	7,500	12,750		22,000
Edwards, J	D-NC			1,000	3,500	4,500
Ensign, J	R-NY	250	3,000	6,000	3,000	12,250
Feinstein, D	D-CA		2,000		2,500	4,500
Fitzgerald, P	R-IL	2,750		1,000	1,000	4,750
Foley, M	R-FL		6,500	4,000	1,000	11,500
Fong, M	R-CA	4,000				4,000
Fossella, V	R-NY		1,000	3,000		4,000
Frist, W	R-TN		9,000		1,000	10,000
Frost, M	D-TX		7,500	4,500	5,500	17,500
Gallegly, E	R-CA	6,500	1,500	1,000		9,000
Gephardt, R	D-MO	4,000	5,000	6,000	13,500	28,500
Gibbons, J	R-NV	500	1,000	1,500	1,500	4,500
Giuliani, R	R-NY		5,500			5,500
Gore, A	D	1,000	20,000			21,000
Gorton, S	R-WA		25,500			25,500
Graham, B	D-FL	21,750			18,250	40,000
Grassley, C	R-IA	9,373		1,000		10,373
Greenwood, J	R-PA	4,000	4,000	5,000	8,000	21,000

Candidate	Party-State		Election Cycle			
		1998	2000	2002	2004	Total
		$	$	$	$	$
Harkin, T	D-IA			5,000		5,000
Hastert, D	R-IL		4,500	1,500	9,000	15,000
Hastings, A	D-FL	5,000	2,000	4,500	8,000	19,500
Herseth, S	D-SD				4,000	4,000
Hollings, E	D-SC	21,000	4,000	10,000	1,500	36,500
Hoyer, S	D-MD	1,000	2,250	1,000	4,000	8,250
Inouye, D	D-HI	9,000		3,000	24,100	36,100
Inslee, J	D-WA	500	2,000	3,000		5,500
Jefferson, W	D-LA			5,000	1,000	6,000
Johnson, T	D-SD	1,000	4,500	3,000		8,500
Kennedy, P	D-RI	1,000	800	2,000	1,250	5,050
Kerry, J	D-MA	5,500	2,500	7,250	81,600	96,850
Kirk, R	D-TX			4,500		4,500
Klink, R	D-PA		5,500			5,500
Lazio, R	R-CA		7,650			7,650
Lewis, J	R-CA				5,000	5,000
Lieberman, J	D-CT		1,500		3,000	4,500
Lobiondo, F	R-NJ			3,000	2,000	5,000
Lott, T	R-MS	14,200	5,000	5,500	5,000	29,700
Lugar, R	R-IN	2,250	1,000	1,250	7,750	12,250
Markey, E	D-MA			1,000	6,000	7,000
McCain, J	R-AZ	21,000	18,000	5,000	12,500	56,500
McCollum, B	R-FL	1,500	8,000		11,000	20,500
McKeon, H	R-CA	1,000	1,500	3,500	1,000	7,000
Meek, C/K	D-FL	5,500	5,000	4,500	7,000	22,000
Menendez, R	D-NJ	500	4,500	7,000		12,000
Mica, J	R-FL	3,946	2,250	8,500	2,000	16,696
Miller, G	D-CA	2,000	2,500			4,500
Miller, Z	D-GA			5,000		5,000
Moakley, J	D-MA	7,000	1,000			8,000
Murkowski, F/L	R-AK	15,250	3,000		45,500	63,750
Murray, P	D-WA	1,500		2,000	16,500	20,000
Nelson, B	D-FL	1,000	61,000	15,500	15,500	93,000
Obama, B	D-IL		2,000	1,000	38,000	41,000
Oberstar, J	D-MN	5,500	9,000	6,500	4,500	25,500
Pelosi , N	D-CA	2,650	2,750	2,500	24,000	31,900
Penelas, A	D-FL				16,301	16,301

Candidate	Party-State	Election Cycle				
		1998 $	2000 $	2002 $	2004 $	Total $
Petri, T	R-WI		6,250	1,500	5,750	13,500
Pickering, C	R-MI	1,500	500	3,000	250	5,250
Pritzker, J	D-IL	26,000				26,000
Pryor, M	D-AR			26,000		26,000
Rahall, N	D-WV	1,000	3,000	1,000	1,000	6,000
Rangel, C	D-NY	2,500	34,000	5,000	11,000	52,500
Redmond, W	R-NM	2,000	2,000			4,000
Reid, H	D-NV	16,000	2,000	9,000	11,000	38,000
Robb, C	D-VA	333	6,000	500		6,833
Ros-Lehtinen, I	R-FL	3,500	4,500	3,500	5,500	17,000
Schultz, D	D-FL			5,000		5,000
Schumer, C	D-NY	4,000	1,000	2,000	2,000	9,000
Serrano, J	D-NY			3,000	1,000	4,000
Shaw, E Clay	R-FL	6,635	8,500	9,000	3,500	27,635
Shelby, R	R-AL	13,000	1,000		4,000	18,000
Shuster, B	R-PA	14,850	10,500			25,350
Smith, A	D-WA	4,000	500	2,000	2,000	8,500
Smith, G	R-OR	1,000		7,000	2,000	10,000
Specter, A	R-PA	1,250			15,249	16,499
Stearns, C	R-FL	1,750	3,000	3,000	5,000	12,750
Stevens, T	R-AK	1,000	10,000	16,100	3,000	30,100
Strickland, T	D-CO			5,000		5,000
Swett, K	D-NH			5,500		5,500
Tauzin, W	R-LA	4,500		6,000	3,000	13,500
Tebelius, D	R-WA				12,000	12,000
Thomas, W	R-CA	4,000	1,500			5,500
Thune, J	R-SD			3,500	1,500	5,000
Thurman, K	D-FL	2,500	1,000	3,500		7,000
Voinovich, G	R-OH				8,000	8,000
Weldon, D	R-FL	1,000	500	1,000	6,250	8,750
Weller, G	R-IL	3,869	4,500		2,000	10,369
Wexler, R	D-FL	500		2,000	3,000	5500
Wolf, F	R-VA			2,000	4,000	6,000
Wyden, R	D-OR	2,750		8,000		10,750
Young, CW	R-FL	500	1,000	2,000	2,004	5,504
Young, D	R-AK	25,000	47,350	42,550	40,300	155,200

Appendix D

Grants From Royal Caribbean's Ocean Fund, 1997–2004

	1997	1998	1999	2000	2001	2003	2004	Total
Alaska Sea Life Center		50,000	50,000	50,000			50,000	200,000
Bahamas Reef Environment Educational Foundation		35,000	35,000	30,000				100,000
Bermuda Biological Station						75,000		75,000
Bermuda Underwater Exploration Institute	50,000					68,000		118,000
C. Darwin Foundation							25,000	25,000
Cabrillo Marine Aquarium		75,000			70,000			145,000
Caribbean Marine Research Centre		30,000						30,000
Clean Islands International	50,000		50,000					100,000
Center for Marine Conservation		50,000		450,000				500,000
Conservation Fund, Alaska					100,000		50,000	150,000
Conservation International							60,000	60,000
Earthwatch			50,000	50,000				100,000
Florida Aquarium		47,000				20,500	25,000	92,500
Florida International University Foundation					75,000			75,000
Harbor Branch Oceanographic Institution	90,000	75,000						165,000
Heinz Centre for Science		50,000						50,000
International Ecotourism Society	50,000							50,000
International Seakeepers Society			100,000					100,000
Island Dolphin Care						50,000	25,000	75,000

Appendix D: Grants from Royal Caribbean's Ocean Fund – continued:

	1997	1998	1999	2000	2001	2003	2004	Total
Marine Animal Lifeline							25,000	25,000
Marine Stewardship Council							50,000	50,000
MAST Academy			50,000		15,000			65,000
Miami Museum of Science				35,000				35,000
Mote Marine Lab					20,000			20,000
National Audubon Society			50,000		450,000			500,000
National Marine Sanctuary Foundation							200,000	200,000
Nature Conservancy	50,000							50,000
Ocean Research and Education Foundation					20,000			20,000
Ocean Watch	25,000							25,000
Perry Institute for Marine Science						31,250		31,250
Reef Relief		75,000						75,000
Smithsonian Tropical Research Institute	20,000							20,000
Southern California Marine Institute			50,000					50,000
St. Croix Environmental Association			30,000					30,000
Tampa Bay Watch					20,000		50,000	70,000
Tongass Coast Aquarium				100,000				100,000
University of Florida, Carr Centre for Sea Turtle Research		50,000	100,000					150,000
University of Miami	100,000						40,000	140,000
University of West Indies						36,000		36,000
Wider Caribbean Sea Turtle Conservation			15,500					15,500
World Wildlife Fund		50,000		450,000		200,000		700,000
Year Total:	435,000	587,000	580,500	1,165,000	770,000	480,750	600,000	4,618,250

Appendix E

Illness Outbreaks* by Cruise Line & Ship, 2002– May 2005

Ship	Date	Reported	Illness	Pax	Crew	Total
Carnival Cruise Lines						
Carnival Conquest	Dec 02	CDC	Noro (2)	224	39	263
	Dec 02			35	23	58
Carnival Legend	Nov 03	CDC	Noro (2)	100	41	141
	Nov 03			73	4	77
Carnival Pride	Mar 02	CDC	Noro			NR
Carnival Spirit	Jan 02	CDC	Noro	102	10	112
Celebration	Feb 04	CDC	Noro	328	20	348
	Feb 05	CDC	Noro (2)	89	35	124
	Feb 05			69	30	99
Fascination	Dec 02	CDC/Media	Noro (2)	190	13	203
	Dec 02					24
Holiday	Oct 03	CDC	Noro (2)	97	53	150
	Oct 03			12	25	37
Celebrity Cruises						
Constellation	Nov 02	CDC	Noro			134
Horizon	Mar 04	CDC	Noro	49	5	54
	Apr 05	CDC	Gastro	42	14	56
Infinity	Jan 05	PAX	Gastro (2)	200		200
	Jan 05			200		200
Mercury	Aug 02	Media	Salmonella			30
	Mar 04	PAX	Gastro			NR
Zenith	Apr 04	CDC	Noro	48	7	55
	Mar 05	CDC	Noro (2)	138	17	155
	Apr 05	PAX		100		100
Clipper Cruise Line						
Clipper Odyssey	Aug 03	CDC	Gastro			NR
Legacy	Jan 04	CDC	Gastro (2)			NR
	Jan 04					NR
Nantucket Clipper	Mar 02	CDC	Noro			NR
	Oct 02	CDC	Sappo			NR
	Jan 03	CDC	Gastro	5	5	10
	Mar 03	CDC	Gastro			NR
	Oct 03	CDC	Gastro			NR

Ship	Date	Reported	Illness	Pax	Crew	Total
Clipper Cruise Line – continued:						
Nantucket Clipper	Jul 04	Media	Gastro	6		6
	Aug 04	CDC	Gastro			NR
Yorktown Clipper	Aug 02	CDC	Gastro			NR
Crystal Cruises						
Crystal Symphony	Apr 05	CDC	Gastro	20	3	23
Cunard Line						
Caronia	Mar 02	CDC	E. coli	225	15	240
QE II	Jan 02	CDC	Noro			NR
	Jan 04	CDC	Gastro	29	46	75
	Feb 04	CDC	Gastro	82	24	106
Queen Mary 2	Feb 04	CDC	Noro	33	55	88
Disney Cruise Line						
Disney Magic	Nov 02	CDC	Noro (2)			275
	Nov 02			164	23	187
	Dec 02	Media	Gastro	25		25
Holland America Line						
Amsterdam	Apr 02	CDC	Gastro			NR
	Oct 02			196	12	208
	Oct 02	CDC	Noro (4)	41	8	49
	Nov 02			163	18	181
	Nov 02			64	18	82
	Aug 03	Media	Gastro	25		25
	Apr 04	CDC	E. coli	75	11	86
Rotterdam	Apr 04	CDC	Gastro	38	7	45
Ryndam	Apr 02	CDC	Noro			NR
	Jul 02	CDC	Noro (2)	167	9	176
	Jul 02			189	30	219
	Feb 04	CDC	Noro	79	10	89
	Jan 05	CDC	Noro	267	30	297
Statendam	Nov 02	Media	Gastro			40
Veendam	Apr 04	CDC	Noro	79	6	85
	Jun 04	PAX	Gastro	40		40
	Oct 04	CDC	Gastro	39	2	41
	Jan 05	CDC	Noro	70	7	77
	Jan 05	CDC	Noro	200	30	230
	Mar 05	CDC	Noro	88	6	94

Ship	Date	Reported	Illness	Pax	Crew	Total
Holland America Line - continued:						
Volendam	Aug 04	PAX	Gastro	75		75
	Dec 03	CDC	Noro	53	11	64
Zaandam	Sep 04	PAX	Gastro	50		50
Zuiderdam	Jul 04	PAX	Gastro	25		25
Norwegian Cruise Line (NCL)						
Norway	Jan 03	CDC	Noro	105	11	116
Norwegian	Apr 04			43	8	51
Crown	Apr 04	CDC	Noro (3)	43	2	45
	May 04			39	6	45
	Feb 05	PAX	Gastro (2)	34		34
	Feb 05			250	75	325
	Mar 05	CDC	Gastro	60	4	64
Norwegian Dream	Aug 02	PAX	Gastro			180
	Sep 02	CDC	Giardia, Shigella	169		169
	Mar 03	CDC	Noro			NR
	Dec 04	CDC	Gastro	73	9	82
Norwegian Sea	Dec 04	CDC	Gastro	44	4	48
Norwegian Sky	May 04	CDC	Noro (2)	90	10	100
	May 04			55	5	60
Norwegian Star	Sep 03	CDC	Gastro			NR
Norwegian Sun	Aug 02	CDC	Gastro			NR
	Sep 02	CDC	Noro	93		93
Norwegian Wind	Apr 04	CDC	Gastro	54	2	56
P&O Cruises						
Aurora	Oct 03	Media	Noro	580	28	608
Oceana	Dec 02	CDC	Noro	269	24	293
	Sep 03	Media	Gastro	95		95
	May 05	Media	Gastro	200		200
Oriana	Feb 04	CDC	Noro	65	9	74
P&O Cruises Australia						
Pacific Sky	Dec 03	Media	Gasto (2)	200		200
	Jan 04			60		60
	May 04	Media	Gastro (2)	140		140
	May 04			32	24	56

Ship	Date	Reported	Illness	Pax	Crew	Total
Princess Cruises						
Coral Princess	Jan 04	CDC	Noro	134	20	154
	Jan 05	CDC	Noro	84	31	115
Dawn Princess	May 05	CDC	Gastro	76	9	85
Golden Princess	Dec 04	CDC	Gastro	84	15	99
Island Princess	Jun 04	CDC	Gastro (2)	375	49	324
	Jun 04			66	19	85
Ocean Princess	May 02	CDC	Noro (2)	40	12	52
	Jun 02			88	39	127
Pacific Princess	Jul 04	CDC	Gastro	22	4	26
Regal Princess	Aug 03	CDC	Noro	301	45	346
	Sep 04	CDC	Gastro	47	7	54
	Mar 05	CDC	Gastro	38	15	53
Royal Princess	Apr 03	CDC	Gastro			NR
	Mar 04	CDC	Gastro	46	12	58
Star Princess	Aug 03	CDC	Noro (2)			
	Aug 03			107	14	121
Sun Princess	Feb 02	CDC	Noro	267	29	296
	Sep 04	CDC	Noro (2)	145	5	150
	Sep 04			101	14	115
	Oct 04	PAX	Gastro			NR
	Jan 05	CDC	Noro	93	5	98
	May 05	CDC	Noro	121	4	125
Royal Caribbean International						
Brilliance of the Seas	Dec 02	Media	Gastro	42	42	
	Feb 04	CDC	Noro	78	16	94
Empress of the Seas	Jan 05	CDC	Noro	68	5	73
Echantment of the Seas	Jan 05	CDC	Noro	103	8	111
Majesty of the Seas	Dec 02	Media	Gastro	71	10	81
Mariner of the Seas	Jan 05	CDC	Noro	276	27	303
Monarch of the Seas	Nov 02	Media	Gastro	35	6	41
Radiance of the Seas	Sep 02	Media	Gastro	46	7	53

Ship	Date	Reported	Illness	Pax	Crew	Total
Royal Caribbean International - continued:						
Rhapsody of the Seas	Jul 03	CDC	Gastro	72		72
Serenade of the Seas	Jun 04	CDC	Gastro	71	9	80
Voyager of the Seas	May 05 May 05	CDC/PAX	Gastro (2)	45 85	14 14	59 99
Seabourn Cruise Line						
Seabourn Pride	Feb 02	CDC	Gastro			NR
	Nov 02	CDC	Gastro			NR
Silversea Cruises						
Silver Shadow	Aug 04	CDC	Gastro	13	5	18
Silver Shadow	Dec 04	CDC	Gastro	11	20	31
Sun Cruises						
Sundream	Jan 03 Feb 03	CDC	Noro (2)	95	12	107 NR
Viking River Cruises						
Viking Spirit	Oct 02	PAX	Gastro			NR
Viking Burgundy	Apr 03	PAX	Gastro	90		90
Other Cruise Lines						
Classic Cruises						
Arabella	Jan 03	CDC	Gastro			NR
Costa Cruises						
Costa Tropicale	Mar 03	PAX	Gastro	30		30
Glacier Bay Cruiseline						
Wilderness Explorer	Aug 02	Media	Noro			18
Mediterranean Shipping						
Melody	Mar 03	CDC	Noro			NR
Mitsui OSK						
Nippon Maru	Apr 03	CDC	Gastro			NR
Phoenix Reisen						
Albatross	Feb 02	CDC	Gastro			NR
Pulmantur						
R6 Blue Star	Aug 04	Media	Gastro	30	2	32

Ship	Date	Reported	Illness	Pax	Crew	Total
Radisson Seven Seas Cruises						
Seven Seas Mariner	Dec 02	CDC	Salmonella	5	16	21
	Feb 05	CDC	Salmonella	1	20	21
Regal Cruises						
Regal Empress	Jan 03	CDC	Gastro			NR
ResidenSea						
The World	Feb 04	CDC	Gastro		8	8
Royal Olympia Cruises						
Olympia Voyager	Jan 03	CDC	Gastro	35	5	40
Semester at Sea						
M/V Explorer	Dec 04	CDC	Gastro	71	1	72
Windstar Cruises						
Wind Surf	Jan 02	CDC	Gastro			NR
	Feb 05	PAX	Gastro	20		20

* An illness outbreak is when 3 percent of passengers (pax) or 2 percent of crew members report ill.

Appendix F

Events at Sea:
All the Things that Can Go Wrong on a Cruise, 2002–2004

Date	Ship	Details of Mishap
American Safari Cruises		
Jun 02	*Safari Quest*	Engine room fire disabled one engine; continues on reduced power.
May 03	*Safari Spirit*	Hit rocks 80 miles north of Vancouver Island and sank in about 30 feet of water. All safely evacuated to lifeboats.
Sep 03	*Safari Quest*	Failed sanitation inspection: 81 points out of 100 (86 required to pass).
American West Steamboat		
Oct 03	*Empress of the North*	The paddlewheel ship hit the gate at Ice Harbor Dam and became stuck in the navigational lock. 200 passengers bussed back to Portland.
Nov 03	*Empress of the North*	Ship ran aground on the Columbia River. Two crew and one passenger suffered minor injuries.
Carnival Cruise Lines		
Mar 02	*Fantasy*	A Picasso etching valued at $12,000 reportedly cut from its frame in front of the casino in the early morning.
Mar 02	*Jubilee*	Sailing canceled due to mechanical difficulties.
Mar 02	*Carnival Pride*	Norovirus outbreak
Apr 02	*Jubilee*	Failed sanitation inspection: 84 points out of 100 (86 required to pass).
Apr 02	*Carnival Spirit*	Air conditioning problems shorten cruise to 9 days from 12; next cruise canceled for repairs.
May 02	*Carnival Destiny*	Power lost for a couple of hours; Aruba replaced St. Lucia.
Jun 02	*Celebration*	Technical problem with propulsion system; stop in Playa del Carmen canceled and Cozumel shortened. Next cruise canceled for repairs.
Jun 02	*Inspiration*	Problem with propulsion system; reduced speed causes late arrival (3 hours) in New Orleans.
Jul 02	*Carnival Destiny*	A 55-year-old man found hanging in a shower stall — an apparent suicide.
Oct 02	*Elation*	Cruise canceled due to propulsion system problems, limiting speed (Cabo San Lucas skipped on previous cruise). Sent to dry dock.

Date	Ship	Details of Mishap
Nov 02	Holiday	Lodged on a sandy bottom .25 miles off coast of Playa del Carmen for 3 days. No injuries or damage. Next cruise canceled.
Dec 02	Fascination	Norovirus outbreaks on 2 cruises in a row.
Dec 02	Carnival Conquest	Norovirus outbreaks on 2 cruises in a row.
Jan 03	Ecstasy	Accidental discharge of 60 gallons of gray water while anchored one-half mile from land at Avalon Bay (Catalina Island, CA).
Jan 03	Carnival Spirit	Norovirus outbreak
Jan 03	Ecstasy	Passengers report an older disabled man jumped to his death from the top of the atrium into the lobby area.
Feb 03	Carnival Legend	Crew member charged with sexual battery after a 28-year-old woman identified him as the man who entered her cabin while she was sleeping and raped her.
Feb 03	Carnival Victory	Ship tilted 5 degrees when a stabilizer malfunctioned. No injuries.
Mar 03	Carnival Conquest	Passengers reported the ship rolled sharply (sending them for life vests and glass crashing to deck) to avoid collision with another ship.
Apr 03	Celebration	A man accidentally fell overboard in the Gulf of Mexico and was rescued 17 hours later by a passing cargo vessel.
May 03	Holiday	Ship left almost 24 hours late after security breaches led the Coast Guard to recheck all passengers, crew, and baggage.
May 03	Carnival Conquest	A 35-year-old man fell from a 10th floor balcony between 12 midnight and 1 AM.
Jul 03	Carnival Conquest	A 25-year-old man was charged with raping a 16-year-old female fellow passenger the final night of the cruise.
Sep 03	Celebration	Because of a malfunction in one of the two propulsion systems, arrives 12 hours late. The next cruise departs a day late.
Sep 03	Celebration	Engine problems continue and one of the two ports are dropped.
Oct 03	Holiday	Two cruises in a row with norovirus outbreaks
Oct 03	Carnival Cruise Line	Paid $200,000 to settle with the California State Lands Commission over the cruise line's noncompliance with state ballast water law.
Nov 03	Carnival Legend	Two cruises in a row with norovirus outbreaks
Feb 04	Celebration	Norovirus outbreak

Date	Ship	Details of Mishap
Feb 04	Holiday	Embarkation/debarkation changed from New Orleans to Mobile, AL, because Mississippi River is blocked.
Feb 04	Carnival Conquest	Embarkation/debarkation changed from New Orleans to Gulfport, MS, because Mississippi River is blocked.
Mar 04	Holiday	Arrived in New Orleans 12 hours late due to a "technical malfunction." Departure also delayed.
May 04	Carnival Victory	Delayed disembarkation at Grand Cayman after bomb threat. Threat traced to an inebriated passenger who was taken into custody.
May 04	Sensation	Four seamen allegedly fell 100 feet during a lifeboat drill when a winch failed while the ship was docked in Cozumel, Mexico. They suffered broken legs, hips, and spines when the lifeboat smashed into the water.
Jun 04	Carnival Miracle	Unscheduled dry dock announced for August 28, 2004, for maintenance on the podded propulsion unit. Cruise canceled.
Jun 04	Carnival Destiny	Passenger reported ship was adrift between St. Thomas to Dominica and delayed 3.5 hours.
Jul 04	Jubilee	Passenger reported engine problems and ports canceled/changed. Key West substituted with Freeport; port calls shortened.
Jul 04	Fascination	Passenger suspected to have fallen overboard.
Jul 04	Carnival Legend	Medical emergency requiring a detour to Bermuda made ship 8 hours late arriving and departing NYC.
Jul 04	Carnival Miracle	At 4 AM, an announcement made over the PA system said, "This is the captain speaking. All crew members abandon ship." A few minutes later a further announcement said all was well and the previous message had been a mistake. A bit later, the captain apologized, stating teenagers had misused the PA system.
Aug 04	Carnival Miracle	Carnival bumped passengers on cruises leaving from Baltimore because ship was overbooked. Hundreds of passengers' cruises canceled.
Aug 04	Carnival Legend	An 8-day cruise from NYC to the Caribbean took a detour to Bermuda where passengers spent 3 days while an electrical component in the Azipod propulsion system was repaired. Passengers returned to NYC from Bermuda without going to the Caribbean.

Date	Ship	Details of Mishap
Aug 04	Carnival Pride	Failed sanitation inspection: 83 points out of 100 (86 required to pass).
Aug 04	Holiday	Rescued 5 people, including a 10-year-old boy, after their fishing boat burned and capsized off the coast of Cancún. A search ensued after ship employees heard someone yell from the water.
Oct 04	Fantasy	Failed sanitation inspection: 83 points out of 100 (86 required to pass).
Nov 04	Holiday	Lost engine power and collided with pilings along the Mobile River before dawn. It eventually regained power and docked.
Nov 04	Carnival Conquest	A 60-year-old German man reportedly committed suicide by throwing himself overboard and into the water when in port at Cayman Islands.
Nov 04	Celebration	A 54-year-old man was reported missing, possibly at sea, after the ship arrived home from a 5-day cruise to the Bahamas.
Dec 04	Carnival Pride	A 37-year-old woman disappeared from the ship while 30 miles off the Mexican coast. A search proved unsuccessful. There is question regarding whether foul play was involved.
Dec 04	Carnival Victory	Failed sanitation inspection: 80 points out of 100 (86 required to pass).
Dec 04	Celebration	Stop at Grand Cayman canceled because, apparently, a crew member was struck by a forklift and broke his back. The ship was re-routed to Cozumel (nearest port) where the injured worker was disembarked.
Dec 04	Holiday	Cruise to Cozumel became a 4-night "cruise to nowhere" because mechanical problems made it impossible for the ship to make it to Cozumel and back. Passengers given a choice to cancel.

Celebrity Cruises

Date	Ship	Details of Mishap
Mar 02	Summit	One sailing canceled for an unscheduled dry dock to repair propulsion pods.
Mar 02	Infinity	Two sailings canceled for an unscheduled dry dock to repair propulsion pods.
May 02	Constellation	Leak in the starboard propulsion pod delays delivery; first cruise canceled.
Jun 02	Infinity	Coast Guard investigated a near miss with Legend of the Seas when both entering Juneau Harbor.
Aug 02	Mercury	Health Canada investigated an outbreak of salmonella on two cruises.

Date	Ship	Details of Mishap
Nov 02	*Millennium*	Two crew members (a plumber and an air conditioning technician) arrested for sexual assault and battery of a female youth counselor.
Nov 02	*Constellation*	Norovirus outbreak.
Feb 03	*Infinity*	Transcanal cruise ends 3 days early in Acapulco instead of San Diego. Next 3 cruises canceled for repairs to the port propulsion pod.
Jul 03	*Summit*	Hull damaged when hitting a rock leaving Hubbard Glacier. Docked at Seward with a 10-foot-long hole in the ballast tank midway along the hull and a 140-foot-long crease. Delayed 2 days while repairs made.
Jul 03	*Millennium*	Cruise canceled for dry dock to have a thrust-bearing unit replaced in the ship's port propulsion system.
Jul 03	*Summit*	Charges filed against a 33-year-old male accused of inappropriately touching a passenger during a massage.
Mar 04	*Infinity*	Reduced speeds caused by propulsion problems affected South America itinerary.
Mar 04	*Infinity* *Millennium*	One *Millennium* cruise canceled to replace the *Infinity* which went into dry dock to repair its propulsion system.
Mar 04	*Horizon*	Norovirus outbreak.
Apr 04	*Zenith*	Norovirus outbreak.
Apr 04	*Galaxy*	380 passengers stranded in Charleston, SC, when ship forced to leave berth because it had failed to file its manifest paperwork on time. It departed, waited outside 12 miles from shore the required time, and returned to pick up those left behind. Fined $32,500.
Sep 04	*Summit*	Will enter dry dock for pre-emptive repair to starboard propulsion system. One cruise canceled, one delayed for 3 days, and one had itinerary adjustments to accommodate ship's top speed.
Sep 04	*Zenith*	Worker arraigned in Bermuda for "unlawful assault and causing bodily harm" to a female co-worker. It is alleged the co-worker received injuries to her face as a result of being attacked with a bottle.
Nov 04	*Century*	Failed sanitation inspection: 79 points out of 100 (86 required to pass).

Date	Ship	Details of Mishap
Nov 04/ Dec 04	Xpeditions	Reports on Cruise Critic of recurring health problems (gastrointestinal illness) on the ship. The ship is not normally inspected by the CDC because it operates outside US waters.

Clipper Cruise Line

Date	Ship	Details of Mishap
Mar 02	Nantucket Clipper	Norovirus outbreak.
Mar 02	Clipper Adventurer	Ran aground on a sand bank in the Essequibo River (Guyana's major waterway) and stuck more than a day.
Jul 02	Clipper Odyssey	Ran aground on St. Matthew Island in the Bering Sea in favorable conditions. After calling for help because attempts to free were futile, ship freed. No damage and no spills.
Aug 02	Yorktown Clipper	Gastrointestinal virus outbreak.
Oct 02	Nantucket Clipper	Sapporovirus outbreak.
Nov 02	Clipper Adventurer	Ran aground near Deception Island in Antarctica. Freed by a Chilean icebreaker. Minor damage but no injuries.
Dec 02	Legacy	Failed sanitation inspection: 82 points out of 100 (86 required to pass).
Jan 03	Nantucket Clipper	Gastrointestinal virus outbreak.
Mar 03	Nantucket Clipper	Gastrointestinal virus outbreak.
Aug 03	Clipper Odyssey	Gastrointestinal virus outbreak.
Oct 03	Nantucket Clipper	Gastrointestinal virus outbreak.
Dec 03/ Jan 04	Legacy	Two cruises in a row with norovirus outbreaks.
Jul 04	Nantucket Clipper	Gastrointestinal virus outbreak.
Jul 04	Legacy	Failed sanitation inspection: 76 points out of 100 (86 required to pass).
Jul 04	Clipper Odyssey	Ran hard aground on rocks in the Aleutian Islands, forcing 153 passengers and crew to transfer to other ships. No injuries reported; ship floated free with the tide next day and proceeded on its own power. Out of service for 2 months.
Aug 04	Nantucket Clipper	Gastrointestinal virus outbreak.

Costa Cruises

Date	Ship	Details of Mishap
Mar 03	Costa Tropicale	50 kilograms (110 pounds) of cocaine found hidden in suitcases of passengers when docked in southern Brazil.
Mar 03	Costa Tropicale	Gastrointestinal virus outbreak
Apr 03	Costa Fortuna	Fire broke out while at the shipyard. Deck 8 was heavily damaged for more than half of its length; damage also reported on decks 7 and 9. The ship was still promised for on-time delivery.

Date	Ship	Details of Mishap
Cruise West		
Jun 02	*Spirit of Endeavor*	Failed 2 successive sanitation inspections: 85 and then 74 points out of 100 (86 required to pass).
Jun 03	*Spirit of Columbia*	Reported that vessel hit bottom and possibly bent the port shaft and propeller in Jackpot Bay, Alaska. Passengers were safely off-loaded in Whittier; the ship was inspected and continued on its way.
Oct 04	*Spirit of Endeavor*	Failed sanitation inspection: 80 points out of 100 (86 required to pass).
Crystal Cruises		
Oct 02	*Crystal Harmony*	Contrary to written promise to not discharge in Monterey Bay Marine Sanctuary, ship discharged 36,000 gallons of treated bilge, treated sewage, and gray water.
Mar 03	*Crystal Harmony*	Banned from Monterey, CA, forever; Crystal Cruises barred for 15 years.
Cunard Line		
Feb 02	*Caronia*	Detained and fined $410,000 after 8,000 gallons of heavy fuel oil spilled into Guanabara Bay near Rio de Janeiro. Delayed 1 day.
Mar 02	*Caronia*	E. coli from water bunkered in Guatemala and ingested with water and ice cubes made from the water is the source of a gastrointestinal virus outbreak.
May 02	*QE II*	A large leak in the aft engine room was stopped after several efforts (over 36 hours, while at sea); several hundred tons of sea water had to be pumped overboard so workers could get at the leaking pipe.
May 02	*QE II*	Departure from NYC delayed more than 13 hours because of a leak in a condenser.
Jun 02	*QE II*	Two workers airlifted (250 miles off Ireland) after being blasted with scalding steam from a faulty boiler valve.
Jan 03	*QE II*	Norovirus outbreak.
Jan 03	*QE II*	Failed inspection by Vessel Sanitation Program after regulators found cockroaches in the kitchen, mold residue on ice makers, and blocked drains in the nursery.
Mar 03	*Caronia*	Three passengers arrested by British police with 20 kilograms (44 pounds) of cocaine in their luggage.

Date	Ship	Details of Mishap
Nov 03	Queen Mary 2	Fifteen people died when a dockside gangway collapsed as visitors were walking onto the liner across a gangway.
Jan 04	QE II	Gastrointestinal virus outbreak.
Feb 04	QE II	Gastrointestinal virus outbreak.
Mar 04	Queen Mary 2	Norovirus outbreak.
Apr 04	Queen Mary 2	Arrived in Southampton 3.5 hours late. Delayed in Lisbon while a problem with a door over a bow thruster was repaired and unable to make up time because one of the back-up engine turbines was not working properly.
Jun 04	Queen Mary 2	Passenger report of a man overboard incident during a Caribbean cruise — rumor was suicide. Disembarkation delayed 3 hours in St. Thomas because "paperwork" not in order.
Jun 04	Queen Mary 2	BBC investigation found panels in 900 of the bathrooms "do not fully meet fire regulation standards"; led to installations of 1,300 additional smoke alarms and plans to install sprinklers in the bathrooms.

Disney Cruise Line

Date	Ship	Details of Mishap
Mar 02	Disney Magic	Smoke stack fire extinguished within 1 hour. Passengers awakened at 5:00 AM and assembled at stations with life jackets. Arrived at next destination 1.5 hours late.
Aug 02	Disney Wonder	Letters sent to more than 15,000 passengers who sailed in the 2 weeks before August 4 and those who planned to cruise the month after August 8, warning of risk of exposure after a crew member came down with rubella. Citing cost, the cruise industry in 1998 ignored CDC recommendations to administer rubella vaccine to all crew without documented immunity.
Nov 02	Disney Magic	Two cruises in a row with norovirus outbreaks. Next cruise canceled for ship to be sanitized and cleaned.
Dec 02	Disney Magic	Media report of gastrointestinal illness.

Festival Cruises (Ceased operations May 2004)

Date	Ship	Details of Mishap
Mar 02	Mistral and European Stars	Mistral pulled from Cuba a month early (4 cruises canceled) to substitute for the European Stars' first 2 or 3 voyages because of late delivery.
Jan 04	Mistral European Stars European Vision	Ships seized in dispute with creditors. Cruises canceled.

Date	Ship	Details of Mishap
Jan 04	*Azur*	Suffered propulsion problems in bad weather off Antalya and unable to enter port. Cut short call to Rhodes, skipped Piraeus, and ended in Ravenna, Italy instead of Venice as planned. Next cruise canceled.
Jan 04	*Bolero Flamenco*	Arrested in Gibraltar on behalf of J.P. Morgan Bank.
Jan 04	*Caribe*	Cruise scheduled for January 31 canceled. All 7 ships owned by Festival Cruises are now idle.

Fred Olsen Cruises

Date	Ship	Details of Mishap
Mar 02	*Black Prince*	Ran aground on sand bank. Passengers were disembarked, bussed to Havana and flown home.
Dec 02	*Black Watch*	Mechanical problems forced the ship to slow down and arrived at Southampton 2 days late. Following cruise delayed.
Mar 04	*Black Prince*	One of the two main engines broke down on the transatlantic crossing. Cruise ended late; ship out of service for a month.
Apr 04	*Black Prince*	En route to first trip after engine repairs, ship broke down and left without power just off Southampton docks. 412 passengers waited hours for the ship's arrival.

Glacier Bay Cruiseline

Date	Ship	Details of Mishap
Aug 02	*Wilderness Explorer*	Media report of gastrointestinal virus outbreak.
May 04	*Wilderness Adventurer*	Evacuated after striking ice and taking on water in SE Alaska. The ice punctured a 3-inch hole in the hull. No injuries and all safely evacuated to another ship.

Hapag-Lloyd

Date	Ship	Details of Mishap
Jan 02	*Europa*	Delayed 26 hours after strong winds blew stern into East Pier when leaving Cape Town.
Dec 02	*Hanseatic*	While on a coastal cruise of New Zealand struck by a rogue wave, which broke out one of the bridge windows and damaged electrical systems. Delayed for repairs.

Holiday Kreuzfahrten

Date	Ship	Details of Mishap
Jul 03	*Mona Lisa*	Evacuated after running onto rocks near Spitsbergen in the Barents Sea. Both propellers and the hull thought to be damaged. Next cruise canceled.
May 04	*Mona Lisa*	Stuck in mud close to St. Mark's Square in Venice, Italy. Freed with no injuries and no damage to the ship,

Date	Ship	Details of Mishap
Holland America Line		
Jan 02	*Noordam*	Failed sanitation inspection: 82 points out of 100 (86 required to pass).
Apr 02	*Ryndam*	Norovirus outbreak.
Apr 02	*Amsterdam*	Gastrointestinal virus outbreak.
Jul 02	*Ryndam*	Norovirus outbreak 2 cruises in a row.
Aug 02	*Ryndam*	Cruise canceled. Ship sanitized and cleaned.
Aug 02	*Statendam*	Five tugboats called to tow ship back to Vancouver after small fire knocked out 4 generators and the ship's 2 main propulsion motors. Efforts to repair the problem took too long so the cruise was canceled. The following cruise was also canceled.
Aug 02	*Ryndam*	A generator stopped running while in the Lynn Canal (Alaska), causing loss of power; ship adrift for approximately 20 minutes. Passengers awoke expecting to be in Glacier Bay but were instead at Auke Bay. Escorted by a tug, the ship docked to undergo inspection then continued.
Aug 02	*Ryndam*	Approximately 40,000 gallons of sewage sludge discharged into Juneau Harbor.
Oct 02	*Statendam*	Bumped by a tugboat towing a barge; damaged above the water line. Departure delayed.
Oct 02	*Amsterdam*	Norovirus outbreak on repositioning cruise from Seattle to Fort Lauderdale.
Oct 02	*Amsterdam*	Norovirus outbreak again; some passengers and crew offloaded at ports during the cruise.
Nov 02	*Amsterdam*	Upon embarkation passengers told ship had been contaminated with Norwalk virus during the previous cruise. Another outbreak on this cruise; passengers disembarked at Bonaire and St. Thomas.
Nov 02	*Amsterdam*	Fourth cruise in a row with norovirus outbreak. Next cruise canceled so ship could be cleaned and sanitized.
Nov 02	*Statendam*	Media report of gastrointestinal illness.
Jan 03	*Statendam*	An elderly man suspected of jumping overboard the night before disembarkation during a roundtrip cruise from San Diego to Hawai'i.
Mar 03	*Oosterdam*	First 2 voyages canceled because of shipyard delays. Inaugural voyage moved from July 10 to August 3.

Date	Ship	Details of Mishap
Mar 03	*Ryndam*	A passenger reported the ship listed to the port side causing injuries to passengers and crew. The pool emptied down the elevator shafts, and put elevators on the port side out of commission for 4 days. The incident was explained as a mechanical failure when going from manual to automatic pilot.
May 03	*Veendam*	A 51-year-old man was missing from the ship when it disembarked passengers in Vancouver; it is presumed he fell overboard.
Aug 03	*Amsterdam*	Gastrointestinal virus outbreak.
Aug 03	*Volendam*	Passenger report of a gastrointestinal virus outbreak.
Aug 03	Carnival Corporation	Carnival's probation officer accused the company of violating terms of its probation by filing 12 false audit reports. Carnival said they fired 3 environmental-compliance employees responsible for the reports.
Sep 03	*Zaandam*	Passenger report of a gastrointestinal virus outbreak.
Oct 03	*Westerdam*	A fire lasting 3.5-hours occurred during construction but did not affect ship's delivery.
Dec 03	*Volendam*	Norovirus outbreak.
Feb 04	*Ryndam*	Norovirus outbreak.
Apr 04	*Amsterdam*	Passengers and crew sickened by E. coli.
Apr 04	*Noordam*	Chief engineers admitted to improperly processing bilge water from Jan 2004 to March 4, 2004. Being pursued by Coast Guard officials in San Juan, Puerto Rico, and Tampa, Florida.
Apr 04	*Rotterdam*	Gastrointestinal virus outbreak.
Apr 04	*Veendam*	Norovirus outbreak.
May 04	*Veendam* *Volendam*	Multiple reports on Internet newsgroups of engine/propulsion problems on *Veendam*. Two cruises skipped College Fjord, cut short the visit to ports, and arrived late into Vancouver (and Seward); many passengers missed scheduled flights home. *Volendam's* right engine was reported not operational on one cruise.
Jun 04	Holland America	Former Vice President Richard K. Softye pleaded guilty to falsely certifying that Holland America Line was performing environmental audits when it wasn't.
Jun 04	*Veendam*	Passengers report a gastrointestinal virus outbreak.

Date	Ship	Details of Mishap
Jul 04	*Zuiderdam*	Passengers report a gastrointestinal virus outbreak.
Sep 04	*Rotterdam*	Ambulances greeted ship in Halifax after enduring monster waves from hurricane Karl in the North Atlantic. Approximately a dozen passengers were taken to hospital with suspected fractures and severe bruising. In total, 90 people reported injury. The ship lost power and for 3 hours was tossed around in high waves and darkness.
Oct 04	*Veendam*	Gastrointestinal virus outbreak
Dec 04	Holland America Line	The company agreed to a $2-million plea agreement in return for its discharge of raw sewage in Juneau Harbor in August 2002.
Dec 04	*Maasdam*	Arrived in Norfolk 8 or 9 hours later than scheduled because of bad weather.

Japan Cruise Line

Jan 03	*Pacific Venus*	Two passengers contracted Legionnaire's disease while on a cruise to Taiwan. The next cruise scheduled for 4 weeks was canceled.
Jun 04	*Pacific Venus*	Failed sanitation inspection: 77 points out of 100 (86 required to pass).

Majestic International

Aug 03	*Ocean Monarch*	A German passenger died, and four others infected with Legionnaire's disease following return to Germany from a cruise to Greenland.
May 04	*Ocean Majesty*	Arrived in Warnemunde and was scheduled to depart for Tallinn that evening, but canceled due to problem with steering gear's hydraulic system. Passengers disembarked.

Mediterranean Shipping Company (MSC)

Mar 03	*Melody*	Norovirus outbreak
Sep 03	*Melody*	Ran into pier at Kusadasi; waited several days for repairs.
May 04	*Lirica*	Failed sanitation inspection: 85 points out of 100 (86 required to pass).

Norwegian Cruise Line (NCL)

Mar 02	*Norway*	Stewardess accidentally fell overboard. Rescued after 10 hours in water; call at St. Maarten canceled.
Jul 02	*Norway*	Wine steward arrested for raping a passenger. Woman and husband both reported to be under the effect of some type of drug.

Date	Ship	Details of Mishap
Jul 02	*Norway*	A crew member fled when met by US Customs agents in Miami. Apprehended with 4.4 pounds (2 kg) of heroin. Disembarkation delayed while drug dogs searched the ship. Four-hour delay in the ship's departure that evening.
Aug 02	*Norwegian Sun*	Gastrointestinal virus outbreak.
Aug 02	*Norwegian Dream*	Passenger reported that as many as 100 people got food poisoning on excursion to Moscow. Ship provided free infirmary services.
Aug 02	*Norwegian Majesty*	Acting on intelligence reports, police raided the ship and seized 33 pounds of cocaine while docked at Bermuda.
Aug 02	*Norwegian Dream*	Passenger reported as many as 15 percent of passengers contracted gastrointestinal illness. Ship provided free infirmary visits.
Sep 02	*Norwegian Dream*	Illness caused by shigella and Giardia. Ship provided free infirmary visits.
Oct 02	*Norwegian Sun*	Norovirus outbreak.
Jan 03	*Norway*	Norovirus outbreak.
Feb 03	*Norwegian Star*	A problem in one of the two Azipod transformers forced ship to operate more slowly; skipped Kiribati but stopped as scheduled at all Hawai'i islands.
Feb 03	*Norwegian Wind*	A couple took photos of glass, plastics, and other waste being tossed into the sea from the back of the ship between Hawai'i and Kiribati.
Mar 03	*Norwegian Star*	An injured crewman airlifted to Oahu after falling from a tender and injuring his legs on the propeller when ship at Kiribati. Ship diverted to Christmas Island and subsequent ports canceled.
Mar 03	*Norwegian Dream*	Norovirus outbreak.
Apr 03	*Norwegian Dream*	Passengers notified at embarkation of schedule change. Instead of going to St. Petersburg, Helsinki, and Tallinn, they were going to Amsterdam, Germany, and Norway.
May 03	*Norwegian Sun*	Discharged 16,000 gallons (40 tons) of raw sewage into the Strait of Juan de Fuca, WA.
May 03	*Norwegian Sky*	Norovirus outbreak.
May 03	*Norway*	A boiler room explosion killed 8 crew members and injured 20 others. No passengers were injured. Cruises canceled indefinitely.
Sep 03	*Norwegian Star*	Gastrointestinal virus outbreak.

Date	Ship	Details of Mishap
Sep 03	Norwegian Crown	Sustained damage to propeller from fishing nets en route from Quebec City to Boston; was delayed 1 day.
Dec 03	Norway	Three engineers indicted on charges of falsifying log books to conceal dumping of waste oil at sea.
Mar 04	Norwegian Crown	Two cruises in a row with norovirus outbreaks.
Apr 04	Norwegian Star	Damage to the forward thrust bearing in the ship's Azipod system, meant stops at Kiribati were canceled. Ship entered dry dock a week earlier than planned — 1 cruise canceled.
Apr 04	Norwegian Wind	Gastrointestinal virus outbreak.
Apr 04	Norwegian Dream	Itinerary changed as a result of a broken crankshaft and ship operated on one engine. Madeira and Genoa dropped; Gibraltar added.
Apr/ May 04	Norwegian Crown	Two cruises in a row with norovirus outbreaks.
May 04	Norwegian Dream	Canceled stop at Genoa, substituting Gibraltar. Afterwards, planned to go to Barcelona but Spanish government enforced law preventing a ship docking at a Spanish port after docking at Gibraltar. Substitute Sete, France for Barcelona.
Jul 04	Norwegian Crown Norwegian Majesty	Hundreds fell violently sick as their Bermuda-bound ships were pounded by 15-foot waves during a fierce storm. All outdoor activities canceled; seasickness drugs, green apples and salt crackers distributed by staff.
Aug 04	Norwegian Sea	En route from Houston to Cozumel, rescued 4 men who had been clinging to a partially submerged fishing boat for 12 days. For almost 2 weeks, they had drifted 520 miles through the Yucatán Strait, catching fish with the help of a t-shirt and drinking rainwater.
Oct 04	Norwegian Majesty	Arrived in Boston 1 day late from Bermuda after going through a storm with 25- to 30-foot waves and horrendous winds.
Dec 04	Norwegian Sea	Gastrointestinal virus outbreak.
Dec 04	Norwegian Dream	Gastrointestinal virus outbreak.

NCL America

Date	Ship	Details of Mishap
Jan 04	Pride of America	Sank at shipyard during a heavy storm. Lower 3 decks under water and engine spaces flooded. Damage extensive.

Date	Ship	Details of Mishap
Jun 04	*Pride of Aloha*	May have dropped anchor over fragile shale beds in Monterey Bay. NCL insists it anchored at one of the 2 permitted locations, but a scientist using lasers and global positioning equipment says otherwise.
Jun 04	*Pride of Aloha*	Maiden call at Hilo met with protest. At issue is NCL's failure to respect and accept responsibility for the impact they will have on the Hawaiian culture and environment.
Aug 04	*Pride of Aloha*	Problems with service, cleanliness, and product quality since the cruise line began led to refunding 50 percent of the mandatory service fee. The service fee was suspended altogether a month later, but will be re-instituted when service is up to standards.

Ocean Club Cruises

May 03	*Mirage*	Failed sanitation inspection: 77 points out of 100 (86 required to pass).
Aug 03	*Mirage*	A 31-year-old steward was arrested for allegedly having consensual sex with a 15-year-old female passenger. He was charged with lewd and lascivious battery on a minor under 16 years of age.
Nov 03	*Mirage*	Next cruise abruptly canceled after ship caught in rough seas that shook up passengers, knocked over equipment, and delayed arrival 2 hours.

Orient Lines

May 02	*Marco Polo*	Unscheduled dry dock to repair main engine. Out of service for 13 days — cruises canceled
Feb 03	*Marco Polo*	Plates welded over cracks found in the hull after ship was pushed by wind on to shallow waters while in the South Shetland Islands.

Plantours and Partners

May 03	*Vistamar*	Ship collided with underwater rocks near the port of Ibiza. Towed by emergency tugs and all evacuated safely. This and 2 additional cruises canceled.
Feb 04	*Vistamar*	Detained in St. Thomas for 36 hours when US Coast Guard found ship lacked certification required by IMO. Held while crew received required training.

Date	Ship	Details of Mishap
P&O Cruises		
Mar 02	*Oriana*	An auxiliary engine failed causing the other 3 engines to stop while crossing the North Pacific. Drifted for 2 hours and then proceeded at reduced speed. Arrived in San Francisco slightly later than scheduled.
Dec 02	*Oceana*	Denied access to St. Maarten after norovirus outbreak.
Sep 03	*Oceana*	Gastrointestinal virus outbreak.
Sep 03	*Oceana*	Nine passengers' hair turned green after using the onboard swimming pool. The cause was not known, but as a gesture of goodwill, the ship's beauty salon provided corrective treatment.
Oct 03	*Aurora*	Norovirus outbreak.
Jan 04	*Oceana*	Ordered out of St. Thomas harbor after failing to provide a list of names and citizenship of its 2,870 passengers and crew. Tenders filled with passengers were sent back to the ship. The ship continued on to Antigua.
Mar 04	*Oriana*	Norovirus outbreak.
May 04	*Caronia*	Passenger reported the ship suffered a total power failure after a leak from a swimming pool took out the main electric board. Drifted for approximately 2 hours before partial power restored. Delay caused revised itinerary.
P&O Cruises (Australia)		
Jan 02	*Pacific Sky*	Two passengers admitted to hospital with meningococcal virus several days after cruise; one dies. P&O stresses infection not related to the ship but to individual contact.
Mar 03	*Pacific Sky*	Returned to Auckland after taking on 165 tons of water from a leak through cracked and corroded plating on the side of the ship. This and following cruise canceled.
Dec 03/ Jan 04	*Pacific Sky*	Two cruises in a row with norovirus outbreaks.
May 04	*Pacific Sky*	Two cruises in a row with norovirus outbreaks.
Nov 04	*Pacific Sky*	Turned back to Brisbane after engine problems prevented it from reaching full speed. The departure had been delayed for more than a day to fix a faulty boiler, and was further delayed to repair a damaged gearbox in the starboard engine.

Date	Ship	Details of Mishap
Nov 04	*Pacific Sky*	Taking on passengers when the engines' water intake became clogged with jellyfish and the engines automatically shut down. Departed 15 hours late.

Princess Cruises

Date	Ship	Details of Mishap
May 02	*Ocean Princess*	Norovirus outbreak.
Jun 02	*Ocean Princess*	Norovirus outbreak.
Oct 02	*Diamond Princess*	Fire swept the ship while being built at a shipyard in Japan. Damage extensive.
Nov 02	*Coral Princess*	Inaugural voyage canceled and rescheduled 10 days later; rescheduled again in December with an additional 3-week delay.
Feb 03	*Sun Princess*	Norovirus outbreak.
Feb 03	*Island Princess*	Ship's delivery delayed 2 months. Inaugural cruise moved from May 13 to July 12.
Apr 03	*Royal Princess*	Gastrointestinal virus outbreak
Aug 03	*Star Princess*	Two cruises in a row with norovirus outbreaks.
Aug 03	*Regal Princess*	Norovirus outbreak.
Aug 03	*Sun Princess*	A 61-year-old man is indicted on 6 felony counts of sexual abuse on a minor. He allegedly forced sexual relations on a 15-year-old boy while both were in the sauna.
Oct 03	*Sun Princess*	A passenger reported one of the 4 engines was not working on this cruise. Left ports early, arrived late, and skipped Princess Cay.
Nov 03	*Sapphire Princess*	Maiden voyage delayed 1 month. Ship's hull was the original *Diamond Princess* damaged by fire in October 2002.
Nov 03	*Royal Princess*	A passenger report says the ship collided with the pier when docking, causing an 8-foot rent in the bow of the vessel and delaying its departure until repairs were completed. Mykonos was skipped as a result; Rhodes had been missed because of sea conditions.
Jan 04	*Coral Princess*	Norovirus outbreak.
Mar 04	*Royal Princess*	Gastrointestinal virus outbreak.
Apr 04	*Diamond Princess*	Five hours late returning to LA because of "technical difficulties." Rumor was a blown engine. The previous cruise had 3 power failures (none longer than 5 minutes) and a water main break in a public washroom.
May 04	*Coral Princess*	A passenger called a San Francisco TV station and reported the ship struck a whale near Golden Gate Bridge.

Date	Ship	Details of Mishap
Jun 04	*Island Princess*	2 cruises in a row with gastrointestinal virus outbreaks.
May 04	*Diamond Princess*	High winds pushed the ship into a pier at Victoria, B.C., when it was docking. Returned to Seattle the next day, 6 hours late. The following cruise dropped Juneau and Victoria because the ship was cruising more slowly.
Jul 04	*Pacific Princess*	Gastrointestinal virus outbreak.
Sep 04	*Sun Princess*	Two cruises in a row with norovirus outbreaks.
Sep 04	*Regal Princess*	Gastrointestinal virus outbreak.
Nov 04	*Sun Princess*	Passenger report of gastrointestinal virus outbreak.
Dec 04	*Sapphire Princess*	As the ship came into the inlet to anchor at Moorea it lost all power and was out of control for about 5 minutes. The only way to stop the ship was to drop an anchor and the ship touched the reef in the process.
Dec 04	*Golden Princess*	Gastrointestinal virus outbreak.
Dec 04	*Coral Princess*	Two workers reportedly got into an argument and one stabbed the other. The wounded man was transferred to hospital in stable condition.

Radisson Seven Seas

Apr 02	*Seven Seas Mariner*	Three cruises canceled for repair of one of its pod propulsion systems.
Jul 02	*Seven Seas Mariner*	Engine problems caused a 6-hour delay in Stockholm. Call at Helsinki for the next day was canceled; ship sailed directly to St. Petersburg.
Dec 02	*Seven Seas Mariner*	Passengers and crew sickened by salmonella.
Mar 04	*Seven Seas Voyager*	Forced to drop anchor in the middle of Victoria Harbor (Hong Kong) — no berths available because *QE II* had extended its port call from 2 to 3 nights. Passengers were upset about having to tender ashore.
Oct 04/ Nov 04	*Seven Seas Mariner*	Canceled Cabo San Lucas on several 7-day cruises to Mexican Riviera. Propeller damaged in Alaska 5 months earlier forced ship to sail at reduced speeds. Similar adjustments were made for future itineraries until the ship was dry docked in December.

Regal Cruise Line (Ceased operations April 28, 2003)

Jan 03	*Regal Empress*	Gastrointestinal virus outbreak
Feb 03	*Regal Empress*	Engine trouble forced cancellation of a 3-day cruise and delayed by a day return of the previous cruise.

Date	Ship	Details of Mishap
Apr 03	*Regal Empress*	Two cruises canceled after the ship is served with arrest warrants over unpaid invoices.

Royal Caribbean International (RCI)

Date	Ship	Details of Mishap
Jun 02	*Legend of the Seas*	Coast Guard investigated near miss with *Infinity* when both entering Juneau Harbor.
Jul 02	*Adventure of the Seas*	A 31-year-old graphic artist somehow boarded the ship in Phillipsburg and the next day died while in custody when the ship was docked in St. Thomas.
Jul 02	*Radiance of the Seas*	While sailing between Juneau and Skagway, two crew members began arguing; one pulled a knife and began slashing the other. Knife victim in serious condition and medevaced.
Aug 02	*Radiance of the Seas*	Ship experienced a 3-minute power outage that disabled steering and propulsion capability while in Frederick Sound. RCI says a crew member accidentally turned off a hydraulic pump, causing a temporary loss of rudder control.
Sep 02	*Radiance of the Seas*	Gastrointestinal virus outbreak.
Oct 02	*Brilliance of the Seas*	Propulsion problems cause Saint John, NB, to be dropped and call at Portland, Maine, to be extended for repairs.
Nov 02	*Monarch of the Seas*	Gastrointestinal virus outbreak.
Dec 02	*Brilliance of the Seas*	Gastrointestinal virus outbreak.
Dec 02	*Majesty of the Seas*	Gastrointestinal virus outbreak.
Feb 03	*Radiance of the Seas*	Ship struck by strong winds as it crossed a squall line and briefly went into a 7-degree list (tilt). No injuries.
Feb 03	*Explorer of the Seas*	A minor fire was discovered at the aft end of Deck 13 and extinguished 13 minutes later. Damage to inline skating facility and the top of the waterslide on Deck 12.
Feb 03	*Monarch of the Seas*	Crew member scalded during routine maintenance on a boiler in the engine room.
Apr 03	*Sovereign of the Seas*	A 30-year-old worker charged with committing sex acts on a 14-year-old girl on a high school band trip. She told chaperones she had sex with the man the last night of the cruise.

Date	Ship	Details of Mishap
Apr 03	*Legend of the Seas*	A 20-year-old woman planted threatening notes around the ship in hopes the cruise would end early. The ship missed Hilo and cut its stop at Kona short because it diverted to Honolulu after the notes were found. Woman arrested and imprisoned.
May 03	RCCL	A suit charged RCI and Celebrity with billing passengers at least $150 million in fraudulent taxes that the companies pocketed as additional fare revenue.
Jun 03	*Legend of the Seas*	The 41-year-old Food and Beverage Manager arrested at Seward, AK and charged with sexually assaulting a 22-year-old female crew member.
Jul 03	*Vision of the Seas*	A 28-year-old male passenger arrested and accused of sexually assaulting a 22-year-old female passenger.
Jul 03	*Rhapsody of the Seas*	Norovirus outbreak.
Aug 03	*Vision of the Seas*	Difficulties with the diesel electric propulsion motors caused the ship to leave Ketchikan 17 hours late.
Jan 04	*Serenade of the Seas*	Made a sharp turn resulting in a 13.5-degree list lasting 20 seconds. Originally, thought to be a malfunction during a required steering test, the list was caused by human error resulting from miscommunication between two areas of the ship.
Feb 04	*Majesty of the Seas*	Passengers were directed to stay at their muster stations for 24 minutes when a galley fire broke out at 5 AM in the Windjammer Cafe. It was extinguished in 21 minutes; no injuries. The ship continued but Windjammer Cafe was closed.
Feb 04	*Grandeur of the Seas*	Trapped in New Orleans when a supply boat capsized near the mouth of the Mississippi River. Departure delayed; turned out to be a 2-day cruise-to-nowhere.
Feb 04	*Rhapsody of the Seas*	Embarkation/debarkation changed from New Orleans to Gulfport, MS because Mississippi River is blocked.
Feb 04	RCI	Calls at private island (Lababee, Haiti) suspended due to unrest in the country.

Date	Ship	Details of Mishap
Feb 04	*Brilliance of the Seas*	Norovirus outbreak
Jun 04	RCI	An ex-crew member charged that RCI failed to respond promptly or properly after she reported having been sexually assaulted by a co-worker. The woman also alleged RCI failed to save any evidence and "subjected her to multiple interrogations," took no action against the accused, and she was subsequently fired.
Jun 04	*Serenade of the Seas*	Gastrointestinal virus outbreak.
Jul 04	*Rhapsody of the Seas*	An underage girl filed suit accusing crew members of giving her alcohol and sexually assaulting her. The incident is alleged to have happened in July 2003.
Aug 04	*Voyager of the Seas*	AP reports a suit claiming sexual assault by an employee on a cruise August 2003. The assault happened when an employee insisted on escorting the woman back to her cabin took her instead to an employees-only area and attacked her.
Aug 04	*Splendor of the Seas*	A woman alleges she was attacked and raped by a senior worker and the cruise line did nothing about it. The incident happened December 2002 — she had only been on the ship for 1.5 days. RCI says it reported her claim to authorities and the incident "appeared to be a consensual relationship on the night of the alleged incident."
Aug 04	*Voyager of the Seas*	A 67-year-old woman committed suicide by jumping overboard after losing money in the casino.
Sep 04	*Empress of the Seas*	Seven crew members seriously injured after a lifeboat plunged 60 feet into the water during a training exercise.
Sep 04	*Jewel of the Seas*	A 62-foot (20-m) finback whale found impaled on the bow on arrival in Saint John, NB.
Oct 04	RCI	Passenger wrote on Internet usenet board that his daughter had been sexually assaulted by another guest and complained that the matter didn't receive the attention needed when on board.
Nov 04	*Enchantment of the Seas*	While docked at Key West, ship struck by a barge leaving an 8-foot hole in the vessel's hull. No injuries; ship repaired and departed on schedule.

Date	Ship	Details of Mishap
Dec 04	*Brilliance of the Seas*	A couple have sued alleging RCI's baby sitter sexually assaulted their 2-year-old son while they were on a cruise. The assault allegedly occurred on Dec. 18, 2003.

Royal Olympia Cruises

April 02	*Olympia Explorer*	After a year-long dispute with the shipbuilder, Royal Olympia announced it will take possession of ship in time for the start of her summer season.
Oct 02	*Olympia Voyager*	Pulled from service for 3 weeks after damage to portside hull below the waterline. Passengers transferred to the *Aegean I* for rest of cruise.
Jan 03	*Olympia Voyager*	Gastrointestinal virus outbreak
Dec 03	*Olympia Voyager*	Christmas/New Year's cruise remained anchored off St. Thomas rather than cruise the Amazon. Next cruise canceled while the company works out its finances.
Dec 03	*Olympia Explorer*	Cruise canceled after cruise line filed for bankruptcy protection.
Jan 04	*Olympia Countess* *Olympia Voyager* *Olympia Explorer*	Ships seized and proceeding to auction. Cruises canceled.

Seabourn Cruise Line

Feb 02	*Seabourn Pride*	Gastrointestinal virus outbreak
Nov 02	*Seabourn Pride*	Gastrointestinal virus outbreak

Sea Escape Cruises

Feb 02	*Island Adventure*	Failed sanitation inspection: 79 points out of 100 (86 required to pass).
Mar 03	*Island Adventure*	Failed sanitation inspection: 81 points out of 100 (86 required to pass).
Apr 03	*Island Adventure*	Fire in storage area on lower deck of the ship forced evacuation of crew. No passengers were on board. Minor damage.

Silja Line

Sep 03	*Opera*	Collided with several ships and a crane at St. Petersburg. Damage not sufficient to delay itinerary.
Nov 03	*Opera*	Collided with an icebreaker at the exit of St. Petersburg. Lifeboats were damaged but was capable of travel.

Silversea Cruises

Jul 04	*Silver Shadow*	Gastrointestinal virus outbreak.
Dec 04	*Silver Shadow*	Gastrointestinal virus outbreak.

Date	Ship	Details of Mishap
Dec 04	*Silver Wind*	A crew member was lost at sea between Montevideo, Uruguay, and Punta Arenas, Chile. A suicide note indicated marital complications.

Stena Line

Date	Ship	Details of Mishap
Feb 03	*Stena Europe*	Adrift for 3 hours in winds of 35–40 knots. Irish Coast Guard called to assist.
Feb 04	*Stena Nautica*	Collided with a cargo ship causing a 34-foot (11-meter) hole in the ship's hull. 91 passengers and 37 crew were evacuated to another ship.

Sun Cruises (Airtours) (Ceased operations April 2004)

Date	Ship	Details of Mishap
Aug 02	*Sundream*	14-year-old girl lured to a crew member's cabin by offer of alcohol and raped by 3 crewmen (dining room waiters). Mother reportedly told that cruise line wasn't responsible because the men weren't acting in their capacity as waiters — this happened on their own time.
Jan 03	*Sundream*	Norovirus outbreak.
Feb 03	*Sundream*	Norovirus outbreak.
Oct 03	*Sundream*	Collided with pier at La Gomera. Some repairs at Tenerife and then an early return to Southampton. The next cruise was shortened to give time needed for repairs.
Mar 04	*Seawing*	Two cruises canceled. Ship under auction as part of the Royal Olympia bankruptcy.
Apr 04	My Travel	All cruise operations were sold to Cyprus-based Louis Cruises.

Transocean Cruises

Date	Ship	Details of Mishap
May 03	*Astor*	Failed sanitation inspection: 79 points out of 100 (86 required to pass).
Feb 04	*Astor*	Grounded in the shipping channel after leaving Townsville, Australia. Delayed for two hours to ensure seaworthiness.

Viking River Cruises

Date	Ship	Details of Mishap
Oct 02	*Viking Spirit*	Passenger report of gastrointestinal virus outbreak.
Mar 03	*Viking Burgundy*	Passenger report of gastrointestinal virus outbreak.
Jun 04	*Viking Europe*	Hit a bridge in Vienna, injuring 19 people — mainly scrapes and bruises. The ship still functioned and damage to bridge was slight.

Windstar Cruises

Date	Ship	Details of Mishap
Jan 02	*Wind Surf*	Gastrointestinal virus outbreak.
Dec 02	*Wind Song*	Engine room fire forced evacuation of the ship's 127 passengers and 92 crew. Ship was a total loss.

Date	Ship	Details of Mishap
Dec 02	*Wind Star*	Until *Wind Star* could assume *Wind Song's* itineraries, 7 Tahiti itineraries canceled. All *Wind Star* Central America cruises were canceled from January 4 forward.
Jan 03	*Wind Spirit*	Passenger reports the ship experienced engine and generator problems that left it adrift for a night and part of a day. Underwent repairs at Tortola.

Other Cruise Lines

American Cruise Line

May 04	*American Glory*	Destroyed a 40-foot section of dock and damaged two yachts when a strong current and tide combination forced the stern into the pier. A door was damaged and 2 windows shattered; delayed 90 minutes and then continued.

Classic Cruises

Jan 03	*Arabella*	Gastrointestinal virus outbreak

Crown Investments

Jun 02	*Crown*	Previously *Norwegian Star I* (*Royal Odyssey*, *Royal Viking Sea*), the ship was delivered by Star Cruises to Crown Investment PRC for 3.5-year charter. Upon inspection swarms of cockroaches were found in the kitchen and other areas — port officials killed more than 10,000 cockroaches.

Cruceros Australis

May 02	*Terra Australis*	Sank off southwest coast of Chile following fire that began in the engine room. No passengers aboard, but 1 crew member died of smoke inhalation.

DFDS Seaways

May 02	*Princess of Scandinavia*	Cruise ferry with 758 passengers, 126 crew has engine fire which spread to funnel. Fire extinguished after several hours. Plans for evacuation canceled.

Hebridian Island Cruises

Jun 03	*Hebridian Princess*	Cruise canceled when half of the ship's 38 crew were struck down with severe tonsillitis.

Island Cruises

May 02	*Island Escape*	Ship flooded with sewage before start of cruise. Canceled.

OSK Passenger Line

Apr 03	*Matsui*	Gastrointestinal virus outbreak.

Date	Ship	Details of Mishap
P&O Ferries		
Apr 03	*Pride of Provence*	Ship hit a breakwater while visibility good and sea conditions fine. Her Master suspended during an investigation. Twenty-eight people suffered minor injuries in the accident which left an indentation from deck 5 to the ship's double-hull bottom.
Peter Dielmann Cruises		
Sep 04	*Berlin*	Entered dry dock for repair to a stabilizer damaged when it collided with a pier at Invergordon. One cruise canceled. Departure of another changed.
Phoenix Reisen		
Feb 02	*Albatross*	Gastrointestinal virus outbreak.
Pullmantur Cruises		
Aug 04	*R6 Blue Star*	Gastrointestinal virus outbreak.
Residensea		
Feb 02	*The World*	After delays, delivery on February 20; will set sail mid-March. Christening ceremony in NYC rescheduled from April 19 to May 17.
Society Expeditions		
Jun 04	*World Discoverer*	Ship's mortgage holders took possession and company ceased operations. Company filed for bankruptcy.
Star Clippers		
Feb 03	*Star Flyer*	Collided with wharf and sustained minimal damage when a small section of wharf collapsed at Port Klang, Malaysia.
Sun Cruise Casino		
May 04	*Sun Cruz V*	Engine room fire extinguished and no injuries. Ship was 3 miles south of Port Everglades and was towed back.
Thomson Holidays		
Aug 03	*Topaz*	Failed sanitation inspection: 72 points out of 100 (86 required to pass).
Travelscope		
Sep 04	*Van Gogh*	Collided with oil tanker in foggy conditions off the southern coast of Spain. No report of injuries or spilt oil, returned to Gibraltar and passengers flown home.

Miscellaneous Vessels

Date	Ship	Details of Mishap
Jan 02	*Walrus*	Collided with Chinese cargo ship in foggy conditions. Undamaged and returned to service.
Nov 02	*Olivia*	Ship detained for more than a day after inspectors in New Zealand found problems with an emergency pump and with equipment that separates oil from water in the ship's bilges.
Aug 03	*MTS Atlantis*	A crewman was killed and 19 others admitted to hospital when a fire extinguisher exploded while ship anchored at the island of Santorini. No passengers were on board when the incident occurred.
Sep 03	*Astoria*	Detained in London after a routine inspection revealed its galleys were infested with cockroaches. Passengers disembarked in London and the ship returned (unauthorized) to Bremerhaven.
Aug 03	*MTS Atlantis*	A crewman was killed and 19 others admitted to hospital when a fire extinguisher exploded while ship anchored at the island of Santorini. No passengers were on board when the incident occurred.
Oct 03	*Kempinski Ganna*	The 2002-built Nile cruise ship suffered a fire sailing from Luxor to Aswan. The captain ordered the ship abandoned. The fire is thought to have broken out in a passenger cabin.

Endnotes

Introduction

[1] See "Mr. easyJet Sets Course for the Cut-Rate Cruise," *Channelnewasia* (March 18, 2004), <www.channelnewasia.com/stories/afp_world_business/view/76044/1/.html>, Accessed March 18, 2004; and Rebecca Tobin, "easyCruise: No Frills Cruising on the Horizon," *Travel Weekly* (February 23, 2004), <www.twcrossroads.com/news/newswrapper.asp?ArticleID=41661&Keyword=Cruise>, Accessed February 23, 2004.

[2] Kelly Yamanouchi, "Cruise Lines Admit Pollution Violations," *Honolulu Advertiser* (December 12, 2003), <the.honoluluadvertiser.com/article/2003/Dec/12/bz/bz021.html>, Accessed December 22, 2003.

[3] See Associated Press, "Ex-Cruise Executive Sentenced in Miami," *Los Angeles Times* (July 1, 2004), <www.latimes.com/business/investing/wire/sns-ap-cruise-pollution,1,6814020.story?coll=sns-ap-investing-headlines>, Accessed July 2, 2004.

[4] See <www.cruisejunkie.com/outbreaks.html>.

Chapter 1: Cruise Tourism Arrives in North America

[1] *Queen Mary 2* is 1,132 feet in length whereas the Washington Monument rises 550 feet. Another point of comparison is the Eiffel Tower, 147 feet shorter than the *Queen Mary 2* is long.

[2] *Princess Patricia* was built in 1949 for Canadian Pacific's Vancouver-Victoria-Seattle service and designed as a day steamer with only 51 cabins. The ship had a major overhaul in 1963 and additional accommodation was built on the car deck and upper deck. It returned for its first summer cruise to Alaska on June 1, 1963.

[3] *Italia* was ordered in 1963, and was launched in April 1965. During fitting out, both the owners and builders declared bankruptcy, and ownership passed to BNL, a creditor bank. BNL chartered the ship to Costa Line in 1967 and Costa subchartered the ship to Princess Cruises. In 1969 *Princess Italia* moved to Alaska cruises out of San Francisco. The subcharter was canceled in 1973, and *Italia* returned to Costa, which purchased it in 1977 and sold it in September 1983 to Ocean Cruise Lines.

[4] *Pacific Princess* and *Island Princess* were both 20,000 tons and carried 640 passengers and a crew of 350.

[5] *Sun Princess* was originally to have been a sibling to Norwegian Caribbean Line's *Southward*, to be named *Seaward*. NCL pulled out of the deal after price rises following the Italian shipbuilders' nationalization and the hull was sold to P&O. The ship was completed in the autumn of 1972 and named *Spirit of London*. It was transferred to Princess Cruises in 1974. The 17,270-ton ship accommodates 800 passengers and 392 crew members.

[6] *Sea Princess* was originally Swedish America Line's *Kungsholm*. It retained the name when sold to Flagship Cruises in 1975. P&O bought the ship in 1979, originally to replace the aging *Arcadia*, but after a major overhaul the ship was renamed *Sea Princess* and assigned to Princess Cruises. The 29,000-ton ship carries 714 passengers and 420 crew. It most recently sailed as *Mona Lisa* for Holiday Kreuzfahrten.

[7] *Royal Princess* was built in 1984. The 45,000-ton ship accommodates 1,200 passengers and 520 crew members.

[8] Bob Dickinson and Andy Vladimir, *Selling the Sea: An Inside Look at the Cruise Industry* (John Wiley and Sons, 1997), p. 24.

[9] Ibid, p. 30.

[10] The 5,000-ton cruise ship *Yarmouth Castle* was built in 1927 as *Evangeline*. In November 1965 it caught fire 60 miles northeast of Nassau. Of the 370 passengers and 175 crew members, 90 were lost. Safety standards on the ship were slipshod, as hearings later pointed out. Interestingly, the ship was referred to in the trade press as a safe "fun ship." See <www.rmstitanichistory.com/yarmouth/yarmouth.html>, Accessed November 12, 2003.

[11] Commodore Cruise Lines filed for bankruptcy in late 2000.

[12] Oivind Mathisen, "25 Years: Royal Caribbean Cruise Line," *Cruise Industry New Quarterly* (Winter 1995/1996), p. 24.

[13] *Song of Norway* was 18,000 tons as built, and carried 724 passengers. In 1978 its length was increased by 85 feet, its capacity expanded to 1,024 passengers, and its weight increased to 23,000 gross tons. The ship was sold to Sun Cruises in 1996 and renamed *Sundream*.

[14] In 1980 *Nordic Prince* underwent the same changes as the *Song of Norway*. The ship was sold to Sun Cruises in 1994 and renamed *Carousel*.

[15] The 18,455-ton *Sun Viking* was the last of three similar ships built for Royal Caribbean. It differed from its two predecessors in that the bow was one deck higher, allowing a few additional cabins. The ship was sold to Hyundai, becoming *Hyundai Pongnae*.

[16] Riklis, who was born in Istanbul in 1922, grew up in Israel and was a schoolmate of Arison's. He had arrived in the US in 1947 and by 1970 was a multimillionaire. He was one of the original corporate takeover artists. His 1966 master's thesis at Ohio State University was on "the effective non-use of cash" in business, and he built a vast fortune running numerous companies, including McCrory Corp. and the Riviera Hotel in Las Vegas. When Arison contacted him, Riklis was chairman of Rapid American Corporation. His Riklis Family Corporation eventually did over a billion dollars in annual sales in the cosmetics field through its Fabergé, Brut, and Elizabeth Arden products.

[17] Though much later, *Forbes* magazine featured an article about the misfortunes that have befallen Riklis' creditors. See Nathan Vardi, "The Check Is Not in the Mail," *Forbes* (September 30, 2002.), <www.forbes.com/forbes/2002/0930/400067_print.html>, Accessed June 5, 2004.

[18] *Empress of Canada* made its maiden voyage from Liverpool to Canada on April 24, 1961, by which time the service had become summer only. It regularly sailed between Liverpool and Quebec and Montreal in summer and ran its first winter Caribbean cruise from New York in December 1961. The number of Atlantic crossings decreased over the years, so that only seven crossings were made in 1969. In 1968 the ship received the latest Canadian Pacific funnel design which was adapted as the Carnival symbol when bought in February 1972. The ship was 27,300 tons and carried 1,048 passengers.

[19] Ted Kissell, "The Deep Blue Greed," *Miami New Times* (February 3–9, 2000), <www.miaminewtimes.com/issues/current/feature3.html>, Accessed February 8, 2000.

[20] Ibid.

[21] *Empress of Britain* was built in 1956 by Fairfields of Glasgow. It was Britain's first fully air-conditioned liner. Initially running on the North Atlantic from Liverpool, it ran its first winter Caribbean cruise from New York in January 1960. Its final Atlantic voyage was completed in October 1963. It was sold to the Greek Line, and re-entered service as *Queen Anna Maria* in 1965, running a fortnightly service to New York calling at Naples and Lisbon. Following the

collapse of the Greek Line, it was sold to Carnival. In 1993 *Carnivale* was renamed *Fiesta Marina* and then in 1994 named *Olympic* by Epirotiki. In 2002 Thomson Tours chartered the ship in the UK and renamed it *Topaz*. A year later it was chartered to Peace Boat (www.peaceboat.org), a Japan-based international non-governmental and non-profit organization that works to promote peace, human rights, equal and sustainable development and respect for the environment.

22 *S.A. Vaal* was launched in 1961 as *Transvaal Castle* by Union-Castle Line, and served on its South Africa–Southampton route from 1962. It remained in Union-Castle colors until 1966, when it was transferred to the South African Marine Corp (UK). In 1969 it transferred to the South African flag. On October 10, 1977, the ship was sold to Carnival Cruise Lines, and rebuilt in Japan. Following the delivery of purpose-built cruise ships to Carnival, it was sold to Dolphin Cruise Line and renamed *Island Breeze*. It was chartered to UK holiday company Thomson during the late 1990s, passed to Premier Cruises with the rest of the Dolphin ships when the companies merged, and was renamed *Big Red Boat III*. On June 4, 2003, the ship steamed from Freeport enroute to the shipbreakers at Alang, India, via Gibraltar. It had the distinction of being the first Carnival Cruise liner to be scrapped. The 38,000-ton ship accommodated 1,146 passengers.

23 Similar in size to the *Festivale*, *Tropicale* was 36,674 tons and accommodated 1,022 passengers. It became *Costa Tropicale* in 2001 and in late 2005 will begin sailing as P&O Australia's *Pacific Star*.

24 See "Honorary Degree for Arison," *Seatrade Insider* (July 21, 2004) <www.cruise-community.com/ShowStory.asp?ID=5971>, Accessed July 21, 2004.

25 Bob Dickinson and Andy Vladimir, *Selling the Sea: An Inside Look at the Cruise Industry* (John Wiley and Sons, 1987), p. 32–33.

26 *Cunard Adventurer* was built in 1971, sold to Norwegian Caribbean Line in 1977, and renamed *Sunward II*. In 1991 it was sold to Epirotiki Line and named *Triton*. Epirotiki later formed part of Royal Olympic Cruises, which is now owned by the Cyprus-based Louis Cruise Line.

27 *Cunard Ambassador* was built in 1972. It was declared a total loss in 1974 after an engine-room fire, and was sold for conversion to the livestock carrier *Linda Clausen*.

28 Established in 1971, Royal Cruise Line was purchased by Knut Kloster, owner of Norwegian Cruise Line, in 1989.

29 Knut Kloster, owner of Norwegian Cruise Line, purchased Royal Viking Line in 1984.

30 The Sitmar Line (Sitmar = Società Italiana Trasporti Marittimi) was formed in 1938 by Russian émigré Alexandre Vlasov. In 1974 the company devoted itself to leisure cruises and started Los Angeles–based Sitmar Cruises, a joint operation of Valsov's Monaco-based V Ships and the Lefebvre family in Rome, which owned the company. In 1988 Sitmar Cruises was sold to Princess Cruises for $210 million. The Lefebvres started Silversea Cruises in 1993. V Ships has been involved in those operations, but there is no indication there was ever joint ownership of Silversea. See George White, "Princess Cruises to Acquire Sitmar in $210-million Deal," *Los Angeles Times* (July 29, 1988), Section 4, p. 1. Also see Peter Plowman, *The SITMAR Liners Past and Present*, (Rosenberg Publishing, 2004).

31 See *Cruise Industry Overview* (Cruise Line International Association, Spring 2004), <cruising.org/press/overview/ind_overview.cfm>, Accessed July 12, 2004.

32 Cruise lines that experienced financial difficulties leading to cessation of some or all of their operations include Premier Cruises, Commodore Cruise Lines, Crown Cruise Line, Cape Canaveral Cruise Line, and the World Cruise Company in 2000; Marine Expeditions,

American Classic Voyages, America Hawaii Cruises, Delta Coastal Voyages, and United States Line in 2001; Regal Cruises in 2003; and Society Expeditions, Festival Cruises, and Royal Olympia Cruises in 2004.

[33] "Who Said It," *Cruise Industry News Quarterly* (Winter 1997/98), p. 104.

[34] In addition to the seven *Destiny*-class vessels operated by Carnival Cruise Lines, Carnival Corporation's Costa Cruises operates two vessels of the same design: *Costa Fortuna* and *Costa Magica*.

[35] Cunard Line Press Release (January 12, 2004), <www.cunardline.com/news/default.asp?Cat=&View=ViewArticle&Mode=News&ContentID=3994>, Accessed July 10, 2004.

[36] See "RCCL Orders Ultra Voyager, Drops Radiance," *Seatrade Insider* (September 19, 2003), <www.cruise-community.com/ShowStory.asp?ID=4377>, Accessed September 19, 2003.

[37] Tony Gray, "Carnival Breaks $1bn and Plans Pinnacle Newbuilds," *Lloyd's List* (September 20, 2004), p. 1, <www6.lexisnexis.com>, Accessed September 18, 2004.

[38] See "Arison: Ultimate Ship Is Now 2 Projects," *Seatrade Insider* (September 29, 2003), <www.cruise-community.com/ShowStory.asp?ID=4418>, Accessed September 29, 2003.

[39] See "Pinnacle Not Possible before 2009," *Seatrade Insider* (December 16, 2004), <www.cruise-community.com/ShowStory.asp?ID=6746>, Accessed December 20, 2004.

[40] "Who Said It," *Cruise Industry News Quarterly* (Winter 1997/98), p. 104.

[41] Jason Cochran, "The Ship Hits the Fans," *MSNBC* (November 24, 2003), <www.msnbc.com/m/pt/printthis_main.asp?storyID=995770>, Accessed November 24, 2003.

[42] Scott Blake, "'Megaship' Set to Sail," *Florida Today* (November 11, 2003), <www.floridatoday.com>, Accessed November 12, 2003.

[43] I was told anecdotally by a cruise director that Royal Cruise Line was the first to formally assume control over bingo after the owner, Pericles Panagopulos, realized the lost opportunity for additional income.

[44] Onboard Media was established in 1989 by Phillip Levine. The company was sold to international conglomerate Louis Vuitton Moet Hennessy in 2000.

[45] J. Norman Howard, "Cruising, Better Than Ever?" *Cruise Industry News Quarterly* (Summer 1993), pp. 62–63.

[46] In 2002/2003 RCCL's net profit was $351 million. The company's vice president for Commercial Development, John Tercek, indicated that $100 million of this is from shore excursions. See Tony Peisley, "Shore Excursions Make Impressive Profits," *Cruise Business Review* (December 2003), p. 5.

[47] Tony Peisley, "Shore Excursions Make Impressive Profits."

Chapter 2: I Never Saw A Cruise Line I Didn't Want to Own

[1] Julia Bornstein, "Carnival Cruise Lines: Cruising for a Bruising?" *Fortune Magazine* (June 9, 2003), <www.fortune.com/fortune/investing/articles/0,15114,454317,00.htm>, Accessed June 10, 2003.

[2] Per-berth cost is drastically reduced when building half a dozen identical ships than when building six individual and unique ships. See "What Does It Cost to Build a Ship?" in the previous chapter.

[3] Julia Bornstein, "Carnival Cruise Lines: Cruising for a Bruising?" *Fortune Magazine* (June 9, 2003), <www.fortune.com/fortune/investing/articles/0,15114,454317,00.htm>, Accessed June 10, 2003.

[4] Rajesh Joshi, "Carnival's $100m Savings on Target Thanks to Takeover Deal," *Lloyd's List* (March 10, 2003), <www.lloydslist.com>, Accessed July 20, 2003.

[5] Since its third ship, *Festivale*, Carnival has used Joseph Farcus to design the interior of its ships. He is a virtual in-house architect — his Joseph Farcus Architects is not part of Carnival, but it works for no other cruise lines and Carnival is his sole client. Micky Arison observes that Farcus consistently delivers the "wow" factor. For example, Carnival's *Fantasy*, which features 15 miles of neon tubing, was compared by one journalist to walking into a giant jukebox. Another journalist referred to it as the only ship in the world whose decor is best described in wattage. See Nancy Huie, "Joseph Farcus: Designing for the Sea," *Cruise Industry News Quarterly* (Summer 1996), p. 72. Also see: "Ship Shape: Joe Farcus Shows What It Takes to Cruise in Style," *Brentwood Magazine Online* (November/December, 2002), <www.brentwoodmagazine.com/nov.dec.02/design/design-1.html>, Accessed November 7, 2004.

[6] See "Carnival Cruise Lines Starts Initial Offering," *Wall Street Journal* (July 24, 1987), p. 1.

[7] This is according to the marketing consultants who undertook a campaign to raise occupancy and to make the property more attractive to potential buyers: "We increased occupancy from 59 percent to 85 percent in three months, sufficient to enable Carnival to unload the white elephant." See <www.burkhardworks.com/idposting.html#Carnival>, Accessed October 3, 2004.

[8] Today the hotel is the Wyndham Nassau Resort and Crystal Palace Casino.

[9] Ted Kissell, "The Deep Blue Greed," *Miami New Times* (February 3–9, 2000), www.miaminewtimes.com/issues/current/feature3.html>, Accessed February 8, 2000.

[10] See Air Line Pilot's Association, "Carnival Air Lines Pilots Vote for ALPA Representation," *Release #96.43* (September 5, 1996), <cf.alpa.org/internet/news/1996news/NR96043.htm>, Accessed July 28, 2004.

[11] See National Mediation Board, *25:NMB 324*, <www.nmb.gov/representation/deter1998/25n324.html>, Accessed July 28, 2004.

[12] See Alexis Muellner, "Arison Just Can't Get Off the Carnival," *South Florida Business Journal* (March 9, 1998), <southflorida.bizjournals.com/southflorida/stories/1998/03/09/story1.html?e=broward>, Accessed July 28, 2004.

[13] Fallout from his involvement with Pan Am continued into 2002. Arison had covered $5.4 million in debt that others (such as generic drug millionaire Phillip Frost and former ambassador Charles Cobb) reneged on their promise to repay. His attempt for a court judgment failed. See Associated Press, "Billionaire Micky Arison on Losing End of Appeal," *South Florida Sun Sentinel* (January 16, 2003), <www.sun-sentinel.com>, Accessed August 7, 2003.

[14] The companies operated *Azure Seas* and *Emerald Seas*. *Azure Seas* was built in 1948 as *Southern Cross*. Converted from an ocean liner to a cruise ship in 1975, it weighed 16,500 tons and accommodated 1,000 passengers. It operated as *Calypso I*, and in 1980 was bought by Western Cruise lines. Dolphin Cruise line bought the ship in 1992, naming it *Oceanbreeze*, and in 1997 was placed under Premier Cruises. *Emerald Seas* was originally built as a troop carrier in 1944. It sailed cruises in Hawai'i in the 1950s and 1960s, first as *Leilani* for the Hawaiian Steamship Company and later as *President Roosevelt* for American President Lines. It passed to Chandris Lines in 1970, but was sold in 1972 to Eastern Cruise Lines because Chandris found the ship's fuel consumption too heavy for long distance cruising. In 1992 *Emerald Seas* was sold to Festival Cruises and sailed for two years as *Sapphire Seas*, was laid

up, and then sailed for two years as *Ocean Explorer* before being scrapped. The ship had experienced a major fire in 1986. See *Fire and Explosions Onboard the Panamanian Passenger Ship Emerald Seas in the Atlantic Ocean near Little Stirrup Cay, Bahamas July 30, 1986* (Government Printing Office, 1987). (NTSB Report Number: MAR-87-04)

[15] Delivered in 1982 as *Scandinavia*, the ship was sold to Stardancer Cruises in 1985 because it was financially unsuccessful in providing cruise-ferry service from New York to Freeport (Bahamas). *Stardancer* became Royal Caribbean's *Viking Serenade* when Admiral merged with RCCL. The 40,132-ton, 1,946-passenger ship was renamed *Island Escape* in 2002 for Island Cruises — a joint venture of Royal Caribbean and First Choice Holidays.

[16] See Michael Allen, "Carnival Agrees to Purchase 70% of 2 Rival Lines," *Wall Street Journal* (September 1, 1988), p. 1.

[17] Thomas Pritzker and his uncle Robert Pritzker are tied at 47 on the 2004 Forbes List of the World's Wealthiest People. They are each worth $7.6 billion. Their partners in Royal Caribbean, Sammy and Yuli Ofer who are worth $2.7 billion and Anders Wilhelmsen who is worth $1.8 billion, place 186 and 310, respectively, on the list. See <www.forbes.com/maserati/billionaires2004/bill04land.html>, Accessed June 5, 2004.

[18] See Michael Allen, "Oslo Ship Firm Plans 70% Stake in Cruise Line – Anders Wilhelmsen to Join with Pritzkers in Offer, Topping Carnival's Bid," *Wall Street Journal* (October 6, 1988), p. 1.

[19] "Ofer Marks 80th Birthday," *Sea Transport and Trading Bulletin* (February 24, 2002), <www.seatransport.co.il/index.php?2&sub=3&nid=17>, Accessed March 13, 2004.

[20] Royal Caribbean Cruises Limited's Form 20-F, Securities and Exchange Commission (April 8, 2002).

[21] "Could Pritzker Breakup Affect RCCL?" *Seatrade Insider* (December 11, 2002), <www.cruise-community.com/ShowStory.asp?ID=2942>, Accessed December 15, 2002.

[22] David Osler, "Pritzker Siblings Sue Father for $5bn over 'Looted' Trust Funds," *Lloyd's List* (July 18, 2003), p. 1, <www.lloydslist.com>, Accessed July 20, 2003. Also see "The House of Pritzker," *Business Week* (March 17, 2003), <www.businessweek.com>, Accessed November 7, 2004.

[23] See "A Pritzker Family Tree" and "Family Businesses," *Business Week* (September 10, 2001), <www.businessweek.com>, Accessed November 15, 2001.

[24] Ameet Sachdev, "Judge Rules Pritzker Suits Can Proceed," *Chicago Tribune* (September 23, 2004), <www.chicagotribune.com/business/chi-0409230282sep23,1,194004.story?coll=chi-business-hed>, Accessed September 23, 2004. Also see Andrew Stern, "Lawsuit between Pritzker Heirs Settled, *Reuters* (January 6, 2005), <www.reuters.com/newsArticle.jhtml?type=domesticNews&storyID=7259988>, Accessed January 7, 2005; and Susan Chandler and Kathy Bergen, "Pritzkers Seal Settlement Deal," *Chicago Tribune* (January 7, 2005), <www.chicagotribune.com/business/chi-0501070205jan07,1,5118383.story?coll=chi-business-hed&ctrack=3&cset=true>, Accessed January 8, 2005.

[25] *Prinsendam* caught fire and sank on October 4, 1980. All 375 passengers and 135 crew were safely rescued. Holland America reported that the ship had no sprinklers and the fire doors had failed. See Robin Herman, "Ship Had No Sprinklers and Fire Doors Failed, Line Says," *New York Times* (October 6, 1980).

[26] *Volendam* was originally built as *Brasil*. After Holland America, it sailed as Monarch Cruise Lines' *Monarch Sun*, American Hawaii Cruises' *Liberte*, Banstead Shipping's *Canada Star*, and Bermuda Star Line's *Queen of Bermuda*. In 1990 the Bermuda Star Line consolidated with

Commodore Cruises, the ship was renamed *Enchanted Seas*. In 1995 the ship was purchased and renamed *Universe Explorer*. It operated regular passenger cruises and the University of Pittsburgh's Semester at Sea program from 1995 until 2004. *Veendam* was originally built as *Argentina*. Later it operated as Monarch Cruises Lines' *Monarch Star*, Bermuda Star Line's *Bermuda Star*, and Commodore Cruise Line's *Enchanted Isle*. The ship was laid up when Commodore went out of business in 2000. Both ships were built in 1957, weighed 23,500 tons, and accommodated 730 passengers.

27 See Oivind Mathisen, "Company Profile: Holland America Line," *Cruise Industry News Quarterly* (Summer 1993), pp. 25–32.

28 Lanterman's Retirement and Consulting Agreement began on November 10, 1997. It is included in Carnival Corporation's annual reports (Form 10-K) filed with the US Securities and Exchange Commission beginning in 1998. The final amount payable at retirement is found in "Schedule 14A," *Carnival plc Directors' Remuneration Report, Annex B* (March 1, 2004).

29 See Carnival Corporation Form 8-K, Securities and Exchange Commission (December 6, 2004).

30 See David Mott, "Carnival's Homegrown Renaissance Man," *Lloyd's List* (October 16, 1993), p. 5, <www.llplimited.com/LLArchive/output.cgi?Sat16 Oct1993-003&cruise%20line>, Accessed January 8, 1999.

31 See Eric Morgenthaler, "Carnival Agrees to Buy Holland America Assets — Price Is about $625 Million for Two Cruise Lines, Hotels, Tour Operator," *Wall Street Journal* (November 28, 1988), p. 1. Also see *Holland America Line Official History, 1980s*, <www.hollandamerica.com/about/history.do?date=1980>, Accessed July 25, 2004.

32 *Noordam* was chartered in November 2004 to Thomson Holidays and sails as *Thomson Celebration*. *Westerdam* was transferred to Costa Cruises in April 2002 and sails as *Costa Europa*. The *Nieuw Amsterdam* was sold to United States Lines in October 2000 and sailed as *Patriot* until the company went bankrupt. It was resold and has sailed since 2002 as *Thomson Spirit*. *Rotterdam* was sold to Premier Cruise Lines in August 1997 and sailed as *Rembrandt* until the company went bankrupt in 2000.

33 When it took over Cunard Line, Carnival Corporation acquired *Royal Viking Sun*. The ship was initially assigned to Seabourn Cruise Line and sailed as *Seabourn Sun* but didn't fit with the company's other ships and within a year was transferred to Holland America Line. As the *Royal Viking Sun*, the 38,000-ton ship carried 756 passengers. The ship was renovated before passing to Holland America — its dining room shrank, some public areas were eliminated, and 20 additional rooms were added.

34 Carnival Corporation Form 10-K, Securities and Exchange Commission (February 14, 2003).

35 "Carnival Sells Masa Stake," *Lloyd's List* (March 23, 1991), <www.llplimited.com/LLArchive/output.cgi?Sat23Mar19991-034&cruise%20line>, Accessed January 8, 1999.

36 *Oceanic* was completed in 1963 for Home Lines' seven-day cruises to Nassau from New York through the summer. In winter it ran longer trips to the Caribbean. The ship was sold to Premier in 1985 and later renamed *StarShip Oceanic*, but was frequently marketed as *Big Red Boat*. This later became her official name. When Premier collapsed in September 2000, *Oceanic* was acquired by Spanish operator Pullmantur.

37 *Sun Princess* was sold to Premier Cruises in 1988, becoming *StarShip Majestic*, one of their "big red boats," and retained the red hull when bought by CTC Lines in 1994 as *Southern Cross*. In 1998 it became the third ship in the Festival Cruises fleet as *Flamenco*.

[38] *Atlantic* joined the *Oceanic* in 1981, of the Home Line fleet. It was sold to Premier Cruises in 1988, shortly after Home Line was bought by Holland America Line, and renamed *StarShip Atlantic*. It was sold again in 1996 and became Mediterranean Shipping Lines' *Melody*.

[39] US participation in the Gulf War began with its air attack on January 17, 1991. A ceasefire was declared February 28, 1991.

[40] See David Mott, "Carnival Calls Off Bid for Premier," *Lloyd's List* (June 1, 1991), <www.llplimited.com/LLArchive/output.cgi?Mon03Jun19991-009&cruise%20line>, Accessed January 8, 1999.

[41] Jim Lamb, "Cruise Giant Pursues Long-Term Alliance," *Lloyd's List* (September 19, 1991), <www.llplimited.com/LLArchive/output.cgi?Thu19Sep19991-004&cruise%20line>, Accessed January 8, 1999.

[42] See "Carnival Links with Seabourn," *Lloyd's List* (February 20, 1992), <www.llplimited.com/LLArchive/output.cgi?Thu20Feb19992-011>, Accessed April 8, 1999. Also see Carnival's Form 10K, US Securities and Exchange Commissions (November 1996).

[43] Royal Viking Line built the *Royal Viking Queen* when it exercised an option Seabourn had not used for a third ship. The ship passed to Royal Cruise Line when Royal Viking Line was sold to Cunard in 1994 and was renamed *Queen Odyssey*. It was sold to Seabourn when Royal Cruise Line was closing down.

[44] The ship had previously been declared a total constructive loss in 1984 when as *Sundancer* it sank after striking a rock in Vancouver. It was operated at the time by Johnson Line.

[45] See Nigel Lowry, "Epirotiki's Trail of Trouble Goes On," *Lloyd's List* (March 25, 1994), p. 5, <www.llplimited.com/LLArchive/output.cgi?Fri25Mar1994-052&cruise%20line>, Accessed January 8, 1999.

[46] In October 1993 Carnival Cruise Lines' *Carnivale* was renamed the *FiestaMarina* and began service with FiestaMarina Cruises, a division of Carnival catering to the Latin America and Spanish-speaking US markets. It departed from San Juan, Puerto Rico and LaGuaira/Caracas, Venezuela for three-, four-, and seven-day cruises. In September 1994 this product was discontinued as the depth of the market could not support the size of the vessel. The ship, which was under charter, was returned to Epirotiki Lines. See Carnival Corporation Form 10 K, US Securities and Exchange Commission (January 23, 1995).

[47] "Carnival Looks for More Market Share," *Lloyd's List* (March 10, 1994), p. 2, <www.llplimited.com/LLArchive/output.cgi?Thu10Mar1994-035&cruise%20line>, Accessed January 8, 1999.

[48] See Nigel Lowry, "Epirotiki Deal Finally Signed," *Lloyd's List*, (February 11, 1995), p. 10, <www.llplimited.com/LLArchive/output.cgi?Fri12Apr1995-040&cruise%20line>, Accessed January 8, 1999.

[49] See Nigel Lowry, "Carnival Sells Epirotiki Stake Back to Greece," *Lloyd's List* (April 21, 1995), p. 1, <www.llplimited.com/LLArchive/output.cgi?Fri21Apr1995-040&cruise%20line>, Accessed January 8, 1999.

[50] According to Jim Parker of Atlanta's Robinson Humphries, the tie-in to Epirotiki has three key benefits: (1) it was procured very cheaply; (2) it allowed Carnival, which gets seats on the Greek company's board for Pam Conover, Micky Arison, and Howard Frank, to learn European cruising; and (3) the Greek company gives Carnival an ideal outlet to dispose of older ships that are no longer suitable for the US and Caribbean markets. See John Prescott, "Carnival Riding Along," *Lloyd's List* (February 2, 1995), p. 5, <www.llplimited.com/LLArchive/output.cgi?Thu02 Feb1995-016&cruise%20line>, Accessed January 8, 1999.

[51] See Nigel Lowry, "Cruising Marriage with a Family Plan," *Lloyd's List* (August 7, 1995), p. 3, <www.llplimited.com/LLArchive/output.cgi?Tue08Aug1995-035&cruise%20line>, Accessed January 8, 1999.

[52] In December 1999 a controlling interest in Royal Olympic was bought by Louis Cruises, a Cyprus company with a dominant position in the eastern Mediterranean short cruises market from Limassol, and in out-chartering ships to tour and travel companies. See "Louis Cruise Buys Stake in Royal Olympic," *Reuters* (October 29, 1999), <biz.yahoo.com/rf/991029/ix.html>, Accessed November 5, 1999.

[53] For details see Nigel Lowry, "Terror Fears Spark Heavy Loss at Royal Olympic," *Lloyd's List* (June 14, 2002), Back Page, <www.lloydslist.com>, Accessed July 31, 2002.

[54] For details see Press Release, "Royal Olympic Cruise Lines Inc Reports Loss for 2002" (Royal Olympic Cruise Line, June 18, 2003), <biz.yahoo.com/prnews/030618/nyw107_1.html>, Accessed June 19, 2003.

[55] See Ina Paiva Cordle, "Olympia Voyager Up for Auction," *Miami Herald* (March 5, 2004), <www.miami.com/mld/miamiherald/business/8108961.htm>, Accessed Mach 5, 2004.

[56] See David Mott, "Carnival Set for Control of Kloster," *Lloyd's List* (November 3, 1995), p. 1, <www.llplimited.com/LLArchive/output.cgi?Fri03Nov1995-012&cruise%20line>, Accessed January 8, 1999.

[57] "Logic behind Carnival Help for Kloster," *Lloyd's List* (November 2, 1995), p. 1, <www.llplimited.com/LLArchive/output.cgi?Thu02Nov1995-046&cruise%20line>, Accessed January 8, 1999.

[58] According to Carnival Corporation's Form 10K (November 1996), approximately $163 million of the acquisition cost of the Airtours transaction was funded by an unsecured five-year $200 million multicurrency revolving credit facility. To fund the remaining purchase price, Carnival issued shares of its class a common stock valued at about $144 million. As of November 30, 1996, the market value of the company's investment in Airtours, based on the closing price of Airtours' stock, was approximately $465 million compared with the $344 million book value of the company's investment in Airtours.

[59] See "Carnival Eyes Europe via Airtours," *Lloyd's List* (January 23, 1996), p. 3, <www.llplimited.com/LLArchive/output.cgi?Tue23Jan1996-043&cruise%20line>, Accessed January 8, 1999.

[60] See Press Release, "Airtours Combines North American Operations" (Airtours plc, November 30, 2000), <biz.yahoo.com/prnews/001130/fl_airtour.html>, Accessed December 8, 2000.

[61] See Louisa Nesbitt, "Mytravel Offloads Cruise Business," *PA News* (April 16, 2004), <business.scotsman.com/print.cfm?id=2790070&referringtemplate=http%3A%2F%2Fbusiness%2Escotsman%2Ecom%2Flatest%2Ecfm&referringquerystring=id%3D2790070>, Accessed April 16, 2004.

[62] See Andrew Clark, "Tour Firm Warns of More Misery," *The Guardian* (March 23, 2004), p. 17.

[63] "Irreconcilable Differences and the Best Way to Make Money," *Cruise News Daily* (September 2, 1997), Received via e-mail September 2, 1997.

[64] See Julian Bray, "Cruise Group Targets European Market; Carnival Set to Take Stake in Airtours," *Lloyd's List* (January 20, 1996), p. 1, <www.llplimited.com/LLArchive/output.cgi?Sat20Jan1996-015&cruise%20line>, Accessed January 8, 1999.

[65] See "What Was Behind the Costa Acquisition?" *Cruise News Daily* (January 2, 1997), Received via e-mail January 2, 1997.

[66] See Carnival Corporation Form 10K, US Securities and Exchange Commission (November 30, 1997).

[67] See "Changes Begin as Costa Buyout Moves Forward," *Cruise News Daily* (March 4, 1997), Received via e-mail March 4, 1997.

[68] "Carnival to Buy Remaining Half of Costa," *Reuters* (August 28, 2000), <biz.yahoo.com/rf/000828/n28527462_2.html>, Accessed August 31, 2000.

[69] See David Mott, "Chandris Completes OSG Cruiseship Deal," *Lloyd's List* (October 22, 1992), p. 1, <www.llplimited.com/LLArchive/output.cgi?Thu22Oct1992-015&cruise%20line>, Accessed January 8, 1999. Also see Julian Bray, "OSG Investments Ensure Profitability," *Lloyd's List* (November 12, 1992), Back Page, <www.llplimited.com/LLArchive/output.cgi?Thu12Nov1992-054&cruise%20line>, Accessed January 8, 1999.

[70] *Cunard Dynasty* was transferred to Norwegian Cruise Line.

[71] See "A Bidder Steps Forward for Cunard," *Cruise News Daily*, November 10, 1997, Received via e-mail November 10, 1997.

[72] Simultaneous with the acquisition, Seabourn Cruise Line (of which Carnival already owned 50 percent) was combined with Cunard. Seabourn's founder and previous owner, Atle Brynestad, became a significant shareholder in the new company and served as the company's chairman of the board. Carnival owned approximately two-thirds of the combined entity. See Press Release, "Carnival Corporation to Acquire Majority Interest in Cunard Line" (Carnival Corporation, April 3, 1998).

[73] See "Carnival Closes the Deal: What They Got and What They Can Make It Into," *Cruise News Daily* (April 3, 1998). The project was for four ships for Carnival Cruise Lines: *Carnival Spirit, Carnival Pride, Carnival Legend, Carnival Miracle* (88,500 tons, 2,124 passengers, $375 million each).

[74] See Press Release, "Carnival Corporation Acquires Remaining Cunard Shares" (Carnival Corporation, October 19, 1999), <biz.yahoo.com/prnews/991019/fl_caniva_1.html>, Accessed October 20, 1999.

[75] "Strategic Fit," *Cruise Industry News Quarterly* (Spring 1999), p. 90.

[76] See "Focus – Premier Courted NCL with Merger Proposal," *Reuters* (December 15, 1999), <biz.yahoo.com/rf/991215/bhc.html>, Accessed December 26, 1999.

[77] See "Star Cruises Raises Norway Stake," *Associated Press* (December 16, 1999), <biz.yahoo.com/apf/991216/Norway_cru_1.html>, Accessed December 26, 1999.

[78] See "Focus – Star Cruises Springs Bid for NCL," *Reuters* (December 17, 1999), <biz.yahoo.com/rf/991217/ep.html>, Accessed December 26, 1999.

[79] "Asian Cruise Line Seeks Norway Line," *Associated Press* (December 17, 1999), <biz.yahoo.com/apf/991217/Norway_cru_1.html>, Accessed December 26, 1999.

[80] See "Focus – Carnival Renews Bid War for Norway's NCL," *Reuters* (January 27, 2000), <biz.yahoo.com/rf/000127/bel.html>, Accessed February 1, 2000.

[81] See "Norway Kistefos Controls 14.97 pct of NCL," *Reuters* (January 13, 2000), <biz.yahoo.com/rf/000113/d1.html>, Accessed January 13, 2000.

[82] See "Norway Govt Likely to Rule on NCL/Star by Friday," *Reuters* (January 31, 2000), <biz.yahoo.com/rf/000131/h7.html>, Accessed February 1, 2000.

[83] See "Oslo Bourse Chairman Quits after NCL Criticisms," *Reuters* (January 31, 2000), <biz.yahoo.com/rf/000131/o6.html>, Accessed February 1, 2000.

[84] If the two were successful in acquiring 100 percent of NCL, the cost to Carnival would be approximately $470 million.

[85] See J.S. Dhaliwall, "Carnival, Malaysia Star End NCL Tie," *Reuters* (March 17, 2000), <daily news.yahoo.com/h/nm/20000317/bs/star_carnival_2.html>, Accessed March 19, 2000.

86 See Press Release, "Star Cruises Acquires 50.2% of Norwegian Cruise Line's Shares" (Star Cruises, December 17, 1999), <www.starcruises.com/newswire/wir17dec.html>, Accessed January 5, 2000.

87 See "P&O Rejected Carnival's 7 Bln Stg Bid – Paper," *Reuters* (August 22, 1999), <biz.yahoo.com/rf/990822/l.html>, Accessed August 23, 1999.

88 See Michael Connor, "Focus – Carnival Says It Held Talks with Rival P&O," *Reuters* (August 23, 1999), <biz.yahoo.com/rf/990823/vc.html>, Accessed August 24, 1999.

89 See Braden Reddall, "Focus – P&O Cruises to Sail Off, Sends Shares Higher," *Reuters* (February 3, 2000), <biz.yahoo.com/rf/000203/bm5.html>, Accessed February 8, 2000.

90 These are the words of Richard Fain, CEO of RCCL. See Sudip Kar-Gupta and Michael Connor, "Cruise Giants to Merge, Create New No. 1," *Reuters* (November 20, 2001), <daily news.yahoo.com/htx/nm/20011120/bs/transport_poprincess_merger_dc_7.html>, Accessed November 21, 2001.

91 Princess brought 18 ships (with 27,370 berths) and Royal Caribbean brought 41 (with 74,770 berths) to the merger. Although Royal Caribbean had more ships and appeared to be a larger company, it also brought a larger proportion of debt.

92 See "EU Officials Object to Carnival Bid," *Associated Press* (May 24, 2002), <story.news.yahoo.com>, Accessed June 3, 2002.

93 See Christopher Mayer. "Terrorist Attacks Tear Hole in Cruise Market," *Lloyd's List* (December 18, 2001), <www.lloydslist.com>, Accessed July 31, 2002.

94 See Press Release, "P&O Princess Cruises plc and Royal Caribbean Cruises Ltd Combine to Create the World's Largest Cruise Vacation Group" (Princess Cruises, November 20, 2001), <biz.yahoo.com/prnews/011120/lntu005_1.html>, Accessed November 20, 2001,

95 See "Is Carnival a Potential Suitor for POC?" *Seatrade Insider* (November 20, 2001), <www.cruisecommunity.com/ShowStory.asp?ID=1378>, Accessed November 21, 2001.

96 See Press Release, "Carnival Corporation: Proposed Combination of Carnival and P&O Princess" (Carnival Corporation, January 24, 2002), <biz.yahoo.com/prnews/020124/lnth009_1.html>, Accessed January 24, 2002.

97 Tony Gray, "Carnival Savages Fain's Track Record," *Lloyd's List* (January 25, 2002), p. 1, <www.lloydslist.com>, Accessed July 20, 2003.

98 Ibid.

99 See Mark Potter, "P&O Shareholders Say Carnival Must Up Bid," *Reuters* (January 15, 2002), <dailynews.yahoo.com/htx/nm/20020115/bs/leisure_poprincess.dc_3.html> Accessed January 16, 2002.

100 See "Carnival Cruises Tries Again with Bid," *Associated Press* (January 30, 2002), <dailynews.yahoo.com/htx/ap/20020130/bs/cruise_merger_1.html>, Accessed January 30, 2002.

101 See "Ratcliffe Details Why Carnival Bid Was Turned Down," *Seatrade Insider* (February 8, 2002), <www.cruisecommunity.com/ShowStory.asp?ID=1644>, Accessed February 13, 2002.

102 "Fain: Adjournment Means No Deal — By Anyone," *Seatrade Insider* (February 13, 2002), <www.cruisecommunity.com/ShowStory.asp?ID=1664>, Accessed February 14, 2002.

103 See Sudip Kar-Gupta, "P&O Princess Investors Steer Toward Carnival," *Reuters* (February 15, 2002), <biz.yahoo.com/rf/020215/sp234028_2.html>, Accessed February 15, 2002.

104 Carnival Corporation Form 10Q, US Securities and Exchange Commission (February 28, 2003).

105 Alistair Osborne, "Upbeat P&O Princess Faces $55m Legal Bill," *Telegraph* (October 9, 2002), <money.telegraph.co.uk>, Accessed October 9, 2002.

[106] "$30m in Merger Costs, RCCL Estimates," *Seatrade Insider* (October 23, 2002), <www.cruisecommunity.com/ShowStory.asp?ID=2685>, Accessed October 24, 2002.

[107] See James Kanter, "EU Antitrust Boss Monti on Defensive after Court Ruling," *Dow Jones Business News* (July 23, 2002), <biz.yahoo.com/djus/020723/200207231301000811_1.html>, Accessed June 24, 2002.

[108] These figures were never cited by the Federal Trade Commission; however, they are contained in *Maritime Law Exemption: Exemption Provides Limited Competitive Advantage, But Barriers to Further Entry under US Flag Remain* (US General Accounting Office, 2004). (Document: GAO – 04 – 421).

[109] The American Antitrust Institute and the National Consumers League both filed briefs opposing the mergers. See Francesco Guerrera, "US Urged to Block Cruise Line Bids," *FT.com* (July 9, 2002), <biz.yahoo.com/ft/020709/1025793445561_2.html>, Accessed July 10, 2002.

[110] "Statement of the Federal Trade Commission Concerning Royal Caribbean Cruises Ltd/P&O Princess Cruises plc and Carnival Corporation/P&O Princess Cruises plc" (FTC File No. 021 0041, October 5, 2002), <www.ftc.gov/os/2002/10/cruisestatement.htm>, Accessed October 5, 2002.

[111] "Dissenting Statement of Commissioners Sheila F. Anthony and Mozelle W. Thompson, Royal Caribbean/Princess and Carnival/Princess," (FTC File No. 021-0041, October 5, 2003), <www.ftc.gov/os/2002/10/cruisedissent.htm>, Accessed October 5, 2002.

[112] See "EGM Now Likely on February 13," *Seatrade Insider* (October 25, 2002), <www.cruisecommunity.com/ShowStory.asp?ID=2710>, Accessed October 25, 2002.

[113] See Press Release, "Result of P&O Princess Extraordinary General Meeting" (Princess Cruises, April 16, 2003), <biz.yahoo.com/prnews/030416/lnw005_1.html>, Accessed April 16, 2003.

[114] See Peter McMullin, "A Highly Satisfactory Investment – 1987–1996," *Cruise Industry News Quarterly* (Winter 1996/97), p. 44.

[115] See "Corporate Profile No 104: Carnival Corporation," *London Times* (February 16, 2004), p. 22, <business.timesonline.co.uk/printFriendly/0,,2020-37-1002930,00.html>, Accessed March 3, 2004.

[116] Diana B. Henriques and Geraldine Fabrikant, "Deciding on Executive Pay: Lack of Independence Is Seen," *New York Times* (December 18, 2002), <www.nytimes.com/2002/12/18/business/18PAY.html>, Accessed December 18, 2002.

[117] "US Share Sales by Executives Top $51 Bln, Highest in 4 Years," *Bloomberg News Service* (December 31, 2004), <www.bloomberg.com/apps/news?pid=10000103&sid=amN7zTIMwta4&refer=us>, Accessed January 2, 2005.

Chapter 3: Representation without Taxation

[1] Business Research and Economic Advisors, *The Contribution of the North American Cruise Industry to the US Economy in 2003* (International Council of Cruise Lines, 2004), <http://www.iccl.org/resources/2003_economic_study.pdf>, Accessed August 24, 2004.

[2] Liz Ruskin, "Senator Seeks Tax Delay for Cruise Ship Companies," *Anchorage Daily News* (May 3, 2004), <www.adn.com/front/v-printer/story/5032642p-4960642c.html>, Accessed May 4, 2004.

[3] Sydney P. Freedberg, "Loophole Inc.: A Special Report on Florida's Corporate Income Tax," *St. Petersburg Times* (October 26, 2003), <www.sptimes.com/2003/10/26/news_pf/State/Loophole_Inc.html>, Accessed October 27, 2003.

[4] Douglas Frantz, "Cruise Lines Profit from Friends in Congress," *New York Times* (February 19, 1999), <www.nytimes.com>, Accessed June 11, 1999.

[5] Jonathan Weisman, "Tax Cut Bill Puts Cruise Lines on Course for Break," *USA Today* (June 6, 2001), <www.usatoday.com/news/Washington/2001-06-06-cruise.htm>, Accessed March 20, 2004.

[6] "Lawmaker Aids Carnival in Customs Fine," *Seatrade Insider* (November 17, 2003), <www.cruise-community.com/ShowStory.asp?ID=4685>, Accessed November 17, 2004.

[7] Though regulations for the tax were drafted in 2002, the cruise industry now claimed that the delay was needed in order to set up accounting procedures to deal with new tax regulations. See "Cruise Ship Tax Delay Is Just Too Sweet a Deal." *Juneau Empire* (May 11, 2004), <juneauempire.com>, Accessed May 11, 2004. Also see "Lines Win More Time to Pay US Taxes," *Seatrade Insider* (October 12, 2004), <www.cruise-community.com/ShowStory.asp?ID=6386>, Accessed October 12, 2004.

[8] The American Federation of Labor and Congress of Industrial Organizations (AFL–CIO) put a proposal on the agenda of the Carnival Corporation annual meeting in June 2003 calling on Carnival to change its corporate jurisdiction from Panama to the US. The initiative did not succeed. See "US Unions Demand Carnival Quit Panama Links," *Lloyd's List* (June 3, 2003), p. 1, <www.lloydslist.com>, Accessed June 20, 2003.

[9] In 1999 the Clinton Administration estimated that the cruise industry avoids billions of dollars a year in federal taxes by being foreign registered. (See Douglas Frantz, "Lawmakers Want I.R.S. Help on Cruise Ships and Tax Laws," *New York Times* (March 15, 1999), p. 14.) In 1993 Representative John Duncan, member of the Public Works and Transport Committee's subcommittee on Investigations and Oversight, called for a change in the "sweetheart" tax deal that Carnival and other foreign-registered cruise lines had, and had his staff research the best remedy to cure the problem. The outcome of this initiative is unknown. See Joel Glass, "US Tax Threat to Cruise Ships," *Lloyd's List* (June 1, 1993), p. 1, <www.llplimited.com/LLArchive/output.cgi?Tue01 Jun1993-040&cruise%20line>, Accessed January 8, 1999.

[10] M.S. Sesit, "US Tax Proposals May Squeeze Multinationals," *Wall Street Journal* (August 9, 2002), p. C14.

[11] "Flag of convenience" refers to situations where the beneficial ownership of a ship is in a country different from where it is registered.

[12] Use of Liberia's ship registry fell off sharply as a consequence of the government's financial support and involvement in the civil war in Sierra Leone. Royal Caribbean and Celebrity moved their ships from Liberian to Bahamian registry. P&O Princess moved AIDA'S ship's from Liberian to UK registry. See John McLaughlin, "UN Report Shows Little Progress from Liberian Register," *Lloyd's List* (April 22, 2002), <www.lloydslist.com>, Accessed July 31, 2002.

[13] See Press Release, "Royal Caribbean Cruises Ltd. Announces Plan to Reflag Six Ships to Bahamian Registry" (RCCL, September 15, 2004), <www.corporate-ir.net/ireye/ir_site.zhtml?ticker=rcl&script=410&layout=9&item_id=614700>, Accessed September 16, 2004. The move will affect about 400 shipboard employees covered by collective bargaining agreements required by the Norwegian International Ship Registry. Royal Caribbean said it plans to keep compensation levels for those employees at or above their current levels during a two-year transition period set to end in January 2007.

[14] See Jim Morris, "'Flags of Convenience' Give Owners a Paper Refuge," *Houston Chronicle* (August 21, 1996), <www.chron.com/content/interactive/special/maritime/96/08/22/part5.html>, Accessed January 4, 2000.

[15] Office of the Deputy Prime Minister, "Queen Mary 2 Flies Flag for Revitalized UK Shipping" (Government News Network, January 8, 2004). Also see David Mott, "Tonnage Tax Rides to Rescue Princess," *Lloyd's List* (July 27, 2001), <www.lloydslist.com>, Accessed July 31, 2002.

[16] "Seetours Switches to Italian Flag," *Seatrade Insider* (September 21, 2004), <www.cruise-community.com/ShowStory.asp?ID=6257>, Accessed September 21, 2004.

[17] David Mott, "Cruise Ship Price Jumps," *Lloyd's List* (April 19, 1991), p. 1, <www.llplimited.com/LLArchive/output.cgi?Fri19Apr1991-011&cruise%20line>, Accessed January 8, 1999.

[18] See H.R. 2056, 102nd Congress.

[19] Jack Adler, "US Shipbuilders Fighting Back," *Los Angeles Times* (May 31, 1992), p. L-6.

[20] Joel Glass, "US Tax Threat to Cruiseships," *Lloyd's List* (June 1, 1993), p. 1, <www.llplimited.com/LLArchive/output.cgi?tue01Jun1993-040&cruise%20line>, Accessed January 8, 1999.

[21] See "Uncertainties Plague French Tax Lease Schemes," *Seatrade Insider* (July 1, 2004), <www.cruise-community.com>, Accessed July 1, 2004.

[22] See *Maritime Law Exemption* (US General Accounting Office, February 2004). (Document GAO-04-421). Note that nearby foreign ports include all foreign ports in North America, Central America, Bermuda, the West Indies (except Aruba, Bonaire, and Curaçao), and the US Virgin Islands.

[23] The American Association of Port Authorities passed a resolution at its annual convention in October 2004 supporting the transportation of passengers by foreign-flagged vessels between US ports. We can expect pressure to mount for cabotage laws to be dismantled. See "AAPA Backs Foreign Ships in Coastwise Trade," *Seatrade Insider* (October 8, 2004), <www.cruise-community.com/ShowStory.asp?ID=6367>, Accessed October 9, 2004.

[24] See Public Law 105-56.

[25] John Porretto, "Sen. Hopeful Ingalls to Honor Contract," *Associated Press* (August 7, 2001), <dailynews.yahoo.com/htx/ap/20010807/bs/stalled_ships_1.html>, Accessed August 7, 2001.

[26] "NCL States Its Stance on Hawai'i," *Seatrade Insider* (August 14, 2002), <www.cruise-community.com/ShowStory.asp?ID=2368>, Accessed August 15, 2002.

[27] The partially completed vessels cost $23 million, while the construction plans cost $6 million.

[28] Tim Ruel, "Senate OKs Inouye Ship Plan," *Honolulu Star-Bulletin* (January 18, 2003), <starbulletin.com/2003/01/18/news/story1.html>, Accessed January 18, 2003.

[29] Derrick DePledge, "Failed Cruise Ship Deal Cost $330M," *Honolulu Advertiser* (April 1, 2003), <the.honoluluadvertiser.com>, Accessed April 3, 2003.

[30] Derrick DePledge, "Cruise Exemption Bolstered," *Honolulu Advertiser* (February 12, 2003), <the.honoluluadvertiser.com/article/2003/Feb/12/bz/bz01a.html>, Accessed February 12, 2003.

[31] Derrick DePledge, "McCain Attacks Inouye's Cruise Deal," *Honolulu Advertiser* (February 22, 2003), <the.honoluluadvertiser.com>, Accessed February 22, 2003.

[32] Janis L. Magin, "Cruise Exemption Passes Congress," *Honolulu Star-Bulletin* (February 14, 2003), <starbulletin.com/2003/02/14/business/story3.html>, Accessed February 16, 2003.

[33] The legislation included S. 668, a bill to increase economic benefits to the US from the activities of cruise ships visiting Alaska; S. 803 (United States Cruise Tourism Act of 1997), a bill to permit the transportation of passengers between US ports by certain foreign-flag vessels and to encourage US-flag vessels to participate in such transportation; S. 2290, a bill to promote the construction and operation of cruise ships in the US; and S. 2507 (United

States Cruise Ship Tourism Act of 1998), a bill to stimulate increased domestic cruise ship opportunities for the American cruising public by temporarily reducing barriers for entry into the domestic cruise ship trade. See *Report of the Committee on Commerce, Science, and Transportation on S. 1510: United States Cruise Vessel Act* (Government Printing Office, 2000), <thomas.loc.gov/cgi-bin/cpquery/T?&report=sr396&dbname=cp106&>, Accessed September 3, 2004.

34   "Congress Threat Clouds World's Largest Market," *Lloyd's List* (January 28, 1994), p. 8, <www .llplimited.com/LLArchive/output.cgi?Fri28Jan1994-019&cruise%20line>, Accessed January 8, 1999.

35   Ina Paiva Cordle, "Carnival Set to Launch a Massive Ad Campaign," *Miami Herald* (December 7, 2004), <www.miami.com/mld/miamiherald/business/10354696.htm>, Accessed December 19, 2004.

36   See Press Release, "Travel Industry Leaders Join the *New York Times* Travel Show" (New York Times Travel, December 19, 2003), <www.nytimestravel.com/pressrelease_pr1.htm>, Accessed February 29, 2004. Carnival returned as a supporting sponsor for the second annual New York Travel Show March 4–6, 2005. See Press Release, "New York Times Signs on New Sponsors" (New York Times, November 17, 2004), <home.businesswire.com>, Accessed November 18, 2004.

37   "5th Annual Mayor's Ball aboard *Carnival Pride* a Success" (United Way of Miami-Dade, January 8, 2002), <www.unitedwaymiami.org/WhatsNewDetails.asp?newsID=40>, Accessed November 3, 2004.

38   "Wine and Food Festival a Smashing Success," *Foundation News* (Summer 2004), <www.baptisthealth.net/vgn/images/portal/cit_449/32/35/32181945FoundationNews.pdf>, Accessed November 3, 2004.

39   According to reports filed with the Secretary of the Senate, ICCL spent on lobbying activities: $500,000 the first six months of 2004, $952,000 in 2003, $915,000 in 2002, $940,000 in 2001, $982,000 in 2000, $567,000 in 1999, and $604,000 in 1998. The figures in Table 3.2 are from income reports filed by Alcalde and Fay, ICCL's lobbyist in Washington, DC, which oddly are different from ICCL's reports.

40   The White Water to Blue Water Conference was held in Miami and co-chaired by the Caribbean Community; Comision Centroamericana de Ambiente y Dessarrollo; United Nations Economic Commission for Latin America and the Caribbean; the United Nations Environment Programme; and the US.

41   According to reports made to the Public Disclosures Commission, State of Washington, Holland America Line spent the following on lobbying activities in Washington state: $37,838 in 1996, $34,636 in 1997, $59,217 in 1998, $46,800 in 1999, $70,445 in 2000, $69,079 in 2001, $97,879 in 2002, $100,050 in 2003, and $96,112 (estimate based on monthly reports) in 2004. These figures include the lobbyist's fee, which in 2004 was $36,000, plus expenses and some of Holland America Line's campaign contributions.

42   "Who Said It?" *Cruise Industry News Quarterly* (Winter 1997/98), p. 104.

43   "Poulides Queries European Association," *Seatrade Insider* (February 26, 2004), <www.cruise-community.com/ShowStory.asp?ID=5182>, Accessed February 26, 2004.

44   "Foschi Elected as Chairman of ECC," *Seatrade Insider* (April 15, 2004), <www.cruise-community.com>, Accessed April 15, 2004.

45   See "Cruise UK Seeks to Amend Light Dues," *Seatrade Insider*, August 7, 2002. <www.cruise-community.com/ShowStory.asp?ID2340>, Accessed August 8, 2002.

[46] Social capital was introduced to sociology by James Coleman in *Foundations of Social Theory* (Belknap Press, 1990). Though the concept has not been picked up in a big way by sociologists, it has become popular in the social work literature. In that context, it refers to social resources and connections that may be used by individuals to achieve their goals and desires.

[47] See John A. Sonquist and Thomas Koenig, "Interlocking Directorates in the Top US Corporations: A Graph Theory Approach," *The Insurgent Sociologist* 5 (Spring, 1975), pp. 196–229.

[48] See J. Allen Whitt, *Urban Elites and Mass Transportation: The Dialectics of Power* (Princeton University Press, 1982).

[49] "Rina Chief Scerni Quits Festival," *Lloyd's List* (February 6, 2003), p. 1, <www.lloydslist.com>, Accessed July 20, 2003.

[50] Arnold W. Donald is chair and CEO of Marisant Company and sits on the boards of Belden Inc., Crown Cork & Seal, The Laclede Company, GenAmerica Insurance Company, Oil-Dri Corporation of America, and The Scotts Company. Sir John Parker is chair of National Grid Transco plc, RMC Group plc, and Lattice Group plc; he is on the board of GKN plc, BG Group plc, Firth Rixson plc, and Lloyds Register.

[51] Heather Tomlinson, "Two Men, Eight Directorships," *The Guardian* (August 28, 2004), <www.guardian.co.uk/executivepay/story/0,1204, 1292758,00.html>, Accessed August 28, 2004.

[52] See Press Release, "Local Charities to Benefit from Introduction of Cunard's Queen Mary" (Cunard Line, November 11, 2003), <cruises.about.com/library/news/blnews031111b.htm>, Accessed November 10, 2004.

[53] *What Is the Cruise Industry Charitable Foundation?* <iccl.org/foundation/history. cfm>, Accessed August 28, 2004.

[54] Donations to the Washington Conference Foundation break down as follow: Alaska ($250,000), Washington, DC ($183,000), New York/Miami ($100,000), New Orleans/Duluth ($100,000), New Orleans/Houston ($91,812), Arizona/Washington ($50,000), Miami ($50,000), New York ($50,000), Texas/California ($50,000).

[55] "Celebrations for Children Inc.," *Disinfodedia* <www.disinfopedia.org/wiki.phtml?title= Celebrations_for_Children_Inc.>, Accessed November 26, 2004.

[56] See Press Release, "Jacksonville Charities to Benefit from Cruise Industry Donation" (Cruise Industry Charitable Foundation, October 27, 2003), <www.iccl.org/foundation/press102703. cfm>, Accessed March 12, 2004. The nine beneficiaries were Children Home Society of Jacksonville, I.M. Sulbacher Center for the Homeless, Special Olympics of Jacksonville, Johnson Family YMCA, First Coast Afro America Chamber of Commerce, Edward Waters College, Community Rehabilitation Center, Mary McLeod Bethune Community Center, and Florida Council for the Blind.

[57] The organizations include M.L. Wilson Boys and Girls Club, Harlem Little League, The Valley (TASA Program), Booker T. Washington Learning Center, East Harlem Council for Community Improvement, Scan LaGuardia, Alianza Dominicana Youth Program, Community Association of Progressive Dominicans, Inwood Community Services, and Harlem Knight's Football League.

[58] See Press Release, "New York Youth Organizations to Benefit from Cruise Industry Donation" (Cruise Industry Charitable Foundation, June 4, 2001), <www.iccl.org/foundation/press14. cfm>, Accessed March 12, 2004.

[59] See Press Release, "Carnival Cruise Lines to Donate $1.2 Million to Gov. Bush's Literacy Initiative; Will Donate All Tax Rebates From State's Qualified Target Industry Tax Refund Program" (Carnival Cruise Lines, June 18, 2002).

[60] Robert McClure and Lise Olsen discuss the conflict when enforcers join the regulators more generally as it applies to all shipping. See "Shipping Industry Attracts Ex-Coast Guard Officers," *Seattle Post-Intelligencer* (November 21, 2002), <seattlepi.nwsource.com/local/96158_coast21.shtml?searchpagefrom=1&searchdiff=774 >, Accessed November 16, 2004.

[61] Ibid.

[62] "Last Night in Miami," *Seatrade Insider* (November 7, 2003), <www.cruise-community.com/ShowStory.asp?ID=4637>, Accessed November 7, 2003. Also see "Last Night in Miami," *Seatrade Insider* (November 10, 2004), <www.cruise-community.com/ShowStory.asp?ID=6551>, Accessed November 10, 2004.

[63] "Success in Seattle," *Coast Guard Foundation Currents* (Fall 2003), p. 1, <www.cgfdn.org/text/newsletter_fall_2003.pdf>, Accessed November 3, 2004.

[64] See *The 1996 Slate 60: The 60 Largest American Charitable Contributions of 1996*, <slate.msn.com/id/2058435/entry/34692/>, Accessed September 3, 2004.

[65] Sherwood Weiser, former Carnival board member and Arison friend, is chair of the board of the Performing Arts Center of Greater Miami Foundation.

[66] "Carnival Pays $1M to Name St. Thomas Center," *South Florida Business Journal* (October 30, 2002), <www.bizjournals.com/southflorida/stories/2002/10/28/daily90.html>, Accessed November 1, 2002.

[67] The Pritzker name was given to the school following a $12 million donation in 1968. In 2002 the family announced an additional gift of $30 million to be invested in the University of Chicago's Biological Sciences Division and School of Medicine. These donations are consistent with the family's involvement with First Health Corporation. See Barbara A. Gabriel, "What's in a Name? Philanthropists' Donations Giving New Names to Medical Schools," *AAMC Reporter* (August 2002), <www.aamc.org/newsroom/reporter/aug02/philanthropy.htm>, Accessed September 3, 2004.

[68] Kathleen Rehbein, School of Business at Marquette University, reports that from a corporate perspective, the effect of campaign contributions is significantly increased when used in concert with lobbying (personal communication, March 9, 2004)

[69] Politicians in Florida received the most ($500,000) followed by Alaska ($250,000) and Washington ($108,000).

[70] Members of the Appropriations Committee who have received campaign funds from the cruise industry include Senators Hollings, Reid, Stevens, Inouye, Burns, Spector, Murray, and Shelby.

[71] Members of the Commerce, Science and Transportation Committee who have received campaign funds from the cruise industry include Senators Nelson, McCain, Boxer, Hollings, Stevens, Inouye, Burns, Cantwell, Lott, Breaux, and Dorgan. In 2003/2004 alone, Dorgan received $9,000.

[72] Douglas Frantz, "Cruise Lines Profit from Friends in Congress," *New York Times* (February 19, 1999), <www.nytimes.com>, Accessed June 11, 1999.

[73] Ibid. Also see Joel Glass, "US Maritime Bills Hit the Deck," *Lloyd's List* (October 17, 1994), p. 7, <www.llplimited.com/LLArchive/output.cgi?Mon71Oct1994-014&cruise% 20line>, Accessed February 8, 1999.

[74] Of the nine co-sponsors in the Senate, the only to receive any money from cruise line sources is Barbara Boxer. On the house side, the lone recipient of industry money among 41 co-sponsors is Eliot Engel of New York.

[75] Members include Senators McCain and Hollings (ex officio), and Stevens, Inouye, Cantwell, Breaux, and Lott.

[76] Members include Senators McCain and Hollings (ex officio), and Stevens, Inouye, Burns, Lott, Boxer, and Breaux.

[77] Veitch also gave Abercrombie $1,000 in the fall of 2002, and $4,000 in 2004. The 2004 contribution was returned because the funds exceeded federal contribution limits. Veitch also had $10,000 returned by the Democratic Party of Hawai'i because the $15,000 given in 2002 exceeded contribution limits.

[78] These eight include Don Young, Bill Shuster, James Oberstar, John Duncan, Sherwood Boehlert, John Mica, and Howard Coble.

[79] The five include Spencer Bachus (AL), Peter DeFazio (OR), Robert Menendez (NJ), Shirley Berkley (NV), and Mario Diaz-Balart (FL).

[80] In addition to Rangel, E. Shaw Clay and Philip Crane are on the Committee. Two other members of the Committee have received less than $15,000 in campaign contributions: Mark Foley of Florida ($11,500) and Xavier Becerra of California ($1,750).

[81] Dingell is joined on the Committee by James Greenwood and Jim Davis. Also on the committee are Billy Tauzin of Louisiana ($11,500), Vito Fosella of New York ($4,000), and George Radanovich of California ($2,500).

[82] Joel Glass, "Congress Cruises into Bribe Row," *Lloyd's List* (March 15, 1993), p. 3, <www.llplimited.com/LLArchive/output.cgi?Mon15Mar1993-025&cruise%20line>, Accessed January 8, 1999.

[83] Joel Glass, "Congress 'Free Trips' Pressure Steps Up," *Lloyd's List* (April 19, 1993), p. 1, <www.llplimited.com/LLArchive/output.cgi?Mon19Apr1993-026&cruise%20line>, Accessed January 8, 1999.

[84] Ted B. Kissell, "The Deep Blue Greed," *Miami New Times* (February 3–9, 2000), <www.miami newtimes.com/issues/current/feature3_p.html>, Accessed February 8, 2000.

[85] Douglas Frantz, "Cruise Lines Profit from Friends in Congress."

[86] Ibid.

[87] "INS Officers 'Given' Free Sea Trips," *Lloyd's List* (June 13, 1994), p. 3, <www.llplimited.com/LLArchive/output.cgi?Mon13 Jun1994-041&cruise%20line>, Accessed January 8, 1999.

[88] House of Representatives, *Coverage of Certain Federal Labour Laws to Foreign Documented Vessels* (Government Printing Office, 1994), p. 1, (House Report #103-818).

[89] Joel Glass, "The Sensitive Subject of Extending the Reach of US Labour Laws to Foreign-Flag Seafarers Is Again in the Capitol Hill Spotlight," *Lloyd's List* (October 10, 1992), p. 4, <www.llplimited.com/LLArchive/output.cgi?Sat10Oct1992-016&cruise%20line>, Accessed January 8, 1999.

[90] In testimony before the Subcommittee on Labor Standards on May 13, 1993, the president of the ICCL, John Estes, stated: "Some have told you that we will not relocate. I am here to tell you that this industry will relocate if the Bill is passed. It won't happen all at once, but it will happen." He pointed out the ease with which cruise ships can be moved from one homeport to another and that: "to keep international costs competitive we do in fact on occasion move from country to country. International shipping will always seek a hospitable economic and political climate from which to operate .... It would be an unfortunate failure of United States policy not to recognize that homeports are unimportant to passengers." (See *Hearings*

before the Subcommittee on Labor Standards, Occupational Health, and Safety of the Committee on Education and Labor of the House of Representatives, May 13, 1993 (Government Printing Office, 1993), Document # Y4 ED8/1 103-9.

91 According to Glacier Bay's visitation statistics, cruise passengers accounted for 26 percent of visitors to the park in 1969. Today, cruise passengers constitute over 80 percent of the park's visitors.

92 See Tom Kenworthy, "Babbitt Orders Park Service to Endorse Increase of Cruise Ships in Glacier Bay," *Washington Post* (December 21, 1994), p. A4. Also see "Babbitt Oks Rise in Glacier Bay Traffic," *Los Angeles Times* (December 22, 1994), p. A-25.

93 Before 1993 both Babbitt and his chief of staff worked for Steptoe & Johnson, the law firm that represented Holland America Line-Westours in a dispute with the Interior Department over whether it could keep its permits rights to Glacier Bay after Carnival's takeover in 1989. In the end, Holland America, which controls 39 of the 107 permits to Glacier Bay, sought and received relief from Congress in an appropriations bill. See Tom Kenworthy, "Tour Operator Was Client of Babbitt's Ex-Law Firm," *Washington Post* (January 24, 1995), p. A3.

94 See Tom Kenworthy, "Babbitt Orders Park Service to Endorse Increase of Cruise Ships in Glacier Bay," *Washington Post* (December 21, 1994), p. A4.

95 Visits during May and September are not included in the quota.

96 Douglas Frantz, "A Question of Regulation," *New York Times* (November 29, 1999), <traveltaax.msu.edu/news/Stories/nytimes2.htm>, Accessed March 20, 2004.

97 See Paula Dobbyn, "Bill Would Aid Glacier Bay Ships," *Anchorage Daily News* (July 13, 2001), Received via e-mail July 17, 2001.

98 "Cruise Lines Give $75,000 to GOP after Judge Lifts Donations Cap," *Juneau Empire* (July 23, 2001), <www.juneauempire>, Accessed July 24, 2001.

99 Douglas Frantz, "A Question of Regulation."

100 Douglas Frantz, "Cruise Lines Profit from Friends in Congress."

101 Liz Ruskin, "Young Singles Out Ship for Special Status," *Anchorage Daily News* (March 29, 2004), <www.adn.com/alaska/v-printer/story/4901277p-4836284c.html>, Accessed March 29, 2004.

102 Joel Glass, "Compromise on US Cruise Tort," *Lloyd's List* (October 1, 1996), p. 1, <www.llplimited.com/LLArchive/output.cgi?Mon01Oct1996-022&cruise%20line>, Accessed January 8, 1999.

103 Guy Gugliotta, "Coast Guard Bill Cruises into Trouble," *Washington Post* (June 11, 1996), p. A15.

104 Joel Glass, "US Wins Its Employment Case against Cruise Lines," *Lloyd's List* (August 30, 1991), p. 3, <www.llplimited.com/LLArchive/output.cgi?Fri30Aug1991-047&cruise%20line>, Accessed January 8, 1999.

105 Larry Fox and Barbara Radin Fox, "Anchored in the Docks," *Washington Post* (October 8, 1995), p. E4.

106 Sean Rowe, "There Oughta Be a Law," *Miami New Times* (March 21, 1996), <www.miaminewtimes.com/issues/1996-03-21/metro.html>, Accessed July 12, 2002.

107 Ibid.

108 Joel Glass, "Compromise on US Cruise Tort," *Lloyd's List* (October 1, 1996), p. 1, <www.llplimited.com/LLArchive/output.cgi?Mon01Oct1996-022&cruise%20line>, Accessed January 8, 1999.

109 Joan Quigley, "Families Allowed to Sue Cruise Line," *Miami Herald* (January 30, 2003), <www.miami.com/mld/miamiherald/business/5060961.htm>, Accessed January 30, 2003.

[110] Noaki Schwartz, a reporter with the *South Florida Sun-Sentinel*, has comprehensively covered the case of the Norway. The district court's decision is covered in: Noaki Schwartz, "Judge: Suits in Fatal Norway Blast Must Be Settled in Philippines," *Sun-Sentinel* (October 15, 2003), <www.sun-sentinel.com/news/local/Miami/sfl-dcruise15oct15,0,4527975.story? coll=sfla-news-miami>, Accessed October 15, 2003. For the appeal court's decision see Noaki Schwartz, "Cruise Ship Workers Lose Case," *Sun Sentinel* (January 20, 2005), <www.sun-sentinel.com/news/local/broward/sfl-cdnorway20jan20,0,5830829,print.story?coll=sfla-news-broward>, Accessed January 20, 2005; or for the decision itself see Docket No. 03-15884 in the US Court of Appeals for the Eleventh Circuit, January 18, 2005.

[111] Catherine Wilson, "Court Revives Suit Against Cruise Line," *Associated Press* (August 28, 2003), <news.yahoo.com/>, Accessed August 28, 2003.

[112] Catherine Wilson, "Ship Doctor Said Not Sheltered from Suit," *Associated Press* (August 20, 2003), <news/yahoo.com/>, Accessed August 20, 2003.

[113] See Chapter 7 for a full discussion of the drawbacks of using a memorandum of understanding. Also see Ross A. Klein, *The Cruise Industry and Environmental History and Practice: Is a Memorandum of Understanding Effective for Protecting the Environment?* (Bluewater Network, 2003), <www.bluewaternetwork.org/reports/rep_ss_kleinrep.pdf>, Accessed November 3, 2003.

[114] The Florida Ocean Alliance includes on its 12- to 13-member board of directors a representative from the Rosenstiel School, at least two representatives from cruise lines. Its chair is a representative from the Florida Ports Council. The Florida Ports Council and ICCL share the same lobbyist — John LaCapra — in Tallahassee.

[115] The amount spent in 2001 is not known, but was undoubtedly substantial.

[116] "Lobbying of Legislature Cost $4.34 Million in 2000," *St. Petersburg Times* (September 13, 2000), <www.sptimes.com/News/091300/State/State_briefs.shtml>, Accessed June 18, 2003.

[117] Gregg Renkes served as Murkowski's chief of staff and chief counsel when he was senator in Washington, DC.

[118] "New Faces in Murkowski's Cabinet: Governor's Staff, State Commissioners Come from Diverse Career, Geographic Backgrounds," *Juneau Empire* (January 19, 2003), <alaska legislature.com/hitchhiker/2003/stories/cabinet.shtml>, Accessed May 12, 2004.

[119] Ernesta Ballard left her position as DEC Commissioner on October 25, 2004, to accept a position as a senior vice president at Weyerhaeuser Company. See "DEC Commission Ballard Leaves State Service," *SITNEWS* (October 16, 2004), <www.sitnews.us/1004news/101604_ballard.html>, Accessed October 24, 2004.

[120] Representative Mulder had received campaign contributions from, among others, Micky Arison (CEO of Carnival), Richard Fain (CEO of Royal Caribbean), and Kirk Lanterman (CEO of Holland America Line).

[121] Mike Chambers, "Ethics Panel Says Mulder Used 'Poor Judgement' in Pushing Bill," *Kenai Peninsula Online* (September 23, 2001), <www.peninsulaclarion.com/stories/092301/ala_092301ala0090001.shtml>, Accessed March 20, 2004.

[122] Martin McOmber, "New Port Commissioner Expected to Make Waves," *Seattle Times* (November 24, 2003), <seattletimes.nwsource.com>, Accessed November 24, 2003.

[123] Larry Lange, "Bill on Cruise-Waste Rules Dies," *Seattle Post-Intelligencer* (February 26, 2004), <seattlepi.nwsource.com/local/162146_cruise26.html>, Accessed February 26, 2004.

[124] "Cruise Bill May Stall in Senate," *Honolulu Star-Bulletin* (February 12, 2003), <starbulletin.com/2003/02/12/business/story2.html#>, Accessed February 16, 2003.

[125] See Chad Blair, "Critics Say Cal Kawamoto Is a Poster Boy for Bad Behavior. The Senators Says He's Just Doing His Job," *Honolulu Weekly* (May 14, 2003), <www.honoluluweekly.

com/archives/coverstory%202003/05-14-03%20Cal/5-14-03%20Cal.html>, Accessed November 3, 2004. Also see Rick Daysog, "Senator Fined for Campaign Violations," *Honolulu Star-Bulletin* July 30, 2004, <starbulletin.com/2004/07/30/news/story3.html>, Accessed November 13, 2004.

[126] Joel Glass, "Congress Clash over Cruise Lines' Tax," *Lloyd's List* (June 15, 1992), p. 1, <www.llplimited.com/LLArchive/output.cgi?Mon15Jun1992-002&cruise%20line>, Accessed January 8, 1999.

Chapter 4: Cruising Cash Cows

[1] *The Caribbean: The Impact of Travel & Tourism on Jobs and the Economy*, World Travel and Tourism Council (June 14, 2004), <www.caribbeanmediaexchange.com/2004/vi/Caribbean FULLTSA.pdf>, Accessed July 5, 2004.

[2] Carla Wilson, "Campbell River Sets Sights on Cruise Ship Visits," *Times Colonist* (July 13, 2004), <www.canada.com/victoria/timescolonist/index.html>, Accessed July 13, 2004.

3 Gerry Bellett, "Campbell River to Get Cruise Terminal," *Vancouver Sun* (December 12, 2003), <www.canada.com/vancouver/vancouversun/index.html>, Accessed December 21, 2003.

[4] McDowell Group, *Cruise Industry Opportunities Assessment and Gap Analysis*, Prepared for Prince Rupert Economic Development Commission (April 2003).

[5] Leanne Ritchie, "Mercury Cruise's Stops in Rupert Shortened," *Prince Rupert Daily News* (May 7, 2004), <www.canada.com/princerupert/index.html>, Accessed May 9, 2004.

[6] Valerie Wilson, "Cruise Success!" *Nanaimo Daily News* (October 14, 2004), <www.nanaimo dailynews.com>, Accessed October 15, 2004.

[7] *Alberni Valley Cruise Ship Society Contribution Request*, Received via e-mail November 7, 2004.

[8] "Saint John Loses Huge Cruise Ship Visit," *CBC News* (August 24, 2004), <nb.cbc.ca/regional/servlet/View?filename=nb_lastcruise20040824>, Accessed August 24, 2004.

[9] "Saint John Starts Construction," *Seatrade Insider* (March 15, 2004), <www.cruise-community.com/ShowStory.asp?ID=5271>, Accessed March 15, 2004.

[10] The handbook was entitled *Cruise Ship Visits: A Handbook for Your Community*. See Sara Minogue, "The Inside Scoop on Cruise Ships," *Nunatsiaq News* (August 20, 2004), <www.nunatsiaq.com/news/Nunavut/40820_05.html>, Accessed August 22, 2004.

[11] Sara Minogue, "Cruise Ship Industry Uneven across Nunavut," *Nunatsiaq News* (August 20, 2004), <www.nunatsiaq.com/news/Nunavut/40820_04.html>, Accessed August 22, 2004.

[12] "Ushuaia Outbids Punta Arenas Port," *Mercosur* (January 26, 2004), <www.falkland-malvinas.com/Detalle.asp?NUM=3177>, Accessed February 24, 2004.

[13] Donna Balancia, "Cruise Ships' Passengers Spend Time, Cash on Land," *Florida Today* (June 15, 2004), <www.floridatoday.com/!NEWSROOM/moneystory/N0616CRUISE.htm>, Accessed June 16, 2004.

[14] Hugh Dellios, "In Popular Resort Cozumel, Demand for Service, Security Increase," *Wichita Eagle* (August 10, 2004), <www.kansas.com/mld/kansas/news/world/9362830.htm>, Accessed August 10, 2004.

[15] Nancy Huie, "The Business of Shopping," *Cruise Industry News Quarterly* (Summer 1995), p. 50. Note that $372 in 1994 is equivalent to $450 in 2004, after adjusting for inflation.

[16] PricewaterhouseCoopers, *Economic Contribution of the F-CCA Member Lines to the Caribbean and Florida* (Florida-Caribbean Cruise Association, July 27, 2001), <f-cca.com/downloads/exsummary.pdf>, Accessed March 5, 2003. The Tourism Department of the US

Virgin Islands reported that average passenger spending in St. Thomas was $225 per passenger and $130 per crew member. See Tim Fields, "WICO Plans Bigger Pier for Bigger Cruise Ship," *Virgin Islands Daily News* (November 12, 2003), <www.virginislandsdailynews.com/index.pl/article_home?id=3071481>, Accessed March 2, 2004.

[17] The figure of $89.72 is an unweighted average. The FCCA study uses a weighted average (meaning that the amount spent is weighted based on the number of passengers visiting each port), which inflates the per-port average. The weighted average of spending per port is $103.83.

[18] Joel Glass, "ICCL Gives Ultimatum to House of Representatives Subcommittee on Relocation of Foreign-Flag Vessels," *Lloyd's List* (May 15, 1993), <www.llplimited.com/LLArchive/output.cgi?Sat15May1993-055&cruise%20line>, Accessed January 8, 1999.

[19] Business Research and Economic Advisors, *The Contribution of the North American Cruise Industry to the US Economy in 2003* (International Council of Cruise Lines, August 2004), <iccl.org/resources/2003econimpact_studies.cfm>, Accessed August 24, 2004.

[20] Adrian Loveridge, "Increased Airline Services Would Boost Local Tourism," *Barbados Advocate* (June 7, 2004), <www.barbadosadvocate.com>, Accessed June 7, 2004.

[21] John C. Martin Associates, *The Economic Impacts of the 2003 Cruise Season at the Port of Seattle* (Port of Seattle, April 13, 2004).

[22] Business Research and Economic Advisors, *The Contribution of the North American Cruise Industry to the US Economy in 2003* (International Council of Cruise Lines, 2004), p.53. <http://www.iccl.org/resources/2003_economic_study.pdf>, Accessed August 24, 2004.

[23] Steven Jackson, "15% of Cruise Passengers Stay on Board," *Jamaica Observer* (March 19, 2004), <www.jamaicaobserver.com>, Accessed March 19, 2004.

[24] In 2003 Halifax, Nova Scotia, reported passenger spending of CDN$102: see *2003 Port of Halifax Cruise Ship Study*, Halifax Port Authority (March 2004); In 2003 Victoria, British Columbia, reported that each passenger spent CDN$88 and each member of the crew spent CDN$62: see *Cruise Ship Survey, 2003*, Victoria A.M. (November 12, 2003); Hawai'i reported cruise passenger spending in 2003 and early 2004 of just over $100 per passenger: see Press Release, "Daily Spending by Cruise Visitors Rose in First Quarter 2004" (Office of Tourism, May 26, 2004), DBEDT News Release 04-16, <www2.hawaii.gov.DBEDT/index.cfm?section=about_DBEDT1009>, Accessed September 20, 2004.

[25] The McDowell Group, *The Economic Impacts of the Cruise Industry on Southeast Alaska* (Southeast Conference, October 2000), p. 11.

[26] *Cruise Ship Passenger Survey: ms Norwegian Sun, September 22, 2001 Visit* (St. John's Economic Development and Tourism Department, March 2002); *2003 Port of Halifax Cruise Ship Study* (Halifax Port Authority, March 2004).

[27] PricewaterhouseCoopers, *Economic Contribution of the F-CCA Member Lines to the Caribbean and Florida* (Florida-Caribbean Cruise Association, July 27, 2001). <http://f-cca.com/downloads/exsummary.pdf> (Accessed March 5, 2003).

[28] The arrival numbers are for 2003 and are provided by the Caribbean Tourism Organization.

[29] In 2002/2003 RCCL's net profit was $351 million. The company's vice president for Commercial Development, John Tercek, said that $100 million of this was from shore excursions. See Tony Peisley, "Shore Excursions Make Impressive Profits," *Cruise Business Review* (December 2003), p. 5.

[30] Hugh Dellios, "In Popular Resort Cozumel, Demand for Service, Security Increase." *Wichita Eagle* (August 10, 2004), <www.kansas.com/mld/kansas/news/world/9362830.htm>, Accessed August 10, 2004.

[31] Katharine Sandiford, "Port Authority: Carrying the Wallets of Thousands of Fun Seekers, the Cruise Industry Receives a Warm Welcome from the Theme Park Named Halifax," *The Coast* (August 14–21, 2003), p. 1. Also see Ross A. Klein, *Cruise Ship Blues: The Underside of the Cruise Industry*, (New Society, 2002).

[32] Hugh Dellios, "In Popular Resort Cozumel, Demand for Service, Security Increase."

[33] David Segal, "Norwegian Cruise Buys Polynesian Tour Bus Line," *Honolulu Star Bulletin* (November 17, 2004), <starbulletin.com/2004/11/17/news/story3.html>, Accessed November 17, 2004.

[34] Jonathan Dahl, "Travel: Why Go Ashore When the Ship's So Nice?" *New York Times* (August 11, 1995), p. B1.

[35] Ibid.

[36] Christopher Reynolds, "Into the Beckoning Arms of Paying Port Merchants," *Los Angeles Times* (September 17, 1995), p. L-2.

[37] J. Martin McOmber, "Most Cruise Passengers Just Dip Toes into Seattle Commerce," *Seattle Times* (May 7, 2004), <seattletimes.nwsource.com>, Accessed May 9, 2004.

[38] Confidential correspondence, March 4, 2004.

[39] J. Martin McOmber, "Study Says Cruise Ship Packs Economic Wallop," *Seattle Times* (April 14, 2004), <seattletimes.nwsource.com>, Accessed April 14, 2004.

[40] "The Financing Challenge," *Seatrade Insider* (February 13, 2004), <www.cruise-community. com/ShowStory.asp?ID=5123>, Accessed February 13, 2004.

[41] A useful comparison of charges by ports in the northeast and the northwest can be found in Pam Parker and Hetty Richardson, *Discharges from Vessels: A Legislative Report Required by Resolve 2003, ch. 79*, Maine Department of Environmental Protection (November 1, 2003).

[42] Bernard Babb, "'Give Us Some More,'" *Barbados Daily Nation* (October 11, 2004), <www.nationnews.com/StoryView.cfm?Record=54239&Section=LO>, Accessed October 11, 2004.

[43] See Ross A. Klein, *Cruising – Out of Control: The Environment, Workers, and Atlantic Canada's Ports* (Canadian Centre for Policy Alternatives, March 2003), pp. 10–11, <www.cruisejunkie. com/cruising.pdf>, Accessed September 3, 2004.

[44] "New Orleans Pledges Power Line Solutions, *Seatrade Insider* (November 26, 2002), <www.cruise-community.com/ShowStory.asp?ID=2864>, Accessed November 27, 2002.

[45] Rebecca Mowbray, "Court Takes Up Dispute on Cruise Ship Relocation," *New Orleans Times-Picayune* (March 9, 2004), <www.nola.com/business/t-p/index.ssf?/base/money-0/10788189 07241480.xm>, Accessed March 10, 2004.

[46] Ibid.

[47] Keith Darce, "Cruise Line Wants Its Moving Costs Paid," *New Orleans Times-Picayune* (March 9, 2004), <www.nola.com>, Accessed March 10, 2004.

[48] According to Dennis Campbell, president of "The Company with the Kilts," his top-selling tour in Halifax is the "Hop On-Hop Off" city tours on double-decker buses, Peggy's Cove, and Lunenberg. See "Halifax Tour Operator Boosts Pierside Sales," *Seatrade Insider* (September 10, 2003), <www.cruise-community.com>, Accessed September 12, 2003.

[49] Peter McLaughlin, "Wanted: Solution to Peggy's Cove Tourist Traffic," *Halifax Daily News* (June 10, 2003).

[50] Quoted in Peter McLaughlin, "Wanted: Solution to Peggy's Cove Tourist Traffic."

[51] Hubbard Glacier is a popular alternative to Glacier Bay, especially for Royal Caribbean and Celebrity Cruises which until 2005 were barred from entering Glacier Bay because of multiple environmental violations.

[52] Kathy Dye, "Lines Fight Head Tax in Yakutat," *Juneau Empire* (May 16, 2001), <www.juneauempire.com>, Accessed May 17, 2001.

[53] Mike Sica, "Yakutat May Protest over Ships, Seals," *Juneau Empire* (January 29, 2001), <www.juneauempire.com>, Accessed January 30, 2001.

[54] Kathy Dye, "Yakutat Assembly Bills Cruise Lines for 2001 Head Tax," *Juneau Empire* (January 4, 2002), <www.juneauempire.com>, Accessed January 4, 2002.

[55] Cathy Brown, "Deal to Skirt Tax," *Juneau Empire* (June 16, 2002), <www.juneauempire.com>, Accessed June 16, 2002.

[56] Masha Herbst, "Juneau Cruise Ship Fee Stands Firm Despite Federal Ban," *Juneau Empire* (April 25, 2003), <www.juneauempire.com>, Accessed May 5, 2003.

[57] Ibid.

[58] Elliott Baron, "Shifting Promotion away from Events," *Solares Hill* (June 18, 1999), p. 9.

[59] Jim Brown, "Lobster Gear Destroyed by Cruise Ships: PEIFA," *Journal-Pioneer* (October 9, 2004), <www.journalpioneer.com/news.aspx?storyID=22687>, Accessed October 9, 2004.

[60] Paul White, "Elizabeth River Run Is Casualty of Norfolk's Cruise Ship Industry," *The Virginian-Pilot* (March 11, 2004), <home.hamptonroads.com>, Accessed March 11, 2004.

[61] "Two Walks This Weekend to Benefit People with MS," *San Diego Union-Tribune* (March 13, 2004), <signonsandiego.com>, Accessed March 13, 2004.

[62] See Mark Adams, "Paddlers Out to Sink Pier Expansion Plan at Harbor, *Maui News* (November 14, 2004), <www.mauinews.com/story.aspx?id=3185> (Accessed November 15, 2004); "Harbor Plan Too Shallow," *Maui News* (November 14, 2004), <www.mauinews.com/story.aspx?id=3184>, Accessed November 15, 2004; Valerie Monson, "Public Weighs Cruise Ship Cost, Benefits on West Side," *Maui News* (November 11, 2004) <www.mauinews.com/story.aspx?id=3088>, Accessed November 12, 2004. Also see Gary Kubota, "Officials Scrap Harbor Plan after Opposition, *Honolulu Star Bulletin* (January 22, 2005), <starbulletin.com/2005/01/22/news/story11.html>, Accessed January 22, 2005.

[63] Joanna Markell, "Jewelry Stores Multiply in Ketchikan," *Anchorage Daily News* (August 3, 2003).

[64] Mike Dunning, "Tourism in Ketchikan and Southeast Alaska," *Alaska History* 15:2 (Fall, 2000), p. 37.

[65] Jennifer Babson, "As the Industry Booms, Key West Considers Limiting Some Cruises," *Miami Herald* (January 5, 2003) <www.maimi.com/mld/miamiherald/4876455.htm>, Accessed January 5, 2003.

[66] Cara Buckley, "Key West Dubbed Victim of Crowding, Poor Planning, Greed," *Miami Herald* (March 12, 2004), <www.miami.com>, Accessed March 13, 2004.

[67] See Timothy O'Hara, "Protesters Cruise Lower Duval," *Key West Citizen* (March 12, 2004), <keysnews.com/280021664867615.bsp.htm>, Accessed March 12, 2004. Also see "Residents Protest Cruise Ships," *Reuters* (March 11, 2004), <edition.cnn.com/2004/TRAVEL/03/11/key.west.reut/index.html>, Accessed March 12, 2004.

[68] Jennifer Babson, "As the Industry Booms, Key West Considers Limiting Some Cruises," *Miami Herald* (January 5, 2003), <www.maimi.com/mld/miamiherald/4876455.htm>, Accessed January 5, 2003.

[69] Ginny Haller, "Cruise Ships: The Good, the Bad and the Ugly," *Keys West Citizen* (January 27, 2003), <www.kyesnews.com/276883752386439.bsp.htm>, Accessed January 28, 2003.

[70] Ginny Haller, "Objection Delays Key West Cruise Ship Study," *Key West Citizen* (May 24, 2003), <www.livableoldtown.com/objection_delays_key_west_cruise.htm>, Accessed January 24, 2004.

[71] Christie Phillips, "FIU Gets Quality-of-Life Study," *Keynoter* (June 7, 2003), <www.keynoter. com/news/20030607s14.html>, Accessed June 9, 2003.

[72] Source: Caribbean Tourism Organization.

[73] "Cruise Ship Contracts Spout Controversy," *San Pedro Sun* (October 7, 2004), <www.sanpedro sun.net/04-342.html>, Accessed October 8, 2004.

[74] See Richard Richtmyer, "State Development Agency Approves Tourism Grant for Hoonah, Alaska," *Miami Herald* (April 8, 2004), <www.miami.com>, Accessed April 9, 2004.

[75] *Proposal for Planning, Development, Financing and Construction of a Large Vessel Marine Berthing Facility at Hoonah, Alaska*, Point Sophia Development Company (October 10, 2001).

[76] Despite Hoonah's apparent success, workers cannot be guaranteed full-time work during the cruise season, and there are reports of infighting in the community over division of jobs. The person who is presently directing the operation is handing out positions to family and friends (personal correspondence).

[77] "Whittier Drops Head Tax to Lure Princess Back," *Juneau Empire* (April 25, 2003), <www. juneauempire.com>, Accessed April 26, 2003.

[78] Haines, Alaska, imposed a tax on shore excursions rather than a passenger head tax. Acting largely in response to the dumping of dry-cleaning fluids and other toxic chemicals in waters adjacent to the town, it introduced a 4 percent sales tax on shore excursions in 2000. Rather than directly oppose the tax, cruise lines quietly told local shore excursion providers that they would have to absorb the tax in the amount they already charge for their product. In other words, the price of shore excursions to the cruise line would remain constant; the local provider would have to deduct from its income the four percent tax. Several years later, after three attempts by local businesses, Haines voters repealed the law.

[79] Bobbi-Jean Mackinnon, "McAlary in Running to Be Country's Craziest Mayor," *Saint John Telegraph-Journal* (January 28, 2004), p. A1/A7, <canadaeast.com>, Accessed January 28, 2004.

[80] Alan Daniels, "RCCL Stresses Commitment to Vancouver as Cruise Base," *Lloyd's List* (June 18, 1997).

[81] "Vancouver to Alaska Cruises at Record Level," *Lloyd's List* (April 18, 2001).

[82] See Press Release, "Cruise Sector Declines for Second Straight Year" (Vancouver Port Authority, October 19, 2004), <www.portvancouver.com/media/dews.html>, Accessed October 24, 2004; "More Business Cruises to Seattle," *Broadcast News* (October 29,2004), <www.canada.com/components/printstory/printstory4.aspx?id=89146e21-552b-444d-be86-8f3b8b2c4477>, Accessed October 30, 2004; Eli Sanders, "Seattle Using Cruise Boom to Navigate through Tough Economy," *Boston Globe* (August 10, 2003), <www.boston. com>, Accessed August 10, 2003.

[83] Elizabeth Sanger, "Mayor Announces Improvements for Cruise Ship Lines," *Newsday* (April 19, 2004), <www.newsday.com>, Accessed May 4, 2004.

[84] Dan Levy, "Pier Plan Cruises Ahead," *San Francisco Chronicle* (December 17, 2003), <www.sf gate.com/article.cgi?file=/c/a/2003/12/17/BUGRQ3OIGI12.DTL>, Accessed December 21, 2003.

[85] "Port Everglades Invests $80m in Cruise," *Seatrade Insider* (October 26, 2004), <www.cruise-community.com/ShowStory.asp?ID=6461>, Accessed October 26, 2004.

[86] Patrick Danner, "Port Everglades to Add Terminal," *Miami Herald* (October 27, 2004), <www.miami.com/mld/miamiherald/business/10021837.htm>, Accessed October 27, 2004.

[87] Harry Minium, "Cruise Ship Terminal Plan Unveiled," *The Virginian-Pilot* (April 21, 2004), <home.hamptonroads.com>, Accessed May 4, 2004.

[88] Garry Mitchell, "Mobile Prepares for the Cruise Crowds," *Tuscaloosa News* (October 9, 2004), <www.tuscaloosanews.com/apps/pbcs.dll/article?AID=/20041009/APN/410090674>, Accessed October 9, 2004.

[89] Frank Vinluan, "Pier 90 to House Berths for Cruise Ships for a Time," *Seattle Times* (May 29, 2002), <seattletimes.nwsource.com>, Accessed June 17, 2002.

[90] J. Martin McOmber, "Port of Seattle Sees Cruise Ships as Economic Anchor," *Seattle Times* (May 18, 2003), <seattletimes.nwsource.com>, Accessed May 22, 2003.

[91] "Four-Ship First for St. John's, Antigua," *Seatrade Insider* (December 20, 2002), <www.cruise-community.com/Show Story.asp?ID=2985>, Accessed December 21, 2002.

[91] Ibid.

[92] Juliet Gill, "Cruise Tourism … St. Maarten's Golden Goose," *Caribbean Cruising* (Second Quarter 2003), pp. 19–20.

[93] John Richardson, "As Terminal Project Begins, Waterfront in a Slump," *Portland Press Herald* (October 8, 2004), <pressherald.mainetoday.com/news/local//041008oceangate.shtml>, Accessed October 8, 2004; "Problems Put Ship Terminal in Jeopardy," *WMTW-TV* (October 8, 2004), <www.wmtw.com/global/story.assp?s=2404756>, Accessed October 8, 2004.

[94] Meredith Cohn, "New Cruise Dock on Hold," *Baltimore Sun* (March 7, 2004), <www.baltimoresun.com/business/bal-bz.cruise07mar07,0,1967234.story?coll=bal-business-headline>, Accessed March 7, 2004.

[95] "Sparks Fly at Passenger Conversion Workshop," *Seatrade Insider* (September 28, 2002), <www.cruise-community.com/ShowStory.asp?ID=2574>, Accessed September 29, 2002.

[96] "Cruise Tourism Impact Forum Keynote Address by Hon. Mark Espat," September 29, 2004, <www.btia.org/news_industry_detail.php?release_id=93>, Accessed October 4, 2004.

[97] Presentation by Sarita Skidmore, principal, Menlo Consulting Group, in "The Future's So Bright … You Gotta Wear Shades," Caribbean Hotel Industry Conference, Punta Cana, Dominican Republic, June 23, 2003.

[98] The 5 percent is based on an assumption that the cruise stops at four ports. Therefore, 20 percent divided by 4 equals 5 percent. Very likely some ports will experience returns rates as high as 10 or 15 percent, but others will see virtually no return of cruise passengers.

[99] Alison Matley, "Cruise Ship Passenger Counts Are Up in Key West," *Keynoter* (August 28, 2002), <keynoter.com>, Accessed August 28, 2002.

[100] Business Research and Economic Advisors, *The Contribution of the North American Cruise Industry to the US Economy in 2003* (International Council of Cruise Lines, 2004), <http://www.iccl.org/resources/2003_economic_study.pdf>, Accessed August 24, 2004.

[101] John C. Martin Associates, *The Economic Impacts of the 2003 Cruise Season at the Port of Seattle* (Port of Seattle, April 13, 2004).

[102] *Survey of Cruiseship Passengers in Hawai'i* (Northwest Cruiseship Association, March 2001).

[103] "By Land, by Sea, or Both?" Caribbean Hotel Industry Conference (Caribbean Hotel Association Annual Meeting), Punta Cana, Dominican Republic, June 24, 2003.

[104] The homeport at Xcaret appears to be "dead in the water" after the local government announced it was considering a head tax of $30 (one-half of what is charged in Bermuda). Carnival Corporation said it was expecting a tax of no more than $2.50. It has now suspended the project "until there is a change in attitude on the part of the local authorities." See Rudy Garcia, "Carnival-Xcaret Homeport 'Dead in the Water' – For Now," *Caribbean Business* (May 29, 2003), <www.puertoricowow.com>, Accessed May 30, 2003.

Chapter 5: A Game of Divide and Conquer

1 "Who Said It," *Cruise Industry News Quarterly* (Winter 1997/98), p. 104.

2 See Ross A. Klein, *Cruise Ship Blues*, pp. 113–144.

3 John Collins, "Cruise Lines Upset with Antigua over Tax Increase," *Caribbean Business* (December 2, 2004), <www.puertoricowow.com/html/cbarchivesdetail.asp?id=14714&highlight=>, Accessed December 19, 2004.

4 Evelyn Guadalupe-Fajardo, "Incentives Package to Cruise Lines Extended to 2004," *Caribbean Business* (April 25, 2002), <www.puertoricowow.com>, Accessed April 28, 2002.

5 See Timothy O'Hara, "Ante Upped for Cruise Ships," *Keys News* (September 13, 2003).

6 Carnival Corporation agreed in February 2004 to bring 500,000 passengers per year for five years (including 80,000 per year to Montego Bay) and in return pay a fixed passenger fee of $7.50. See "2.5m Cruise Passengers for JA under 5 Year Pact with Carnival," *Jamaica Observer* (February 7, 2004), <www.jamaicaobserver.com>, Accessed February 6, 2004.

7 Pam Parker and Hetty Richardson, *Discharges from Vessels: A Legislative Report Required by Resolve 2003, Ch. 79* (Maine Department of Environmental Protection, November 1, 2003).

8 "Mexico's Head Tax Proposal Is Dead," *Seatrade Insider* (November 12, 2004), <www.cruise-community.com/ShowStory.asp?ID=6569>, Accessed November 12, 2004.

9 See Port of Colon Website, <www.colon2000.com>, Accessed August 7, 2003.

10 In the past cruise lines earned substantial income directly from "port charges." A class action lawsuit in 1996 changed advertising practices. Most companies agreed to stop stating additional charges in small print at the bottom of the page or the back of a brochure. Instead, they included port charges and fees in the advertised prices. Estimates of the amount overcharged were $600 million. For details see Ross A. Klein, *Cruise Ship Blues*, p. 45.

11 Mark Stevenson, "Cruise Industry Faces Caribbean Revolt," *The Globe and Mail* (September 8, 2004), p. R8.

12 "Cruise Ship Contracts Sprout Controversy," *San Pedro Sun* (October 7, 2004), <www.san pedrosun.net/04-342.html>, Accessed October 8, 2004.

13 "Is This for Real?" *Belize Times* (September 2, 2003), <www.belizetimes.bz/news/story/2414.shtml>, Accessed January 4, 2004.

14 Cruise Tourism Impact Forum Speech by Belize Tourism Industry Association President Steven Schulte, September 28, 2004. <www.btia.org/news_industry_detail.php?release_id=91>, Accessed October 4, 2004.

15 Wallace Immen, "Sailing in Search of Uncrowded Ports," *Globe and Mail* (October 9, 2004), <www.theglobeandmail.com/servlet/ArticleNews/TPStory/LAC/20041009/EXOTICCRUISE0 9/TPTravel/TopStories>, Accessed October 9, 2004.

16 Karen Heusner, "Belize Tourist Industry Challenges Cruise Ship Contract," *Associated Press* (November 10, 2004), Received via e-mail November 10, 2004.

17 See Molly Morris, "VIPA Agrees to Crown Bay Dock Expansion," *St. Thomas Source* (August 15, 2001), <www.onesource.com/stthomasvi/>, Accessed August 20, 2001.

18 Ibid.

19 Molly Morris, "VIPA, WICO, Chamber Share Views on Crown Bay," *St. Thomas Source* (December 17, 2001), <http://www.onesource.com/stthomasvi/>, Accessed January 3, 2002.

20 The Senate debated considerably about whether the proposed plan should be given final approval. The background and debate on the issue are described in the following articles

printed in the *St. Thomas Source*: Molly Morris, "Cruise Lines: Crown Bay Must Expand, or Else" (November 12, 2001); Molly Morris and Jean Etsinger, "Cruise Lines' Crown Bay Deal a Leveraged Buy-In" (November 22, 2001); Molly Morris, "Dowe: Crown Bay a No-Go without Senate OK" (December 7, 2001); Jean Etsinger, "Cruise Industry Upheaval Affecting V.I. – Part 2" (December 21, 2001); Molly Morris, "Key Crown Bay Question May Be 'Who,' Not If" (January 11, 2002). <www.onepaper.com/stthomasvi/>, Accessed January 20, 2002.

21 Molly Morris, "Turnbull Halts Cruise Lines-Crown Bay Deal," *St. Thomas Source* (March 13, 2002), <www.onepaper.com/stthomasvi/>, Accessed March 17, 2002.

22 Molly Morris, "WICO Chief: Crown Bay Idea Rejected Elsewhere," *St. Thomas Source* (December 17, 2001), <www.onepaper.com/stthomasvi/>, Accessed December 20, 2001.

23 See "Carnival Hopes for Return to St. Croix," *Seatrade Insider* (August 23, 2002), <www.cruise-community.com/ShowStory.asp?ID=2404>, Accessed August 23, 2002.

24 Tanya Mannes, "Winter Will Usher in Small Boost in Cruise Passengers," *Virgin Islands Daily News* (October 10, 2004), <www.virginislandsdailynews.com/index.pl/article?id=7607770>, Accessed October 10, 2004.

25 "Royal Caribbean to Stop in St. Croix for Overnight Refueling," *Canadian Press* (November 9, 2004), <www.canada.com/components/printstory/printstory4.aspx?id=d007c919-29df-4c74-b7bd-68416690e0c5>, Accessed November 10, 2004); Patrick Joy, "Tourism Touts Plans for Tempting Passengers in Frederiksted," *Virgin Islands Daily News* (November 16, 2004), <www.virginislandsdailynews.com/index.pl/article_home?id=776494>, Accessed November 16, 2004.

26 Bob Jaques and Mary Bond, "Italian Ports: New Trend Afoot," *Seatrade Cruise Review* (September 2004), pp. 87–91.

27 "Changing Face of Lines' Investment in Ports," *Seatrade Insider* (June 7, 2004), <www.cruise-community.com>, Accessed June 7, 2004.

28 "Lines May Fight Legality of Juneau Passenger Levy," *Lloyd's List*, October 8, 1999, p. 5.

29 Yereth Rosen, "Alaska Officials Plan Crackdown on Cruise Ships," *Reuters News Service* (February 22, 2000).

30 Ann Chandonnet, "Cruise Line to Halt Gifts of Cash," *Juneau Empire* (March 11, 2002), <www.juneauempire.com>, Accessed March 20, 2002.

31 Paula Dobbyn, "Cruise Ship Association Questions Signatures," *Anchorage Daily News* (January 7, 2005), <www.adn.com/front/v-printer/story/5989323p-5888669c.html>, Accessed January 7, 2005. Also see Sean Cockerham, "Voters to Settle Ship Tax," *Anchorage Daily News* (December 18, 2004), <www.adn.com/front/v-printer/story/5924969p-5832072 c.html>, Accessed December 19, 2004; Matt Volz, "Suit Filed to Stop Tax on Ships," *Anchorage Daily News* (January 19, 2005), <www.adn.com/business/v-printer/story/6038748p-5928014 c.html>, Accessed January 19, 2005.

32 "Carnival in J/V to Build Port near Cancun," *Seatrade Insider* (November 7, 2001), <www.cruise-community.com>, Accessed November 7, 2001.

33 In clearing a channel through a gap in the reef to the proposed dock at Xcaret, developers moved 45 small islands of coral. Ecological activists insist such action is illegal, but developers cite a loophole that allowed them to do so. In either case, survival of the transplants is not guaranteed. See James Varney, "Tourism, Ecology at Odds in Mexico," *New Orleans Times-Picayune* (February 9, 2003), <www.nola.com>, Accessed February 12, 2003.

34 Rudy Garcia, "Carnival-Xcaret Homeport 'Dead in the Water' – for Now," *Caribbean Business* (May 29, 2003), <www.puertoricowow.com>, Accessed July 31, 2003.

[35] Ibid.

[36] "Mayor Calls for Cancun Homeport," *Seatrade Insider* (November 8, 2003), <www.cruise-community.com/ShowStory.asp?ID=4643>, Accessed November 9, 2003.

[37] Anne Kalosh, "Costa Maya: Golden Opportunity," *Seatrade Cruise Review* (September 2004), p. 55. For a discussion of sustainability issues around development of Costa Maya see Rebecca Lynn Greenberg, *Toward Sustainable Coastal Tourism Development: The Case of Costa Maya* (University of Miami, December 2004), (Masters Internship Report, Rosenstiel School of Marine and Atmospheric Science).

[38] Lee K. Cerveny, *Preliminary Research Findings from a Study of the Sociocultural Effects of Tourism in Haines, Alaska* (July 2004, US Department of Agriculture), p. 80, Technical Report PNW-GTR-612.

[39] See Iver Peterson, "Port of Embarkation: Bayonne, N.J.," *New York Times* (September 26, 2004), <travel2.nytimes.com/2004/09/26/travel/26rep.html>, Accessed September 26, 2004.

[40] Meredith Cohn, "Snazzier Cruise Terminal Is Sought," *Baltimore Sun* (August 13, 2004), <www.baltimoresun.com/business/bal-bz.cruise13aug13,1,4412807.story?coll=bal-business-headlines>, Accessed August 13, 2004.

[41] "Port of Los Angeles Poised for Renewal," *Seatrade Insider* (October 1, 2004), <www.cruise-community.com/ShowStory.asp?ID=6329>, Accessed October 4, 2004.

[42] Irwine Clare, "Cruise Line Impact on Caribbean Questioned," *Heartbeat News* (October 19, 2004), <www.heartbeatnews.com/details2336.htm>, Accessed October 19, 2004.

[43] Many ports give water away or charge a nominal hook-up fee. Bayonne agreed to give Royal Caribbean only one-fourth of the volume of water it asked for. For details see Ronald Leir, "Cruise Line Gets Deal for Water," *New Jersey Journal* (March 4, 2004), <www.nj.com>, Accessed March 4, 2004.

[44] Mark Stevenson, "Cruise Industry Faces Caribbean Revolt," *Globe and Mail* (September 8, 2004), p. R8.

[45] Evelyn Guadalupe-Fajardo, "Royal Caribbean Carries 33% of Island's Cruise Visitors," *Caribbean Business* (February 10, 2000), <www.puertoricowow.com>, Accessed February 12, 2000.

[46] Evelyn Guadalupe-Fajaro, "F-CCA Member Lines Say Puerto Rico Ignores the Cruise Industry," *Caribbean Business* (March 28, 2002), <www.puertoricowow.com>, Accessed March 29, 2002.

[47] Ibid.

[48] Evelyn Guadalupe-Fajaro, "Cruise Ships to Get Entertainment and Provisions at Port," *Caribbean Business* (August 29, 2002), <www.puertoricowow.com>, Accessed August 30, 2002.

[49] Evelyn Guadalupe-Fajaro, "Royal Caribbean Seeks Cheap Hotel Rooms for Pre- and Post-Cruise Passengers," *Caribbean Business* (April 18, 2002), <www.puertoricowow.com>, Accessed April 19, 2002.

[50] Evelyn Guadalupe-Fajardo, "Incentives Package to Cruise Lines Extended to 2004," *Caribbean Business* (April 25, 2002), <www.puertoricowow.com>, Accessed April 26, 2002.

[51] John Collins, "Turks and Caicos Islands Entering Cruise Trade," *Caribbean Business* (January 15, 2004), <www.puertoricowow.com>, Accessed March 1, 2004.

[52] Statement by the Secretary General of CTO, Mr. Jean Holder, on the Proposed Cruise Levy (September 18, 2003), <www.onecaribbean.com>, Accessed September 18, 2003.

[53] Hayden Boyce, "Cruise Liners Seeking to Divide and Rule the Caribbean," *Nassau Guardian* (October 23, 2003), <www.thenassauguardian.com/editorial/33177441 7855056.php>, Accessed October 24, 2004.

[54] "Papua New Guinea Upset Tourist Wrote about Fears of Ending Up in Cannibal Soup," *Canadian Press* (March 3, 2004), <www.canada.com>, Accessed March 4, 2004.

[55] See Press Release, "CHA, CTO, and F-CCA Establish Tripartite Committee for Cooperation in Regional Tourism Development," (Caribbean Tourism Organization, May 3, 2004).

[56] <f-cca.com/pages/foundation.html>, Accessed October 3, 2004.

[57] "The 2000 F-CCA Foundation for the Caribbean Children's Essay Contest," *Entre Nous – Bonaire's Bi-weekly Newsletter* (Issue #6, April 21 2000).

[58] "Students from Belize and the Bahamas Take Top Prizes in the F-CCA Foundation Children's Essay Contest" (September 16, 2000), <democrat.freeservers.com/democrat/archives/09162000.html#15>, Accessed April 11, 2004.

[59] "Ketchikan Students Learn about the Visitor Services Industry," *SITNEWS* (September 17, 2004), <www.sitnews.us/0904news/091704/091704_ship_tour.html>, Accessed September 17, 2004.

[60] Bruce Potter, Keynote Presentation, Whitewater to Bluewater Partnership Conference, March 24, 2004, Miami, FL.

[61] The account was given by a journalist from Cayman Islands at the Caribbean Media Exchange, St. Lucia, June 2004.

[62] "Carnival Classic Raises $50,000 for Charity," *Seatrade Insider* (June 8, 2004), <www.cruise-community.com>, Accessed June 8, 2004.

[63] Other consultants commonly used are the McDowell Group in Alaska, Gee & Jenson in the Caribbean, and G.P. Wild in Europe.

[64] According to Baron, B&A provided architectural, interior design, engineering, cost estimating, and construction management services for headquarters of both Carnival and Royal Caribbean as well as the development of a 260-acre destination resort for Royal Caribbean in Haiti.

[65] Elliott Baron, "City Taken on a Sea Cruise," *Solares Hill* (January 22, 1999), pp. 1, 6–9.

[66] Ibid.

[67] Elliott Baron, "City Gets Fare Representation," *Solares Hill* (January 29, 1999), pp. 1, 4–5.

[68] Michael Crye, president of the International Council of Cruise Lines, made the distinction between "good media" and "bad media" at the World Cruise Tourism Summit held on March 5, 2001. The session entitled "Cruise Industry in the Media" used stories by Douglas Frantz in the *New York Times* as an exemplar of the "bad media."

Chapter 6: Squeezing to the Last Drop

[1] See Mary Lu Abbott, "Extras Can Cost More Than the Cruise," *New Orleans Times-Pacayune* (November 7, 2004), <www.nola.com/printer/printer.ssf?/base/living-0/109981480177200.xml>, Accessed November 7, 2004.

[2] Steven Mihailovich, "Game Maker Sails into Big Deal," *Las Vegas Business Press* (October 7, 2004), <www.lvbusinesspress.com/artciels/2004/10/07/news/news04.prt>, Accessed October 8, 2004.

[3] Discussed by Bob Dickinson, Carnival Cruise Lines president, State of the Industry Debate, Seatrade Cruise Shipping Convention, Miami Beach, March 12, 2002.

[4] "Mr. easyJet Sets Course for the Cut-Rate Cruise," *Channel News Asia* (March 18, 2004), <www.channelnewsasia.com/stories/afp_world_business/view/76044/1/.html>, Accessed March 18, 2004.

[5] For a discussion of casino income see Dale K. Dupont, "Casinos Boost Onboard Spending," *Miami Herald* (May 1, 2004), <www.miami.com/mld/miamiherald/business/8562781.htm>, Accessed May 2, 2004.

[6] While most pieces of art cost less than $1,000, many are in the tens of thousands. While it is difficult to know what happens on every ship, one news report cited a couple that spent $34,000 on artwork, including $26,430 for a print by Pablo Picasso. See James Kogutkiewicz, "Child Abuse Case Grows," *Waukesha Freeman* (October 9, 2004), <www.gmtoday.com/news/local_stories/2004/October_04/10092004_03.asp>, Accessed October 9, 2004. Other news reports over the years have described the additional charges, overpricing, and misleading nature of shipboard art auctions: Daniel Grant, "Art Auctions: A Seaworthy Enterprise," *Plain Dealer* (June 27, 2004), <www.cleveland.com/living/plaindealer/index.ssf?/base/living/1088155829139501.xml>, Accessed June 29, 2004; Will Bennett, "Hoisting Sales on the High Seas," *Daily Telegraph* (May 3, 2004), <www.telegraph.co.uk/arts/main.jhtml?xml=/arts/2004/05/03/bawb03.xml&sSheet=/arts/2004/05/03/ixartleft. html>, Accessed May 4, 2004; Kitty Bean Yancey, "Cruise Lines Draw Profits from Selling Works of Art," *USA Today* (February 9, 2001), <www.usatoday.com/life/travel/leisure/ 2001/2001-02-09-auctions.htm> and Kitty Bean Yancey, "Art Auctions at Sea Could Soak You," *SA Today* (February 9, 2001), <www.usatoday.com/life/ travel/leisure/2001/2001-02-09-cruise-auctions.htm>, both accessed February 9, 2001.

[7] Jonathan Siskin, "Passengers Are No Longer Asking 'Where's the Beef?'" *Cruise Industry News Quarterly* (Spring 2003), pp. 112–114.

[8] Rebecca Tobin, "Royal Caribbean: Eats at Johnny Rockets Get a Surcharge," *Travel Weekly Crossroads* (October 25, 2004), <www.travelweekly.com/printarticle.aspx?pageid=45985>, Accessed October 25, 2004.

[9] Rob Marjerison, "Maximizing Onboard Revenue," *Cruise Industry News Quarterly* (Winter 1995/96), p. 82.

[10] See "Exclusive Destinations Concept an Economic Necessity for 1990s: Out-Islands the In-Thing," *Lloyd's List* (October 18, 1991), <www.llplimited.com/LLArchive/output.cgi?Fri18 Oct1991-005&cruise%20line>, Accessed January 8, 1999.

[11] Rebecca Tobin, "Seatrade Panel Talks Directly About Trend," *Travel Weekly Crossroads* (March 16, 2004), <www.twcrossroads.com/PrintArticle.asp?ArticleID= 42011>, Accessed March 17, 2004.

[12] Crystal Sets Grand Prize," *Travel Weekly Crossroads* (October 5, 2000), <www.twcrossroads.com/cruise/Cruisewrapper.asp?ArticleID=23328>, Accessed November 4, 2000.

[13] Michele San Filippo, "Agents Irate Over Major Cruise Lines' Pays," *Travel Weekly Crossroads* (September 7, 2001), <www.twcrossroads.com>, Accessed September 8, 2001.

[14] Ernest Blum, "CCL to End Preferred Deals for Online Agencies," *Travel Weekly Crossroads* (July 21, 2003), <www.twcrossroads.com/PrintArticle.asp?ArticleID=38751>, Accessed November 22, 2003.

[15] Rebecca Tobin, "Agent Finds Out Carnival Prices Not Always Even," *Travel Weekly Crossroads* (February 9, 2004), <www.twcrossroads.com/PrintArticle.asp?ArticleID=41470>, Accessed February 11, 2004.

[16] Rebecca Tobin, "Cruise Analysis: When a Level Playing Field Isn't Necessarily Level," *Travel Weekly Crossroads* (August 24, 2004), <www.travelweekly.com/printarticle.aspx?pageid= 44667>, Accessed August 24, 2004.

[17] It is common for cruise lines to offer promotions to residents of certain states, but these discounts are not available to others. As a result, one passenger may pay significantly more

than another simply because he lives in Iowa rather than Illinois. The same inequities in cost are also found across country borders. Pricing for US passengers is often different from pricing for Canadians on the exact same cruise ship.

[18] Evan Perez, "Cruise Lines Crack Down on Consumer Discounts," *Wall Street Journal* (August 12, 2004), p. D1. See also Rebecca Tobin, "Retailers Hail Carnival, RCCL Plans to Squelch Rebating," *Travel Weekly Crossroads* (August 22, 2004), <www.travelweekly.com/printarticle. aspx?pageid=44570>, Accessed August 22, 2004)

[19] James Gilden, "2 Cruise Lines Try to Simplify Rates by Halting Rebate Ads," *Los Angeles Times* (September 12, 2004), <www.latimes.com/travel/la-tr-insider12sep12,1,1642938.story>, Accessed September 12, 2004.

[20] "UBS: Agent Commission Ripe for Cost Savings," *Travel Weekly Crossroads* (August 6, 2004), <www.twcrossroads.com>, Accessed August 6, 2004.

[21] Holland America Line, *Know before You Go* (Fall 1999/2000).

Chapter 7: The Art of Greenwashing

[1] "'Sovereign of the Seas' Operator in Two Key Defensive Moves against Coast Guard Oil Dumping Charges," *Lloyd's List* (December 23, 1996), p. 3, <www.llplimited.com/LLArchive/output.cgi?Mon23Dec1996-019&cruise%20line>, Accessed January 8, 1999.

[2] Ibid.

[3] See Joel Glass, "Royal Caribbean Indicted after Alleged Oil Discharge off Puerto Rico," *Lloyd's List* (December 21, 1996), p. 1, <www.llplimited.com/LLArchive/output.cgi?Sat213Dec1996-022&cruise%20line>, Accessed January 8, 1999.

[4] Douglas Frantz, "Gaps in Sea Laws Shield Pollution by Cruise Lines," *New York Times* (January 3, 1999), <www.nytimes.com/library/national/010399cruise-industry.html>, Accessed June 11, 1999.

[5] "Royal Admits to Dumping," *CNN* (June 1, 1998), <www.cnn.com>, Accessed June 2, 1998.

[6] See Press Release, "Royal Caribbean Sentenced for Fleet-Wide Conspiracy of Dumping Oil and Lying to the Coast Guard" (Department of Justice, September 17, 1998), <www.usdoj. gove/opa/pr/1998/Septempber/429_enr.htm>, Accessed July 5, 2002.

[7] In October 1992 the US government "told the International Maritime Organization's Marine Environmental Committee meeting that it had reported MARPOL violations to the appropriate flag states 111 times, but received responses in only about 10% of the cases." See "US Cracks Down on Marine Pollution," *Lloyd's List* (April 17, 1993), p. 3.

[8] See US General Accounting Office, *Marine Pollution: Progress Made to Reduce Marine Pollution by Cruise Ships, but Important Issues Remain,* (GAO, February 2000), p. 4, (Doc #GAO/RCED-00-48).

[9] These figures are based on information provided by Royal Caribbean International. They are confirmed in Linda Nowlan and Ines Kwan, *Cruise Control: Regulating Cruise Ship Pollution on the Pacific Coast of Canada,* (West Coast Environmental Law, 2001), p. 21. Also see *Report to the Legislature: Regulation of Large Passenger Vessels in California,* (Cruise Ship Environmental Task Force, August 2003).

[10] See "After Apology and $9 Million Punishment, Royal Caribbean Dumps Again," *Washington Post* (October 25, 1998), p. E3.

[11] See Press Release, "Royal Caribbean to Pay Record $18 Million Criminal Fine for Dumping Oil and Hazardous Chemicals, Making False Statements" (Department of Justice, July 21, 1999), Received via e-mail July 22, 1999.

[12] James Vicini, "Focus – Royal Caribbean to Plead Guilty to Pollution," *Reuters* (July 21, 1999), <dailynews.yahoo.com>, Accessed July 23, 1999.

[13] "Cruise Line Will Pay $3.5 Million to Alaska," *New York Times* (January 15, 2000), <proquest. umi.com>, Accessed January 19, 2000.

[14] "Crewman Rewarded for Reporting Pollution," *Juneau Empire* (October 9, 1998), <www. juneauempire.com>, Accessed January 3, 1999.

[15] A number of explanations were explored for finding fecal coliform in gray water, but no consensus was reached. A report showed that fecal coliform counts in gray water being higher than 9 million per milliliter. The allowable limit is 200 per milliliter. See "Knowles Steps Up Pressure on Congress for Action on Cruise Ship Discharges," *Press Release #00252* (Office of the Governor, October 6, 2000), <www.gov.state.ak.us/press/00252.html>, Accessed October 10, 2000.

[16] See Bill McAllister, "A Big Violation on Wastewater: Some Ship Readings 100,000 Times Allowed Amount," *The Juneau Empire* (August 27, 2000), <www.juneauempire.com>, Accessed September 2, 2000.

[17] See McAllister, Bill, "Cruise Initiative Brought about Federal, State Lows," *Juneau Empire* (November 18, 2001), <www.juneauempire.com>, November 19, 2001.

[18] The regulations required that the geometric mean of the samples from discharge during any 30-day period does not exceed 20 fecal coliform per 100 milliliters and not more than 10 percent of the samples exceed 40 fecal coliform per 100 milliliters. See *H.R. 5666, Making Miscellaneous Appropriations for the Fiscal Year Ending September 30, 2001, and for Other Purposes, Section 1404 (C.3)*

[19] Bluewater Network Fact Sheet, March 2004.

[20] See Press Release, "ICCL Environmental Statement" (International Council of Cruise Lines, July 27, 1999), <iccl.org/pressroom/press13.cfm>, Accessed July 31, 1999.

[21] Figures are from an estimate of charges for disposal of gray water and sewage at Pier 66 in Seattle, Washington, June 8, 2001.

[22] Robinson Shaw, "Suit Filed over Cruise Line Pollution," *Environmental News Network* (July 6, 2000).

[23] Wendy Doscher, "Rough Seas for Cruise Line," *Miami Daily Business Review* (July 18, 2000).

[24] Rajesh Joshi, "Model Suspect NCL Escapes with $1.5 m Pollution Fine," *Lloyd's List* (August 2, 2002), <www.lloydslist.com>, Accessed August 5, 2002.

[25] Marilyn Adams, "US Cracks Down on Cruise Ship Pollution," *USA Today* (November 8, 2002), <www.usatoday.com/travel/news/2002/2002-11-18-cruise-dumping.htm>, Accessed November 8, 2002.

[26] See Press Release, "Norwegian Cruise Line Admits to Environmental Crime" (Department of Justice, July 31, 2002), <www.usdoj.gov/opa/pr/2002/July/02_enrd_441.htm>, Accessed September 16, 2002.

[27] Rajesh Joshi, "Model Suspect NCL Escapes with $1.5 m Pollution Fine."

[28] Marilyn Adams, "US Keeps Wary Eye on Cruise Ships for More Pollution," *USA Today* (November 8, 2002), <www.usatoday.com/travel/news/2002/2002-11-18-cruise-dumping. htm>, Accessed November 8, 2002.

[29] Gary T. Kubota, "Maui-Bound Cruise Ship Investigated for Dumping," *Honolulu Star-Bulletin* (March 8, 2003), <starbulletin.com/2003/03/08/news/story6.html>, Accessed March 14, 2003.

[30] See Sharon L. Crenson, "Cruise Ship Inquiry Expands," *Associated Press* (February 15, 2001), <story.news.yahoo.com>, Accessed February 15, 2002.

[31] "Carnival Pleads Guilty to Charges," *Associated Press* (April 19, 2002), <story.news.yahoo. com>, Accessed May 8, 2002. Also see Department of Justice Press Release, July 31, 2002, <www.usdoj.gov/usao/fls/Carnival.html>, Received via e-mail July 31, 2002.

[32] Joanna Markell, "Ryndam Spill Estimate Jumps to 40,000 Gallons," *Juneau Empire* (August 28, 2002), <juneauempire.com>, Accessed August 28, 2002.

[33] Tony Carroll, "Cruise Line Apologizes for Sewage," *Juneau Empire* (December 14, 2004), <www.juneauempire.com>, Accessed December 19, 2004.

[34] Letter from E. Heldewier, Carnival's director, Environmental Programs to N. Kampas, California Water Resources Control Board, January 16, 2003.

[35] See Press Release, "Carnival Cruise Lines to Pay $200,000 for Illegal Dumping of Ballast Water" (Bluewater Network, October 21, 2001), Received via e-mail October 21, 2003.

[36] Dale K. DuPont, "Pollution Case Haunts Carnival," *Miami Herald* (July 24, 2003), <www. miami.com/mld/miamiherald/6369543.htm>, Accessed July 24, 2003.

[37] Evan Perez, "Carnival Fires Pollution Auditors," *Wall Street Journal* (August 28, 2003), <online.wsj.com>, Accessed August 28, 2003.

[38] See Carnival Corporation Form 10Q (US Securities and Exchange Commission, April 8, 2004).

[39] "Former HAL Exec Sentenced for False Reports," *Seatrade Insider* (July 1, 2004), <www. cruise-community.com>, Accessed July 5, 2004.

[40] See James P. Walsh *v.* Carnival Corporation, Case No. 02-018326 (08) in the Circuit Court for the Seventeenth Judicial Circuit in and for Broward County, Florida.

[41] Sharon L. Crenson, "Cruise Lines Set Environmental Rules," *Associated Press* (June 10, 2001), <dailynews.yahoo.com/htx/ap/20010610/us/cruise_pollution_1.html>, Accessed June 11, 2001.

[42] Kathy Dye, "Ship Pumps Laundry Water into City Harbor," *Juneau Empire* (June 19, 2001), <juneauempire.com>, Accessed June 20, 2001.

[43] See Press Release, "New Mandatory Environmental Standards for Cruise Ships" (International Council of Cruise Lines, June 11, 2001), <iccl.org/pressroom/press55.cfm>, Accessed June 12, 2001.

[44] Kelly Yamanouchi, "Cruise Lines Admit Pollution Violations," *Honolulu Advertiser* (December 12, 2003), <the.honoluluadvertiser.com/article/2003/Dec/12/bz/bz02a.html>, Accessed December 21, 2003.

[45] Scott Harper, "Line Touts Strides to Clean Up Its Act," *The Virginian-Pilot* (October 4, 2004), <home.hamptonroads.com/stories/print.cfm?story=76366&ran=24890>, Accessed October 4, 2004.

[46] Geoff Johnson, *Don't Be Fooled: The Ten Worst Greenwashers of 2003*, (The Green Life, April 2004), <www.thegreenlife.org/dontbefooled.html>, Accessed April 5, 2004.

[47] See words of DeeVon Quirolo at Reef Relief in Key West, as quoted in David Conway, "Time to Clean Up Cruise Pollution," *Florida Sportsman* (November 2004), <www.floridasportsman.com/confron/C-0407/index.html>, Accessed November 9, 2004.

[48] Bluewater Network Fact Sheet, March 2004, Received via e-mail March 1, 2004.

[49] See Ocean Fund History <www.oceanfund.org/about.html>, Accessed January 7, 2004.

[50] See Press Release, "RCCL Donates Funds to Ocean Protection" (Royal Caribbean Cruises Limited, October 18, 1996).

[51] Michael Herz and Joseph Davis, *Cruise Control: A Report on How Cruise Ships Affect the Marine Environment*, (The Ocean Conservancy, May 2002).

⁵² Oceans Blue Foundation similarly lost its funding after it issued a report critical of the cruise industry. While it didn't receive funds from industry sources, the industry lobbied and pressured those that did fund the organization and in a very short time Oceans Blue Foundation had folded. See Ross A. Klein, *Charting a Course: The Cruise Industry, the Government of Canada, and Purposeful Development* (Canadian Centre for Policy Alternatives, September 2003), <www.cruisejunkie.com/ccpa2.html>, Accessed October 1, 2003.

⁵³ See Timothy O'Hara, "Cruise Money Goes to Marine Sanctuary Visitor Center," *Key West Citizen* (January 29, 2004).

⁵⁴ In comparison, consider that Royal Caribbean was prepared to give $500,000 to $1 million a year to Golden Gate Bridge officials in San Francisco in return for free advertising at its ferry terminals, on at least 20 buses, and in each issue of the transit guide produced by the bridge district. The plan fell through after a public outcry. The cost for RCCL's advertisements on the walls of Boston's Red Line "T" (subway) is not known. See Mark Prado, "A Landmark Way to Raise $500,000," *Marin Independent* (September 10, 2004), <www.marinij.com/stories/0,1413,234~24407~2392625,00.html>, Accessed September 10, 2004; Naomi Aoki, "Next Stop, Ad Buzz," *Boston Globe* (August 18, 2004), <www.boston.com/business/articles/2004/08/18/next_stop_ad_buzz>, Accessed August 22, 2004.

⁵⁵ See Press Release, "International Council of Cruise Lines and Conservation International Announce Joint Initiative" (International Council of Cruise Lines, December 10, 2003), <iccl.org/pressroom/pressrelease.cfm?whichrel=38>, Accessed December 22, 2003.

⁵⁶ James E.N. Sweeting and Scott L. Wayne, *A Shifting Tide: Environmental Challenges & Cruise Industry Responses* (Conservation International, March 2003).

⁵⁷ "Cruise Ships Shouldn't Dump Raw Waste, Say US Tourists," *Forbes Magazine* (March 4, 2003), <northamerica.oceana.org/index.cfm?sectionID=10&fuseaction=41.detail&pageID=1003>, Accessed October 5, 2004.

⁵⁸ Ocean Conservation and Tourism Alliance, "Interview with Michael Crye," distributed March 2004 at Seatrade Cruise Shipping Convention and at White Water to Blue Water Partnership Conference, Miami.

⁵⁹ See <www.cruisejunkie.com> for a list of environmental offences and fines.

⁶⁰ "Quick and Dirty: A Notebook of News and Politics," *Las Vegas Mercury* (October 30, 2003), <www.lasvegasmercury.com/2003/MERC-Oct-30-Thu-2003/22428503.html>, Accessed November 12, 2003.

⁶¹ Ibid.

⁶² George Monbiot, "Greens Getting Eaten," *The Guardian* (January 15, 2002), <www.monbiot.com>, Accessed March 27, 2004.

⁶³ Carmelo Ruiz-Marrero, "The Troubled Marriage of Environmentalists and Oil Companies," *CorpWatch* (December 22, 2003), <www.corpwatch.org/issues/PID.jsp?articleid=9448>, Accessed January 8, 2004.

⁶⁴ Aziz Choudry, "Tarzan, Indiana Jones and Conservation International's Global Greenwash Machine," *Z Magazine* (October 10, 2003), <www.zmag.org/sustainers/content/2003-10/10 choudry.cfm>, Accessed October 20, 2003.

⁶⁵ See *Tourism and Biodiversity: Mapping Tourism's Global Footprint* (Conservation International, 2003).

⁶⁶ Aziz Choudry, "Tarzan, Indiana Jones and Conservation International's Global Greenwash Machine."

[67] See Press Release, "Marine Biologist Sylvia Earle Joins Conservation International" (Conservation International, January 31, 2002), <www.biodiversityscience.org/xp/news/press_releases/2002/013102.xml, Accessed April 2, 2004.

[68] Dr. Earle has also been on the board of directors of the Center for Marine Conservation/Ocean Conservancy, though she was not a member the year the study that ruffled Royal Caribbean's feathers was released. She had been on the board at least from 1997 to 2001, and was again elected to the board to begin a term in May 2002. It is not known whether she stepped down because of the report, or simply sat out a year to comply with the organization's constitution, which prohibits more than two-consecutive three-year terms. In either case, presumably Royal Caribbean's anger at The Ocean Conservancy did not extend to her.

[69] "Business/NGO Partnerships — What's the Payback," *Ethical Corporation* (April 2004), <www.greenbiz.com/news/reviews_third.cfm?NewsID=26712>, Accessed May 11, 2004.

[70] Described by ICCL and CI at the White Water to Blue Water Conference, Miami (March 24, 2004).

[71] See Press Release, "Statement: Clean Cruise Ship Act" (International Council of Cruise Lines, April 1, 2004), <iccl.org/pressroom/pressrelease.cfm?whichrel=40>, Accessed April 3, 2004.

[72] Form letter from J. Michael Crye to members of Congress, May 11, 2004. (Copy sent to me by its recipient on May 17, 2004.)

[73] Form letter to members of Congress, re: Clean Cruise Ship Act and Cruise Industry Opposition Letter, May 24, 2004.

[74] <www.ips-dc.org/ecotourism>, Accessed April 10, 2004.

[75] "Cruise Ship Settlement to Fund Girls Athletics," *Los Angeles Times* (October 27, 1999), p. B4, <www.latimes.com/archives/doc/rArchive/temptemp.20913>, Accessed November 8, 1999.

[76] See Press Release, "Surfrider Foundation Settles Lawsuit with Carnival Cruise Lines" (Surfrider Foundation, June 1, 2001), <www.surfrider.org/press_releases/press_releases_page.asp?which_one=45>, Accessed October 5, 2004.

[77] Gary T. Kubota, "Port Calls by Cruise Ships Split Moloka'i," *Honolulu Star Bulletin* (October 29, 2002), <starbulletin.com>, Accessed November 3, 2002.

[78] Accounts relating to OBF are drawn from media and from members of the ENGOs involved, including the principal players in OBF.

[79] Organizations contacted reported this back to OBF.

[80] Though the relationship between Hoggan and the David Suzuki Foundation appears to some to be a conflict of interest, the foundation defends the connection saying its concern is with the oceans, not with cruise ships (as though the two can be separated). Accounts relating to OBF are drawn from media and from members of the NGOs involved.

[81] *Blowing the Whistle and the Case for Cruise Ship Certification* (Oceans Blue Foundation, October 2002), <oceansblue.org/bluetourism/chartacourse/cruiseship/cruisereport.html>, Accessed on January 5, 2004.

[82] See Tracy Tjaden, "Cruise Lines Blasted: Tourism-Industry Funded Oceans Blue in Hot Water Following Critical Report on Industry," *Business in Vancouver* (November 12–28, 2002).

[83] Co-sponsors were Save our Shores, Friends of the Sea Otter, and The Ocean Conservancy-Monterey Bay.

[84] Letter from Joseph L. Valenti to Lynn Young of Save Our Shores, January 17, 2003. It was copied to M. Crye (ICCL); G. Michel (President, Crystal Cruises); M. Weisband (Public Relations, Crystal Cruises); D. Laidman (Reporter, Monterey Herald); and S. Scheiblauer (Monterey Harbormaster).

[85] Dan Laidman, "Cruise Line Says Rookie Mistake Led to Ship's Waste Dumping," *Monterey Herald* (March 6, 2003), <www.montereyherald.com>, Accessed March 6, 2003.

[86] Ed Fletcher, "Cruise Ships Are in the Cross Hairs," *The Sacramento Bee* (June 23, 2003).

[87] Nick Madigan, "Monterey Bans a Cruise Ship over Dumping" *New York Times* (March 6, 2003), <www.nytimes.com>, Accessed March 6, 2003. Also see Dan Laidman, "Crystal Ships Banned from Monterey for 15 Years," *Monterey Herald* (March 18, 2003), <www.monterey herald.com>, Accessed March 19, 2003.

[88] Volumes are based on Carnival Corporation estimates for newbuilds in 2002.

[89] Alaska Department of Environmental Conservation, *Assessment of Cruise Ship and Ferry Wastewater Impacts in Alaska* (ADEC, January 28, 2004).

[90] "Pollution Solutions Lack Science," *Seatrade Insider* (March 26, 2004), <www.cruise-community.com>, Accessed March 26, 2004.

[91] This was clearly stated during the ICCL panel on *Cruising, Voyage to Environmental Stewardship: Miles Traveled,* World Cruise Tourism Summit, March 3, 2003, Miami Beach, Florida.

[92] Azipod (short for *azimuthing podded*) propulsion systems are mounted on the underside of the ship's hull (rather than inside the hull). Because the pod can be turned up to 360 degrees, it eliminates the need for long shaft lines (from the engines to the propellers), rudders, and stern thrusters common to all conventional cruise ships. Benefits of an Azipod system include excellent maneuverability, elimination of a number of main components which reduces breakdowns and maintenances costs, fuel savings because of greater hydrodynamic efficiency, reduced capital cost of ship construction, and freeing space for up to 50 additional cabins.

[93] One member of the Science panel writing the Alaska report was subsequently appointed to OCTA's science panel.

[94] Transport Canada, *Pollution Prevention Guidelines for the Operation of Cruise Ships under Canadian Jurisdiction* (Transport Canada, 2004). (Document # TP 14202 E)

[95] Ken Weiss, "Cruise Line Pollution Prompts Legislation," *Los Angeles Times* (August 18, 2003), <www.latimes.com>, Accessed August 19, 2003.

[96] Organization for Economic Co-operation and Development, *Voluntary Approaches to Environmental Policy: Effectiveness, Efficiency, and Usage in Policy Mixes* (OECD, 2003).

[97] See <www.dhs.state.or.us/news/2004news/2004-1001b.html>, Accessed October 7, 2004.

[98] See <www.dhs.state.or.us/news/2004news/2004-1006a.html>, Accessed October 7, 2004.

[99] Larry Lange, "State, Port Reach Deal with Cruise Ships," *Seattle Post-Intelligencer* (April 21, 2004), <seattlepi.nwsource.com/local/170003_cruiseships21.html>, Accessed May 4, 2004.

[100] Robert McClure, "Cruise Ships Not Using Low-Pollution Fuels after All," *Seattle Post-Intelligencer* (September 11, 2003), <seattlepi.nwsource.com/local/139108_cruise11.html?searchpagefrom=1&searchdiff=475>, Accessed September 12, 2004.

[101] Ibid.

[102] Ibid.

[103] In June 2004 Washington State Ferries, the largest ferry fleet in the US, shifted to low-sulfur diesel fuels. As a result they will reduce sulfur dioxide emissions by 412 tons (90 percent) and particulate matter by 75 tons (30 percent). See <www.ens-newswire.com/ens/jun2004/2004-06-03-09.asp#anchor5>, Accessed June 6, 2004.

[104] Ibid.

[105] See Ross A. Klein, "Left in Its Wake," *Alternatives Journal* (Fall 2002) 28:4, p. 24.

[106] See "Draft Cruise Ship Pollution Rules Studied," *Bangor Daily News* (November 5, 2004), <www.bangornews.com/editorial/news/printarticle.cfm?ID=441678>, Accessed November 5, 2004. Also see "Maine Restricts Ship Pollution," *Bangor Daily News* (April 22, 2005), <www.bangornews.com/news/templates/?a=112463&z=178>, Accessed May 1, 2005.

[107] Ken Weiss, "Cruise Line Pollution Prompts Legislation." Also see *Report to the Legislature: Regulation of Large Passenger Vessels in California* (Cruise Environmental Task Force, August 2003).

[108] See Press Release, "Cruise Ship Dumping and Trash Burning Banned along California Coast" (Bluewater Network, September 23, 2004), <www.bluewaternetwork.com>, Received via e-mail, September 23, 2004. Also see Associate Press, "California Gets Tougher on Cruise-Ship Pollution," *Seattle Times* (September 29, 2004), <seattletimes.nwsource.com>, Accessed October 3, 2004.

[109] According to "Industry Sees Irony in California Sewage Bill," *Seatrade Insider* (August 27, 2004), the industry saw AB 2672 as problematic given its prohibition of discharges in state waters from AWTS and pointed its concerns out to the governor. Michael Crye, ICCL president, said the new law ignores the new technology that the industry uses to treat sewage. Those wastewater purification systems "discharge water that is close to drinking-water quality." (See "California Gets Tougher on Cruise-Ship Pollution," *Associated Press* (August 27, 2004.) "Close" is not the same as drinking water quality.

Chapter 8: Paradise Lost at Sea

[1] Stuart Roberts and Eloisa Mayers, "Crew Injured as Lifeboat Plunges from Ship," *Royal Gazette* (September 9, 2004), <www.royalgazette.com>, Accessed September 10, 2004; "Four Crewmen Still in Hospital after Accident," *Royal Gazette* (September 15, 2004), <www.royal gazette.com>, Accessed September 15, 2004.

[2] According to James Walsh's complaint filed against Carnival Corporation, two Holland America cruise ships had "insufficient operating and or certified lifesaving equipment: e.g., life rafts on which the certifications had expired, lifeboats that were inoperative due to a lack of spare parts and maintenance issues, and a lifeboat on the *Nieuw Amsterdam* that was used to ferry passengers to shore notwithstanding that it had a reported crack in the bow." See *First Amended Complaint, Case # CACE 02-018326(08), 17th Circuit Court, Broward County Florida.*

[3] Paul Nyhan, "Cruise Ship Becomes a Wild Ride in the Atlantic," *Seattle Post-Intelligencer* (October 7, 2004), <seattlepi.nwsource.com/business/194061_cruise07.html>, Accessed October 7, 2004; Bill Power, "Roughed Up on the High Seas," *Halifax Chronicle Herald* (September 29, 2004), <www.herald.ns.ca/stroies/2004/09/29/f303.raw.html>, Accessed September 29, 2004.

[4] Brian Major, "Arison: Hostile Media Hurts Cruising," *Travel Weekly* (October 6, 2000), Received via e-mail, October 6, 2000.

[5] Media statement from Michael Crye, president of the International Council of Cruise Lines concerning the incident on the cruise ship *Nordic Empress*, ICCL, June 16 2001, <iccl.org/pressroom/press57.cfm>, Accessed October 25, 2004.

[6] See National Transportation Safety Board, *Marine Accident Report: Fire On Board the Panamanian Passenger Ship Universe Explorer in the Lynn Canal near Juneau, Alaska, July 27, 1996* (NTSB, 1998). (Document #NTSB/MAR-98/02)

[7] Open letter from senior executives of the International Council of Cruise Lines, July 27, 1999, <iccl.or/pressroom/press14.cfm>, Accessed October 25, 2004.

[8] See the articles written by Douglas Frantz for the *New York Times* in the late 1990s and 2000.

[9] Douglas Frantz, "Cruise Line Reports 62 Alleged Sexual Assaults over 5 Years," *New York Times* (July 14, 1999). Also see Douglas Frantz, "Cruise Line Says It Underreported Allegations of Sexual Assault," *New York Times*, July 29, 1999, <www.nytimes.com>.

[10] Billy Shields, "Stowaway's Family Angry over V.I.'S Refusal to Prosecute," *Virgin Islands Daily News* (December 23, 2002), <www.virginislandsdailynews.com>, Accessed March 2, 2003.

[11] "Urgent Safety Work Starts on QM2," *BBC News* (June 26, 2004), <news.bbc.co.uk/go/pr/fr/-/2/hi/uk_new/England/Hampshire/dorset/3837063.stm>, Accessed June 27, 2004.

[12] "Another Ship Sprinkler Problem," *Seatrade Insider* (June 5, 2001), <www.cruise-community.com>, Accessed June 5, 2001.

[13] Karl Ross, "Norway Calls Off Seven-Day Journey," *Miami Herald* (May 30, 2001), <www.herald.com>, Accessed May 30, 2001.

[14] Brittany Wallman and Peter Bernard, "Coast Guard Cites Safety Concerns in Keeping Cruise Ship in Miami Port," *Sun-Sentinel* (May 27, 2001), <www.sun-sentinel.com/news/local/southflorida/sfl-cruiseship527.story?>, Accessed May 28, 2001.

[15] "Marco Polo in Antarctic Emergency," *Merco Press* (February 19, 2003), Received via e-mail February 19, 2003.

[16] *Pacific Sky* was built by Sitmar Line in 1984 and originally named *Fair Sky*. It became Princess Cruise's *Sky Princess* in 1988, and *Pacific Sky* in 2001 when it began service in Australia. The 64,000-ton ship accommodates 1,600 passengers and 535 crew members.

[17] Mathew Dearnaley, "Leaking Liner Cuts Pacific Cruise Short," *New Zealand Herald* (March 17, 2003), <www.nzherald.co.nz/stroyprint.cfm?storyID=3201114>, Accessed March 16, 2003.

[18] "P&O Cruises Maintenance Reform after Pacific Sky," *Lloyd's List* (March 21, 2003), <lloyds list.com>, Accessed July 20, 2003.

[19] "Cruise Passengers Close to Mutiny," *TVNZ News* (November 5, 2004), <tvnz.co.nz/view/news_travel_story_skin/457298%3fformat=html>, Accessed November 5, 2004.

[20] Daniel Knowles, "Cruise Blues: This Time It's Jellyfish," *Sunday Mail* (November 14, 2004), <www.thesundaymail.news.com.au/common/story_page/0,5936,11379968%255E903,00.html>, Accessed November 13, 2004.

[21] Douglas Frantz, "Getting Sick on a Cruise May Mean Medical Care with Few Standards," *New York Times* (October 31, 1999), <www.nytimes.com>, Accessed January 8, 2000.

[22] Chris McGinnis, "While on Vacation, Don't Let the Bedbugs Bite," *CNN News* (February 10, 2004), <cnn.com/2004/TRAVEL/ADVISOR/02/10/hln.adviser.bedbugs/index.html>, Accessed February 11, 2004. See also Joseph Farah, "US Not Sleeping Tight as Bedbugs Renew Bite," *World Net Daily* (December 13, 2004), <worldnetdaily.com/news/printer-friendly.asp?ARTICLE_ID=41894>, Accessed December 19, 2004; "Hundreds of Bed Bug Bites Sicken Couple on Cruise," *Local6.com* (April 11, 2005), <www.local6.com/print/4365719/detail.html>, Accessed April 11, 2005; "Couple Wakes Up to Bed Bugs During Cruise," *Firstcoastnews.com* (April 25, 2005), <www.firstcoastnews.com/printfullstory.aspx?storyid=36131>, Accessed May 1, 2005.

[23] "The Insider: Cruise Line Tries to Get Out of Sick Bed," *Seattle Post-Intelligencer* (January 13, 2003), <seattlepi.nwsource.com>, Accessed January 13, 2003.

[24] An article in *The Lancet* reported a striking increase in norovirus outbreaks in Europe, which coincided with the detection and emergence of a new predominant norovirus variant. See Ben Lopman et al., "Increase in Viral Gastroenteritis Outbreaks in Europe and Epidemic Spread of New Norovirus Variant," *The Lancet* (February 28, 2004), pp. 682–688.

[25] Marvin Hokstam, "Cruise Ship with Sick Passengers Abandons Visit to St. Maarten," *Miami Herald* (December 10, 2002), <www.miami.com>, Accessed December 15, 2002.

[26] See "'Bug Ship' Passengers to Sue," *BBC News* (November 6, 2003), <news.bbc.co.uk/go/pr/fr/-/2/hi/uk_news/England/Hampshire/dorset/3246481.stm>, Accessed November 6, 2003). Also see Tom Worden and David Wooding, "Spain Shuts Out Sick Brits," *The Sun* (November 4, 2003), <www.thesun.co.uk/article/0,2-2003511026,00.html>, Accessed November 4, 2003.

[27] T. Ando, J.S. Noel, and R.L. Fankhauser, "Genetic Classification of Norwalk-Like Viruses," *Journal of Infectious Disease* (May 2000), pp. S336–348.

[28] "As Many as 30 Percent of Travelers Don't Wash Hands after Using Public Restrooms at Airports," *Science Daily* (September 16, 2003), <www.sciencedaily.com/releases/2003/09/030916074111.htm>, Accessed September 17, 2003.

[29] "Norwalk-Like Viruses," *Morbidity and Mortality Weekly Report* 50:RR-9 (June 1, 2001).

[30] See Elaine H. Cramer, David X. Gu, and Randy E. Durbin, "Diarreal Disease on Cruise Ships, 1990–2000," *American Journal of Preventive Medicine* (December 2002), <www.ajpm-online.net>, Accessed December 2, 2002.

[31] The CDC estimates norovirus affects 180,000 people annually. In 2002 only one-third of one percent of cruise passengers from North America reported norovirus. See "Keeping Viruses at Bay," *Cruise Industry News Quarterly* (Spring 2003), p. 16.

[32] Spencer Morgan, "Virus Gives Cruise a Sinking Feeling," *New York Daily News* (September 1, 2003), <www.nydailynews.com>, Accessed September 2, 2003.

[33] See *CDC Telebriefing Transcript: Outbreak of Gastrointestinal Illness Aboard Cruise Ships* (November 27, 2002), <www.cdc.gov/od/oc/media/transcripts/t021127.htm>, Accessed November 28, 2002.

[34] Elaine H. Cramer, David X. Gu, and Randy E. Durbin, "Diarreal Disease on Cruise Ships, 1990–2000."

[35] See *CDC Telebriefing Transcript, Outbreak of Gastrointestinal Illness Aboard Cruise Ships* (December 12, 2002), <www.cdc.gov/od/oc/media/transcripts/t021212.htm>, Accessed December 15, 2002.

[36] Ibid.

[37] "Outbreaks of Gastroenteritis Associated with Noroviruses on Cruise Ships – United States 2002," *Morbidity and Mortality Weekly Review* 51:49 (December 13, 2002), pp. 1112–1115.

[38] Bob LaMendola and Tom Steighorst, "Cruise Line Blames Passengers for 3rd Viral Outbreak on Ship," *Sun-Sentinel* (November 12, 2002), <www.sun-sentinel.com/news/yahoo/sfl-rxship12nov12,0,6638757.story?coll=sfla%2Dnewsaol%2Dheadlines>, Accessed November 12, 2002.

[39] See <www.cruisejunkie.com/outbreaks2004.html>.

[40] Lisa Lindesmith et al., "Human Susceptibility and Resistance to Norwalk Virus Infection," *Nature Medicine* 9:5 (May 2003), pp. 548–553.

[41] Message posted at rec.travel.cruises usenet newsgroup, April 15, 2004. 00:47 GMT.

[42] "Norwegian Star – The Plot Thickens," *Rolling Pin Daily News* (July 15, 2003), <www.rollingpincruise.com/news.html?nid=355>, Accessed July 24, 2003.

[43] For an interesting look at all that is possible and that makes it into the court system, see Justice Thomas A. Dickerson, *The Cruise Passenger's Rights & Remedies: 2003* (January 29, 2004), <www.classactionlitigation.com/Cruise%20Passenger%20Web.htm>, Accessed January 9, 2004. This annual publication should be easily found with a search engine.

[44] Dale K. DuPont, "Cunard Stiffed Me, Contestant Charges," *Miami Herald* (July 2, 2004), <www.miami.com>, Accessed July 7, 2004.

[45] Mary Lu Abbott, "At Sea, It's a Booking — Not a Berth Right," *Los Angeles Times* (September 26, 2004), <www.latimes.com/travel/la-tr-cruise26sep26,1,681797.column?coll=la-travel-headlines>, Accessed September 26, 2004.

[46] "Passenger Speaks of Aurora Fiasco," *BBC News* (January 20, 2005), news.bbc.co.uk/go/pr/fr/-/2/hi/uk_news/england/hampshire/4193237.stm>, Accessed January 21, 2005.

[47] See Carol Pucci, "Ports of Call Changed? Welcome to Tough Luck Island," *Philadelphia Inquirer* (October 5, 2003), <www.philly.com>, Accessed October 15, 2004; "Mutiny on the Norwegian," *Washington Post* (June 8, 2003), p. P1. Other details in this account are drawn from personal correspondence with passengers on the cruise.

[48] Emily Frankel *v.* Norwegian Cruise Line, Superior Court of California, Ventura County (May 26, 2004), Case: SH99710, <courts.countyofventura.org/civcase/actions.asp?CASE_TYPE= SH&CASE_NUMBER=099710>, Accessed October 15, 2004.

[49] Joel Glass, "Concern over US Ship Safety Plan for Disabled," *Lloyd's List* (August 26, 1996), <www.llplimited.com/LLArchive/output.cgi?Mon26Aug1996-012&cruise%20line>, Accessed January 8, 1999.

[50] Cynthia Corzo, "Suit Says Carnival Ships Fail to Comply with Disabilities Act," *Miami Herald* (December 23, 1998), p. 3C.

[51] "Cruise Line Settles Disability Suit," *Yahoo News* (November 2, 2001), <dailynews.yahoo.com/htx/wplg/20011102/lo/940448_1.html>, Accessed November 3, 2001.

[52] Catherine Wilson, "Court: Cruise Ships Covered by ADA," *Associated Press* (June 3, 2000), <biz.yahoo.com/apf/000623/cruise_dis.html>, Accessed June 26, 2000.

[53] Catherine Wilson, "Feds Want ADA to Apply to Cruises," *Associated Press* (August 24, 1999), <biz.yahoo.com/apf/990824/cruise_dis_1.html>, Accessed August 25, 1999.

[54] See Press Release, *ICCL and Cruise Industry Respond to ADA Ruling* (International Council of Cruise Lines, June 27, 2000), <iccl.org/pressroom/press37.cfm>, Accessed June 28, 2000.

[55] "DOJ Going after NCL," *Travel Weekly* (January 24, 2001), Received via e-mail, January 24, 2001.

[56] Josh Richman, "MTC Member Sues Cruise Line over Accessibility," *Alameda Times-Star* (March 19, 2004), <www.timesstar.com>, Accessed March 19, 2004.

[57] L. M. Sixel, "Cruising Uncharted Waters," *Houston Chronicle* (September 25, 2004), <www.chron.com/cs/CDA/printstory.mpl/business/2813782>, Accessed September 26, 2004.

[58] "Industry Open to Disability Ruling" *Seatrade Insider* (September 29, 2004), <www.cruise-community.com>, Accessed September 29, 2004.

[59] "ICCL Seeks More Time on Access Guidelines," *Seatrade Insider* (December 15, 2004), <www.cruise-community.com/ShowStory.asp?ID6740>, Accessed December 15, 2004.

Chapter 9: Prospects for Positive Change

[1] "Carnival's Asia Strategy," *Seatrade Insider* (November 5, 2004), <www.cruise-community.com/ShowStory.asp?ID=6524>, Accessed November 5, 2004.

[2] See Sean Cockerham, "Voters to Settle Ship Tax," *Anchorage Daily News* (December 18, 2004) <www.adn.com/front/v-printer/story/5924969p-5832072c.html>, Accessed December 19, 2004.

[3] Workers also risk being sent home and denied medical care in the US if they ware injured on the job. See Forrest Norman, "Crewed If by Sea," *Miami New Times* (November 11, 2004), <www.miaminewtimes.com/issues/2004-11-11/news/feature_print.html>, Accessed November 12, 2004.

[4] Justin Stares, "Arison Warns Fincantieri Workers on Pay Demands," *Lloyd's List* (July 1, 2003), <www.lloydslist.com>, Accessed July 20, 2003.

[5] "Who Said It?" *Cruise Industry News Quarterly* (Winter 1997/98), p. 104.

[6] Some of the social issues are well developed in Robert E. Wood, "Caribbean Cruise Tourism: Globalizations at Sea," *Annals of Tourism Research* 27:2 (2000), pp. 245–370.

[7] See Ross A. Klein, "Sweatships: The Cruise Industry and the Socialist Agenda," *Socialist Studies Bulletin* 70 (Spring-Summer, 2003), pp. 5–18; Ross A. Klein. "High Seas, Low Pay: Working on Cruise Ships," *Our Times: Canada's Independent Labour Magazine,* (December/ January, 2001), 29–34. Also see War on Want's 2002 Sweatships campaign, <waronwant. org>.

[8] See H.R. 4975, <thomas.loc.gov>. Also see Shawn Cumberbatch, "Cruise Tax Proposals," *Barbados Advocate* (November 16, 2004), <www.barbadosadvocate.com/NewViewNewsleft. cfm?Record=19327>, Accessed November 17, 2004.

[9] Saul Alinsky was a social activist and community activist during the 1950s and 1960s who authored two books. *Rules for Radicals* (Vintage, 1972) is a bit lighter and more entertaining than *Reveille for Radicals* (University of Chicago, 1946), which is thicker and gives the foundation for his methods and approach. The National Film Board of Canada produced a film, "Saul Alinsky Went to War," which is both a historical artifact and a good representation of Alinsky.

[10] In 2002 Pew Charitable Trusts awarded more than $165 million in grants; almost $40 million was devoted to the environment program under the direction of Joshua Reichert.

[11] See Felice Pace, "How the Pew Charitable Trusts Is Smothering the Grassroots Environmental Movement," *Counterpunch Magazine* (October 9/10, 2004), <counterpunch.com/pace 10092004.html>, Accessed October 11, 2004.

[12] See Mark Dowie, *American Foundations: An Investigative History,* (MIT Press, 2001).

[13] Erik Wemple, "Abandon Ship," *Washington City Paper* (June 20-26, 2003), <www.washington citypaper.com>, Accessed February 7, 2004). See also Alex Kuczynski, "Supporting the Cause on a Cruise," *New York Times* (December 11, 2000), <www.nytimes.com>, Accessed February 7, 2004.

Index

About the Author

ROSS KLEIN BEGAN CRUISING AS A YOUNGSTER although he didn't think about writing about the industry until the late 1990s. He was spending as many as 50 days a year on cruise ships as a passenger and got to know the industry in a way that few others had. Through his research he came to know the industry even better.

Ross is a sociologist whose previous work had little to do with the cruise industry. He has written about child abuse prevention, the strength of nonviolence in resolving conflict, and fostering labor force attachment. His community-based social research has been extensive. He began researching the cruise industry in 2000 and since has published three books, three reports for Canadian Centre for Policy Alternatives, one report for Bluewater Network, and numerous articles in academic and mainstream venues.

Ross lives with his partner and their dog, Lucca, in St. John's, Newfoundland. He teaches research methods in the School of Social Work at Memorial University of Newfoundland. He is also board chair of Family Service Canada, a not-for-profit, national, voluntary organization representing the concerns of families and family-serving agencies across Canada. He hasn't taken a cruise since December 2001 and continues to advocate for positive change in the cruise ship industry. In the meantime he is accumulating wonderful experiences with a range of land-based (often island-based) vacations.

Ross is online at <www.cruisejunkie.com>.

If you have enjoyed *Cruise Ship Squeeze*, you might also enjoy other

BOOKS TO BUILD A NEW SOCIETY

Our books provide positive solutions for people who want to make a difference. We specialize in:

Sustainable Living • Ecological Design and Planning
Natural Building & Appropriate Technology • New Forestry
Environment and Justice • Conscientious Commerce
Progressive Leadership • Resistance and Community • Nonviolence
Educational and Parenting Resources

New Society Publishers

ENVIRONMENTAL BENEFITS STATEMENT

New Society Publishers has chosen to produce this book on recycled paper made with 100% post consumer waste, processed chlorine free, and old growth free.

For every 5,000 books printed, New Society saves the following resources:[1]

37	Trees
3,364	Pounds of Solid Waste
3,702	Gallons of Water
4,828	Kilowatt Hours of Electricity
6,116	Pounds of Greenhouse Gases
26	Pounds of HAPs, VOCs, and AOX Combined
9	Cubic Yards of Landfill Space

---

[1]Environmental benefits are calculated based on research done by the Environmental Defense Fund and other members of the Paper Task Force who study the environmental impacts of the paper industry.

For a full list of NSP's titles, please call 1-800-567-6772 or check out our web site at:

www.newsociety.com

NEW SOCIETY PUBLISHERS